# Absenteeism

*New Approaches
to Understanding,
Measuring, and Managing
Employee Absence*

*Paul S. Goodman*
*Robert S. Atkin*
*and Associates*

# Absenteeism

## Jossey-Bass Publishers

San Francisco • Washington • London • 1984

ABSENTEEISM
*New Approaches to Understanding, Measuring, and Managing Employee Absence*
by Paul S. Goodman, Robert S. Atkin, and Associates

**Library of Congress Cataloging in Publication Data**
Main entry under title:

Absenteeism.

(The Jossey-Bass management series) (The Jossey-Bass
social and behavioral science series)
Includes bibliographies and index.
1. Absenteeism (Labor)—Addresses, essays, lectures.
I. Goodman, Paul S.    II. Atkin, Robert S., 1945–
III. Series.    IV. Series: Jossey-Bass social and
behavioral science series.
HD5115.A175  1984      658.3'14      84-47985
ISBN 0-87589-617-0

Manufactured in the United States of America

The paper in this book meets the guidelines for
permanence and durability of the Committee on
Production Guidelines for Book Longevity of the
Council on Library Resources.

JACKET DESIGN BY WILLI BAUM

FIRST EDITION

*Code 8428*

*A joint publication in*
The Jossey-Bass Management Series
*and*
The Jossey-Bass Social and Behavioral Science Series

# Preface

Employee absenteeism is a pervasive phenomenon that cuts across industries and national boundaries. It has broad-ranging consequences for managers, union officials, workers and their families, the government, and other social institutions. Some estimates place the annual cost of absenteeism in the United States at around $30 billion. Despite the importance of absenteeism, we know little about its causes or how to manage it.

Although there have been many studies on absenteeism, most reviewers of this literature (see, for example, Atkin and Goodman, 1983) would say that a cumulative body of research based on sound theory, measurement, and analytic procedures has not been developed and that many of the findings do not inform practice. Indeed there is little relationship between theory and research on absenteeism and the practice of managing employees. While this observation may also be true of other topics in the organizational literature, it seems particularly true of studies of absenteeism, and there appear to be a number of causes. First, a portion of the literature has a strong empirical orientation with very little specification of the theory of absence behavior. Second, while researchers' current theories about absenteeism are more differentiated than the simple hypothesis that job dissatisfaction produces absenteeism, there has still been little consideration of the fundamental processes that cause absentee behavior. Third, research findings will not build on each other in a coherent way until some of the basic issues about measuring absenteeism are clarified and resolved. Fourth, while current research on absenteeism has moved toward more multivariate procedures, there is little consideration of how the distributional qualities of absenteeism should dictate the choice of statistical procedures. Fifth, very little research has focused on the policy and institutional rules governing absenteeism. And sixth, while absenteeism is typically understood at the individual level, its effects at other levels (for example, group, organization, economic section, and nation) have not been systematically explored.

Our goal in writing about absenteeism is to stimulate new avenues of theoretical research and management practice. While our primary target is the researcher, we also want to influence how senior line and staff managers think about absenteeism. Our strategy is to delineate a set of fundamental issues in the areas of theory, measurement, and employee relations and to respond to the questions that surface as we go along. These will concern the definition of absence, the theoretical assumptions about absence behavior, alternative operational specifications of absence behavior, measurement properties of absence indices, statistical models for representing absence behavior, the relationships of absence behavior to other withdrawal behaviors, consequences of absence for other organizational indicators (for example, productivity), strategies for reducing absences, and so on. Most of the chapters in this book map out new approaches to resolving these issues and questions.

## Critical Issues and Questions

Seven critical issues and related questions provide the basic structure for this book. We will briefly review each to provide the reader a way to think effectively about absenteeism. The issues represent the basic dilemmas and problems that will confront anyone interested in absenteeism in the 1980s. Some of the issues derive from theory, others from the current literature on absenteeism, and others from practical consideration.

1. *Theoretical Specification.* The need for a well-developed theory is one of the most important problems underlying any new developments in understanding absenteeism. This means specifying (a) a clear definition of absenteeism that will have an operational counterpart, (b) the construct space of absentee behavior, and (c) the fundamental mechanisms that explain absence taking. By fundamental mechanisms we do not mean a listing of variables that predict absenteeism. Rather, we want to get at the basic psychological processes that explain absence taking.

2. *Measurement.* The issue of selecting the appropriate measures of absenteeism permeates the whole literature. The question of whether frequency or duration is the best measure arises often. Other researchers have worried about the best way to estimate reliability of absentee measures. Our position is that many of the methodological investigations on absenteeism have been studies of convenience. The researchers have data sets with alternative indices and the problem is to select the appropriate indices. Our view is that one should step back and view the fundamental properties of absenteeism in the light of current measurement theory before launching any methodological investigations. For example, an argument developed later in this book (Chapter Two) is that the properties of most absentee measures may preclude estimating reliability coefficients. That is, many of the past studies estimating reliability of absence measures may have inappropriately applied the concept of reliability. The basic idea is that we need to think carefully about what reliability means in the light of a clear concept of absenteeism. The measurement chapters in this book (Chapters Two and Three) highlight the major questions in this area and offer some new strategies for advancing our understanding of absenteeism.

3. *Statistical Models.* The bulk of the absentee literature aims at explaining causes of absenteeism—that is, estimating the magnitude of different variables' effects on absenteeism. The selection of the appropriate statistical model is a prerequisite for identifying the predictors or causes of absenteeism, and the selection process has become more sophisticated over the last ten to fifteen years. We no longer find studies that relate a single factor (such as job dissatisfaction) to absenteeism. The acknowledgment of more complicated

models has in turn led to more sophisticated analytic procedures. The question remains, however, whether the current set of models are appropriate. The answer to this question rests in our theoretical assumptions about absenteeism. This book will present some new approaches to selecting statistical models that have not typically been used in research on absence.

4. *Absence and Other Forms of Withdrawal Behavior.* Much of our discussion — and the current literature — has focused solely on absenteeism as a dependent variable. Another quite different focus of both theory and research on absenteeism concerns its relationship to other forms of withdrawal behavior. In this view, absenteeism is seen as part of a broader construct and the issue is to understand the relationships among different forms of withdrawal (for example, absenteeism, turnover, tardiness, daydreaming). *Absenteeism* examines this point of view because if one embraces the withdrawal concept, the theory, measurement, and analytic models will differ from those in an approach that focuses on modeling absenteeism.

5. *Predictors of Absenteeism.* How to predict absenteeism is the central question in most research on the topic. Researchers want to explain why people do not go to work, and managers want to find out why so that they can control absenteeism. While we believe that finding predictors will remain a central research issue, we do not believe that it should be the major focus of absenteeism research. The current body of empirical data will inform the development of the needed basic assumptions about absenteeism, and progress on theory, measurement, and analysis will open new ways to understand predictors.

6. *Consequences of Absenteeism.* The majority of research treats absenteeism as a dependent variable. We thought an important new avenue would be to explore absenteeism's effects at different levels of analysis (for example, individual, group, and organization). That is, we want to treat absenteeism as an independent variable and explore its consequences. Understanding theoretically and empirically the effects of absenteeism may shed new light on the phenomenon.

7. *Managing Absenteeism.* Anyone managing an organization faces the problem of how to deal with absenteeism. There are a growing number of reports on organizational interventions designed to control absenteeism, some through disciplinary programs, others

through incentives. We are interested in these developments because we want research to contribute to the accumulation of knowledge *and* to inform practice. We think the results of organizational interventions designed to reduce absenteeism can inform theory because one important way to learn about a phenomenon is to try to change it.

These seven issues are both independent and interdependent. If one is interested in the consequences of absenteeism, it is possible to review the current literature on consequences and theoretical frameworks about consequences of absenteeism without exploring the other issues. Also, if one is interested in techniques to control absenteeism, it is possible to learn about them. At the same time, the themes underlying all these issues link them. For example, the definition of absenteeism (rarely specified in the literature) is common to all the issues. Identifying the fundamental assumptions underlying absenteeism is really a precondition to understanding its measurement, models, cause, and so on.

## Overview of Contents

This book is organized around the seven critical issues detailed in the previous section. It consists of original chapters written by scholars working on various aspects of absenteeism. Their aim has been to provide new avenues for thinking about research and practice.

Mark Fichman begins by providing an alternative theoretical framework for the concept of absenteeism. After reviewing the current status of theoretical work, Fichman proposes a set of criteria for absence theory construction. He then advances a theory drawn from work in human motivation and economics that conceives of individual absence as a dynamic form of motivated behavior.

The next two chapters concern the measurement of absenteeism. Robert Atkin and Paul Goodman chart some of the fundamental questions that must be considered in the measurement of absenteeism. The topics addressed include recording the raw data set, metrics by which absence events can be measured, different perspectives for interpreting absence events, aggregating levels of analysis and time frames, and reliability and validity of absence measures.

Frank Landy, Joseph Vasey, and Frederick Smith focus on

two major methodological issues: (1) problems inherent in analyzing low-base-rate phenomena (a characteristic of absenteeism) and the need to explore other distributions in order to understand the properties of absence-taking behavior and (2) the stability of absence behavior—whether individual absence behavior is stable and whether absence rates at one period can be predicted by absence rates at a prior period. This chapter differs substantially from the one by Atkin and Goodman in its intellectual orientation.

Chapter Four, by Robert Avery and V. Joseph Hotz, concerns statistical models for estimating absenteeism. Both authors are economists who have done research on phenomena that have some of the characteristics of absenteeism. Their contribution is twofold. First, they identify a set of statistical models that have not been used in absenteeism research but that are relevant. Second, they identify a set of theoretical assumptions that provide a guide to the selection of a relevant statistical model. Specifically, the categories of models are (1) models without historical dependence (that is, absenteeism at one time period is independent of absenteeism at a prior time), (2) models with observed sources of heterogeneity (across individuals), (3) models with historical dependence, and (4) models with unobserved sources of heterogeneity.

In Chapter Five, Joseph Rosse and Howard Miller treat absenteeism as a specific manifestation of the more general construct "withdrawal behavior" and examine it in the context of other withdrawal behaviors (for example, turnover, tardiness). They open their chapter with a brief review of the empirical predictors of employee withdrawal behavior and then identify five "implicit" conceptual models underlying most of the research on employee withdrawal behavior. They outline a new adaptation cycle model, which can be used to explain individual withdrawal behavior, and discuss its implications for research and practice.

In 1978, Richard Steers and Susan Rhodes published a major research paper in the absentee literature. One of its contributions was to organize a large number of empirical studies into a systematic framework; another was to stimulate empirical testing of that framework. In Chapter Six, Steers and Rhodes assess the literature on predictors of absenteeism since their previous paper, revise their framework in the light of new empirical evidence, and provide some new directions for studying predictors of absenteeism.

Chapter Seven, by Paul Goodman and Robert Atkin, examines consequences of absenteeism. It opens by noting that absenteeism can have consequences for a variety of constituencies and that these consequences are likely to be positive *and* negative. Much of the literature implies absenteeism has only negative effects. The major portion of this chapter looks at a specific set of indicators that may be affected by absences, such as productivity, safety, grievances, and costs. The authors consider the current empirical evidence for each indicator and present alternative theoretical perspectives and new strategies for research.

Increasing employee attendance is the topic of Chapter Eight, by Gary Latham and Nancy Napier. They address the questions How can we get people to come to work? and How do we know what efforts are successful? The chapter enumerates a variety of intervention techniques that have been used to increase attendance, such as job preview, measurement of performance and attendance, different types of training, flextime, behavior modification, and so on. The chapter describes each intervention technique and examines the empirical evidence of its impact on increasing attendance.

The last two chapters are integrative in nature. They are written by Gary Johns and Charles Hulin, who have contributed important work in the area of absenteeism and other withdrawal behaviors. Each author identifies the common themes and discusses the diverse viewpoints expressed in the first eight chapters. But they do more than just react to the ideas presented in this book. They identify the points that have not been addressed, indicate where we should be going in the future, and characterize significant forms of research on absenteeism. Their positions are different and stimulating.

## Genesis of the Book

The unique feature of this book is the caliber of the contributors. Robert Avery, Mark Fichman, V. Joseph Hotz, Charles Hulin, Gary Johns, Frank Landy, Gary Latham, Howard Miller, Nancy Napier, Susan Rhodes, Joseph Rosse, and Richard Steers have produced chapters that are significant contributions to the field.

It is important for the reader to understand the process by which this book was created. We, as organizers of the effort, decided on an approach based on theory, methods, research, and practice. We then identified the best people in the field to address those content areas and contracted with each author or team of authors for an original chapter. When the initial drafts were completed, they were circulated to all contributors. We then met at Carnegie-Mellon University for two days of intensive discussion to generate new ideas on each chapter. Tapes of the workshop discussion were given to the contributors to use in revising their chapters.

The intellectual effectiveness of the workshop format in generating new ideas was based on our work with a group of Carnegie-Mellon faculty who served as "provocateurs" for the discussion of the chapters. This group included Linda Argote, Stephen Fienberg, Eric Johnson, Charles Kiesler, Lance Kurke, and Andrew Mitchell. They made significant contributions to this book.

The major support for this endeavor came through a contract with the U.S. Bureau of Mines. This contract is part of a larger research program called the Carnegie-Mellon Coal Project, which is involved in investigations of absenteeism, group productivity, and safety. We appreciate the interest and support of our project officers, James Peay and Robert Peters. Marilyn Samples Hersh, the administrative assistant of the Coal Project, was responsible for all administrative aspects relevant to the workshop and the completion of this book. Her work was invaluable.

This book is dedicated to our mothers, Lillian and Ida.

*Pittsburgh, Pennsylvania*                          Paul S. Goodman
*July 1984*                                         Robert S. Atkin

# Contents

# The Authors

Paul S. Goodman is a professor of industrial administration and psychology at the Graduate School of Industrial Administration, Carnegie-Mellon University, Pittsburgh. Previously he was on the faculty at the Graduate School of Business at the University of Chicago and was a visiting professor at Cornell University. He was educated at Trinity College (Hartford, Connecticut), where he received a B.A. degree in economics in 1959. His master's work was done at the Amos Tuch School at Dartmouth College in 1961, and he received his Ph.D. degree from Cornell University in organizational psychology in 1966.

Goodman's main professional interests are in research on work motivation and attitudes, organizational design, productivity, and organizational effectiveness. Some of this research has concerned the effects of pay inequity on performance, motivation of scientists and engineers, designing organizations to retain disadvantaged workers, and the effects of new forms of work organizations on organizational effectiveness. His research has been published in many professional journals including the *Journal of Applied Psychology, Organizational Behavior and Human Performance,* and *Human Relations.* Recent books include *Assessing Organizational Change* and *Change in Organizations.*

Paul Goodman is on the editorial board of *Organizational Behavior and Human Performance* and he also serves in a consulting capacity for private industry and the government. His current research includes a large-scale study on group productivity and absenteeism, new forms of work organizations, the impact of robotics on the work force, and organizational effectiveness.

Robert S. Atkin is associate dean and director of the master's program at the Graduate School of Industrial Administration at Carnegie-Mellon University. He received the B.Eng. degree in mechanical engineering (1967) and the M.S. degree in management science (1971) from Stevens Institute of Technology, and he has done doctoral work at the University of Illinois at Champaign. Prior to joining Carnegie-Mellon in 1976, Atkin held positions at Union Carbide, Stevens Institute of Technology, and State Farm Insurance.

Atkin's teaching and research interests include manufacturing and work-force management, productivity and quality, compensation and incentive systems, and performance appraisal. Current research includes a multiyear study of the human resource aspects of the coal industry, with particular emphasis on safety, productivity, turnover, absenteeism, and employee assistance programs; a study of organizational responses to economic shocks; and a study of the effect of union seniority and job-bumping rules on productivity during cyclic layoffs.

Robert B. Avery in on the Board of Governors of the Federal Reserve System.

Mark Fichman is assistant professor of organizational behavior, Graduate School of Industrial Administration, Carnegie-Mellon University.

V. Joseph Hotz is assistant professor of economics, Graduate School of Industrial Administration, Carnegie-Mellon University, and research associate in economics research at the National Opinion Research Center.

Charles L. Hulin is professor of psychology, Department of Psychology, University of Illinois.

Gary Johns is associate professor of management, Department of Management, Concordia University.

Frank J. Landy is professor of psychology, Department of Psychology, Pennsylvania State University.

Gary P. Latham is a member of the faculty, Management and Organization Department, University of Washington.

Howard E. Miller is assistant professor of industrial relations, Industrial Relations Center, University of Minnesota.

Nancy K. Napier is assistant professor of management and organization, Management and Organization Department, University of Washington.

Susan R. Rhodes is associate professor of personnel and industrial relations, School of Management, Syracuse University.

Joseph G. Rosse is assistant professor of industrial relations, Industrial Relations Center, University of Minnesota.

Frederick D. Smith is a doctoral candidate in the Department of Psychology, Pennsylvania State University.

Richard M. Steers is professor of management, Graduate School of Management, University of Oregon.

Joseph J. Vasey is a doctoral candidate in the Department of Psychology, Pennsylvania State University.

# Absenteeism

*New Approaches
to Understanding,
Measuring, and Managing
Employee Absence*

# 1

# A Theoretical Approach to Understanding Employee Absence

R R R R R R R R R R R R R R R R R R R R R R R R R R R R R R R R R R R R R R R R R R R R R R R R R R

*Mark Fichman*

Setting the theoretical stage for the study of absence presents interesting problems. Do we use all the props developed over the years or rethink this from the beginning, starting with a bare stage? Have we combined the props in the right way? Should we even be doing this? (Gupta and Jenkins, 1983).

This metaphor applies with equal vigor to studying absence in organizations. Given our prior beliefs from intuitions and empirical results, should we continue down the same research paths? Johns and Nicholson (1982, p. 128) argue that "a heavy investment

*Note:* Support for this chapter was provided by the U.S. Bureau of Mines under contracts J0100069, J0328033, and J0123040.

I extend my thanks to the editors, Robert S. Atkin and Paul Goodman, for their useful substantive and editorial suggestions and the opportunity to participate in the absenteeism conference and to the members of the conference who provided useful comments and feedback on the original draft of this paper. James Lindsey provided much appreciated editorial and bibliographical help throughout. Thanks also to V. Joseph Hotz for many useful discussions and digressions on absences and event histories.

1

absence." Given the sufficiently large number of studies in the absenteeism literature (Steers and Rhodes, 1978), we have a reasonably precise prior expectation for the results of a "traditional" approach to absenteeism (that is, correlating rates of types of absence with demographic and intrapsychic variables using an organizational convenience sample). If we concur with Johns and Nicholson's (1982) appraisal of the literature, we must conclude that a "traditional" study of absenteeism is not designed to be very informative.

What can we do? We may either abandon the study of absence, develop new methods within the traditional framework, or develop a new theoretical approach. Our recommendation is exploring new theory and considering other methods. Since method proceeds from theory, the study of absence requires essaying new theory (if the knowledge and insights generated by current views are not compelling). An interesting issue here is why some areas such as absence engender very high levels of persistence in pursuing only a few research paths. Johns and Nicholson's (1982) arguments about the consequences of cognitive appraisal of an absence incident touch on the problem. The effects of labeling absences as casual, voluntary, or attitudinal and the strong tacit beliefs people have that absence is a result of dissatisfaction both support the narrow fashion in which the problem has been studied, despite the early identification of problems and alternatives that are now receiving attention (Walker, 1947; Kerr, Koppelmeier, and Sullivan, 1951). Walker had suggested that absence may be a group phenomenon related to norms. Kerr, Koppelmeier, and Sullivan suggested that absence measures did not reflect an underlying unidimensional construct.

Costs and benefits should be considered. Predicting behavior measures in organizations (for example, turnover, health, performance, and absence) is quite difficult. Consequently, other approaches to understanding absence from work are tempting. The cost-benefit analyst says, "What is there to lose?" However, we should not be so cavalier. If absences are costly (a plausible, untested assumption, which may be controversial; Staw and Oldham, 1978; Moch and Fitzgibbons, 1982) and if we can reliably predict absence, changing a weakly correlated predictor can have substantial cost ramifications (Mirvis and Lawler, 1977; Terborg and others, 1982). Absence events and their measures, given the complex matrix of events and forces in which they are embedded, may be intrinsically noisy, making even small gains in understanding difficult to attain. Having noted these considerations, we will attend only to developing theory necessary to understanding absence. Later chapters by Goodman and Atkin and by Latham and Napier address the consequences, costs, and control of absence.

## Plan for the Chapter

The goal of this chapter is to identify and begin to map an alternative theoretical framework for studying absence. To do this, we will first briefly review the literature on absenteeism, focusing on work and criticism generated since the reviews of Muchinsky (1977) and Steers and Rhodes (1978). This will help identify the underlying assumptions and premises in current absence work, building on the contribution of Johns and Nicholson (1982).

The next task will be *defining absence*. We will ask:

- Can absence be treated as a theoretical construct? If so, how, and if not, why not?
- What definitions do different theoretical approaches imply?
- What are we trying to explain, given a definition of absence or some related construct? Can we move from individual-level absence behavior to group phenomena to differences between firms? Does it matter whether we look at absence over time statically or dynamically? (Roberts, Hulin, and Rousseau, 1978).

This will complete the critic's role. We will propose conceiving of individual absence as a dynamic form of motivated behavior, a problem in time allocation across activities. Using work in human motivation and economics, we will sketch a conception of the motivational dynamics of behavior and its ramifications for understanding absence. We will then illustrate potential applications of the dynamic concepts offered. We will evaluate our theory against the criteria and criticisms generated in the first section. To complete the chapter, unanswered questions and implications for practice will be noted.

## Theoretical Perspectives and Developments

A difficulty with absence research is that "little in the way of comprehensive theory building can be found, with the possible exception of Gibson (1966)" (Steers and Rhodes, 1978, p. 392). Consequently, problems of method and theory often characterize earlier work. This lamentable situation became clear in several reviews (Steers and Rhodes, 1978; Muchinsky, 1977; Nicholson, Brown, and Chadwick-Jones, 1976). Porter and Steers's (1973) finding of little relation between absence and turnover in their review contributed as well to increased interest in absenteeism as a behavior worth studying in its own right.

The piecemeal quality of the research literature is evidenced by the finding that job satisfaction and absence are very weakly related in twenty-nine studies (Nicholson, Brown, and Chadwick-Jones, 1976). This quality has led to a search for situational constraints moderating attitude-absence relationships (for example, Morgan and Herman, 1976; Smith, 1977; Steers and Rhodes, 1978; Ilgen and Hollenback, 1977; Herman, 1973), culminating in the Steers and Rhodes attendance model. The Steers and Rhodes model extends earlier attitude-behavior models, with attendance behavior a function of *motivation to attend* and *ability to attend*. Steers and Rhodes accept the tacit theoretical premise that absence events reflect the balance of rewarding and aversive forces operating in the individual's life space. Their contribution is explicating the factors people have looked at, identifying constraints that may attenuate the attitude-behavior relationship, and emphasizing the need for multivariate studies of absence. The univariate studies they review are weak, often nonsignificant, and frequently contradictory. No studies they review approach a reasonable test of their model.

The Steers and Rhodes model has generated substantial research interest. Watson (1981) found mixed support for the Steers and Rhodes model, with job satisfaction showing little effect on a time-lost measure of absence, while some demographic characteristics did show the anticipated effects. Clegg (1983) found little evidence for the model and raised the possibility of reverse causation (behavior → attitudes) as a plausible alternative explanation. For example, he found some indication of unauthorized absence behavior predicting subsequent affective responses, such as job satisfaction. Terborg, Davis, and Smith (1980) found little support for Steers and Rhodes in a homogeneous population of retail stores. Hammer, Landau, and Stern (1981) explicitly contrasted Steers and Rhodes's model with an alternative model—the Exit, Voice, and Loyalty (EVL) model of Hirschman (1970). They did not find strong support for either model. Frechette (1981) found some support in an explicit partial test of the Steers and Rhodes model. However Frechette's analysis strategy and lack of any measures of pressures to attend make his test weak. Fitzgibbons and Moch (1980) tested a number of relationships in Steers and Rhodes's model using multiple measures of absence taking. Their results were mixed, and their positive findings often failed to replicate. Mowday, Porter, and Steers (1982) review the research, reporting marginal support for the model. Similar weak effects were estimated by Johns (1978), using job satisfaction, leadership, job characteristics, and demographics to predict frequency of absence and time lost. Ilgen and Hollenback (1977) examined a model of job satisfaction and pressure to attend to predict sick leave and unexcused absence. They found that pressure to attend did not moderate the job satisfaction–absence relationship. The Steers and Rhodes model to date both has theoretical problems and lacks strong empirical support.

Muchinsky (1977) reported a lack of absence-measure validity studies (and the nomological net required to do them), a lack of reliable absence measures, and substantial variability across studies in the quality of absence measures, all exacerbated by the lack of good reporting of measurement procedures. Substantively, Muchinsky claimed that an overall job satisfaction–absence relationship did hold, disagreeing with Nicholson, Brown, and Chadwick-Jones, (1976). However, Nicholson, Brown, and Chadwick-Jones's review and findings are quite convincing, while Muchinsky's reviewing procedure is not as clear or rigorous. Muchinsky calls attention to measurement problems. "More than any other consideration, the methodological 'hodgepodge' surrounding absenteeism indices

plagues the evaluation and interpretation of absenteeism research"
(Muchinsky, 1977, p. 320). Muchinsky finds that the research difficulties arise from lack of attention to conceptualizing absence,
reflecting inadequate theoretical development. Both Muchinsky
(1977) and Steers and Rhodes (1978) find that absence continues to
be "a social fact in need of a theory" (Ås, 1962).

The most telling critiques are those of Chadwick-Jones,
Johns, Nicholson, and their colleagues. Johns and Nicholson
(1982) claim that "the implicit boundaries within which absence
research has been conducted, drawn by metatheoretical assumptions and unstated premises, are overly restrictive and inappropriate. . . these boundaries have led to theoretical and empirical vacu-
ity" (p. 128). They question the fundamental, unstated premises in
absence research, arguing that the impoverished quality of absence
research is due to the lack of theory. Chadwick-Jones and colleagues find that most absence models tacitly accept the assumptions of previous researchers and do not confront alternative explanations.

Chadwick-Jones, Nicholson, and Brown (1982) cite two
examples of useful theory. First, Gibson's (1966) exchange framework and the use of the notion of the informal psychological contract to build a theory of absence are positive steps. The evolution
of the psychological contract reflects an *adjustment* of the person to
the environment. Unfortunately, the theory is difficult to operationalize and test. The second example is Hill and Trist's (1953)
suggestion that absence represents withdrawal from the stress of
work. For Hill and Trist, withdrawal shows a developmental progression, reflecting individual learning of culturally shared organizational absence norms. A consequence of this progression is that
the individual is now better fitted to the social environment. Building on this type of work, absence norms and cultures in an exchange
framework are developed by Chadwick-Jones, Nicholson, and
Brown (1982) to put absence in a social context.

Chadwick-Jones and colleagues assert that most absence
models focus primarily on the individual, without sufficient attention to exchange and social context. They suggest that absence
events vary systematically within persons over time and vary across
groups and organizations as a function of cultures and norms.

While their data are consistent with their exchange theory, their finding of distinctive occupational and organizational correlations with absence does not require their particular framework to explain it. For example, differences in industrial policies, contracts, labor markets, or ownership policies could explain differences between organizations. The value of their social-exchange emphasis is that it calls attention to different aspects of absence and to the fact that absence can be looked at usefully at different levels.

Nicholson (1977) proposes asking what functions an absence event serves for the individual. Absence effects and consequences and social beliefs and values about absence are the constraints on the individual. One must consider the *meaning* of an absence event from the perspective of the social actors involved. A situation-specific idiographic functional analysis of absence may often be warranted. He assumes that attendance is an individual's normal *inertial* state.

Nicholson proposes an avoidability-of-absence scale, ranging from unavoidable (A) to avoidable (B). One can then develop individual and occupational profiles on this A–B continuum. The impact of situational variables on an individual would be contingent on their profile on the A–B continuum. The profile would indicate the threshold for absence to occur given a particular instigating variable. For example, there may be differences across occupations in the degree to which job stress affects absence taking. Nicholson proposes using attendance motivation, defined as the likelihood that stimuli can induce absence taking (see Steers and Rhodes, 1978, for another treatment). He operationalizes attendance motivation as attachment, defined as the "degree to which the employee is dependent upon the regularities of organizational life" (Nicholson, 1977, p. 246). Attachment should reflect habitual organizational attendance, bureaucratic sanctions, commitment, and identification. In Nicholson's framework, the impact of the A–B continuum would be mediated by the level of attachment. This position is supported by Cheloha and Farr's (1980) finding that job involvement better predicts absence taking than does job satisfaction.

Nicholson's proposal, unlike other theory, justifies a priori the choice of absence measure for theory testing. He argues that absence frequency, not duration, is an appropriate absence measure. To explain duration, one needs a *theory for predicting return to work,* a different theoretical problem from being absent from work. While others have certainly made this argument ad hoc, his claim is from a theory of the measure. Secondly, Nicholson drops the "voluntary" versus "involuntary" absence distinction often used in the literature. This label implies an internal state of the absentee, he argues, and an assumption of some "will" to be absent. These measurement assumptions may not obtain. If so, the classification should be dropped or made an explicitly testable part of the theory. In addition, a particular absence in a particular category may not have equivalent "meaning" across individuals.

Johns and Nicholson (1982) extended these ideas, focusing on the meaning of absence for a theory of absence as a dependent variable. They note, as do others (Roberts, Hulin, and Rousseau, 1978; Steers and Rhodes, 1978), the need to address absence as a dynamic process. Muchinsky's (1977) observation that absence measures are often psychometrically unreliable has been taken as evidence for the need to aggregate over longer time frames (Hammer and Landau, 1981). The problem with aggregating is that the underlying processes influencing absence may not be stable (which fits the developmental and functional perspective) over time and hence will not meet standard psychometric assumptions (Mowday, Porter, and Steers, 1982). Johns and Nicholson want absence researchers to reexamine absence as a dynamic process, with past absence having causal consequences for future absence events.

Johns and Nicholson ask why absence should be viewed as an *organizational behavior.* By this, Johns and Nicholson mean that most research on absence takes the view that absence is determined by organizational membership and exposure to organizational factors. A number of authors acknowledge the impact of other elements in an individual's life space (Steers and Rhodes, 1978; Morgan and Herman, 1976; Roberts, Hulin, and Rousseau, 1978; Smith, 1977), yet few couch the study of absence in other than organizational terms. Given that absence is organizational behavior, it has further been assumed to be a management problem. Since absences have organizational ramifications, they are treated as a problem for management control. This may not be true or appropriate, but the "management problem" orientation helps effect a view of absence as within the control of the manager.

A theory-building problem noted by Johns and Nicholson (1982), echoing Steers and Rhodes (1978), is the focus of study on blue-collar absence, with little attention to white-collar and managerial absence. Since absenteeism occurs also among managers and upper-level white-collar employees, the lack of interest in these occupational strata is curious.

While psychologically oriented models have garnered most attention in organization behavior, others studying absence have taken an economic view. Allen, using the concepts of work-leisure trade-off, compensating differentials, and income and substitution effects, has developed empirical models of work attendance (1981b) and the relationship between absence and safety (1981a). Absence is treated as a behavior that allows the worker control of the level of wages and other work rewards received relative to desired levels of work, leisure, and risk. For example, if work is dangerous, the employer may be willing to tolerate greater employee absence as a price for the danger on the job. The employee is willing to accept the bargain where absence compensates for job risk.

Economists have introduced other useful concepts (Dalton and Perry, 1981; D. R. Winkler, 1980; Chelius, 1981; Deitsch and Dilts, 1981). One set of useful insights is in the area of the formal, contractual wage and benefit structure. For example, since fringe-benefit packages are not tied to hours worked (Deitsch and Dilts, 1981), as hours of work decrease, the paid benefits per hour increase (since benefits are constant and hours are decreasing), creating an incentive for absence. This is only partially tied to the relative strength of income effects and substitution effects on the individual. While income effects foster absence and substitution effects dampen absence, fringes, untied to hours worked, have a positive income effect and no substitution effect (Chelius, 1981). Since income and substitution effects cannot be independently estimated, such predictions as that increased wages result in reduced absence are unsupportable. In several studies, increases in fringe benefits were found to be associated with increased absences (Allen, 1981a, 1981b; Chelius, 1981). Similar arguments and findings have been reported for income protection through paid sick and absence days (D. R. Winkler, 1980; Dalton and Perry, 1981). These results support both the use of labor economic approaches to analyzing absence and attention to the constraints imposed on behavior by contractual and wage structure agreements. Two difficulties should be noted with some of these reported results. First, the measurement of and concern for quality of absence data are meager in some of these studies, casting doubt on the utility and meaning of some of the results (for example, Allen, 1981b, specifies a very complex model to predict self-reported absence behavior for the prior two weeks). Another issue is that findings often involve firms as units of analysis. While difficulties with aggregation problems are acknowledged, caution in interpretation of firm results as reflecting individual processes is warranted (for example, Allen, 1981b, D. R. Winkler, 1980; Dalton and Perry, 1981).

The labor-economics analysis supports Nicholson's (1977) functional approach, since absence is treated as a part of the income stream, exchangeable for safety or leisure or other goods. The notion of withdrawal or some other single function being served by absence becomes problematical with this analysis.

Hammer and her colleagues, using Hirschman's EVL model, propose that a dissatisfied worker has an alternative to *exit* (that is, withdrawal). The person can *voice* objections, attempting to ameliorate the situation. "The choice between exit and voice strategies depends on the loyalty to the work organization and belief in the possibility of improvement in the dissatisfying conditions" (Hammer, Landau, and Stern, 1981, p. 562). Interestingly, this viewpoint suggests situations where dissatisfaction increases pressure to attend, yielding a positive correlation of attendance and dissatisfaction. While their results are mixed and only mildly support their hypothesis, the concept of voice as an alternative means of dealing with "presumed absence causes" is theoretically useful. Hammer, Landau, and Stern (1981) also observed that the amount of absence did not change after a shift to employee ownership, but the distribution showed more involuntary and fewer voluntary absences. Similarly, requiring proof of illness changes the pattern and/or the amount of absence, adjusting for the more personally costly procedure of having one's absence behavior examined (Nicholson, 1976; Dalton and Perry, 1981; D. R. Winkler, 1980).

Interest in withdrawal continues. Gupta and Jenkins (1983) recommend that withdrawal be reformulated as escape behavior. They argue that escape is the underlying construct of interest for withdrawal studies. They suggest examining the escape function for absence as well as other behaviors. This refines the pain-avoidance approach by focusing on the escape component across behaviors. Like Johns and Nicholson, Gupta and Jenkins are questioning the stability of absence classification across time and persons. While some earlier work on withdrawal progression (Gupta and Jenkins, 1982) is noteworthy for its clear model specification, the underlying theoretical dynamics and assumptions of the escape concept are not clear. For example, why not take the voice option in the presence of a noxious organization stimulus? What are the consequences of an escape behavior for subsequent escape? Do some escape behaviors (such as drug abuse) create a need for more escape, rather than being pain reducers? The escape concept, while clarifying withdrawal both conceptually and operationally, also has the drawback, as pointed out by Clegg (1983), that withdrawal or escape may reflect not work avoidance but rather approach to attractive nonwork outcomes (Morgan and Herman, 1976, have made similar arguments in a different context).

The recent work on absence has several features. The first is the pessimistic tone, despite testing of refinements and incorporation of criticism (Fitzgibbons and Moch, 1980). Second, absence phenomena are unstable, often not replicable, and difficult to treat statistically (Hammer and Landau, 1981). Third, difficulties are being recognized in defining absence events operationally and conceptually (Muchinsky, 1977; Chadwick-Jones, Nicholson, and Brown, 1982; Mowday, Porter, and Steers, 1982). Fourth, there is greater attention to constraints such as norms, culture, sanctions, and contractual arrangements on the amount and distribution of absences. Fifth, there is increased acknowledgment that an absence model requires a dynamic structure to accommodate observed variations in absence. Economic and functional models can extend the range of ideas available to theories of organizational behavior, providing new insights and alternative models (Hammer, Landau, and Stern, 1981; Johns and Nicholson, 1982).

Interestingly, very little theory and research to explain absence uses organizational-level variables. Excepting some work on group and organizational size (Porter and Lawler, 1965) and technology (Chadwick-Jones, Nicholson, and Brown, 1982), very little attention has been paid to structural factors (Berger and Cummings, 1979). We take no position on why this occurs or whether this omission is warranted. It is noteworthy that most explanatory assumptions are individual-level hypotheses, while some suggested controls are structural.

## Underlying Theoretical Assumptions in Absence Research

A useful way to summarize the absence literature is to classify work by the implicit assumptions made. This approach (following Nicholson, 1977) yields the categories below. (Nicholson suggests three categories that partially overlap with the categories we suggest — pain-avoidance, adjustment, and decision models.)

- Absence is an approach-avoidance behavior. Withdrawal research uses this premise (Beehr and Gupta, 1978; Gupta and Jenkins, 1982, 1983). Most work using satisfaction with job aspects is really about avoidance behavior. Steers and Rhodes (1978) are using decision-making or expectancy model elements to study approach-avoidance behavior. Expectancy models are classified separately below, since avoidance-oriented studies make predictions that expectancy approaches do not. For example, job satisfaction is not a predictor in some versions of expectancy theory (absence consequences should influence job satisfaction), while it frequently is a predictor in absence studies.
- Absence is the result of a decision process. Expectancy models (Vroom, 1964) and some attitude models (Fishbein and Ajzen, 1975) are decision models where the action or object that is most attractive across attributes is chosen. In the idealized model, the person decides on any given day whether or not to attend work. Economic analysts using a utility-maximizing approach or work-leisure trade-offs are doing similar theorizing (Allen, 1981b; Chelius, 1981; R. C. Winkler, 1980; Deitsch and Dilts, 1981).
- Absence is the outcome of an adjustment process. One can describe the models of Gibson (1966) and Hill and Trist (1953) as adjustment models. As job conditions change, one renegotiates the psychological contract in response to those changes,

adjusting the fit of the organization and the employee. This is congenial with a labor-economic approach in which absences are compensation for unattractive aspects of the job (for example, hazards on the job, with absence as a compensating differential) (Allen, 1981a). Normative control of absence (Johns and Nicholson, 1982) requires social control via rewards and punishments by group members to adjust some desired equilibrium. Absence cultures effect control similarly, as the individual adjusts to cultural expectations.

- Absence is a habit. Atkin and Goodman (1983) suggest that some absences represent the generalization of learned responses to previous organizational conditions. While largely untested, this hypothesis is intuitively appealing. Habit is implicit in the suggestion that a few workers (the absence-prone) are responsible for most absence. Garrison and Muchinsky (1977) were unable to find substantiation for absence-proneness. Predicting present absence on the basis of past absence is consistent with but does not directly support the habit hypothesis (Breaugh, 1981; Waters and Roach, 1979; Morgan and Herman, 1976). Some unobserved variable(s) could account for these results, and the tests were not explicitly of the habit hypothesis. An explicit test would require hypotheses about the impact of environmental change on the rate and magnitude of absence.

- Absence is a consequence of an apparently unrelated event. Unrelated or apparently unrelated events, such as a stressful family crisis (for example, divorce or death in the family) or some behavioral disorder (for example, alcoholism), may lead to absence. These "causes" may be unrelated to organizational conditions. Additionally, they may have an internal dynamic of their own. For example, we know that addictive behaviors such as alcoholism or drug abuse may generate behavior patterns driven by the dynamics of addiction (Solomon, 1980).

- Absence is phenomenologically unique. Whether Johns and Nicholson's idiographic orientation is termed a view about theory or a view about method, a functional approach is a distinct theoretical view. Ostensibly similar actions may have different causes and consequences and different meanings for the individual and should be treated as distinct. One can look at withdrawal behavior fruitfully this way. Gupta and Jenkins (1983) suggest looking at escape and asking to what degree absence provides escape. Their argument is that behaviors can share common surface features while having different underlying structures, and vice versa. One should study the underlying structures, such as escape. While some would despair at the idiographic approach, its functionalist underpinnings make it an acceptable theoretical category for classifying research. The key distinctive feature is the cognizance of multiple functions.

These different assumptions encompass most work on absence. One can now group apparently unrelated studies that share the same underlying tacit beliefs about absence.

### Absence Theory Construction Criteria

Several past shortcomings needing attention from any absence theory are identifiable. We will not undertake a lengthy philosophical excursion into general criteria for theory construction. Rather, the following issues require particular attention when absence is studied.

- Does the theory *define* absence or the underlying construct for which absence is a proxy? If absence is a proxy for a concept such as withdrawal or escape (Gupta and Jenkins, 1983), are both clearly defined and operationalized? Are the conceptual and operational linkages between absence and the underlying concept clear?
- What is the *conceptual and psychological space for absence?* Johns and Nicholson (1982) note problems with defining absence as organizational behavior. Morgan and Herman (1976) found that "Many of the motivating consequences that employees who are frequently absent consider to be justifiable indicate a need for free time. This is an outcome over which organizations normally exert little control" (p. 742). Most investigators look at absence in an organizational space, disregarding nonwork variables. The nonorganizational causes and consequences of absence require systematic attention or explicit delimiting of the scope of an absence model.

- Does the theory present *disconfirmable* predictions and explanations? Only if the theory can make this claim can it be useful. If the theory is infinitely flexible and pliable and can take on new hypotheses and results without embarrassment, then it will not provide useful predictions and explanations. If the theory is disconfirmable, then its utility can be tested and judged by confronting alternative explanations. Too little of this has been done (see Hammer, Landau, and Stern, 1981, for a notable exception). In effect, we want to know what evidence helps confirm the theory and what data disconfirm the theory. It is also reasonable to ask what the boundaries are of the theory's capacity to explain and predict. Is it intended to deal with some kinds of absence events or all kinds, and what predictions can it make about those events?
- Does the theory characterize absence *dynamically*? The possibility that absence is a dynamic process changing in its characteristics through time needs consideration. Given that absence is a priori defined in time, we should ask whether it is a static or dynamic process over time. Two related issues are involved.
  1. Can the theory explain the *instability* (whether the pattern of events is invariant over time) in its domain of absence? Are current absence events dependent on past events? If so, we may need to look at the absence process through time, within and across indivduals. Garrison and Muchinsky (1977) found no evidence of absence-proneness (that is, stability), and others have found that their results are not replicated (Fitzgibbons and Moch, 1980) over time and samples.
  2. Does the theory deal with the *consequences* of absence? There are two questions here. First, can absence consequences matter in the theory? If absence should be treated dynamically, then the answer is yes. The dynamics of absence aside, are there immediate consequences that can affect subsequent absence events? For example, Johns and Nicholson (1982) note that absence is a clear, salient behavior that other organizational members may encode, facilitating attributions and judgments. These cognitive responses may influence subsequent behavior directed toward the absentee, influencing subsequent absence and other behavior. Atkin

and Goodman (1983) discuss the effect of absences on organizational productivity, costs, safety, and attitudes. These
effects are of interest in their own right and may have direct
and indirect effects on subsequent absence. Staw and
Oldham (1978) argue that absence can sometimes have
positive consequences for both the individual and the organization.

• Should group- and organizational-level policies and properties
matter in an absence theory? Little work has been done on
structural effects on absence. Yet researchers have become
aware of the possible effects of labor contracts (Dalton and
Perry, 1981; D. R. Winkler, 1980), management sanctions
(Nicholson, 1976; Baum, 1978), and other control and management policies. These concepts can help explain absence and
allow control of exogenous influences when studying individual-
level explanations of absence. There are two related issues
here. We may study absence as individual behavior and not
worry about levels of analysis, just treating group and organizational effects as control variables. Alternatively, we may take
Johns and Nicholson (1982) seriously and worry about whether
we are studying absence at the right level (for example, whether
we need to look at absence cultures).

While not constructed to be exhaustive, this criterion set is
useful for evaluating theoretical and empirical developments in the
area. These criteria capture the thrust of the critical appraisals of
absence research offered here and by others.

### Problems in Defining Absence

Two issues need attention: *is absence, or some category system of
absence, a meaningful construct,* and, if so, *do different theoretical approaches
imply different definitions?* The number of operational definitions and
absence categories that people have developed is staggering.
Following a review of some definitional difficulties, a definition will
be offered.

Absence is a socially defined event. However, absence is
socially defined more than once. A person who fails to appear at

work is defined as absent by someone in the organization. Without the organization and its concept of attendance, absence has no meaning. Absence immediately exists only as defined by the organization and its relationship to the employee. Absence is frequently categorized by the organization. Researchers often find the firm's category system unsuitable and devise another category system. These categories and the context in which they place absence often differ from researcher-defined variables. (The measures are generally organizational records designed by managers for different purposes. Researchers rarely can claim that acceptable coding and reliability controls were applied. Often, a well-defined, reliable coding system is lacking.) Absence requires two state changes, from present to absent and from absent to present, and is not presumed to be an enduring attribute in the same way as is satisfaction with working conditions or performance quality. As Nicholson (1977) notes, we do not have a theory about returning to work, but some process is required to return the person to work, and it may influence our observations. For example, suppose people's willingness to return to work is premised upon when they next expect to be absent. Then understanding the next absence-taking incident requires understanding the process of returning to work. The relative complexity of the absence event may require definitional attention to its components.

Can absence be treated as a meaningful construct, even with a complex category scheme for partitioning absence events into homogeneous categories? Absence may be a socially interesting index of uncertain quality reflecting underlying dynamic processes that yield complex behavior patterns of which absence is only one component. A more useful view may be that absence is a socially defined event leading to interesting social responses (Johns and Nicholson, 1982). Studying how the absentee and others in his or her life space respond to the absence may be a fruitful way to look at absence for itself. We may discover more consistency and clarity in the social definitions, categorizations, and responses to absence than in the event itself.

Since absence is defined by time and place, several kindred definitional problems surface. If an absence exists only because an organizational relationship was not fulfilled, then if the causes of an

absence exert their influence when a person is not in that organizational relationship, we will not observe the absence substitute. For
example, family pressures have been hypothesized to pull a person
from the job (Steers and Rhodes, 1978). Those pressures exist on
weekends, exerting the same force, but the weekend obviates the
possibility of observing an absence. This organizational bounding
is true for other behavioral events, such as job performance. The
difference lies in the causal explanation and when the observed
behavior can be manifested. While work performance is organization bound, its nomological network includes only organizational
events having direct effects on performance. In contrast, most tacit
absence nomological networks have nonorganizational elements,
since the forces "causing" absence often are not organizationally
bounded in time or space.

A functional approach also generates some definitional
problems. Absence can serve multiple functions simultaneously, so
defining absence as expressing one underlying function (such as
withdrawal or leisure seeking) is inappropriate. Even if an absence
is an attempt to serve some particular function, it does not follow
that the absence will serve only that function. For example, if I am
absent for reasons of illness, I may get an opportunity to be with
my family, a function not implied by the putative absence cause.
Therefore, the absence fulfills two functions, getting well and being
with family. If this argument is correct, then *absence category schemes*
*that attempt to identify the cause of an absence are conceptually flawed in a*
*fundamental way,* rather than merely being noisy and unreliable (that
is, requiring refinement).

Let us turn the argument around and ask about activities
substituting for absence. Gupta and Jenkins (1983) note that
escape is a motive that can be served by a multitude of behaviors,
behaviors that may be partially substitutable for one another. Consequently, if absence is defined in functional terms, we need to
coordinate the absence definitions of functions and behavioral
modalities that serve those functions. We then have absence serv-
ing multiple functions and each function being served by a set of
behaviors, of which absence is only one. That is, *absence itself may*
*best be treated as one possible behavioral event in a multivariate conceptual*
*space of multiple motives and behavioral alternatives jointly determining the*
*allocation of time and effort across activities.*

Absence is conditioned by contractual obligations and constraints imposed on individuals. For a given year, over 33 percent of the days in the year are enforced absence, if you will. One may get 104 days of absence for weekends, 10 holidays, and 14 vacation days. Frequently, we pay people to be absent by offering sick days that expire if unused within a calendar year. These enforced absences, which are rarely declined or may not be declinable even if one wanted, constitute (assuming 5 sick days) 36.4 percent of a calendar year. These days are opportunities to serve some of the functions we presume absences serve, though they may not be well timed from the point of view of some job incumbents. In effect, the imposition of fixed schedules, while clearly beneficial, may provide absence opportunities inefficiently from the absentee's point of view. Certainly, interest in flextime reflects this intuition.

An interesting problem that external schedule constraints create is estimating what the ambient rate of absence would be before variation in causal factors. That is, absences we observe are conditioned on the unobserved effects of current work schedules. For example, absence defined as withdrawal is conditioned on the availability of regularly timed withdrawal opportunities at some rate (28.4 percent for weekends). As in any other motivational context, we would like to know what the ambient rate of absence would be, holding the causal factors that influence it constant. This is particularly true if there is a strong behavioral inertial tendency to continue attending work, slowing behavioral change and reducing the detectability of some "true" underlying tendency to be absent. In a multiple regression model, the constant term is an estimate of the ambient absence rate, holding other factors constant. This ambient rate estimate is very difficult to obtain under external schedule constraints, but the problem needs attention. Smith's (1977) study of attendance during a snowstorm implicitly acknowledges the powerful constraints imposed on an individual's attendance behavior. Smith's snowstorm was an opportunity to observe attendance with all constraints removed.

Johns and Nicholson (1982) point out that most definitional schemes (both the organization's and the researcher's) have tacit theories, untested attributions, assumptions, and operational problems built into their construction. The idea of short-term absences as attitudinal is a clear example. The category *attitudinal* (implying that the absence reflects a voluntary response to a disposition to avoid work) is an untested assumption and may have little foundation in fact.

The definition of absence is clearly difficult. Few writers actually go to the trouble of defining it. Gibson (1966) makes a valiant effort, offering that *"an absence from work* means an *inability,* an *inappropriateness,* or an *unwillingness* to work" (p. 112). Earlier, he notes that "absence events are a subclass of the events that constitute the behavior of workers" (p. 110–111). Despite the care taken to define terms, Gibson needs legitimacy, roles, willingness to work, and other concepts to help define whether an absence event occurs. The difficulty of characterizing behavior that is signaled by a nonevent is apparent. It is necessary to impute motives and causal factors to give meaning to absence events.

When definitions are offered (and they generally are not), they are tacit theories of absence bound to specific measures (which are often poor operationalizations of the intended meaning of the concept). The question of whether different theories offer different definitions is rendered moot by the failure to clearly define absence. Most definitions reiterate tacit theories of absence rather than conceptual definitions derived from theory. Absence definitions should be bound to theory, not data. Data should be ordered by theory and definition.

Absence can be defined as *the allocation of time across nonwork activities when an individual is expected to be working.* This definition is consistent with Gibson but makes no causal attribution. The definition allows one to look at the full range of time allocations of the individual and the functions that they serve when examining the allocation of time away from work. The definition permits us to study absence duration and the process of returning to work. This definition highlights absence as allocation of time and a *change from one activity to another* (Atkinson, 1981b). This definition can help organize the criticisms raised earlier and guide study of the inception and duration of absence and the behaviors and motives engaged during the absence episode. We can look at imposed schedule effects and their interaction with spells of absence in a time-allocation framework. A time-allocation framework steers us toward dynamic modeling of absence and away from the static models that currently prevail. By couching absence as a change from one activity to another in a time-allocation framework, the researcher must consider other activities in the behavior stream, the statistical conditioning effects of those activities, and whether those other activities affect the relationship of absence to stable individual or group properties.

Using this definition, we will outline a framework for analyzing time allocation to absence and the duration of absence behavior. We reviewed five theoretical perspectives that shared the idea that absence, or the functions fulfilled by absence, reflected motivated behavior. We share that belief and will view *time allocation and absence as aspects of motivated behavior*. Our theory will be at an individual level. As we construct our theory, we acknowledge that between-group and between-organization effects exist; however, we believe those effects have detectable individual-level consequences and can be thought of as between-group differences in an individual-level analysis. Essentially, we are trying to model an individual response process underlying absence. Understanding absence requires looking at behavior and time allocation dynamically, and the appropriate analytic strategy is partitioning an individual's stream of behavior. This individual stream can be affected by group and organizational variables and events.

### Theoretical Framework for Motivated Behavior

Having defined absence as a problem in individual time allocation, we will present a theoretical model of time allocation as motivated behavior. The framework is a general one and is best presented initially as a general model.

The initial premise is that the key problem in the study of motivated behavior is a change in activity. Atkinson and Birch (1970, p. 23) make this the centerpiece of motivation theory: "The behavioral life of an individual is a constant flux of activity. There are no behavioral vacuums except when the individual is literally inactive and unconscious—yet still alive in a medical sense—as in the case of extreme illness or after a severe blow on the head. Otherwise, his behavioral life (which constitutes the subject matter of psychology) is, as Barker (1963) has described it: a continuous stream characterized by change from one activity to another without pause from birth until death (p. 1).... A change in the activity of an individual, from some initial activity that is already in progress when the interval of observation begins to another activity later, defines the fundamental problem for a psychology of motivation.... The two classic problems of motivation, persistence of an activity and initiation of an activity, are two sides of the same coin — a change in activity."

Any particular behavior in an organization, or any other sphere of life, is one behavior among many, a piece of "behavioral chatter" (Atkinson and Birch, 1970). Yet most thinking about organizational motivation ignores the "motivational paradox, that is, the conjecture that people do not always choose the genotypically preferred alternative" (Kuhl and Blankenship, 1979, p. 149). Traditional motivation theory assumes that some stochastic component causes a change in the relative strengths of motives, leading to a change in behavior. No real attempt has been made in organizational psychology to predict changes in molar activity. Most theories beg the question or demand constant re-estimation of the decision process by the individual.

Naylor, Pritchard, and Ilgen (1980), having reached a similar conclusion, suggest that: "Motivation is defined as the process of allocating personal resources in the form of time and energy to various acts in such a way that the anticipated affect resulting from these acts is maximized... we are talking about a *resource allocation process.* The motivation process is one whereby the person takes the time and effort resources at his or her disposal and uses or distributes these resources to the various acts he or she could emit" (pp. 159–160).

Similar ideas have evolved within economics, particularly in behavioral psychology, where economic models of choice are used for motivational analysis. For example, Lea (1978) has argued that consumer demand theory and reinforcement theory make reasonably similar predictions and that demand theory may be applied to problems traditionally reserved for reinforcement approaches. Collier (1981) asserts that "choice as it has been studied does not permit the psychologist or physiologist to understand the underlying process of choice solutions.... Only an analysis of choice that recognizes the time/energy allocation problem will suffice" (p. 71). Hursh

(1980) and Collier (1981) distinguish between an "open economy" and a "closed economy" in experimental motivation. An open economy is characterized by experimental control of the intake and pattern of rewards, while a closed economy is characterized by subject control of the pattern and intake of rewards. Collier's experimental results with animals show that behavior is radically different in the two kinds of economies. Most studies have been in open economies and have led to classical learning and motivation theory. In a closed economy, the response distributions are radically different. The allocation of time and effort across activities seems to minimize the costs of obtaining rewards while simultaneously maintaining the needed variety of rewards (for example, types of nutrients). This excursion into behavioral motivation theory illustrates the value of looking at motivation in terms of allocation of time and effort across activities.

In an economic analysis of behavior, choice behavior is best understood as the outcome of an individual's utility analysis of a commodity bundle. Choice behavior is the distribution of resources (of which time is both a resource and an index) across a bundle of rewarding activities with associated utility functions (reflecting the costs and benefits of those activities). In this context, there is no meaning to a statement about motivation to do some activity without asking what the bundle of activities is that the person is contemplating. One cannot ask how much ice cream you would like without looking at what other delicacies are available. Additionally, in a closed economy with a bundle of foods, we would not expect someone to eat ice cream all night but to eat some of the other available foods as he or she gets tired of ice cream. Similarly, one cannot ask how much of any particular food will be eaten without knowing what other foods are available at what cost. The Naylor, Pritchard, and Ilgen (1980) and Atkinson and Burch (1970) models share the central theme of resource distribution as a function of costs and gains. The economic reasoning of Naylor, Pritchard, and Ilgen (1980) is captured in their concept of *motivational force*, which has a marginal utility assumption shared by the behavioral economic analysis. Naylor, Pritchard, and Ilgen (1980, p. 189) define *motivational force*. . . " as the slope of the function describing a composite contingency relationship between resources committed to an act and the amounts of affect anticipated from the committing of

various levels of resources to that act." This is the essential requirement for examining resource allocation across activities. Motivational force theoretically predicts when an individual will switch
from one activity to the next. Unless the utility for an activity is
greater for any unit increase in resource allocation compared to
every other activity in the bundle of activities the person can
choose, at some point the return on increased effort at one activity
will be less than the return on some other activity. If activities have
marginally decreasing utility functions, then at some point, the
motivational force for one activity will be less than the prospective
return for engaging in another activity. In the Naylor, Pritchard,
and Ilgen model, the information needed to predict switching is
forbidding, requiring knowledge of contingency relationships and
utility functions for the complete bundle of activities of concern.
The model is instructive. It eliminates the motivational paradox
and opens up the allocation of resources for motivational analysis.

While economic models are attractive, we will initially use
the Atkinson and Birch (1970) model for thinking about absence.
The Atkinson and Birch "dynamics of action" model aspires to
explain the full range of behavioral effects an absence theorist
might be interested in (while proposed as a general model for
behavioral action, most of the research it has been used for involves
achievement motivation or learning and motivation in the animal
laboratory), which were discussed above.

The dynamics of action theory is too rich and complex to
present here in detail (the reader is referred to Atkinson, 1981b;
Atkinson and Birch, 1970, 1978, for details). We will introduce
Atkinson and Birch's terms and an explanation of their theory that
should make its applicability to absence clear. An initial premise of
the theory is that a person frequently changes behavior as motivational forces and their internal consequences fluctuate. That is,
when we study a person's behavior stream, we are observing a person already motivated to behave in some fashion. Our attention is
on what forces cause a shift from one activity to another. Like Collier's closed economy, the dynamics of action theorist asks how the
individual distributes resources over activities. If we are predicting
changes from one behavior to another, we are trying to look at
behavior in a closed economy.

*The Dynamics of Action.* Atkinson and Birch posit that a stimulus situation affects behavior through the effects of *instigating* and *inhibitory* forces to engage in actions. Past rewarding experiences strengthen instigating forces, and past aversive experiences strengthen inhibitory forces. The stronger the force, the stronger the *action tendency* (for instigating forces) or *negaction tendency* (for inhibitory forces). The stronger the force, the greater the strength of its corresponding tendency. In a constant stimulus environment, the tendencies aroused by the forces will increase in strength at some constant rate. The hypothesis is: "A behavioral tendency (either action or negaction), once it has been aroused, will persist in its present state until acted on by some force that either increases or decreases its strength... we begin with the assumption of inertia applied to behavioral tendencies... to capture the fundamental insight of Freud... that a wish or intention, once aroused, will persist until it is expressed in behavior and satisfied" (Atkinson and Birch, 1970, p. 10).

These two tendencies (the action and negaction tendencies), specific to an activity, are combined additively to determine the net or *resultant action tendency*. This combining of tendencies is simultaneously occurring for all other activities cued by the stimulus situation. The strongest resultant action tendency at some moment is acted upon by the person, producing the associated action. As in any motivation theory, the taking of action yields certain reward consequences, termed a *consummatory force*. This is the product of the action's consummatory value and resultant action tendency. The stronger the consummatory value or the resultant action tendency, the greater the consummatory force of the action taken. The consummatory force reduces the resultant action tendency. "Similarly, resistance to an action tendency, produced by the opposition of a negaction tendency, constitutes an analogous *force of resistance* (R), which reduces, in a comparable way, the strength of the negaction tendency" (Atkinson, 1981b, p. 177).

This relatively simple structure for a particular action can yield some fairly complex behavioral outcomes. For every action being instigated or inhibited by the stimulus setting, we have associated values for the various terms outlined above. The activity with the greatest initial resultant action tendency will be observed at the beginning of an interval of time. This produces consummatory force, which may increase, decrease, or leave unaffected the strength of the resultant action tendency. The stronger the consummatory force, the weaker the action tendency will become. Meanwhile other resultant action tendencies that initially were weaker are becoming stronger, since there is no consummatory force to dampen them. Consequently, at some point in the interval of time, if it is long enough, we will observe some unexpressed action tendency overtaking the currently expressed action tendency. This will result in a change in behavior. Now the new activity will have some consummatory force acting on it, and the previous activity will not. Of the initially unexpressed tendencies, the one with the largest positive acceleration (that is, the greatest instigating force acting on it relative to inhibitory force) will be the first activity expressed, assuming that the unexpressed tendencies start with the same initial value. (If a resultant action tendency has a smaller rate of acceleration and a higher initial value, it may be expressed, though it would not have the highest motivational force, to use Naylor, Pritchard, and Ilgen's terminology.)

Atkinson and Birch look at when changes in behavior will occur and the duration of behaviors. In the case outlined above, the rate of relative growth in the two tendencies (one expressed, one unexpressed) determines when to switch activities. Forces for action and resistance to an action combine additively. Action and resistance forces operate in similar fashions. Sometimes, a tendency is blocked by some *incompatible* activity (meaning the taking of that action precludes some other action or actions). When an incompatible tendency is unexpressed, it will grow in strength. If an incompatible tendency exceeds the strength of the currently expressed tendency, it will be expressed, and we will observe a change of behavior.

Atkinson and Birch develop the concept of families of tendencies, linking concepts in economics and behavioral psychology. We may have tendencies that are partially compatible (that is, substitutable), not incompatible, instigated by the stimulus situation. Tendencies that are partially substitutable are in the same family of tendencies. Tendencies to eat different kinds of foods are all part of a tendency family, for example.

This family concept can explain situations where absence does not occur though the instigating forces may be quite powerful.

Some other action tendency can substitute for the absence action tendency. A related concept is *displacement* (Atkinson and Birch, 1970). The forces effecting one action tendency may indirectly instigate another action tendency, though the stimulus situation itself may not elicit that second tendency. For example, suppose the stimulus situation elicits an action tendency to escape from work. The thought of leaving work increases thoughts of home and family, thoughts elicited not by the stimulus situation but by the escape action tendency. This pairing and displacement may increase the likelihood of leaving. As in Freudian displacement, taking some action may increase the strength of some other motive. This touches on the problems of enforced schedules and their consequences. The concepts of substitution and displacement can prove quite useful in looking at this effect.

*The Dynamics of Absence Events.* Absence, in a dynamic framework, occurs in a context of simultaneous action tendencies elicited by the stimulus situation. An individual can be examined in two settings, the work setting and some nonwork setting (for example, home). In any setting, instigating and inhibitory motivation forces affect the strength of the set of elicited action tendencies. At work, we can imagine resultant action tendencies toward doing the task, engaging in social interaction, and going on a coffee break. Assume one of the actions (for example, doing the task) is currently being taken. Consequently, that path has some consummatory force. The other paths have increasing resultant action tendencies, since they have no consummatory effects. At some point, either the coffee break tendency or the social interaction tendency will overtake the tendency to do the task, assuming no change in the stimulus situation. Suppose the social interaction tendency overtakes the task tendency and is expressed in action. Depending on its consummatory force and the relative magnitudes of the slopes of the other two tendency functions, the resulting social interaction could last a long time or just a moment. If the coffee break and social interaction tendencies are partially substitutable for each other, then the coffee break tendency may be dampened by the consummatory force of the social interaction. Further suppose that the break turns to talk of work and how people are doing at their work tasks. This could have a displacement effect, increasing the unexpressed resultant action tendency toward the task. This complex interplay leads to a precipitous return to the task, forgoing a coffee break.

This microanalysis illustrates several interesting effects observable from a dynamic perspective:

- The choice of behaviors and their duration are derivable from the assumptions of the model.
- Some behaviors for which there is motivation (for example, taking a coffee break) are never taken because of substitution effects or the ever-present impact of alternative tendencies that are consistently more powerful.
- Some behaviors, such as social interaction, through the process of substitution, serve multiple functions.
- Some behaviors instigate other behaviors through the process of displacement, as when the talk at the break turned to work, accelerating the motivational force for task behavior.
- The mixture and distribution of behavior were functions of the bundle of action possibilities in the stimulus situation. If there had not been the possibility of social interaction, the coffee break would have been taken. If the coffee break had been taken, there would have been no displacement effect due to the social interaction. With no displacement effect, the resultant action tendency toward the task is lessened. The variation in the taking of coffee breaks, whose motivational force (in the sense of rate of change in motivation per unit time) is constant whether or not there is social interaction is attributable to the bundle of possible actions in the stimulus situation.

Let us examine a situation closer to an actual absence event. A set of resultant action tendencies develops in response to the home stimulus situation. There is some tendency for going to work. There are forces toward doing various activities outside of work. Let us assume it is Saturday afternoon. The resultant action tendency toward work is a somewhat strong (neither the weakest nor the strongest) tendency. It is not expressible in behavior, since there is no work available on Saturday. Hence, we see no direct behavioral evidence of that motive state. The action tendency will continue to grow in strength, since it is unexpressed. Other tendencies evoked by the home situation are expressible, and the strongest one (for example, going out for a run, playing with the children) will be acted on and be observable. As the day wears on, the interplay of forces, consummatory forces, and other effects will yield a behavioral chatter such as one frequently sees on a weekend. Meanwhile, the action tendency for work, even if it is growing slowly, is getting stronger. By Monday, the person, even if not powerfully motivated by work, will go to work because of how powerful, relative to the others, that action tendency has become.

Observed on Monday morning, the individual seems quite eager and ready to attack work. If the force (the slope of the action tendency) is small and/or if the consummatory value of work activity is high, we may find our individual eager to escape work by Wednesday as those unexpressed weekend tendencies start up (evoked by being at home in the evening). If we interviewed our organization member on Monday, we would find a high absolute level of motivation and misclassify the person as highly motivated toward work. A Wednesday motivation measure would suggest a lower motivation level. Even if the person were more motivated to attend, the lack of opportunity to express those nonwork action tendencies that are expressible over the weekend might still lead to absence or withdrawal. To adequately explain an absence or lack of absence for this person, we need to know the full set of behavioral action options in the life space, not just the level of motivation. (We assumed a fixed schedule. Contrast this with a person with a less constrained schedule, such as a manager or professor, and the same set of forces and parameters will yield a different stream of activities.)

What is the heuristic and empirical value of this complex system of tendencies and forces? A first answer is that people's behavior is probably as complex as or more complex than the model. A constructive answer is that a dynamic model has several useful properties when mapped onto absence. The assignment of "meaning" to absence is facilitated. The concept of substitution and displacement within families of tendencies allows an absence to serve multiple functions. We can ask what action tendencies were fulfilled by the absence event and assign meaning on that basis. A second, related insight is that a function can be served by multiple behaviors. In our coffee break example, we saw another activity substituting for coffee breaks.

Previous results are now seen in a different light. Reliability, which has annoyed absence researchers (Muchinsky, 1977), is less salient now. Certain forms of the absence process, when absence is one alternative in a large bundle of action alternatives, can lead to unreliable absence taking across time. Clearly, the person who first did not take coffee breaks and then did was not evidencing an unlawful behavior pattern. Rather, it was not reconcilable with the classic psychometric true-score model (Atkinson, 1981a). In some sense, nothing about the individual's underlying attributes and states had changed, just the behavioral outcroppings (see also Chapter Two, by Atkin and Goodman, in this volume.).

The suggested approach also allows us to look at both frequency and duration, integrating the onset, offset, and duration of absence into one framework. The theory raises doubts about our measures. Types and categories of absence (for example, excused, voluntary) become social-psychological issues differing fundamentally from the issue of time distribution per se. The assignment of meaning by the self and others to absence events and the consequences that flow from them may feed back to the stimulus situation, altering the balance of instigating and inhibitory forces. This changes the parameters, not the fundamental workings of forces and action tendencies. In that sense, Ilgen and Hollenback's (1977) argument for different models for different absences may be inappropriate. Different absences (in the category sense, such as excused or unexcused) may differ in the mixture of motives that operate when they occur but not in the fundamental motivational process underlying them. Different types of absence may reflect different mixtures of motives, not different processes. While this is counterintuitive when one views absences as different labeled categories, it is less so when viewed in a multimotive, multiaction space. Thus, even in an extreme situation such as an extended layoff due to illness, the dynamic model should still operate. Certain tendencies are affected by the stimulus situation, while others are not. One might find that after an extended illness, which presumably should lead to a greater motive tendency to attend work, absence rates may not change. Some illness-related activities may have satisfied work motives (for example, disability insurance may have satisfied compensation requirements), so that the absolute level of motivation to attend is not as high as might be anticipated. Secondly, the illness may have blocked other incompatible (with work) activities that have strong resultant action tendencies.

Motivation and absence are conceived of in a multivariate space, with multiple motives and multiple behavior options available. This is consistent with the claim that absence behavior is multivariate and can serve different functions at different times. The multivariate behavior space accommodates the withdrawal concept that links absence events to other behaviors, such as accidents, drug taking, and psychological withdrawal. (The only difficulty here is that a drug addiction or alcohol problem may generate its own dynamic, with different functional forms and motive behavior.) The appropriate unit of study is that multivariate space and the relationships within it rather than one element in that multivariate space.

If we analyze several action tendencies operating simultaneously, we begin to see patterning of behavior and complex outcomes in activity duration and switching as different action tendencies are expressed and then overtaken by other tendencies. The kinds of action tendencies that are operating are due in part to the stimulus situation and the kind of behavioral tendencies it evokes and the nature of the individual's motives. The formation of utility functions and contingency relationships and beliefs, as in other motivation theory, is a given and requires separate attention as a developmental and learning phenomenon. Hence, one can map various theories of motivation onto the dynamic structure without sacrificing the value of the dynamic structure.

There is a great deal of space to build theory within this framework. For example, Kuhl and Blankenship (1979) have used the dynamic of action to look at changes in achievement motives in a computer simulation. Several of their results fit empirical findings well. Similar kinds of work can be done in the absence area. That is, one can construct theory about the formation and development of the model's parameters and predict changes over time in the distribution of behavior (as Naylor, Pritchard, and Ilgen, 1980,

argue), not the timing of absence events. The value in this kind of
approach is that it does not make demands of the theory that are
empirically intractable because of the potentially large number of
unobservable variables and parameters.

Certain kinds of theory can provide testable bases for looking at the stability of absence taking over time. For example, the
Nicholson (1977) A–B model has some significant commonalities
with the model offered here. He argued for a threshold model for
absence events. In the dynamics of action, we will observe those
kinds of threshold effects, since an action tendency, while continuous in its underlying action tendency in the multivariate space,
will demonstrate significant discontinuities at the behavioral level,
as other expressed incompatible tendencies dominate that focal
resultant action tendency for some period of time. The Nicholson
(1977) A–B model idea of thresholds is a phenomenon that the
dynamics model would generate. Both the threshold model and the
dynamics model allow for changes in parameters, both endogenously and exogenously, though Nicholson is not explicit on this
point. Consequently, one can look at absence events changing in
their form and distribution over time. This may be due to endogenously generated parameter changes, such as some developmental or learning process generated by the events themselves, or due
to exogenous constraints or shocks (for example, changed work
schedule, no more social interaction).

The relative advantage of the dynamics framework is that it
is better grounded in psychology, often allowing for more realistic
assumptions about individual motives and behavior. For example,
Houston and McFarland (1980), in a demand analysis of motivation, make assumptions about the variation in behavior individuals
are willing to tolerate. They make the homeostatic assumption that
people are not willing to allow their internal environment to
diverge from some set point. The greater the divergence, the more
motivating a behavior option will be that allows the person to
regain their homeostatic set point. While we are not ready to assert
that set points are involved in the patterning of absence, the introduction of such psychological parameters is admissible within these
classes of models. Finally, these economic models and their
dynamics of action forms can potentially accommodate the imposi-

tion of budget constraints. That is, one can ask about the substitutability of commodities or activities under the constraint of limited time and resources in which to pursue both activities. This may be another way to handle the imposition of schedules on absence taking (Rachlin, Kagel, and Battalio, 1980).

*Integrating Tacit Theories with a Dynamic Approach.* We suggest some tacit theories of absence (that is, absence is a result of approach-avoidance, decision making, adjustment, habit, an apparently unrelated event, or phenomenologically unique considerations). The dynamics approach is certainly able to accommodate the tacit theories offered (excepting absence as a consequence of unrelated events). It can explicitly handle withdrawal and approach-avoidance quite readily, since the underlying conception is derived from traditional approach-avoidance theory. We would claim, as argued earlier, that the notion of phenomenological uniqueness, when interpreted as a functionalist view, is well handled by the dynamics of action view. The habit formulation suggested in discussions of proneness and by Atkin and Goodman (1983) would not require radical revision in the theory, since we have made no claim about the motive space driving absence; therefore, the motive could be a habitual one. Certainly most habit formulations in classical learning theory would predict variation in habit strength in a fashion similar to the one we have presented.

The more difficult tacit theories are those based on an adjustment process and those based on a decision calculus such as expectancy theory. The adjustment, or exchange, view claims that there are reliable developmental or implicitly negotiated changes that occur over time in the relationship between the individual and the firm. In one sense, this is not a problem, since the dynamic model will be testable if we can observe all the relevant variables. Unfortunately, that is extremely difficult to do. An adequate test of an exchange formulation may require more specification of the nature of the developmental process and how it will influence motives that are then expressed as instigating and inhibitory forces and then in turn as action tendencies. The specification of an explicit learning process makes the situation very much more complex, since we are not predicting some time-varying change in the consequences of entering the stimulus situation. For example, one might claim that certain instigating forces increase in magnitude after some unit of time as the socialization process takes effect. Given these conditions, the adjustment model should be accommodated.

The expectancy model is actually easier to think about, since we can use the expectancy model to generate for us the values of the forces evoked by the stimulus situation. Higher motivation values for some particular behavior option should index the strength of forces instigating and inhibiting an action. Some of Atkinson and Birch's work illustrates the use of an expectancy formulation (the theory of achievement motivation) in the dynamics of action framework.

### Does a Dynamic Approach Fit Our Theory Criteria?

We developed criteria for absence theory. Is the dynamic framework useful given those criteria?

1. *Does the theory deal with the definition of absence?* Yes, we provided a definition of absence that is coordinated with the theory and fits how we want to model absence behavior. The structuring of absence as a change from presence to absence (or vice versa) addresses problems raised by Muchinsky (1977) and Atkin and Goodman (Chapter Two of this volume) concerning the lack of coordination between theories of absence and operationalizations of absence.

2. *Does the theory define the conceptual and psychological space for absence?* Yes and no. The theory does not *explicitly* define the psychological space but explicitly acknowledges the need to broaden the conceptual space. As in any theory, the particular specification of the space depends on the particular application of the theory. There is no generic motivation-behavior space implicit or explicit to this theory. We have tried to avoid defining absence as organizational behavior. Absence events occur in different stimulus situations, and only some are dominated by organizational influences. Given the well-founded criticism of the traditional narrow organizations focus, and that the determinants of absence are often outside the purview of the firm (Morgan and Herman, 1976), this seems reasonable. Since the stimulus situation and the forces it evokes are crucial, and the absence event occurs away from work, as does the return to work, it seems reasonable to worry about the

structure of the stimulus situation at home, for example. Additionally, since the motivation toward any particular behavior option is a function of the complete bundle of behavioral options, it is necessary to examine nonorganizational behavior options.

3. *Can the theory be tested against alternative explanations?* The theory can accommodate the various tacit theories presented above. However, the tacit theories are concerned more with individual outcomes and less with the actual process by which an absence event occurs. Consequently, it is difficult to provide a clear example of the dynamic theory pitted against another theory. One approach is to take the implications of several formulations for the distribution of absences and run them through the model to test for differences in implications. For example, the adjustment formulation clearly indicates that, holding the environment constant, we should observe differences in individual absences over their organizational life. A habit formulation generates a different prediction. The implication within a dynamic theory is that we will see substantially greater variation over time in absence taking in the former case than the latter. That is a testable proposition. For testing the dynamic process theory itself and propositions such as substitutability and displacement, we can alter the bundle of rewards available and see whether the changes in behavior we observe reflect the impact of substitution and displacement effects. Some of that work, though not well executed empirically (see D. R. Winkler, 1980, for a notable exception), has begun to appear. As in the previous example, the test is of a particular version of the dynamic theory, with hypotheses and constructs for the motivational effects of various components of a particular bundle of rewards. These subhypotheses are necessary to generate testable, disconfirmable predictions. Given an explicit version of a dynamic theory of absence, one can generate disconfirmable hypotheses. As in any theory, we try to generate studies that allow for disconfirmation with the particular set of constructs designed for that study. It is at this level that disconfirmability has meaning for a dynamic theory of absence.

4. *Does the theory deal with the instability of absence?* Yes, the theory explicitly allows for variation in the stability of absence behavior as a function of the stability of the action bundles facing

the individual and his or her past history in the stimulus situation. We see stability of absence events within an individual as a less serious issue, given the nature of the model. If we were building a model that had static predictors of an underlying stable behavioral tendency, we would be concerned. However, if organizational constraints reduce absence variation (Herman, 1973), and relatively small changes in the array of behavioral options faced by the individual can change absence patterns, then stability is not expected in the classic psychometric sense.

5. *Does the theory deal with the consequences of absence?* Yes and no. One can distinguish two uses of the term *consequences.* There are individual-level direct consequences of absence. If I am absent, there are certain rewarding and punishing consequences for me in my motive-behavior space. This type of direct consequence is of concern here. A second sense, which Goodman and Atkin address in Chapter Seven of this volume, is indirect, usually aggregate consequences of absences. These indirect consequences, such as accidents, safety, and efficiency, are not touched on here. When absence events have an impact on the various motives and resultant action tendencies evoked by the stimulus situation, the theory does deal with consequences. Presumably, if we can map the full set of behavior options and their associated parameters (for example, substitutability coefficient, displacement coefficient, consummatory value), we can begin to model the motivational and action consequences of absence. If we are concerned about the broader array of indirect consequences, such as safety or grievances, the theory is not designed to handle these phenomena. In a fully specified version of an absence model such as we suggest, we can expect to look at only the motivational and behavior space. To the extent that absence has safety consequences and those consequences influence the multivariate space we are trying to understand, there is a gap. It is difficult to imagine the scope of a theory that could fully specify the causal and functional relations among all the consequences of absence. The secondary consequences flowing from absence events probably require a different theory, cast in terms (such as those Goodman and Atkin discuss) that accommodate organization-specific characteristics.

6. *Does the theory take into account organizational- and group-level policies and properties?* As we noted earlier, if absence norms and cul-

tures are distal stimuli that are mediated by motivational mechanisms such as rewards and sanctions, then the dynamics of action framework should accommodate the impact of group forces. Similarly, to the extent that organization policies influence the consequences of absence, the motivational forces influencing absence behavior should reflect this effect. Some of these effects may not be readily accountable in the dynamics framework, since they may be exogenous variables that need to be explicitly specified. Some events and policies may cause shifts in parameters that reshape the multivariate space, altering all the relationships in the motive-behavior space. A change in organization policy may have that effect. This sort of situation would require re-examining parameter values and, possibly, re-estimating the various relationships in the model. However, within the framework outlined, the nature of those effects is not identified and probably cannot be identified given our current knowledge of the motivation-behavior space we are defining and exploring.

Understanding absence is very difficult, and the way we have set up the problem may make it look even more difficult. In fact, we believe that other structures for the problem probably ensure continued frustration and little empirical or theoretical gain, since the full scope of the absence problem is not identified.

## Implications for Theory and Practice

There are some questions that arise in the dynamics framework for looking at absence, and we would like to briefly relate them.

*Exogenous Shocks.* It is very difficult to incorporate exogenous shocks, particularly those that are random. Industrial accidents, shutdowns, and illness can have these properties of being random shocks. While some configurations of motives and their associated parameters would lead to no apparent effect due to accident, it is difficult to imagine this always being the case. The discontinuity often introduced may be difficult to model, since the motive-behavior space has often been radically altered for some time interval. If the change in the motive-behavior space is identifiable, we may be able to predict some effects of an exogenous shock. This is a problem that we think can be treated with some gain in knowledge, but we are more sure that the knowledge is incomplete. However, this is an improvement over claiming that absences due to illness and accident (leaving aside the accident that is withdrawal in disguise, for example) are sufficiently different that we will avoid modeling them, or model them separately.

*Aggregate Effects.* Given that the model requires a number of individual parameters and can generate large variance in behavior over a narrow range of individual parameter values, it is difficult to talk about testing aggregate effects. One test might be to introduce a new behavior alternative or change the payoff for some option. If the other options remain the same in their parameters, we may be able to model the change at the aggregate level in proportion and duration of absences. However, studying aggregate effects runs into the same questions discussed earlier. What is the space of behaviors and motives we are considering, for example? These analytical thorns are still there to be stepped on at aggregate levels.

*Time Span.* We are uncertain about the appropriate time span for looking at a dynamic process such as the one we have outlined. One is tempted to say that the time span should be quite long to allow variation to occur in absence behavior, so that we can see variation due to the model. However, it really depends upon what is being observed and the rates of change in the set of action tendencies we observe. We may find few absences but enough variation in other components of the activity bundle that we do not need to wait for an absence event. If one takes the view that we in fact observe a great deal of imposed absence and can estimate parameter values from the behavior in work and nonwork settings using imposed absence, then we may not need to wait for everyone to show what is organizationally labeled an absence. The choice of time frame will be dictated by the budget constraints (in terms of time) individuals operate under and the rapidity of observed changes in behavior. The tighter the constraint (that is, the less time people have to take some action), the fewer the behavior options to choose from, and the farther away they are from some extreme asymptotic value on an indifference curve of the activities possible, the less time we will need to look at absence and the other behavioral options in the motive-behavior space. If one dominates another completely and we cannot observe behavior changes, we will be unable to examine absence.

*Planning Absences.* Atkin and Goodman (1983) suggest that some people may plan some of their absence taking. Knowing how many absences they can take with no penalty, they will conscientiously schedule their absences and act on the plan. A forward planner is difficult to deal with in this model. Unfortunately, none of the other tacit models really could handle this concept very well. Thaler and Shefrin (1981) suggest likening economic actors to the Freudian ego and id; Thaler and Shefrin call them planners and doers. The planner looks out into the future, trying to husband resources so they can be expended to maximize utility over the long term. The doer would like to maximize utility now and pays no attention to the future. Tension develops between the planner and doer, as the planner tries to control the doer. Thaler and Shefrin show evidence for this dualistic model, since economic actors frequently do show economically rational planner behavior mixed with some idful doer behavior. The idealized planner requires great foresight to anticipate future behavior options. To plan absences, the planner must consider possible behavior options available now and in the future, making planning difficult. Furthermore, testing for planning is difficult, since planning may be confounded with other explanations (for example, is it planning or responding to social pressure if one takes off the first day of deer hunting season, since everyone else does?). Further, how small a time frame distinguishes a planner from a doer? Unless doers show instantaneous behavior in response to wishes, is it planning behavior if I plan today to take off tomorrow, or is it doer behavior? After all, tomorrow is not very far away. Making the distinction is quite difficult. However, if the distinction has meaning and can be mapped onto the motive-behavior space, it creates problems for the dynamics model. We now have some motive force in place that does not operate (that is, is quiescent) until some day. In other words, we have a specification for a particular day for a particular absence lying outside the ongoing stream of behavior.

There are some implications for practice generated by a dynamic model.

*Measuring Absence and Absence Tendencies.* In order to influence and change behavior events, if that is desired, one needs to measure those behavior events. As Latham and Napier (in Chapter Eight of this volume) suggest, measurement alone is an intervention. We suggest that measuring types and categories of absence is fraught with problems, though for different reasons from those suggested by Latham and Pursell (1975). If absences result from the resolution of several motivating forces, then measures should identify and characterize those forces. Morgan and Herman (1976) gave an example of measuring nonwork influences in an expectancy framework. The dynamic approach requires attention to the full range of possible activities that influence absence events. Using time diaries that log the full range of activities is a way of estimating absence tendencies. This allows investigation of the time-allocation decisions people make. With this information, one can try to calibrate an intervention to influence attendance.

Another measurement technique is trade-off analysis (Shapira, 1981). Since absence is partially influenced by available alternatives, we can try to investigate the trade-offs people are willing to make, either using judgment studies or deriving individual empirical estimates from absence records and time diaries.

The message of the dynamic approach for measurement is that we should measure the multivariate behavior-motive space and begin to estimate the relationships in that space. Since this implies that we can influence absence events by changing the parameters of forces instigating other behaviors, we should measure those other behaviors (Morgan and Herman, 1976). Finally, we should find measures to capture the changing relationships in that space over time. Static, infrequent measures will probably not do.

*Influencing Attendance.* To influence attendance, the resultant action tendencies for work should be dominant. One ready way to influence attendance should be to loosen the restrictions on when attendance is required. If flextime and other scheduling innovations can be applied, they should have a positive effect on absence if there are resultant action tendencies blocked because of scheduling. If flextime leads to strengthened nonwork resultant action tendencies, we may reduce actual attendance.

The theory calls for rewarding (increasing the attractiveness of) desired behavior (coming to work) rather than punishing undesired behavior (not coming to work). A second implication is that the attractiveness of alternatives should be reduced. This provides a theoretical rationale for "well pay" rather than "sick pay" as a way to increase attendance. These implications are not unique to a dynamic motivation theory. The major distinction is that absence events are inevitable unless the action tendency toward some incompatible activity is either (1) made compatible with work or (2) allowed to occur when it will not interfere with work. The provision of day care for parents is an example of (1). Flextime is an example of (2).

Using the concepts of substitution and displacement, we can try to identify individual trade-offs and use that information to design schedules and rewards that minimize the conflict between activities for individuals. If absence is a compensating differential for some risk, such as accidents, then a firm can consider reducing the on-the-job risk, moving individuals along their indifference curve. A second example is to find activities at work that are substitutable for nonwork activities. If these activities can be identified, they should reduce the need to be absent to express some nonwork action tendency. In all these cases, the continued effectiveness of such strategies requires monitoring of individual parameters and their changing values.

There are a number of difficulties in developing, operationalizing, and testing this model. However, it calls our attention to the full array of concepts needed to model absence. On the positive side, work in behavioral psychology and in behavioral and labor economics indicates the potential of using some of the concepts underlying the framework we have offered here.

## References

Allen, S. G. "Compensation, Safety, and Absenteeism: Evidence from the Paper Industry." *Industrial and Labor Relations Review,* 1981a, *34* (2), 207–218.

Allen, S. G. "An Empirical Model of Work Attendance." *The Review of Economics and Statistics,* 1981b, *63* (1), 77–87.

As, D. "Absenteeism: A Social Fact in Need of a Theory." *Acta Sociologica,* 1962, *6, 278–285.*

Atkin, R. S., and Goodman, P. S. "An Issue-Oriented Review of the Research on Absenteeism." Unpublished report to the U.S. Bureau of Mines, Carnegie-Mellon University, 1983.

Atkinson, J. W. "Studying Personality in the Context of an Advanced Motivational Psychology." *American Psychologist,* 1981a, *36* (2), 117–128.

Atkinson, J. W. "Thematic Apperceptive Measurement of Motivation in 1950 and 1980." In G. d'Ydewalle and W. Lens (Eds.), *Cognition in Human Motivation and Learning.* Hillsdale, N.J.: Erlbaum, 1981b.

Atkinson, J. W., and Birch, D. *The Dynamics of Action.* New York: Wiley, 1970.

Atkinson, J. W., and Birch, D. *Introduction to Motivation.* New York: D. Van Nostrand, 1978.

Barker, R. G. *The Stream of Behavior.* New York: Appleton-Century-Crofts, 1963.

Baum, J. F. "Effectiveness of an Attendance Control Policy in Reducing Chronic Absenteeism." *Personnel Psychology,* 1978, *31,* 71–81.

Beehr. T. A., and Gupta, N. "A Note on the Structure of Employee Withdrawal." *Organizational Behavior and Human Performance,* 1978, *21,* 73–79.

Berger, C. J., and Cummings, L. L. "Organizational Structure, Attitudes, and Behavior." In B. M. Staw (Ed.), *Research in Organizational Behavior.* Greenwich, Conn.: JAI Press, 1979.

Breaugh, J. A. "Predicting Absenteeism from Prior Absenteeism and Work Attitudes." *Journal of Applied Psychology,* 1981, *66* (5), 555–560.

Chadwick-Jones, J. K., Nicholson, N., and Brown, C. *Social Psychology of Absenteeism.* New York: Praeger, 1982.

Chelius, J. R. Understanding Absenteeism: The Potential Contribution of Economic Theory." *Journal of Business Research,* 1981, *9,* 409–418.

Cheloha, R. S., and Farr, J. L. "Absenteeism, Job Involvement, and Job Satisfaction in an Organizational Setting." *Journal of Applied Psychology,* 1980, *65* (4), 467–473.

Clegg, C. W. "Psychology of Employee Lateness, Absence, and Turnover: A Methodological Critique and an Empirical Study." *Journal of Applied Psychology,* 1983, *68* (1), 88–101.

Collier, G. H. "Determinants of Choice." In D. J. Bernstein (Ed.), *Nebraska Symposium on Motivation: Response Structure and Organization.* Lincoln: University of Nebraska Press, 1981.

Dalton, D. R., and Perry, J. L. "Absenteeism and the Collective Bargaining Agreement: An Empirical Test." *Academy of Management Journal*, 1981, *24* (2), 425–431.

Deitsch, C. D., and Dilts, D. A. "To Cut Casual Absenteeism: Tie Benefits to Hours Worked." *Compensation Review*, 1981, *13*(1), 41–46.

Fishbein, M., and Ajzen, I. *Beliefs, Attitude, Intention and Behavior: An Introduction to Theory and Research.* Reading, Mass.: Addison-Wesley, 1975.

Fitzgibbons, D., and Moch, M. K. "Employee Absenteeism: A Multivariate Analysis with Replication." *Organizational Behavior and Human Performance*, 1980, *26*, 349–372.

Frechette, H. M. "An Investigation of the Utility of Steers and Rhodes' Process Model of Attendance Behavior." Paper presented at 41st annual meeting of the Academy of Management, San Diego, Calif., Aug. 1981.

Garrison, K. R., and Muchinsky, P. M. "Evaluating the Concept of Absenteeism-Proneness with Two Measures of Absence." *Personnel Psychology*, 1977, *30*, 389–393.

Gibson, R. O. "Toward a Conceptualization of Absence Behavior of Personnel in Organizations." *Administrative Science Quarterly*, 1966, *11*, 107–133.

Gupta, N., and Jenkins, G. D., Jr. "Absenteeism and Turnover: Is There a Progression?" *Journal of Management Studies*, 1982, *19* (4), 395–412.

Gupta, N., and Jenkins, G. D., Jr. "Behavioral Outcomes in Organizational Research: A Reconceptualization." Unpublished paper, University of Texas at Austin, 1983.

Hammer, T. H., and Landau, J. C. "Methodological Issues in the Use of Absence Data." *Journal of Applied Psychology*, 1981, *66* (5), 574–581.

Hammer, T. H., Landau, J. C., and Stern, R. N. "Absenteeism When Workers Have a Voice: The Case of Employee Ownership." *Journal of Applied Psychology*, 1981, *66* (5), 561–573.

Herman, J. B. "Are Situational Contingencies Limiting Job Attitude-Job Performance Relationships?" *Organizational Behavior and Human Performance*, 1973, *10*, 208–224.

Hill, J. M. M., and Trist, E. L. "A Consideration of Industrial Accidents as a Means of Withdrawal from the Work Situation." *Human Relations*, 1953, *6* (4), 357–380.

Hirschman, A. O. *Exit, Voice, and Loyalty: Responses to Decline in Firms, Organizations, and States.* Cambridge, Mass.: Harvard University Press, 1970.

Houston, A. I., and McFarland, D. J. "Behavioral Resilience and Its Relation to Demand Functions." In J. E. R. Staddon (Ed.), *Limits to Action: The Allocation of Individual Behavior.* New York: Academic Press, 1980.

Hursh, S. R. "Economic Concepts for the Analysis of Behavior." *Journal of the Experimental Analysis of Behavior,* 1980, *34,* 219–238.

Ilgen, D. R., and Hollenback, J. H. "The Role of Job Satisfaction in Absence Behavior." *Organizational Behavior and Human Performance,* 1977, *19,* 148–161.

Johns, G. "Attitudinal and Nonattitudinal Predictors of Two Forms of Absence from Work." *Organizational Behavior and Human Performance,* 1978, *22,* 431–444.

Johns, G., and Nicholson, N. "The Meanings of Absence: New Strategies for Theory and Research." In B. M. Staw and L. L. Cummings (Eds.), *Research in Organizational Behavior.* Vol. 4. Greenwich, Conn.: JAI Press, 1982.

Kerr, W. A., Koppelmeier, G. I., and Sullivan, J. "Absenteeism, Turnover and Morale in a Metals Fabrication Factory." *Occupational Psychology,* 1951, *25,* 50–55.

Kuhl, J., and Blankenship, V. "The Dynamic Theory of Achievement Motivation: From Episodic to Dynamic Thinking." *Psychological Review,* 1979, *86* (2), 141–151.

Latham, G. P., and Pursell, E. D. "Measuring Absenteeism from the Opposite Side of the Coin." *Journal of Applied Psychology,* 1975, *60* (3), 369–371.

Lea, S. E. G. "The Psychology and Economics of Demand." *Psychological Bulletin,* 1978, *85* (3), 441–466.

Mirvis, P. H., and Lawler, E. E. III. "Measuring the Financial Impact of Employee Attitudes." *Journal of Applied Psychology,* 1977, *62* (1), 1–8.

Moch, M. K., and Fitzgibbons, D. E. "Automation, Employee Centrality in the Production Process, the Extent to Which Absences Can Be Anticipated, and the Relationship Between Absenteeism and Operating Efficiency: An Empirical Assessment." Unpublished manuscript, University of Texas at Dallas, 1982.

Morgan, L. G., and Herman, J. B. "Perceived Consequences of Absenteeism." *Journal of Applied Psychology,* 1976, *61* (6), 738–742.

Mowday, R. T., Porter, L. W., and Steers, R. M. *Employee-Organization Linkages: The Psychology of Commitment, Absenteeism, and Turnover.* New York: Academic Press, 1982.

Muchinsky, P. M. "Employee Absenteeism: A Review of the Literature." *Journal of Vocational Behavior,* 1977, *10,* 316–340.

Naylor, J. C., Pritchard, R. D., and Ilgen, D. R. *A Theory of Behavior in Organizations.* New York: Academic Press, 1980.

Nicholson, N. "Management Sanctions and Absence Control." *Human Relations,* 1976, *29* (2), 139–151.

Nicholson, N. "Absence Behavior and Attendance Motivation: A Conceptual Synthesis." *Journal of Management Studies,* 1977, *14* (3), 231–252.

Nicholson, N., Brown, C. A., and Chadwick-Jones, J. K. "Absence from Work and Job Satisfaction." *Journal of Applied Psychology,* 1976, *61* (6), 728–737.

Porter, L. W., and Lawler, E. E. III. "Properties of Organization Structure in Relation to Job Attitudes and Job Behavior." *Psychological Bulletin, 1965, 64* (1), 23–51.

Porter, L. W., Crampon, W. J., and Smith, F. J. "Organizational Commitment and Managerial Turnover: A Longitudinal Study." *Organizational Behavior and Human Performance,* 1976, *15,* 87–98.

Porter, L. W., and Steers, R. M. "Organizational, Work, and Personal Factors in Employee Turnover and Absenteeism," *Psychological Bulletin,* 1973, *80,* 151–176.

Rachlin, H., Kagel, J. H., and Battalio, R. C. "Substitutability in Time Allocation." *Psychological Review,* 1980, *87* (1), 355–374.

Roberts, K. H., Hulin, C. L., and Rousseau, D. M. *Developing an Interdisciplinary Science of Organizations.* San Francisco: Jossey-Bass, 1978.

Shapira, Z. "Making Trade-Offs Between Job Attributes." *Organizational Behavior and Human Performance,* 1981, *28,* 331–355.

Smith, F. J. "Work Attitudes as Predictors of Specific Day Attendance." *Journal of Applied Psychology,* 1977, *62* (1), 16–19.

Solomon, R. L. "An Opponent-Process Theory of Acquired Motivation." *American Psychologist,* 1980, *35* (8), 691–712.

Staw, B. M., and Oldham, G. R. "Reconsidering Our Dependent Variables: A Critique and Empirical Study." *Academy of Management Journal,* 1978, *21* (4), 539–559.

Steers, R. M., and Rhodes, S. R. "Major Influences on Employee Attendance: A Process Model." *Journal of Applied Psychology,* 1978, *63* (4), 391–407.

Terborg, J. R., Davis, G. A., and Smith, F. J. "A Multivariate Investigation of Employee Absenteeism." Unpublished paper, University of Houston, 1980.

Terborg, J. R., and others. "Extension of the Schmidt and Hunter Validity Generalization Procedure to the Prediction of Absenteeism Behavior from Knowledge of Job Satisfaction and Organizational Commitment." *Journal of Applied Psychology,* 1982, *67* (4), 440–449.

Thaler, R. H., and Shefrin, H. M. "An Economic Theory of Self-Control." *Journal of Political Economy,* 1981, *89* (2), 392–406.

Vroom, V. H. *Work and Motivation.* New York: Wiley, 1964.

Walker, K. J. "The Application of the J-Curve Hypothesis of Conforming Behavior to Industrial Absenteeism." *Journal of Social Psychology,* 1947, *25,* 207–216.

Waters, L. K., and Roach, D. "Job Satisfaction, Behavioral Intention, and Absenteeism as Predictors of Turnover." *Personnel Psychology,* 1979, *32,* 393–397.

Watson, C. J. "An Evaluation of Some Aspects of the Steers and Rhodes Model of Employee Attendance." *Journal of Applied Psychology,* 1981, *66* (3), 385–389.

Winkler, D. R. "The Effects of Sick-Leave Policy on Teacher Absenteeism." *Industrial and Labor Relations Review,* 1980, *33* (2), 232–240.

Winkler, R. C. "Behavioral Economics, Token Economies, and Applied Behavioral Analysis." In J. E. R. Staddon (Ed.), *Limits to Action: The Allocation of Individual Behavior.* New York: Academic Press, 1980.

# 2

# Methods of Defining
# and Measuring Absenteeism

⌧⌧⌧⌧⌧⌧⌧⌧⌧⌧⌧⌧⌧⌧⌧⌧⌧⌧⌧⌧⌧⌧⌧⌧⌧⌧

## *Robert S. Atkin*
## *Paul S. Goodman*

This chapter is concerned with the methodological issues that underlie the operationalization and measurement of absenteeism. As such, it sets the stage for the chapter by Avery and Hotz (Chapter Four), who consider the specification and estimation of models of absenteeism. That is, the present chapter considers the characterization of the absence variable, while Avery and Hotz address the problems of how to build causal models of absenteeism and how to estimate the relative effects of the various explanatory variables. Both this chapter and the chapter by Avery and Hotz are consistent with the theoretical framework developed by Fichman (Chapter One), although both develop concepts somewhat independent of the specifics of Fichman.

Another focus of this chapter is a general examination of the reliability and validity of various measures of absence. Landy, Vasey, and Smith (Chapter Three) complement this discussion

*Note:* Support for this chapter was provided by the U.S. Bureau of Mines under contracts J0100069, J0328033 and J0123040.

with their chapter, which reviews two specific empirical studies of the measurement and the reliability of absences. In a number of ways, however, this chapter is also different from that of Landy and his colleagues. They are concerned with the analysis of a specific data set, while we are interested in general principles applicable to all absence data; they proceed in a generally atheoretical fashion, while we establish a very specific theoretical base; they appear to assume that "proneness," or stability, of absence behavior is a critical issue, while we explicitly do not assume that absence behavior is necessarily stable over time; and, finally, they concern themselves primarily with the issues of absence-behavior distributions and reliability, while we explore these topics within a context of the information available in absence measures, the realities of absence data, and the complexity of defining reliability and validity for absence data.

The chapter will be organized around the following four questions:

1.  What do we know about the measurement of absenteeism, and what are the limitations of this knowledge?
2.  How can the current limitations be overcome?
3.  What do we mean by "the reliability of absenteeism measures"?
4.  What do we mean by "the validity of absenteeism measures"?

Our answer to the first question has two parts: first, we pose a theoretical framework within which to view absenteeism; and, second, we overview the current literature, with particular emphasis on a number of unresolved issues. Question 2 is also addressed in two parts, with the first examining the information available to the researcher in a typical absentee data set and the second developing a classification scheme for various types of absentee measures. This section will also consider some problems associated with the various types of aggregation that must often be applied to absenteeism data sets. In response to the third question, we propose a scheme within which various approaches to the assessment of reliability and consistency can be discussed and evaluated. Finally, question 4 will be discussed in terms of the various alternatives available to the researcher to assess the validity of absenteeism measures.

The problems just previewed are of considerable importance to both the researcher and the practitioner. For the researcher, the goal is to understand absenteeism. To accomplish this, we need to step back from the methods that have become commonplace and throw "light on their limitations and resources [and clarify] their presuppositions and consequences" (Kaplan, 1964, p. 24). Inquiries of this form are difficult, because they scrutinize current practices and, as a by-product, often evoke desultory notes. To combat this inherent randomness, we will proceed toward a precise end, namely, an evaluation of current methods and a discussion of alternatives. Examples are chosen to highlight the limits of many current methods, not to cast doubt on the scientific prowess of particular researchers.

For the practitioner, the usual goal is not understanding but control. That is, we view absenteeism as a real problem to all organizational members if it results in lowered benefits to all members because of systematic production disruptions or increased costs (see Chapter Seven for an extensive discussion of the "downstream" effects of absenteeism). By definition, all organizational members surrender some opportunities for behavioral control for the benefits of steady remunerative and psychological rewards. What is critical, then, is that the control mechanisms (at all levels in the organization) adequately reflect appropriate reasons for absence, while exacting sufficiently great penalties to discourage cavalier absences. Attaining this end, however, is unlikely unless the control basis is understanding. Hence, even to the practitioner, the importance of methodologically sound results is at least as poignant as it is to the scientist.

### Question 1. What Do We Know About the Measurement of Absenteeism, and What Are the Limitations of this Knowledge?

Our response to this question will consist of two parts, one focusing on theory and the other on the empirical literature. Our discussion of the empirical literature will highlight a number of themes that appear to characterize the current research effort. A more thorough review of recent work is presented in a later chapter by Steers and Rhodes (Chapter Six). Our selected review will then provide the basis for a brief discussion of the theoretical assumptions that underlie a number of methodological decisions that the researcher must make.

*Empirical Themes in the Current Literature*

This section will characterize the current literature in terms of four themes important to the measurement of absence: (1) the choice of time period (2) the characterization of the raw data base, (3) the choice of absence types, and (4) the choice of a measure of absence events. The reader more interested in a general review of absence research should see Muchinsky (1977), Steers and Rhodes (1978; Chapter Six of this volume), or Johns and Nicholson (1982). Our review consisted of more than forty articles that have appeared in major research journals in the last decade. While this review is not exhaustive, we believe that it is representative of the themes posed above.

Our strategy was to operationalize the above four themes by enumerating a set of questions about each. These questions are provided in Table 2.1. As can be seen by observation of the table, these questions vary from rather abstract to quite pragmatic and from somewhat general to very precise. This inquiry produced predictable results. In general, no reported study passed muster on all of these questions. The details follow.

*Choice of Time Period.* Few studies provided any rationale for the time period over which absenteeism was studied. Periods vary from several weeks to several years. Rarely was there any linkage provided between the period chosen and any concept of a "natural time frame" that might exist within any particular firm or industry. An exception is Hammer and Landau (1981), who at least correctly note that the "appropriate time interval of measurement is a function of the organizational and environmental context within which the absenteeism takes place, the behavior patterns of the research sample, and the index of measurement used" (p. 580). They do not, however, appear to apply this principle in their study.

The concept of a natural time frame is both appealing and elusive. That is, many organizations experience periods of relatively high and relatively low absence taking. During relatively low periods, absences are more likely to be the result of accidents or illnesses or to be associated with individuals whose absence-taking behavior is in some way different from that of their peers. A natural interest of both researchers and managers is understanding why absence taking during low periods may occur more frequently

Table 2.1. Research Themes Investigated and General Questions
Asked During Review of the Empirical Literature Pertaining
to the Measurement of Absence.

---

Theme 1: Choice of Time Period (researcher defined)

1. Is the definition of time period examined?
2. Did the researcher provide a rationale for the time period chosen?
3. Did the rationale include company-based issues of importance, such as shutdowns? seasonality effects? shift or job rotation effects? building of long holidays by taking absences adjacent to scheduled off days? the institutional rules for "cashing in" or "losing" vacation or personal days?

Theme 2: Raw Data Characterization (company determined; possibly researcher modified)

1. What are the company policies concerning the recording of absence, including such items as:
   a. What is recorded (that is, does the record explicitly note days present or does it only note days absent? does it note the reason for an absence?)?
   b. When is the absence recorded, and how are modifications made if the record is not accurate?
   c. Do the formal policies remain constant over time?
   d. Who actually does the recording, is there an audit procedure, and who authorizes adjustments?
2. What are the provisions of the formal policy?
   a. How many sick days, if any, are individuals allowed? Are they paid or unpaid? What certification procedure exists?
   b. How many legitimate nonsick absences are allowed? Are they paid or unpaid? Are they for specific reasons only (for example, death in family; birthday), or are they at the individual's discretion?
   c. Are there "cash in" procedures for legitimate days not taken? At what rate?
   d. Are there carry-over provisions, or are legitimate days not taken lost?
   e. How easy is it to get overtime hours or days in exchange for regular days missed?
   f. Is there a formal absenteeism-control plan? If so, what are its provisions?
3. How is the company policy applied, including such items as:
   a. How consistent is the recording over different recorders?
   b. How consistently are the formal policies actually applied across different members of the work force?
   c. How consistently are the formal policies actually applied over time?
   d. Are there side payments or special deals? What are they?
4. How were the data "cleaned" to make them amenable to the research purpose?

Table 2.1. Research Themes Investigated and General Questions
Asked During Review of the Empirical Literature Pertaining
to the Measurement of Absence, Cont'd.

---

Theme 3:   Choice of Absence Categories (company defined and researcher
           redefined)

   1.   What categories were used? Were they adequately defined?
   2.   Were the categories used linked to an underlying theory?

Theme 4:   Choice of a Measure of Absence Events (researcher defined)

   1.   What measures of absence events were used? Were they
        adequately defined?
   2.   Were the measures linked to the underlying causal models?

---

among certain individuals when most are generally present. Several specific items may affect the occurrence and "appearance" of natural time frames, and we will briefly consider four: (1) policy related, (2) demand related, (3) seasonally related, and (4) shift related.

Three key elements of absence policy may affect natural time frames: (1) whether sick leave (or other legitimate leave) must be used within a fixed period (usually a calendar year) or whether it can be cashed in or carried over; (2) whether holiday pay is lost if the day preceding or following the holiday is an absence day; and (3) whether there are stipulations concerning the total number of absence days that can occur within a fixed time period. Natural time periods are more likely to develop and persist when legitimate leave must be used within a fixed period (or lost), when there is no loss in holiday pay for absences preceding or following the holiday, and when there are no stipulations concerning the maximum number of absences within a fixed time period. Indeed, the presence of these last three conditions encourages individuals to take absences when they are most convenient for the individual. If individuals, either because of implicit norms or because of chance, happen to "agree" on the time during the year that absence taking is "most convenient" (a situation enhanced by restricting sick or vacation days to a fixed period), the organization has, in effect, created a natural time frame during which absence taking is likely to be different from other times in the year (which would then be a second natural time frame).

This effect can be observed in the following example. The authors have found that absence taking in two mines in the coal industry is substantially more frequent in the late fall period (Thanksgiving to New Year) than during the remaining ten and a half months of the year. This appears to be attributable to the combined effects of deer season, a tendency to add on days to the regularly scheduled Thanksgiving, Christmas, and New Year holidays, and an absence policy that does not discourage these behaviors. For those particular mines, it may be the case that there are two natural periods over which to examine absenteeism, namely, January through mid-November, during which the expectation of absenteeism in the aggregate work force is relatively lower, and mid-November through year-end, during which the expectation of absence taking in the aggregate work force is relatively much higher.

To see how complex the effects of demand can be, consider the following example. For many firms, the demand for their products or services varies over time, and it may very well be the case that absenteeism is a function of a number of factors that vary with output demand. Increased demand might increase perceived job stress or sheer exhaustion (thereby increasing absenteeism), but increased demand might also tighten management's absenteeism-control system, resulting in a reduction of absenteeism. Hence, the summary effect might be difficult to discern. Even this somewhat complex model may be underspecified in the sense that increased management control might reduce the frequency of short absences but increase the tendency of individuals to lengthen long-term absences that are accident or sickness related (see Smulders, 1980, for a brief discussion of some of the possible causes of the length of absences due to sickness). Under these circumstances, natural time frames may result from the interplay of additional job stress (or exhaustion) and the differential application of absence policy.

Seasonal effects are likely to be the result of two factors: (1) a common vacation period and (2) weather conditions. The first may cause some individuals to take vacation at a time during the year other than when they would prefer it. When this happens, these individuals may tend to take a "second vacation" at some other time. To the extent that this other time is attractive to many persons in a given work force, the absence rate may be unusually high at the "other time." The possible effect of weather in certain parts of the country may also create periods of relatively high absence. In these examples, the natural time frames are those associated with these seasonal effects.

The fourth possible reason is shift. Absence on certain shifts may be higher than on other shifts. It may also be the case that absence is higher on the first day of a new shift, independent of which shift is examined. Under these circumstances, it may be that the natural time frame is the period of one complete rotation.

An important caveat, which will receive more thorough treatment later, should be noted here. *Natural time period,* as used in these examples, is sometimes defined from the point of view of the researcher and at other times from the point of view of either the organization or the employee. Which of these is used may produce very different "definitions" of natural time period.

*Characterization of the Raw Data Base.* Across the reviewed studies, little consideration has been given to the formal absentee policies of the company, to the manner in which the policies are applied, or to how the raw data are collected (see Ilgen and Hollenback, 1977; Cheloha and Farr, 1980; and Hammer, Landau, and Stern, 1981, for some of the better examples). For example, few studies indicate the number of allowable sick days or personal days an individual has available, although Allen (1981) has demonstrated that such policy variables may be important. Within a company, different classes of individuals may have different numbers of available days (perhaps because of seniority, carry-over from previous years, or job class), and this would be expected to affect absence taking at the individual level. The formal policies may be differentially applied, and there may be complex but important side payments or deals. That these phenomena exist has itself not been the subject of serious study, but there are few of us who as employees have not seen "the system" distorted by implicit agreements, favoritism, and other realities of work life.

One additional topic deserves comment at this point, namely, the process by which raw information about absences gets organized into research data sets. Field-based data in general are not in a form directly amenable to the scientists' analytical methods. The process by which they become useful is known as *cleaning* (a term that probably defies proper definition). When applied correctly, cleaning procedures should "sanitize" the data by ridding them of certain reporting anomalies without inducing any bias. Absence data are notoriously in need of cleaning, but few if any of the published research items describe whether cleaning occurred and, if so, how. For example, let us assume that the actual recorder of absence records was absent on a given day and replaced by a fill-in not completely cognizant of the recording system. The fill-in may use conventions or symbols for various types of absence in a manner different from the regular recorder. This might produce a symbol for a particular form of absence different from that the regular recorder ever used. The researcher subsequently might observe a unique type of absence that has been recorded only on one day of a year. Should the researcher accept this symbol as denoting a unique event, or should the researcher attempt to find out what "it really means" and, upon determination, recode the data point on the research data set? The point to be made is obvious: "we should insist on great detail in specifying how absence data are... cleaned" (Johns, personal communication). Detailed discussions of how absence data were cleaned simply do not occur in the literature.

*Choice of Absence Categories.* Most organizations that record absences distinguish among various types of absence. For example, absences due to "certified" sickness are often distinguished from absences due to other reasons. We assume that organizations will develop absence typologies that are generally relevant to perceived needs. Companies that are unionized, for instance, will tend to use a category scheme that addresses those types of absence defined in a collective bargaining agreement. In practice, the number of categories used may be numerous (in the coal industry, we have observed some companies that define twenty-five to thirty-five different types of absence). Many of these categories differ in only subtle ways (for example, absence due to on-the-job injuries versus absence due to injuries occurring off the job). Others are more reflective of local definitions of what constitutes absence. For example, in the coal industry, federal law requires that each miner receive one day of safety training per year. Attendance at such a training session (which is usually at the mine site) is noted by some mines as "absence due to training," while other mines do not record this event at all in the miner's absence record.

To the researcher, many of these differences are not important. Hence, the researcher must decide on the set of research-based categories that will be used (for example, legitimate versus nonlegitimate; paid versus unpaid; voluntary versus involuntary). In essence, the researcher must decide how to translate what is on the absence record to a smaller set of categories. Clearly, this process will differ from study to study, if only because the companies studied will likely have different recording conventions. Although some studies do provide sufficient information to discern the translation rules used by the researcher, our review suggests that most do not. Even those that do report these rules often base their new categories on attributions about the cause of an absence rather than on objective characteristics (for example, whether an absence was "voluntary" is more likely an attribution of the researcher than it is a definitive characteristic obvious from the data).

*Choice of Absence-Event Measures.* More will be said about this in a later section, but for the present let us note that most studies provide only the skimpiest of rationales for the choice of the measure actually used to operationalize absence events. Most common are measures of magnitude (total days absent over some time period), frequency (the average number of absence events over some time period), and duration (the average length of absence events). In a later section, we develop in detail the observation that these three absence measures capture only a subset of the basic information available in most data sets. Given this observation, it is not clear why these measures are employed almost exclusively in the literature. In some instances, the reason may be theoretical. More likely, however, is some combination of a general misunderstanding of the richness of the information contained in most absenteeism data sets, a lack of knowledge of the statistical tools to apply to these data, and/or an overreliance on the literature about the relative psychometric properties of certain absenteeism measures.

*Implications.* This selected review of the empirical literature focused on a number of issues that affect the measurement of absence. Our reading of the literature strongly implies that, at minimum, incomplete reporting of information about time periods, characterization of the raw data, choice of absence categories to study, and choice of absence measures is common. This, coupled with questions that others have recently posed about the inappropriateness of commonly employed statistical techniques (Hammer and Landau, 1981; Landy, Vasey, and Smith, Chapter Three) and the inadequacy of theoretical formulations of absenteeism (Johns and Nicholson, 1982; Fichman, Chapter One), suggests that the study of absenteeism has been characterized more by convenience than by scientific merit.

Correction of this situation requires advances in how we think about absenteeism, in the tools we use to study absenteeism, and in how we employ these tools to advance our understanding of both the causes and the effects of absenteeism. The remainder of this chapter will focus on the linkage of how we think about absenteeism and the tools used to study absenteeism. To accomplish this task, we will first present a brief theoretical framework, and then we will examine how this framework helps us understand choices among the tools that are available.

*A Theoretical Point of Departure*

We begin with the assertion that work behavior is a composite of many behaviors linked together by location and time. Only a subset of the actual behaviors enacted in the work location during working hours is actually devoted to the production of a good or service. Many workplace behaviors have little or nothing to do with the task at hand. To be certain, many of these nontask behaviors are indirectly instrumental to the long-term accomplishment of work, either because they affect interpersonal relations or because they provide direct opportunities to enjoy the work setting. A prudent observer would also probably conclude that, even given a relatively high degree of routinization, the behaviors emitted at work differ over person, time, and setting.

Absenteeism is a specific composite of behaviors linked by expectations about the location of an individual given a particular time. That is, the individual is expected to be at a particular location at a particular time. Within this framework, then, absence is a composite of behavioral events that happen to share a common characteristic, namely, that the person is away from work during hours normally predictive of work attendance. Variation in expectations about the presence or nonpresence of the individual at the expected location is to be expected. We will use the term *absence event* to mean any incident in which the individual is not at the expected location at a given time. This point of view represents a theoretical bias on the part of the authors and thus may affect the methodological positions to be discussed below. Since this position is based on a number of assumptions, it may be appropriate here to sketch them prior to the main discussion. The six assumptions are as follows:

1.  Absence events can be classified into types.
2.  Each type may be the outcome of a different set of underlying causes, and each of these sets can be represented by a model that specifies how the various causes combine.
3.  The underlying causes can change in terms of their relative importance over time.
4.  Certain specific causes are more variable over time than are others.
5.  The set of causes for any particular type of absence may vary from individual to individual (or subgroup to subgroup).
6.  Some types of absence events are more predictable than are others.

Taken jointly, the first two assumptions argue that absence events are separable into different types, with each potentially the result of a different mix of causal variables (that is, there are potentially several different models each predictive of a different type of absence event). These variables may be under the control of the individual (endogenous) or under the control of some other agent (exogenous). While disaggregation into types may be difficult to perform in practice, in theory such separation should be possible. (Whether such separation has theoretical utility is another question; see Fichman, Chapter One.)

The mix of causal variables can be represented symbolically as a model. A *model*, as used here, refers to a formal statement of the relationship between some dependent variable and the explanatory variables thought to cause, control, or predict the dependent variable. In effect, the model is a metaphor or analogy to the theory, presented in a form that is more useful for study than the underlying theory (Kaplan, 1964). Specification is the act of determining the set of explanatory variables, and estimation is the act of determining the relative predictive power possessed by the set of variables and by each variable as a member of the set. The exact mathematical relationship that each explanatory variable has to each other and to the dependent variable is known as the functional form of the model. For example, we may have a theory that suggests that frequency of absence events is the result of job stress and family size, with absence frequency linearly decreasing with family size and exponentially increasing with job stress.

Assumptions 3 and 4 state that the explanatory variables may take different values at different times and that the amount of time-dependent variation may differ for different variables. That is, in the above example, we might also believe that job stress may vary substantially from day to day, while family size changes only very slowly. At any given instant of time, the model has some "value," which is computed by weighting the value of each variable at that instant by the parameters of the model (where the parameter weights have been determined by a statistical process such as regression).

We do not assume that the underlying model for any type of absence is identical across individuals. That is, the model for absence event type $i$ may take different specifications for different individuals or different groups of individuals. This fifth assumption provides us with a context in which to consider an individual-ideographic or a subgroup-ideographic argument of the form urged by Johns and Nicholson (1982). In a statistical sense, this is roughly equivalent to saying that there exists a set of all possible explanatory variables, many of which will have parameter values of 0.0 for any particular individual and any particular type of absence.

Finally, the last assumption implies that some absence events are more predictable than others, even if the underlying models are completely specified. This is equivalent to saying that some types of absence events are simply more the result of chance than are others.

In toto, these assumptions suggest that absence events may be of different types, that each type may be the behavioral outcome of different underlying models, that each model may contain variables whose value changes over time, that the variability in the functional value over time of each model may differ, and that some types of absence events are more predictable than others.

As noted above, the theoretical propositions just enunciated represent a particular point of view. Others exist, and the most popular of these can be labeled (1) the dissatisfaction/withdrawal model and (2) the proneness model. Satisfaction models assume that absence, especially frequent short-term absence, increases with increasing levels of dissatisfaction. At least one further assumption seems to be made by researchers in order to drive a prediction of consistency in absence taking over the aggregate work force: either satisfaction is a relatively long-term chronic state, or it cycles in some fixed way over time. That is, a chronic level of dissatisfaction will periodically produce an absence, or each time dissatisfaction reaches some critical value, an absence will ensue. Proneness models assume that individuals demonstrate consistency in absence taking because of the presence of a chronic element, such as a personality factor, or because of learned patterns. Rarely, however, is the "third party" well characterized from a theoretical point of view. Although both of these theoretical frameworks have been examined on many occasions, neither has added much to our knowledge about the causes of absenteeism.

A new approach, different from the one we propose, that may hold promise for future research is to characterize absenteeism as a latent variable. This approach would begin with the assumption that there exists an underlying response syndrome of which absence events are but one manifestation. Such a framework clearly asks us to specify quite exactly "what theoretical construct is represented by an observed absence" (Hulin, private communication). Our approach in this chapter is to sidestep this issue by concentrating on the observed behavior of absence per se, although other chapters (for example, those by Fichman, by Landy, Vasey, and Smith, by Rosse and Miller, and by Hulin) do provide some insight into underlying response tendencies.

*Implications of the Theoretical Framework.* What does this theoretical framework buy us? Quite a bit, we believe. First, it fixes clearly in our minds the concept of absenteeism as a summary, composite phenomenon. Any absence event may be different from any other absence event. This follows from the proposition that both the mix of causes and the relative importance of each cause may change over time. Although certain types of absence events may be more closely linked to certain sets of causes (assumption 2, above), these relationships may continually vary over time. Absenteeism — the "track record" of absence events over time — is a bouillabaisse whose exact ingredients are in constant flux. Second, we make no assumption of homogeneity of causal models across individuals. Different causes can and do produce similar types of absence events in different individuals. It may be the case, however, that the models for some subset of the population are reasonably homogeneous over some period of time. In this case, aggregation over the homogeneous subset may be an appropriate strategy to increase statistical power. A possible problem here is that homogeneity is not necessarily permanent, and, hence, subset membership may change over time.

The reader should note, however, that aggregation of this type is conceptually and statistically different from consideration of absenteeism as a group- or organizational-level variable. This can be best understood by examining the work reported by Scheflen, Lawler, and Hackman (1971). Their interest was to demonstrate the effects of changes in department-level absence policies. That is, they hypothesized that different department-level policies would cause different department-level absenteeism. In this situation, individual-level heterogeneity was treated as "noise" within groups, reflected by variability in the error terms. Although the point is subtle, the issue is important: if the focus of the study is an understanding of individual behavior, then aggregation over individuals requires a common underlying model; if the focus of the study is an understanding of a group's behavior, then individual heterogeneity may (given some distributional assumptions) be treated as due to sampling error.

Third, we make no assumption of stability of causal models over time. The causes of absence can and do change over time. It may be the case, however, that models may be relatively stable over certain time periods. In this case, aggregation over time may be an appropriate strategy to increase statistical power. Again, as was the case in the previous paragraph, the conceptual level of analysis is the individual, whether or not this type of aggregation occurs.

This discussion provides us with two central methodological problems: How do we deal with models that vary over time, and how do we deal with heterogeneous sets of models? These two problems will serve as an organizing device for our subsequent discussion of "what we mean by reliability of absenteeism measures."

At this juncture, however, we can note the interplay of theoretical assumptions and methodology from Table 2.2. As depicted in this table, there are essentially four different cases that we need to consider. Case 4 follows directly from our preceding discussion, in which we assumed both that a given sample may exhibit multiple underlying causal models (heterogeneity is present) and that these models could change over time (models are dynamic). Under certain circumstances, the researcher may be willing to assume that the underlying models are heterogeneous but stationary. That is, the sample under consideration is assumed to be composed of individuals who differ in terms of their underlying causal models, but these models are assumed to be unchanging over time. This situation is depicted as Case 3 in Table 2.2. Case 2 represents the set of assumptions corresponding to a single common causal model of

Table 2.2. Classification of Assumptions Concerning Homogeneity of Causal Models and Stationarity of These Models.

| Homogeneity Assumption | Stationarity Assumption | |
| --- | --- | --- |
| | Static | Dynamic |
| Homogeneous | Case 1 (one causal model that does not change over time) | Case 2 (one causal model that does change over time) |
| Heterogeneous | Case 3 (multiple causal models that do not change over time) | Case 4 (multiple causal models that do change over time) |

absenteeism that is expected to change over time in the sample under consideration. Finally, we have Case 1. In this case, the researcher must assume that there is a single underlying causal model that does not change over time. Although this case appears to be accepted implicitly in most reported empirical studies of absenteeism, a solid theoretical basis for these restrictive assumptions simply does not exist.

The implications of the assumptions discussed above and displayed in Table 2.2 are particularly important when we pose the question "under what circumstances would we expect individuals to demonstrate consistency in absence taking?" Case 1, the "traditional" set of assumptions, implicitly assumes that all individuals have consistent absence-taking patterns at all times, given a sufficiently long period of observation. Case 4, our favored set of assumptions, does not assume that consistency exists but allows it to be observed if and when it occurs.

A detailed discussion of the implications of these assumptions will be found in a later section. Before that, however, we will summarize this section and consider a number of other general issues concerning (1) the measurement of absence events, (2) the interpretation of absence-event histories from the points of view of the employee, the company, and the researcher, and (3) some additional issues of aggregation.

At the onset of this section, we posed the question "what do we know about the measurement of absenteeism, and what are the limitations of this knowledge?" We indicated that the answer had two parts, one theoretical and the other empirical. Based on our review of the empirical research pertaining to measurement themes, there would appear to be sizable gaps in our knowledge of the appropriate time period over which to study absence types, and the choice of a measure of absence events. These observations led us to the conclusion that advances are required in how we think about absenteeism, in how we develop methodological tools to study absenteeism, and in how we employ these tools to advance our understanding of both the causes and the effects of absenteeism. The first portion of our response to this challenge was to propose a theoretical framework sufficient to focus our thoughts about absenteeism. This framework allowed us to identify two important problems, previously not discussed in the literature, that provide an interface between theory and methodology, namely, homogeneity of individual-level causal structures and stationarity of these structures over time.

### Question 2. How Can the Current Limitations Be Overcome?

The theoretical issues and empirical themes posed in the previous section provide a rich problem set for the methodologist to explore. In this section, we provide a beginning for this discovery process by first considering the entire question of how absence events may be measured. To accomplish this end, we examine (1) the process by which absence-event data sets are generated, (2) the information content of absence-event data sets, and (3) the set of different measures that capture varying amounts of this information. We then build on this discussion to consider a second point, namely, how the interpretation of absence-event data may vary as a function of the frame of reference from which it is viewed. The point here is that the information content of the absence-event data set may take on different meaning when examined by the individual, the organization, and the researcher. A third topic, that of aggregation and time frame, concludes this section and sets the stage for the final two sections, which consider the questions of what we mean by reliability and validity of absence measures.

*Measurement of Absence Events*

Although Gaudet (1963) identifies more than forty different measures of absenteeism, Muchinsky concluded in 1977 that the "single most vexing problem associated with absenteeism as a meaningful concept involves the metric or measure of absenteeism" (p. 317). Of the possible metrics that have been identified, the most commonly used are measures of magnitude, measures of simple frequency, and measures of duration. Indeed, to at least one author (Smulders, 1980), "all other measures. . . are in fact derivations of one of these (latter) two basic aspects" (p. 368).

As will be seen shortly, we disagree with Smulders's premise.

However, before we develop this argument, there may be value in first stepping back and trying to understand the information available in the raw data. Therefore, the first part of this section will consider three issues (1) the process by which absence events are recorded to form the raw data set, (2) the information contained in absence-event data, and (3) a number of possible measures of absence taking. It is in this latter discussion that we will consider Smulders's quotation.

*Recording the Raw Absence-Event Data Set.* Each organization develops its own unique procedures for recording absence events. To provide a sense of the issues involved, we have drawn the following example from our current work in the coal industry.

At any particular mine, three actors are important in the recording process: the employee, the mine clerk, and the superintendent (or his or her representative). Let us assume that an employee is ill and cannot attend work. For purposes of this example, let us assume that the employee is a member of the United Mine Workers of America (UMWA). Contractually, the individual should notify the appropriate mine official (usually the clerk) before shift start, if possible, or as soon thereafter as is possible. Let us assume that the notification occurs before shift start, and the individual has available a leave day that could be used for sickness or personal reasons (a "contract day," in coal jargon). Depending on mine policy, the individual may have the option to have the absence recorded as either a paid personal day or an unpaid excused day. (Although it may seem strange to the reader that an individual might choose to take an unpaid leave day when it would be possible to take a paid leave day, we have often observed this practice in the coal mines we have studied.) If notification does not take place until after shift start, the mine clerk may automatically record the absence as AWOL ("absence without official leave"). Subsequent notification may result in an updating of the recorded reason for the absence to either a personal day or an unpaid excused day. Although it is the mine clerk who actually performs the updating, if any, it is likely to be the superintendent who makes the determination.

The determination may be done unilaterally, or it may involve negotiation between the individual and the superintendent. For example, a miner with a "good" absence record may be able to

convince the superintendent that timely notification was not possible; a miner with a "bad" absence record may not be as successful.
That is, the superintendent may be willing to bend company policy
in some cases but not in others. The circumstances under which
bending might occur may be dependent upon whether similar
exceptions have produced grievances in the past (perhaps because
of alleged favoritism). In general, we might expect that the actual
determination is probably a function of the individual's absence history, the company's policy, and the grievance history of earlier,
similar cases. The matter may be further confused in the coal
industry, because many mines do not distinguish between personal
days and floating vacation days (although the UMWA contract
does). Also common is the situation in which a sick or injured miner
misses a day or more (not calling in) and then presents a valid doctor's excuse covering not just the days missed to date but also additional days into the future.

Although the discussion could easily become more detailed,
the general point is clear. Recording the cause of a particular
absence is complex and may depend on any or all of the following:
(1) the company's absence policy, including contractual arrangements, if any, and the actual rules by which the policy is applied;
(2) the employee's absence history; (3) the grievance history of the
mine; (4) negotiations between the employee and the management;
and (5) the default rules used by the recorder. Clearly, the resolution of the issues may vary over time. Under these circumstances,
it becomes extremely difficult to make comparisons across various
organizational units, whether they are individual mines within the
same company or different mines in different companies. The significance of these differences notwithstanding, however, most
absence data sets do tend to contain a generic set of information.
The next section will focus on this information.

*Information Content of Absence Data Sets.* Absentee data are
categorical in nature. As such, the data represent a set of mutually
exclusive and exhaustive states into which behavioral events may
be classified. The basic information contained in these data are
type of event, the timing of each event, the number of each type of
event, and the sequence of events. After we consider each of these
types of information, we will discuss the various types of absence
measures that can tap aspects of this information.

1. Type of event. At a minimum, only two states, representing presence or absence, may be observed. The maximum number of states is not bounded and cannot be determined without explicit examination of the recording system. Typically, absence reporting systems use five to fifteen categories, although systems using more than twenty-five have been encountered by the authors. The additional categories are used to represent type of absence. In practice, many category schemes contain overlapping or repetitive categories. Although the category scheme usually reflects union agreements (if any), firms with a common union may have markedly different schemes. Indeed, even multiple sites of a single company may have different schemes.

2. Timing of event. Transition from one state to another can, in theory, occur at any time. For example, an individual who is present at the start of the workday may become ill or injured during the course of the day and, as a result, be sent home. Some firms capture this information by recording the actual number of hours worked. More common, however, is the case in which the absentee record would indicate either present or absent (or absent due to a particular cause). The specific information typically available, then, is an indication of the workday on which an event becomes salient, not the exact time of the occurrence of the event within the day or between workdays. Since the record provides information about the timing of the event, information about the time between events is also captured. Intertemporal periods between events of the same type or of different types, which on the surface represent rich information, are not frequently used in the literature.

3. Number of events. Over time, the system provides a record of the number of times each event has occurred. Two issues are of importance when counting the events: (1) the time period over which the count will be taken and (2) whether each observation of an event is counted or whether temporally contiguous events are treated as a single event. For example, it is a common research practice to consider a three-consecutive-day absence due to illness as a single event, while three nonconsecutive days due to illness are treated as three events. The ability to determine the number of events also permits the development of cumulative measures of a particular class of events over multiple time periods.

4. Sequence of events. Since most systems record events

along a time line, the sequence of events is preserved. As noted in the discussion of number of events, sequence information may affect the measure of number. Sequence information, however, also provides the opportunity to examine the precedence relationships of one type of absence relative to another or of presence to absence (or absence to presence). Precedence relationships may be valuable devices for understanding the trade-off of types of absenteeism over time or the effects of a policy change that affects only a limited number of absence types.

The purpose of this discussion was to characterize the type of information contained in most absentee record systems. Admittedly, concentration on existing record-keeping systems may appear to be an acceptance of absenteeism as a blue-collar issue (Johns and Nicholson, 1982). Our perspective, however, is more general. That we chose to characterize the information in a typical absence-event record system does not preclude a similar analysis being performed for any particular system, whether a traditional one common in blue-collar settings or one uniquely designed for professional or managerial occupations. The only differences we would expect to see involve level of detail (more detail for lower-level employees is likely) and definition of absence event (it is probably the case, for example, that higher-level employees may have multiple locations that are defined as legitimate work locations).

Having discussed the recording of the basic data and the information content of the data, we now turn to a presentation of possible measures of absence taking.

*A Fresh Approach to the Measurement of Absence Taking.* We have just suggested that at least four types of information are available in absence-event data sets. Earlier, we noted that not all of this information is actually exploited by the commonly used absence-event metrics. The spirit of the following discussion is one of contemplation of a possible universe of generic measures, each of which captures a somewhat different set of the available information. We recognize that this strategy may cause some readers to argue that "too often, we ask how to measure something without raising the question of what we would do with the measurement[s] if we had [them]" (Kaplan, 1964, p. 214). Such an exercise has importance, however, for at least two reasons: (1) it may suggest absence-event operationalizations that are superior to those presently in use, and (2) it may suggest additional directions for theoretical development.

We have identified seven different generic measures that can be applied to absence events. They are measures of occurrence, duration, magnitude, return, building, intertemporal lag, and run type. One convenient device for previewing the material in this section is provided by Table 2.3, in which the information contained in absence-event data sets is cross-tabulated with the generic absence-event measures. Reference to this table suggests that those most commonly used (that is, occurrence, magnitude, and duration) typically capture only part of the available information. The purpose of this section is to develop ideas concerning how new measures that capture different portions of the available information may be constructed and what role they may play in better understanding absence events. Each of the seven new measures will now be discussed in some detail. Within each discussion, we first describe the measure, then review current usages (if any), and finally offer some suggestions as to how they may be used. The reader is forewarned that this section is long, and, at times, somewhat tedious going.

One additional note is in order at this point: the measures

Table 2.3. Cross-Tabulation of Absence-Event Information and Generic Absence-Event Measures.

| Generic Type of Measure | Information Type | | | |
|---|---|---|---|---|
| | Type | Timing | Number | Sequencing |
| Occurrence | C | N | Y | N |
| Duration | C | Y | Y | N |
| Magnitude | C | C | Y | C |
| Return | C | Y | Y | N |
| Building | C | Y | Y | N |
| Intertemporal lag | C | Y | Y | C |
| Run type | Y | Y | Y | Y |

Code: Y = Measure contains this type of information.
  C = Measure could contain this type of information.
  N = Measure does not contain this type of information.

proposed below should not be confused with the statistics that might be applied to the measures. For example, the variance (or some other dispersion index, such as range) may be an appropriate statistic to apply to a measure of duration if one is interested in assessing the effects of a change in absence policy. In other instances, however, the appropriate statistic might be the mean or median of duration. In general, both the choice of measure of absence and the choice of an appropriate statistic must be guided by theory, by purpose, and by the pragmatics of the distribution of the measure of interest.

1. Measures of occurrence. As the name implies, occurrence measures focus on the number of absence events that occur within a particular time period and the frequency with which such events occur. Four problems surround the use of such measures, namely, definition of an event, determination of the time period, determination of days that should be omitted from the count, and determination of the level of analysis.

Event definition concerns (1) whether to consider a run of consecutive absences of a single type as one event or as multiple events (2) whether to consider a run of consecutive absences of different types as a single event or as multiple events, (3) whether to consider runs interrupted by a weekend, holiday, shutdown day, or strike day as a single run, and (4) whether to consider long-term absences at all in the frequency count.

Although the level of explicitness often varies, it appears that those authors who employ frequency measures consider a consecutive run of a single type of absence as a single event. For example, Hammer, Landau, and Stern (1981) are more explicit when they note that "frequency is the count of instances of absenteeism irrespective of duration" (p. 565) than are Hammer and Landau (1981), who define frequency as "a count of the number of times a person was absent" (p. 577). Whether a consecutive run of absences of multiple types is treated as a single event or multiple events is simply not reported by most authors (see Cheloha and Farr, 1980, for an exception). A similar comment can be made about the effect of "natural interruptions" due to weekends, strikes, vacations, and shutdowns.

Before exiting the discussion of definition, note should be

made of a variant of the occurrence measure used by Newman (1974). Based on a theory that should predict whether any absence event occurred in a particular time period, Newman's occurrence measure "was scored as 0 or 1 depending on whether the employee was (1) or was not (0) absent... at all during the two-month period" (p. 612).

The issue of whether to include long-term absences in the frequency count has been addressed by several authors, with the central issue being whether "the count of one- and two-day absences [is an] index of chosen absences" (Chadwick-Jones, Nicholson, and Brown, 1982, p. 58). Chadwick-Jones, Nicholson, and Brown (1982), Nicholson, Brown, and Chadwick-Jones (1976), and Terborg and others (1982) provide examples of studies that chose to report data for both a frequency count of all absences and a short-term index for one- and two-day absences. Although the use of a separate long-term absence frequency would seem feasible as a measure of "nonchosen" absence events, only Froggatt (1970) seems to have used such a measure.

Time frame as an issue has been mentioned by Hammer and Landau (1981) and Garrison and Muchinsky (1977). Most authors, however, simply do not provide any rationale for the time period over which the frequency counts are conducted, although many periods have been used (for example, Chadwick-Jones, Nicholson, and Brown, 1982, use a one-week period; Latham and Pursell, 1975, use a three-week period; Hammer, Landau, and Stern, 1981, use a one-month period; Terborg and others, 1982, use an eleven-week period; and Garrison and Muchinsky, 1977, use a three-month period). As observed by Fichman (private communication), two subtly different aspects of time frame can be identified. The first is a "theoretically based time frame," or the time required by the underlying theory to study a particular aspect of absence taking. For example, if our interest were to study the effects of a contractual change in an absence policy, a natural time frame might be the time period over which certain absence benefits (such as sick days) must be taken or otherwise forfeited. The second is the time frame chosen to examine the consistency of absence taking, which is usually longer than the theoretically based time frame.

Two final issues need to be considered, choice of days to delete from the computation and level of analysis. Most studies that employ occurrence measures apparently consider all weeks (or months) to contain the same number of workdays. Obviously, this is not true (a point also made by Landy, Vasey, and Smith in Chapter Three). Indeed, the number of available workdays per week or month may vary substantially because of vacation shutdowns, holidays, and other calendar anomalies. The current literature review did not disclose a single study that adjusted frequency counts for the number of working days actually possible in a period (although Chadwick-Jones, Nicholson, and Brown, 1982, made adjustments to reflect standard six- and seven-day work weeks, and Ilgen and Hollenback, 1977, made adjustments to reflect turnovers). Yet the magnitude of this adjustment could be substantial: for example, in the coal industry, the number of available working days could vary from a low of ten to twelve in July (due to shutdown for vacation and the Fourth of July holiday) to a maximum of perhaps twenty-two or twenty-three.

Level of analysis can also be an issue in occurrence measures. Most such measures appear to be conceptualized and measured at the individual level. At least two sets of authors— Chadwick-Jones and his colleagues and Latham and Pursell (1975)— do not. The latter develop an occurrence-type measure at the level of the work group, while the former appear to develop measures at the firm level. At issue here is not whether the level of analysis chosen was correct from a theoretical view (a thorny problem in its own right) but simply that there is nothing inherent in occurrence measures that binds them to individual levels of analysis.

To summarize this section, it is sufficient to note that occurrence measures, while simple to understand and easy to use, capture only a small portion of the data contained in absence records (see Table 2.3). Specifically, these types of measures do not capture information concerning the type of event, the timing of events (except in the somewhat trivial sense of defining whether a run or consecutive absences constitutes a single event), or the sequencing of events (except, again, in the same trivial sense as just noted). Furthermore, the simplicity of these measures may be more apparent than real, as the number of problems just discussed suggests.

2. Measures of duration. Two generic forms of this type of measure can be found in the literature. The first is the average length of absences (total days absent divided by absence frequency), and the second is percentage of work time lost (total days absent divided by scheduled workdays). Many of the problems that affect duration measures are similar to those that affect occurrence measures. That this is so for average length of absences is evident from this measure's definition. The problems that will be discussed include definition of the numerator, definition of scheduled workdays, issues involving very long absences, and the possible effects of natural "anchors" (for example, weekends).

Total days lost, the numerator in both generic definitions, can be subject to a number of biases. Of these, the most critical concerns the definition of an absence day. As correctly noted by Hammer and Landau (1981), inclusion of partial days worked as "days present" produces an underestimate of days lost, while inclusion of partial days as "days lost" produces an overestimate of days lost. Since loss of a partial day is usually not reported (especially if the partial day was the result of an accident or sickness that occurred after the individual reported for work), this problem is likely to persist (see Chapter Three for reports of a study that did measures of half-days absent). Exacerbating the entire issue, however, are two items: (1) the magnitude of the bias and (2) whether the bias is consistent across all individuals or co-varies with absence taking in general. An estimate of the magnitude of the bias problem can be obtained from the data provided by Hammer and Landau (1981). For voluntary absences, 5.422 hours were lost, on average, for each event, while consideration of each partial day lost as a whole day produces an average of 0.996 days per event. Similar computations for involuntary absence events yield 30.238 hours per event and 4.151 days per event. Assuming an eight-hour day, the ratio of the hours-lost measure to the days-lost measure is 0.678 for voluntary events and 0.911 for involuntary events. Based on this one sample, the bias is potentially large, especially for voluntary events.

Whether the bias is uniformly distributed over all individuals who take absences cannot be determined from the data provided. At first blush, it would seem reasonable to assume that the bias is not so distributed and, further, that it might actually be endogenously controlled. Since insufficient information about company policy toward voluntary absence events is given, it cannot be determined whether such events were sanctioned. However, clearly, if there were no sanctions or if sanctions were under the differential control of immediate supervisors, certain individuals might have absented themselves from portions of the workday that were particularly onerous.

Scheduled workdays, the dominator in the second generic measure, also pose problems. The major issue is how to treat work on overtime days and during shutdown periods. It would seem that all days actually worked should be included, although this item is not reported in the literature (for example, neither Chadwick-Jones, Nicholson, and Brown, 1982, nor Ilgen and Hollenback, 1977, address the issue). This problem is often exaggerated by the fact that many companies report only absence events on the absence record, and hence there often is no easily available positive record to determine number of scheduled days. This suggests that construction of absence data sets may require access to payroll data, which usually do provide positive records of attendance.

The third problem concerns the treatment of very long absences. At issue are two points—first, that a few very long absences can distort a duration measure and, second, that some companies automatically reclassify individuals who experience long absences in ways that can confound the data. The current review found that only Ilgen and Hollenback (1977) actually described a procedure for deleting subjects from the sample population because of very long absences (they used a $+3$ standard deviation cutoff), although it is likely that other methods have been used and not reported. Reclassification is a complicated issue. For example, during our research we found one coal mine that actually removed individuals from company roles after a four- or five-week absence due to injury, only to rehire them (with seniority and other benefits presumably intact) after they were able to return to work. This practice would not have been discovered without very detailed study of the patterns of absence events, because the code used to indicate this type of removal was identical to that used to indicate termination for cause.

A final problem, which the research literature apparently

has not addressed, concerns the possible "adhesive effect" that weekends or other natural anchors might exert on choice of day to return to work after an absence event. For example, it is likely that an individual who was injured on the job will not choose to return to work on a Friday if Saturday and Sunday are nonwork days. Similar comments also hold for the day before a scheduled holiday and shutdown. The frequency of this phenomenon could probably be estimated by observation of the relative frequency of returns as a function of day of the week. Whether adhesion actually produces a significant bias is not, however, presently known.

3. Measures of magnitude. Magnitude measures are measures of total time lost per employee during some period due to all absence events or due to particular types of absence events. The time metric may be hours (for example, Ilgen and Hollenback, 1977; Hammer and Landau, 1981) or days (for example, Winkler, 1980; Baum, 1978). It appears that magnitude measures are quite popular among both researchers (Chadwick-Jones, Brown, and Nicholson, 1973) and companies (Chadwick-Jones, Nicholson, and Brown, 1982). The problems with measures of this type are very similar to those observed for frequency measures, namely, determination of the proper time period, determination of days to exclude, and determination of the level of analysis. As with other measures discussed earlier, the key item underlying the time-period issue is a definition of a "naturally correct" period. Most researchers chose a time period with no rationale offered or even explicitly defined. An exception is provided by Chadwick-Jones, Nicholson, and Brown (1982), who develop magnitude measures at both the week and the year.

It should be noted that, as used in the previously cited studies, magnitude measures are static in the sense that they capture only the "end point" of a potentially dynamic measure. To understand this point, let us consider for a moment the type of data collected during a traditional study of instrumental reinforcement. At any particular time, three pieces of information are collected: the time, the presence or absence of a reinforcement, and the presence or absence of a behavior. The data are usually characterized by graphing time on the abscissa and cumulative behaviors on the ordinate, producing an upward-sloping curve familiar to all students in an introductory course in psychology. Information about the cumulative number of behaviors as a function of time is preserved, and this information can then be related to the frequency and timing of the reinforcements. Such an approach could be applied to absence-event data, not only preserving the dynamic aspect of magnitude but also providing a rather different framework within which to view consistency of absence taking over time. This concept will be developed further in the following section on alternative approaches to measuring the consistency of absence taking.

4. Measures of return. Absence events have distinct beginnings and distinct ends. This suggests that measures could be built that characterize when an individual returns to the work situation. No such measures were observed, however, in the current review of the literature, although Nicholson (1977) does talk to the need for a theory that addresses the act of returning to work. The basic requirement of a measure of return would seem to be a means of estimating the conditional probability that an absence event on day $t$ would not be observed given that the individual had an absence event on days $t$-1, $t$-2, and so on. Such a measure would also have to account for the adherence effect, discussed earlier, which might increase (for example, Mondays) or decrease (for example, Fridays) the conditional probability of return. Return measures would seem to be the measure of interest for a model that spoke to the attitudes of medical officials, the duration of sick pay and other benefits, company policy concerning extended absences, job dissatisfaction, and labor market conditions.

5. Measures of building. To introduce the concept of building, a rhetorical question will be posed: how often has the reader "made" a three-day weekend by absenting himself or herself from work on a Monday or Friday, or built a four-day weekend by absenting himself or herself on the Friday after Thanksgiving? In general, the concept of building refers to the process of extending an unbroken period of absence by the judicious use of a relatively few absence events. If a workplace usually is shut down, for example, on Thursday and Friday of Thanksgiving week, three absence events (the preceding Monday, Tuesday, and Wednesday) produce a nine-day break from work.

Although such situations probably are quite common, relatively few researchers have tried to operationalize and to use them in their empirical work. It is also curious that what little work has been done in this area has been European in origin (Behrend, 1959; see Chadwick-Jones, Nicholson, and Brown, 1982, for a brief review; see also Winkler, 1980, for a U.S. study). The European studies focus on the "Blue Monday Index" and the "Worst Day Index." "Blue Monday" is the frequency of absences that occur on Mondays, while the "Worst Day" measure is the difference between the highest and the lowest absentee days in the week (and is not a true measure of building unless the highest day is a Monday or Friday).

Alternative measures of building are possible, and the authors of this chapter have begun to explore use of some of them. The first of these might be labeled the adjacency measure and can be defined as the number of one-day absences that occur adjacent to a nonwork day, such as weekends, holidays, and known shutdowns. A variant is the ratio of such days to all such possibilities in the work year. This latter measure is an expression of the frequency with which such opportunities are exploited. A second variant is the ratio of adjacent one-day absence events to the total number of one-day events that an individual takes in a year. When adjusted for the probability of such events occurring by chance is made, this may be a measure of the likelihood that absences are for personal or planned reasons rather than due to sickness. For example, at one of the coal mines studied by the authors, this ratio has varied dramatically at the individual level, from a low of 0.00 to a high of more than 0.90.

Another possible measure of this generic type is the ratio of absence events after an unscheduled shutdown (due to weather or strike) to those on the day preceding the shutdown observed at the individual level. The rationale here is that days after the shutdown represent possible building, while the day before (unless it is a day after a natural building anchor) cannot be considered as a building day.

6. Measures of intertemporal lag. Absence events are spaced over time, suggesting that measures of the lag between such events may be developed. Intertemporal lag may be important to measure, because it may help determine whether there are individual-level

cyclic aspects to absence events. To the best of the authors' knowledge, such measures have not been reported in the literature.

One way of considering lag between absence events is to think of lag as a measure of the duration of attendance events. From this point of view it becomes nothing more than a duration measure of the complement of absence events, subject to all of the problems discussed earlier for measures of duration. However, since attendance events tend to be substantially more common than absence events, measures other than the average length of attendance and average days worked are feasible. (Note that the average-days-worked measure contains no information not already contained in the average-days-absent measure if the latter includes all possible types of events; see Latham and Pursell, 1975; Ilgen, 1977; Latham and Pursell, 1977; Smulders, 1980, for an interesting exchange of ideas concerning an absence- versus an attendance-event focus).

Another way to think of lag is in terms of the average observed lag for an individual relative to the expected lag given some random distribution of $n$ total absence events during the course of a time period. A third way to think of lag is in terms of the number of individuals in the work force who have lags of sufficient magnitude that they are not absent during a particular time period. For example, one possibility is the number of individuals who show no absence events within a particular period of time, say thirty, sixty, or ninety days. Another possibility is the ratio of average length of absence events to the average length of attendance event. Although discussed under measures of lag, the former could be thought of as a frequency type measure (that is, the number of individuals showing a frequency of zero absence events during a fixed time period), and the latter could be thought of as a duration measure.

7. Measures of run type. If we assume that absence events can be differentiated as to type (see the discussion in the following section), then it appears that runs of absence events may consist of different absence types. Of particular interest may be combinations of paid and unpaid days and of sickness (or accident) days and non-sickness (nonaccident) days. At two coal mines, the authors have noted at least ten different types of "mixed" runs. Although these have not yet been well analyzed, one possible inference that sug-

gests itself at this point is that at least some individuals use sickness or accident runs as building blocks by combining them with one or more AWOLs or paid personal days.

At the onset of this section, we suggested that a review of possible absence-event measures was important to the degree to which it might improve current operationalizations or identify new theoretical directions. Four of the measures reviewed—those of return, intertemporal lag, building, and run type—are not commonly used. They do appear to imply alternative directions for theory construction. For example, measures of building may provide a convenient means of operationalizing an information set partially explainable by a theory linking the psychological phenomenon of stress reduction (if we assume that a three-day weekend is more likely to reduce stress than a single isolated absence event) and the labor-economic phenomenon of leisure-work trade-offs (if we assume that a three-day weekend produces more leisure than a weekend plus an isolated absence event). Part of the review focused on the issues that underlie choice of a particular measure. For example, our discussion of duration measures noted the biases introduced by whole-day versus part-day data and further explored how duration operationalization is affected by decisions concerning what days to include as absence events, how to treat very long absences, and how to treat natural absence-event anchors. Our belief is that this type of discussion may result in more considered operational definitions of absence-event durations.

We also distinguished between a measure of absence and a choice of the statistic for the measure. That caveat urged that choice of statistic should be guided by the same principles that guide choice of measure, namely, theory and purpose. One can imagine many situations in which the appropriate choice of statistic is one of central tendency (means or medians) and other situations in which the appropriate choice is one of dispersion (variance, range, and so on). Choice of statistic is, however, also affected by the distributional characteristics of the measure of interest. We simply do not know very much about the sampling distributions of most measures, and what we do know suggest that they are not likely to be normally distributed. Hence, if the purpose of a study is to assess the statistical significance of some aspect of an absence measure relative to some hypothesis, we may be forced to consider techniques that are distribution free (that is, nonparametric) or those that explicitly incorporate distributional assumptions more appropriate to the data (for example, logit, probit, hazard rate, or event-study models).

*Interpretation of an Absence-Event History from Three Perspectives*

Any particular absence event may occur for a myriad of reasons, although the manifestations of that event to the company is that the individual is not available for work. The simplicity and objectivity of absence data may be deceptive. Why an individual is absent, the implications of that event to the individual and to the company or work group, and whether the formal typology superimposed by the recording system is "accurate" in any sense constitute a thorny set of problems. Two items seem clear, however, First, the meaning attached to any single absence event or to the entire history of events may differ when viewed from the vantage of the individual, the company, and the researcher. Second, there has been little discussion of this matter in the literature until the recent papers by Johns and Nicholson (1982) and Fichman (Chapter One of this volume). The purpose of this section, then, is to focus on this problem.

*Organizational Vantage.* From an organizational point of view, any particular absence event is either legitimate or not, payable at regular rate or at some lower rate (perhaps zero), payable by the company or some third party, subject to discipline or not, expected or not, and controllable or not. For example, a company may allow an individual some number of legitimate absence events for any reason. If prior notification is required, non-notification may result in an AWOL, even if all legitimate days have not been expended. A single day of AWOL may not result in discipline, but the second day might. The AWOL day is not likely to be a paid day, although it is likely that the company will pay its fringe-benefit contribution for the AWOL day. Certain absence events may be paid at a reduced rate (for example, absence events due to jury duty may be paid at the difference between the regular rate and that received for working on the jury; a similar scheme may be used for absence due to military duty) or at a reduced rate paid by a third party (for example, Worker's Compensation).

The point is that absence events have meaning to the organization, and hence most organizations will develop recording systems and devices to attribute meaning to any absence event, to record that meaning, and to monitor the events over time. Whether the outcomes of the attribution, of the recording, or of the monitoring of the events are consistent over individuals, time, supervisor in charge of recording, and recorder is quite a different matter. Indeed, it may be more reasonable to begin with the hypothesis of nonconsistency than with one of consistency.

*Individual Vantage.* Absence events also have meaning for the individual who experiences the absence. We cannot assume, however, that the meaning an individual attaches to a particular absence is the same as that attached by the organization. For example, let us assume that an individual is absent to attend to the needs of a sick family member. Such an absence may "always" be legitimate in the eyes of the employee yet not legitimate from the company point of view. Other issues that may flavor the meaning an individual attaches to a particular absence include the trade-off of multiple single absence events for blocks of time off; whether certain times of the week, month, or year have greater absence-event value than other times; the perception that the formal absentee policy does or does not apply to a particular absence event; the amount of "negotiating power" that an individual believes may exist over the classification of a particular event; the normative aspects of the individual's work group or boss; the role played by absence events in the incentive system (if any); and a host of other possibilities.

At issue here is that absence events have meaning to individuals, and, as Johns and Nicholson (1982) and Fichman (Chapter One) argue, this meaning has rarely been integrated into studies of absence taking. As a simple hypothesis, it seems reasonable to expect that the absence-event classification system used by the company and that perceived by the individual are not congruent.

*Researcher Vantage.* Those who study absenteeism seem rarely to have included the richness of either of the above two vantages in their research. Often this is the result of a lack of data, although it may be the case that a more common reason has been the lack of a well-developed understanding of how the realities of the organization and the individuals in the organization contribute meaning to the data.

For example, in our work in the coal industry, we frequently observe "mixed runs" recorded on the absence record. A mixed run is a string of consecutive days absent with different days coded as due to different reasons. One common case is an individual who has one or two AWOLs followed by a number of sick days; for the present discussion, let us assume that the actual codes for a ten-day period beginning on Monday are "no code, AWOL, AWOL, sick, sick, weekend, weekend, sick, no code, no code." "No code" is presumed to mean "present." To the researcher, the data probably will represent a single incident of absence, five days in length, or perhaps two incidents, one of two days due to AWOL and one of three days due to sickness. To the organization, the data may mean that this individual has exceeded some rule concerning AWOLs and is subject to discipline. To the individual, however, the story may be as follows: A legitimate illness actually began a few days before the first AWOL (he or she tried to "shake it" over the previous weekend), and it got worse on Monday while the miner was at work. This resulted in the miner spending Tuesday in the emergency room (and hence being unable to contact the mine in a timely manner). The miner attempted to attend work on Wednesday but got sick again on the trip and returned home, again missing a timely call-in, and then, still sick on Thursday and Friday, stayed home and called in. By Saturday, our friend was almost recovered, but on Sunday, he or she heard that the company had recorded Tuesday and Wednesday as AWOLs. Frustrated at being listed AWOL when a legitimate sickness was at fault, the miner called in sick again on Monday and spent the day at the hospital trying to obtain documentation of the emergency room visit.

To be certain, many studies have explicitly isolated certified sick days, legitimate personal days, or extensive periods of industrial injury in their computations of absence-event measures. What is disturbing in the literature, however, is the lack of discussion of the formal absentee policy, an examination of how the system actually works or is applied, or any apparent interest in what actually happened from the individual's point of view.

Our disquiet is heightened because we do have evidence that absence taking varies as a function of the characteristics of the formal absentee policy (Winkler, 1980; Dalton and Perry, 1981; Scheflen, Lawler, and Hackman, 1971; Baum, 1978). Further, most researchers have good anecdotal evidence to suggest that what "really happened" is rarely reflected in the formal data. Rather than pursuing either formal policy or an incumbent's view of reality, it appears as though it is de rigour for the researcher either to accept the data as fully laden with all necessary information or to attribute meaning to the data (apparently) independent of what the absence events mean to the organization or to the individual.

The bottom line of this discussion is that absence data are generated from the organization's point of view. This implies that the researcher must, at minimum, fully understand the formal policy that produces these data. A second implication is that these data probably do not represent well the individual's point of view concerning the cause of any particular absence. Finally, the typology game played by the researcher is no more likely to map onto the classification scheme of either the company or the individual than is that of the individual likely to map onto that of the company. Indeed, Fichman (Chapter One) argues that this problem is so complex that all "absence category schemes that attempt to identify the cause of an absence are conceptually flawed in a fundamental way." Our position is a bit more sanguine, namely, that there is a rich area of exploration here waiting for the researcher willing to be inculcated with the complexities involved.

*Aggregation, Level of Analysis, and Time Frames*

An absence event is a low-base-rate, individual-level behavior that is not homogeneously distributed over all individuals in a given work setting. It is plainly a difficult variable to model, especially for industrial/organizational scientists who have been trained in methods applicable to variables that can be assumed to have normal distributions. Although a few studies in the literature attempt to face this problem (for example, Hammer and Landau, 1981, suggest tobit models; Clegg, 1983, uses a square-root transformation on his absentee data; Allen, 1981, uses both a logit and an adjusted logit model; Landy, Vasey, and Smith, in Chapter Three of this volume, consider both Poisson and negative binomial distributions), most have not heeded the warning of Hulin and Rousseau (1980) that "because infrequent events are often tantalizing or threatening. . . we cannot afford to allow appropriate analysis of these events to be an infrequent event in itself" (p. 18). Naturally occurring low-base-rate phenomena pose intriguing analytical problems, many of which are discussed by Avery and Hotz (Chapter Four of this volume). The purpose of this section is to highlight some of these, with particular attention to issues of aggregation.

Roberts, Hulin, and Rousseau (1978) have suggested that aggregation can occur at the conceptual level, over samples, over time, over measurements, during data analysis, and during interpretation of results. The first three of these have been addressed briefly in our discussion of the possible measures of absence events. They are particularly important in the study of absence events and require some additional commentary.

*Conceptual Aggregation.* Absence events are, in most circumstances, nearly decomposable. That is, in the short run, the absence-event behavior of one individual can be treated as though it were independent of the absence-event history of other individuals in a given work system. In the long run, however, excessive absence events by a few individuals may very well result in a company-level adjustment in absence-event policy. That is, action at one level of analysis (the individual) may result in action at a different level of analysis (the company), which may, in turn, affect action at the original level of analysis. A number of studies (for example, Scheflen, Lawler, and Hackman, 1971; Baum, 1978) have examined the impact of policy changes on absence taking, but, to our knowledge, none have examined how absence taking might affect policy making. More importantly, as is pointed out by Goodman and Atkin (Chapter Seven of this volume), the link from individual absence events to organizational-level outcomes (and presumably attempts by the organization to control these outcomes) can be quite complicated. Finally, although absence events are infrequent events, they are probably many times more common than are policy changes. The issue at hand, then, is twofold:

(1) a need to recognize explicitly that the nearly decomposable aspect of absence behavior does not imply that the behavior of all individual units of analysis are independent over all time horizons and (2) a need to focus, theoretically and empirically, on the linkages between the individual and organizational (or other aggregate) level over time to capture the dynamics of the entire system.

*Aggregation over Samples.* The caveat that "selection of samples is rarely based on units of theory" (Roberts, Hulin, and Rousseau, 1978, p. 91) is perhaps nowhere better exemplified than in absence-event studies. Choice of samples appears to be determined by convenience and data availability. For example, most studies focus on one-time views of single companies with no discussion as to why those particular companies or those particular times conveyed any specific theoretical meaning. Even simple propositions—for example, that two companies whose absence-event policies differ in certain significant ways should also differ in terms of observed absences—have rarely been tested (although this particular hypothesis has been examined by Winkler, 1980).

A second aspect of this problem is the apparent assumption by most researchers that an arbitrarily drawn work-force sample is, in fact, a homogeneous sample. Two items are important here. First, if Johns and Nicholson (1982) are correct in their contention that "absence means different things to different people at different times in different situations" (p. 134), then it may be more reasonable to assume a priori that a given work force is at minimum a combination of several different subpopulations. If this is so, then the imperative of the researcher is to provide a theory addressing the aggregate population and a separate theoretical statement concerning the subpopulations. Second, aggregating across all subpopulations is more likely to obscure systematic relationships than to highlight them (Hulin and Rousseau, 1980). For example, several studies suggest that a majority of the absence events in a company are likely to be accounted for by a minority of the individuals in that company. Expecting that the absence-taking behavior of both high and low absence takers should be systematically related to the same set of explanatory variables may be wishful hypothesizing.

*Aggregation over Time.* By definition, only one absence event at most can occur on any given day for any given individual. Hence, absence data are typically cumulated over time. Addressing this issue, Hulin and Rousseau (1980) note that this procedure trades off increased likelihood of observing the phenomenon of interest at the cost of at least three inherent problems: (1) fluctuations in relations, (2) history/maturation, and (3) lack of synchronicity. Although the first two of these issues have been discussed in the earlier section on the choice of absence measures, it seems important to restate the arguments. Choice of time interval may affect the empirical findings, because the chosen interval may not correspond well to the natural cycle in the phenomenon. That is, natural fluctuations in absenteeism may occur, and unless these fluctuations are well understood and explicitly made part of the choice of time interval, it is unlikely that the resultant data will be an appropriate characterization of the absenteeism. Furthermore, a phenomenon such as absence taking is likely to vary as a function of previous absence events and other time-dependent variables. Unless these variables are well understood and modeled, relations over time are likely to be distorted. The final concern of Hulin and Rousseau, synchronicity, is concerned with the temporal matching of explanatory and dependent variables. Their essential point is that causal modeling requires that the explanatory variables measured represent phenomena that precede the dependent variable in time. This is particularly important when the researcher attempts to relate data collected at one point in time (for example, from questionnaires) to absence data collected over a long period of time.

As a summary statement, aggregation produces some positive effects (such as increasing the likelihood of observing the event), but always at a cost. Since all absence-event studies that were reviewed engage in some form of aggregation, it seems reasonable to expect that these problems would have received some attention in these studies. Unfortunately, that is more the exception than the rule. Even those that do address the issues (for example, Hammer and Landau, 1981) focus primarily on the aggregation-over-time problem. Clearly, more direct attention to these issues is required.

The nature of this attention has already been introduced in our earlier discussion of a theoretical framework and will again be examined in our discussion of the consistency of absence-taking behavior over time. Essentially, choice of aggregation requires an explicit statement about the theoretical assumptions that the researcher is willing to make about a particular sample. As we noted earlier, we begin with the assumption that absence events are likely to be the result of individual-level, heterogeneous, dynamic models. This requires that we explicitly justify all aggregation over samples and over time. While the challenges that this proscription brings are difficult to meet, we believe that they are more likely to provide an increase in our understanding of absenteeism than are the traditional assumptions of homogeneous, static models.

### Question 3. What Do We Mean by "The Reliability of Absenteeism Measures"?

To this point, we have posed and attempted to answer the following two questions:

1.  What do we know about the measurement of absenteeism, and what are the limitations of this knowledge?
2.  How can the current limitations be overcome?

In response to the first question, we identified two fundamental theoretical problems with important methodological implications (whether causal models of absence are heterogeneous and whether these models are dynamic) and commented on a number of gaps in the literature. Question 2 allowed us to explore the process by which absence-event data are generated, the information content of the data, the possible measures that may be superimposed on the data, the variation in meaning of the information as a function of frame of reference, and the implications associated with several forms of aggregation. As a result of this exploration, we observed that the researcher needs to understand the process by which absence data are generated; that most data sets contain more information than most researchers ever use; that at least seven generic measures of absence can be constructed to use this information, even though most researchers use only two or three; that the meaning attached to an absence event is often more complex than that assumed by researchers; and that aggregation of absence data over time and individuals requires theoretical justification.

We may view the response to question 1 as analytical in that we dissected the literature to identify key topics in need of further discussion. Question 2 produced a response that had roughly equal measures of analysis and synthesis. Our concern now is purely synthesis — given what has been developed to this point in the chapter, what can we now say constructively about the assessment of absence-event reliability (this section) and validity (next section)?

Let us begin by asking "reliability for what purpose?" (Johns, personal communication). Are we interested in the traditional concept of the reliability of the measuring instrument (that is, the degree to which repeated uses of the measuring instrument produce similar observed scores), the consistency of behavior (that is, the degree to which the behavior of an individual or group of individuals remains invariant over time), or what (Rosse, personal communication)?

Our belief is that the traditional concept of reliability is *not* the appropriate focus. The rationale for this belief is straightforward and is based on two propositions: (1) The traditional concept of reliability assumes (a) that there exists an "existentially 'true' value" (Runkle and McGrath, 1972, p. 156) for the phenomenon of interest (absence taking in this instance) and (b) that this phenomenon retains this true value over time in the absence of a specific change in conditions. (This comment is based on a parallel-test model of reliability; a domain-sampling model is less restrictive but also requires certain assumptions of temporal invariability. These will later be discussed briefly. A detailed discussion of this topic is long overdue in the literature but is beyond the scope of the present chapter.) (2) Since we have limited our discussion of absence to behavioral events (recall our comment about latent traits earlier in this chapter), and since we believe that conditions are subject to continual change at the level of each individual (see assumptions 3, 4, and 5 earlier in this chapter), *we believe that there is no difference between "true value" and observed events* and that the observed events may vary constantly due to changing, individual-level events not always observable.

We do believe that the appropriate question to ask is "how consistent is behavior over time?" Our choice of the term *consistent* (or *consistency*) should be understood to refer to two issues: (1) the degree to which absence behavior demonstrates systematic or random shifts from one time period to another and (2) the degree to which an order relationship between two individuals or two groups remains constant over time. We can restate this position in somewhat less technical jargon by noting that we do *not* begin with the assumption that absence-taking behavior is consistent over time; indeed, we do expect to observe substantial inconsistencies. Our inquiry as scientists and as managers should then be properly focused on the question "under what circumstances would we expect to observe consistency?"

To answer this question, we need methods to measure consistency. The purpose of the remainder of this section is to explicate a number of such methods. We have organized these methods according to the scheme provided in Table 2.2. That is, our organization is based on two assumptions that the researcher believes are appropriate to the sample being studied: Does the researcher believe that absence in the sample is the result of a single set of underlying causes or of multiple sets (what we earlier called the homogeneity assumption), and does the researcher believe that these models are stable over time or do they vary in complex ways (what we earlier called the stationarity assumption)?

We begin with a discussion of the "standard approach," which is to cast the problem as one of test-retest reliability. Following these introductory comments, we then proceed through the four cases presented in Table 2.2. For the reader's convenience, these four cases, together with suggested methods, are presented in Table 2.4.

**Table 2.4. Classification of Possible Consistency Measures as a Function of Assumptions Concerning Homogeneity of Causal Structures and Stationarity of Structure.**

| | Stationarity Assumption | |
|---|---|---|
| *Homogeneity Assumption* | *Static* | *Dynamic* |
| Homogeneous | 1. Test-retest | 1. Analysis of variance |
| | | 2. Event history model |
| Heterogeneous | 1. Subgroup test-retest | 1. Single-case techniques |
| | 2. Morrison and Schmittlein model | 2. Event history model |

*Case 1: Homogeneous, Static Assumptions.* The standard approach is to construe the behavior-consistency problem as one of traditional reliability assessment, with the technique most frequently observed being that of a test-retest of absence-event measures. Typically, absence-event measures from one period of time are correlated with measures from a second period of time, and the resultant correlation is taken as the measure of consistency (see Muchinsky's 1977 review; Fitzgibbons and Moch, 1980; Ilgen and Hollenback, 1977; Hammer and Landau, 1981). Chadwick-Jones, Nicholson, and Brown (1982), using logic developed from test theory, adjust this type of estimate upward by the Spearman-Brown technique. The magnitude of the test-retest correlations appears to be sensitive to the length of the time base chosen and to the measure and the type of absence event (Hammer and Landau, 1981). In particular, extension of the time base from one month to about fifteen months has been found to result in increasingly large test-retest correlations (Hammer and Landau, 1981; our own work in progress). Occurrence measures seem to demonstrate higher consistency than magnitude measures, and voluntary absence events appear to be more consistent than involuntary absence events. In general, test-retest correlations for occurrence metrics have reported ranges of 0.40–0.60. Given our earlier comments concerning the problems mitigating against the observation of substantial consistency, these numbers seem fairly reasonable.

The first major problem in this approach is that, as noted earlier, the assumptions underlying the test-retest reliability model are not likely to be met by absence-event data. Moreover, discrepancies between the assumptions and the realities of the data are probably substantial. Why this is so from a parallel-tests construal of reliability was discussed a few paragraphs earlier. The argument from a domain-sampling approach begins by noting the need to assume an underlying stable domain, that is, absence events can be represented by an unchanging factor structure (or perhaps one changing in a linear manner). An unchanging factor structure is equivalent to an assumption of stationarity as discussed earlier. The second assumption is that individual scores on the domain are either invariant or all changing in a homogeneous linear fashion. The third assumption is that the factor structure for the population is equivalent to the factor structure for all individuals. These last two assumptions are equivalent to what we earlier called the assumption of homogeneity. There are a few other assumptions, but they are not germane to the present discussion.

The first problem that is apparent when we consider the reliability of an absence measure is that we cannot well characterize the underlying factor structure. Johns and Nicholson (1982) and Fichman (Chapter One of this volume) would argue that this is due to theoretical issues. Even if this were not the case, absence events are such that only a single observation is available for any particular day. Hence, estimation of internal consistency is not possible. If aggregation over days is performed to obtain the analogue to a multiple-item measure, we require the additional (stationarity) assumption that the cause of the absence event on each day (or, for that matter, the cause of the attendance event) is identical (or a linear transformation). This is an assumption that may hold for any two arbitrarily drawn days but is unlikely to hold for all occasions (Horst, 1963).

The second problem concerns the assumption of a common-factor model over all individuals being examined. This is equivalent to the (homogeneity) assumption that the causal structure producing absence (or attendance) events is theoretically identical for all individuals in the sample. While the resolution to this issue hinges on a choice of theoretical position, it is likely, as discussed in the theory section of the chapter, that the observed sample is a potpourri of subsamples, each with a different causal structure.

There is also a third problem. As noted above, we have reason to believe that absence-event measures are not likely to be distributed normally. Clearly, one can compute a sample correlation among two measures regardless of the underlying distribution. What is not so clear, however, is how to interpret test-retest correlations of measures characterized by non-normal distributions. More specifically, our rules of thumb for a "good" test-retest correlation are based on experience with normally distributed random variables, and they may not be appropriate for measures having other distributions.

Indeed, one might interpret the findings of Hammer and Landau (1981) cited earlier in light of this discussion of distributions.

For very short time periods, the distribution of absence measures probably departs markedly from a normal distribution, and the observed "low" correlations may actually be close to their theoretical maximums. As the time base is increased, the distributions may more closely approximate that of the normal, allowing the theoretical maximum to approach 1.00. One implication of this is that a correlation of 0.20 for a short time period may be as good as one of 0.60 for a longer time period (in the sense that each may be equally close to its respective theoretical maximum). Of course, this interpretation is highly speculative, but it does point to the need to understand much better the interaction between the distributions of the sample statistics of absence measures and the interpretation of test-retest correlations. Landy, Vasey, and Smith (Chapter Three of this volume) provide a somewhat different approach to this problem by constructing an empirical sampling distribution for test-retest correlations.

Given the problems just discussed, are there ever situations in which the rest-retest logic is appropriate? The answer is a qualified "yes." For example, work in the area of human learning (Alvares and Hulin, 1973) suggests that well-learned behavior subject to random variation will demonstrate a particular pattern of correlations between time 1 and successively lagged periods (periods 2, 3, 4 and so on). This pattern is the "simplex" pattern, in which the correlations monotonically decrease in magnitude with increasing time lag between periods. Such a pattern might be an appropriate baseline to expect if absence results from well-practiced habits for a particular sample of individuals or a particular type of absence. It may also be the case that, under certain circumstances, the stationarity and homogeneity assumptions can be made with fair confidence; under these conditions, one could use rank-order techniques to determine the consistency of the rank ordering of individuals in terms of an absence measure, thereby avoiding the distributional problems that have been discussed. Other examples could be constructed. The major point, however, is not whether we can construct specific contexts with which the test-retest logic is appropriate; rather, it is that, in most circumstances, test-retest logic is not justified.

*Case 2: Heterogeneous, Static Assumptions.* A more reasonable set of assumptions about individual behavior begins with the admission of multiple distinct subgroups within the sample. If we could independently ascertain subpopulation membership, then we might be able to employ test-retest logic for each separate subpopulation. An obvious problem with this approach is the need to determine subgroup membership on theoretical grounds. Membership identification aside, this approach still requires the stationarity assumption and to that degree is still subject to the criticisms enunciated under Case 1. Distributional issues also remain as a problem, as does the threat that group membership may change over time as some individuals experience modification in their underlying causal models. Although this approach is superior to Case 1, it, too, has a number of problems.

A second approach, which seems especially worth examining, is a procedure suggested by Morrison and Schmittlein (1981). This procedure begins with the assumption that the event of interest can be approximated as being generated by a Poisson process with rate lambda (see Hulin and Rousseau, 1980, for some coments about the applicability of Poisson processes to absence events). Individuals, however, are heterogeneous with regard to lambda. That is, individuals may have lambdas different from that of the entire population; this is equivalent to saying that individuals may have unique heterogeneous underlying models all of which can be thought of as being Poisson in nature. Given this characterization, Morrison and Schmittlein then develop a straightforward method for estimating the number of individuals in time period 2 who will have exactly 0, 1, 2, and so on, absence events given an observation of the number of individuals with 0, 1, 2, and so on, absence events in time period 1. The method is particularly good at estimating what will happen in time period 2 to the individuals who were observed to have event occurrences of 0 in time period 1, a common occurrence in absence data sets. Other, similar techniques, assuming negative binomial distributions (Goodhardt and Ehrenberg, 1967) and condensed negative binomial distributions (Chatfield and Goodhardt, 1973), also exist.

It should be noted that this method more fully talks to a measure of consistency than does test-retest logic. Specifically, the application of the procedure does not result in a single index characteristic of consistency within the entire population; rather, it produces an estimate of the distribution of behavioral events in one time period given the distribution in the previous time period. It is also superior to the subgroup test-retest logic in that (1) it does not require a priori specification of subgroup membership, and (2) there may be as many subgroups as there are individuals.

*Case 3: Homogeneous, Dynamic Assumptions.* Dynamic models differ from static models in at least two ways. First, time is an explicit parameter, and, second, the outcome at one point in time can enter as an explanatory variable at a later point in time. In the context of consistency measures of absence events, this means that previous absence events may affect future events, and one time during a period can have an effect different from other times during a period.

The time dependency of later absences on previous absence events means that the variation in absence measures from one time period to the next period is a function of both random error and actual change. For example, if the absence measure were frequency, the frequency measure during period 2 would be different from that in period 1 because of random fluctuations and because the time 2 frequency is dependent on the time 1 frequency. Test-retest logic assumes that all change from one time period to another is due to measurement error. Since the present case includes two variance components, one due to error and the other due to history, test-retest logic is inappropriate unless the effect of the history component can be partialed out or modeled separately. Unfortunately, this has not been attempted in the absence literature.

If we can assume that the underlying change is "systematic and constant for all subjects" (Winer, 1971, p. 296), then we can use the standard analysis of variance method for the computation of reliability (see Winer, 1971, pp. 283–296), adjusted "by eliminating variation due to change from the within subject variation" (Winer, 1971, p. 296). This would amount to a partitioning of the individual by time-period data into four variance components, one between individuals, one within individuals, and a subsequent partitioning of the within-individual component into one due trend and a residual. If the researcher has a strong a priori model to identify the likely trend component (say, only a linear trend), then variance due to this trend may be obtained by orthogonal polynomials.

This component may then be subtracted from the within-individuals components to satisfy the adjustment suggested above.

The major drawback of this approach is that we assume that all individuals undergo change at the same rate; that is, that the change in absence measure is dependent on time only, rather than on time and the number of previous absence events. Lindman (1974, pp. 234–238) has suggested an approximate method that may overcome this problem by estimating individual trends separately. Such estimates could then be directly subtracted from individual frequencies to provide the necessary adjustment. This procedure, however, also has several drawbacks, which are best summarized by Lindman's own words: "The procedure is far from satisfactory in many of its aspects [although] it is sometimes useful when no other procedure is available" (p. 326).

So the question then becomes "are there more satisfactory methods available?" Perhaps the procedures that are most applicable are based on the event-history models presented by Avery and Hotz in Chapter Four of this volume. Since the treatment there is quite extensive, the discussion here will be brief. Avery and Hotz begin by positing a model in which the probability of an absence event depends only on whether the individual was absent on the previous day. Posing the problem in this form explicitly differentiates it from the test-retest logic, which assumes that the probability of an absence event on one day is independent of the probability of an absence event on any other day.

After a discussion of the basic model, they extend it to include the probability of an absence of a given type given an absence of any type on the previous day. This form of the model is not convenient, however, because it does not include the entire history of absence events. Avery and Hotz note this as a limitation and then extend the basic model to include this history. In the process, they distinguish two forms of the extended model, one that focuses on occurrences and the other that focuses on durations. Finally, they outline a more general procedure that can deal with the issue of historical dependency, known exogenous differences between individuals (for example, age, job), and unobserved differences between individuals (for example, individual "persistent idiosyncracies."

The procedure discussed by Avery and Hotz is very general

and appears to be the most promising approach to the assessment of consistency of absence taking yet proposed. It does, however, bring with it a number of new problems. The first of these can be thought of as being on the interface between theory and methodology. The estimation procedure requires a much more careful specification of the problem than the literature has generally exhibited in the past. While more attention to specification is "good," it is also more difficult and will require a more systematic reflection on the implications of various theoretical formulations. Such refocusing is difficult, and, given the inertial proclivity of behavioral science research, it is not likely that the "goodness" of the above approach will be easily or rapidly accepted. The second problem, which is technical, can best be stated by noting that existing behavioral science software (such as SPSS and BMDP) does not allow analysis of the general problem. Avery and Hotz do note that certain forms of the problem can be attacked by BMDP (for example, proportional hazard rates), but these forms are somewhat limited. Special-purpose software is available for the general problem, but relative to existing techniques, it is substantially more complicated and expensive to use.

*Case 4: Heterogeneous, Dynamic Assumptions.* The last case to be considered concerns assumptions involving both heterogeneity of the sample and nonstationarity of the phenomena. The procedure discussed by Avery and Hotz (Chapter Four) is generalizable to meet such assumptions, and therefore we will not devote any more space to it. We will, however, discuss one other approach that is available, which concerns single-case research designs.

The extreme example of an assumption of heterogeneity is that each individual is different from each other individual. This is the possibility that Johns and Nicholson (1982) have asked us to consider, although they "do not deny that valid generalizations may be made (p. 134). This latter point has been given eloquence by Garmezy (1982), who detailed how single-case studies have provided the bases for generalizable statements about learning, reaction time, perception, associational processes, and development.

To the best of our knowledge, no formal research focusing on the in-depth study of single cases has been reported in the area of absenteeism. Yet the data for such studies seem to be available, and they can be made to meet the following two criteria set forth by Kazdin (1982a) for use in single-case studies: (1) The behavior of interest must be continually assessed over time, and (2) "intervention effects are replicated within subjects over time" (pp. 38–39). Clearly, the first condition is well approximated by daily, individual-level absence-event data. Condition (2) is not quite so straightforward, since the exact meaning of intervention is complex. Policy changes in an absence-control plan are interventions, but they are not likely to occur very often. Individual-level "deals" may change and hence are interventions, but they are not likely to be observable; even if they were, they would not likely occur frequently.

There are circumstances, however, in which interventions may be observed. Some organizations have formal warnings that occur after some number or type of absence events. These would seem to be reasonable interventions, in that they are issued with the explicit purpose of trying to modify behavior. Another possibility may be present in those firms that have some type of bonus system keyed to continuous attendance. The point of this discussion is not to detail a methodology of single-case studies; several good discussions of this subject already exist (for example, Herson and Barlow, 1976; Kazdin, 1982b). Rather, we wish to identify alternate approaches that may prove fruitful in the study of absence.

To conclude this section, let us recall that our mission was to present alternative ways of conceptualizing and assessing reliability of absence-event measures. We began with the statements "the traditional concept of reliability is not the appropriate focus," and "the appropriate question to ask is 'how consistent is behavior over time?'" Drawing on material from earlier in the chapter, we then formulated a fourfold context, based on the assumptions about homogeneity of sample and stationarity of model that the researcher was willing to make. From this we proceeded to develop methods of assessing behavioral consistency that were compatible with the various possible sets of assumptions. Out of this exploration have come a number of approaches that have not yet been applied to absence data. Particularly interesting suggestions include the procedure developed by Morrison and Schmittlein (1981), the models discussed by Avery and Hotz, and the single-case approach.

## Question 4. What Do We Mean by
## "The Validity of Absenteeism Measures"?

The validity of absence measures is a subtle and complex issue. To psychologists, the term *validity* usually refers to the degree to which the measure of interest is a true representation of the phenomena of interest. When applied directly to absence events, the literal interpretation is "if the absence record states that some person was absent on a particular date, was that person indeed absent?" Given that most absence records record only absence from work and not presence, perhaps a more telling form of this question in the present case is "if the absence record indicates nothing, was the person indeed present?" Anecdotally, we have observed situations in which an injured individual was physically present but unable to work (and spent the day in the "lamp room" of a mine, doing nothing). By our earlier definition of absence (being in a specified place at a specified time), the individual was not absent, and yet somehow, were it not for a particular company's desire to make its absence-due-to-injury rate look small, we would expect this person to be absent. At the mine in question, no mark would appear in the absence record, implying that the person was present. If that is what we mean by validity, then we do not have (to the authors' knowledge) any relevant studies, although it is easy to see how one could be conducted.

Another aspect of validity, derivative from the preceding discussion, concerns the recording of type of absence. As suggested in our example of the process of recording absences, the recording of type is dependent upon what the absentee claims the reason to be, what the management interprets the reason to be, and what the recorder actually notates. Without doubt, many claims of absence of one type are indeed not accurate in that the stated reason is not the "real" reason for the absence. (The senior author recalls a cartoon that a colleague had posted on his wall: An obviously sick man was in bed surrounded by a concerned-looking doctor and a nearly desperate spouse. The caption, spoken by the ill man as he was attempting to arise from his bed, was "I can't waste a sick day being sick.") It is probably also the case that deals between a particular individual and management might result in one type of absence being recorded when another was actually the case. If this is what we mean by validity, then again we do not have (to the authors' knowledge) any relevant studies, although, in principle, one could be conducted.

A rather different approach to the issue of validity in the case of absence events is the degree to which absence measures at one time and under one condition are predictive of absence at other times or under other conditions. The astute reader will quickly note that this topic has already been discussed in part under the heading of the consistency of behavior. This "blurring" of consistency and validity is akin to the important thesis that frames the work of Cronbach and others (1972) on generalizability theory. Perhaps the best simple explanation of this thesis has been provided by Runkle and McGrath (1972), who note:

> What we really want to know about a set of observations is to what extent (and with respect to what properties) they are like other sets of observations we might have taken from a given universe of potential observations; and to what extent (and with respect to what properties) they differ from other observations we might have taken from that (or some other) universe of potential observations. When we ask this question in the limited sense of the likeness of the observations to another, near-identical set of observations with the same forms and conditions of measurement and the same population of respondents, we find ourselves within the bounds of the traditional reliability or repeatability concepts. But if we ask the likeness question with respect to a set of observations drawn from a universe considered as some kind of "criterion" set of potential observations, we are inclined to treat the results in the vein of traditional validity concepts [p. 168].

In the present context, this thesis asks us to estimate, as our measure of validity, the degree to which our knowledge of absence behavior is robust over predictions of absence behavior during time frames not observed or under conditions not observed. For example, does our knowledge of run building under one absence-control policy tell us anything about run building under a different absence-control policy? Does our knowledge of total days absent due to sickness in one time period tell us anything about total days absent due to sickness in another time period? Generalizability is, in essence, the ability to generalize the findings observed at one time, in one population, and under one condition to other times, other populations, and other conditions.

The model does make many distributional assumptions that may not be tenable in the current setting, and it also appears to make assumptions of stationarity that may not be tenable. As such, the explicit statistical basis may not be applicable directly. Our point, however, is not necessarily to apply the model of Cronbach and others directly but rather to suggest that the questions they ask are the correct ones.

## Question 5. So, What's New?
### A Brief Review and Some Implications

The purpose of this chapter was to examine the broad methodological issues that underlie the study of absence events. To accomplish this end, we first reviewed a number of central theoretical issues and concluded that the methodology necessary would have to be robust over a heterogeneous population and capable of dealing with models that were time and history dependent. Our examination of the empirical literature suggested that there were many gaps that had not been well researched or well characterized. We then turned our attention to the process by which an absence data set is generated in the organizational setting, the information content of the data set, and a number of possible measures by which various chunks of this information could be captured. This was then followed by a discussion of methods by which the consistency and validity of absence-event data could be assessed.

Three major conclusions were reached. First, the absence literature has tended to employ very weak methodology — methodology that is weak because it (1) does not follow from theory, (2) does not exploit much of the information in the standard absence-event data set, and (3) does not seem appropriate for the complexity of the phenomena. Indeed, the bulk of the literature seems somewhat pervaded by lazy acceptance of inappropriate methodology applied casually to a poorly conceptualized phenomenon.

The second conclusion is more optimistic: The typical absence-event data set is rich in information, and there are numerous methods that are available to exploit this information. We have focused particularly on those that may be appropriate to the assessment of consistency and validity, although other chapters extend these and other ideas to model estimation. Caveats about frame of reference and aggregation were provided along the way to help alert the researcher to possible problems they may pose regarding the data and the interpretation of results obtained based on these data.

Finally, a third conclusion was reached: There is no substitute for a good theory. Much of the methodological difficulty inherent in the literature is at least partially a response to the generally inadequate development of theory that seems endemic to this field. Only a miniscule portion of the literature has been devoted to a discussion of theory. Most of the reported work has consisted of empirical studies not likely to provide a cumulative knowledge base. Recent papers by Johns and Nicholson (1982) and by Fichman (Chapter One of this volume) have begun to sharpen our theoretical wit. Methods discussed above and those detailed by Avery and Hotz (Chapter Four) complement the conceptual developments and help point out new research directions. The opportunities for a fresh wave of more robust studies seem great.

We will conclude this chapter by considering a few of the implications of our discussion.

1. Measuring absence events. Absence data contains much information that is potentially quite useful to both the manager and researcher. Presently, however, most of this information lies fallow. In our discussion of the information content of absence data, we noted that data regarding the timing of absence events and the sequencing of absence events are rarely captured by the commonly used measures of absence. Both of these represent complex aspects of human behavior that may provide unique insight into the relative allocation of work and nonwork.

To the manager, these aspects of absenteeism may be the keys to understanding patterns of absence taking. As such, they provide, first of all, information for making informed decisions about the allocation of personnel, especially temporaries or fill-ins. Second, these aspects of absence taking may be particularly important in understanding the absence behavior of persons such as managers whose work is not likely to be absorbed by fill-ins. For example, managers or others whose work is project based may tend to be absent more immediately after the completion of a project than in the few weeks prior to a deadline. Third, these two types of information may provide an understanding of the effects, if any, of job stress on absence taking, especially among individuals not covered by rigid or formal absence-control policies. For example, following from the logic of Herman (1973) and Smith (1977), when behavior is not rigidly constrained by company policy, individuals are more likely to demonstrate behavior consistent with their feelings about work. That is, when individuals have substantial latitude in terms of the workplace behavior they can display (more typical of managerial than production workers), they are more likely to act in concordance with their feelings: when dissatisfied or stressed, they are more likely to be absent (if that helps reduce the dissatisfaction or stress) than are their colleagues who must also consider possible constraints on absence taking (that is, a maximum number of days or possible sanctions).

To the researcher, the discussion of the measurement of absent events should pose both a paradox and a challenge. Although the paradox is easily stated — why, if these data are available, have they not been used? — the resolution is not. Our belief is that researchers have been aware of these data but have shied away from any investigation of them for two reasons: (1) theory about absence taking has been simplistic and has not talked to the complex realities of why and how people take absences, and (2) the methodology to deal with these complex data has not been readily available.

These two items, then, provide the new challenge to the researcher. With the work of Johns and Nicholson (1982) and Fichman (Chapter One) and our own modest contribution in this chapter, new theoretical ideas are beginning to emerge. These may provide the context within which to propose meaningful hypotheses about the timing and sequencing of absence events. We also now have available, with the work of Avery and Hotz (Chapter Four), Landy, Vasey, and Smith (Chapter Three), and Atkin and Goodman (this chapter), new approaches to the possible set of tools with which to study absence taking.

2. Psychometric properties of the measures of absence taking. We have argued that the traditional views about the reliability and validity of standard behavioral science measures are not applicable to measures of absence taking. What we have suggested is that we substitute behavioral "consistency" for reliability and "generalizability" for validity. Further, we believe that neither consistency nor generalizability can be tacitly assumed as the null case; indeed, it is the researcher's task to demonstrate the conditions under which either consistency or generalizability of absence-taking behavior would be expected to occur. Let us restate this last point in the active voice: We believe that absence taking is not, in general, consistent, nor are findings about absence taking likely to generalize except in certain conditions. We do not know what these conditions are, but we do believe that discovery of them is a primary agenda item for current and future work in absence research.

Although this topic may, on the surface, appear to be of importance only to researchers, it is also important to practitioners. As noted on the opening pages of this chapter, the goal of the practitioner is the judicious control of absence taking, and the basis of control is understanding. As we noted earlier in this chapter, control implies policy that is designed to allow "appropriate reasons for absence, while exacting sufficiently high penalties to discourage cavalier absences." At this point, we simply do not know enough about the relationship between policy and absence-taking consistency. That is, we know neither whether absence-taking consistency should be the goal nor whether policy can be employed to encourage absence-taking consistency, if that should be a goal. As a topic of interest, exploring this will require close collaboration between practitioners and researchers.

Further, we know very little about the degree to which policy in one setting produces similar results in another setting (although Chapter Eight, by Latham and Napier, provides some interesting insights). This issue is what we referred to in the previous paragraph as the question of generalizability. Again, problems of interest to the researcher and to the practitioners converge, and their resolution may require a better working relationship between these parties in the future.

3. Information systems. Our observation is that absence-

data collection and reporting rarely take place in a manner that is conducive to report generation. That is, absence events are typically recorded on paper records, and few regular reports are developed. Further, absence records are usually kept only for production and nonmanagerial personnel. If absence taking has important organizational consequences (see Chapter Seven, by Goodman and Atkin), then records concerning its occurrence should be kept for all individuals, and the manner in which the data are recorded should be amenable to regular reports. This suggests to us the integration of absence data into computer-based personnel systems.

The economic justification for computer-based information systems begins with a belief that the data of interest are important and have a time-based value. Aside from the need to integrate absence taking with pay and perhaps with discipline, it would appear that many organizations do not believe that absence data are important or timely. We are not so certain. At the aggregate level, there might be relatively short-term personnel assignment adjustments that could be effectively accomplished if absence trends were monitored more closely. (This implies that absence trends at the aggregate level be somewhat consistent; this does not violate our oft-stated comment about the probable lack of consistency at the individual level.) More effective auditing of equitable application of absence policy might also be observed by techniques feasible only if absence data were "on line." Other possibilities also exist, but the basic point is unchanged: absence data might be better utilized by organizations to assess the status of their work force (managerial as well as nonmanagerial) *if* the data were on line and reasonable procedures were developed to analyze these data.

4. Future research. We have addressed a number of different issues and at most junctures raised more questions and problems than perhaps we have resolved. Indeed, this is somewhat of a theme throughout this entire book. We believe this accurately addresses the state of current absence research and obviously believe that current research should be redirected from its traditional vein. We recommend more focus on

- the process by which absence data are actually generated at the organizational level,

- the details and application of formal absence-control policies,
- the informal aspects of absence policies (especially supervisor discretion in effecting deals),
- the specific information contained in absence data,
- the development of alternative measures of absence,
- the complex patterns of absence taking,
- the interplay between the different meanings attached to absence taking by the individual and the organization, and
- the generalizability of policy effects and the effects of policy on individual and aggregate behavior.

The list should be longer, but we believe the message is clear: absence behavior is complex and we should begin to study its complexities.

## References

Allen, S. G. "Compensation, Safety, and Absenteeism: Evidence from the Paper Industry." *Industrial and Labor Relations Review,* 1981, *34* (2), 207–218.

Alvares, K. M., and Hulin, C. L. "An Experimental Evaluation of a Temporal Decay in the Prediction of Performance." *Organizational Behavior and Human Performance,* 1973, *9,* 169–185.

Atkin, R. S., and Goodman, P. S. "An Issue-Oriented Review of the Research on Absenteeism." Unpublished report to the U.S. Bureau of Mines, Carnegie-Mellon University, 1983.

Baum, J. F. "Effectiveness of an Attendance Control Policy in Reducing Chronic Absenteeism." *Personnel Psychology,* 1978, *31,* 71–81.

Behrend, H. "Voluntary Absence from Work." *International Labour Review,* 1959, *79,* 109–140.

Chadwick-Jones, J. K., Brown, C., and Nicholson, N. "Absence from Work: Its Meaning, Measurement and Control." *International Review of Applied Psychology,* 1973, *22,* 137–156.

Chadwick-Jones, J. K., Nicholson, N., and Brown, C. *Social Psychology of Absenteeism.* New York: Praeger, 1982.

Chatfield, C., and Goodhardt, G. J. "A Consumer Purchasing Model with Erlang Inter-Purchase Times." *Journal of the American Statistical Association,* 1973, *68,* 828–835.

Cheloha, R. S., and Farr, J. L. "Absenteeism, Job Involvement, and Job Satisfaction in an Organizational Setting." *Journal of Applied Psychology*, 1980, *65* (4), 467–473.

Clegg, C. W. "Psychology of Employee Lateness, Absence, and Turnover: A Methodological Critique and an Empirical Study." *Journal of Applied Psychology*, 1983, *68* (1), 88–101.

Cronbach, L. J., and others. *The Dependability of Behavioral Measurements: Theory of Generalizability for Scores and Profiles.* New York: Wiley, 1972.

Dalton, D. R., and Perry, J. L. "Absenteeism and the Collective Bargaining Agreement: An Empirical Test." *Academy of Management Journal*, 1981, *24* (2), 425–431.

Fitzgibbons, D., and Moch, M. K. "Employee Absenteeism: A Multivariate Analysis with Replication." *Organizational Behavior and Human Performance*, 1980, *26*, 349–372.

Froggatt, P. "Short-Term Absence from Industry. III. The Inference of 'Proneness' and a Search for Causes." *British Journal of Industrial Medicine*, 1970, *27*, 297–312.

Garmezy, N. "The Case for the Single Case in Research." In A. E. Kazdin and A. H. Tuma (Eds.), *Single-Case Research Designs.* San Francisco: Jossey-Bass, 1982.

Garrison, K. R., and Muchinsky, P. M. "Evaluating the Concept of Absentee-Proneness with Two Measures of Absence." *Personnel Psychology*, 1977, *30*, 389–393.

Gaudet, F. J. *Solving the Problem of Employee Absence.* New York: American Management Association, 1963.

Goodhardt, G. J., and Ehrenberg, A. S. "Conditional Trend Analysis: A Breakdown by Initial Purchasing Level." *Journal of Marketing Research*, 1967, *4*, 155–162.

Hammer, T. H., and Landau, J. C. "Methodological Issues in the Use of Absence Data." *Journal of Applied Psychology*, 1981, *66* (5), 574–581.

Hammer, T. H., Landau, J. C., and Stern, R. N. "Absenteeism When Workers Have a Voice: The Case of Employee Ownership." *Journal of Applied Psychology*, 1981, *66* (4), 561–573.

Herman, J. B. "Are Situational Contingencies Limiting Job Attitude–Job Performance Relationships?" *Organizational Behavior and Human Performance*, 1973, *10*, 208–224.

Herson, M., and Barlow, D. H. *Single-Case Experimental Designs: Strategies for Studying Behavior Change.* New York: Pergamon, 1976.

Horst, P. "Multivariate Models for Evaluating Change." In C. Harris (Ed.), *Problems in Measuring Change.* Madison: University of Wisconsin Press, 1963.

Hulin, C. L., and Rousseau, D. M. "Analyzing Infrequent Events: Once You Find Them Your Troubles Begin." In K. H. Roberts and L. Burstein (Eds.), *Issues in Aggregation.* San Francisco: Jossey-Bass, 1980.

Ilgen, D. R. "Attendance Behavior: A Reevaluation of Latham and Pursell's Conclusions." *Journal of Applied Psychology,* 1977, *62,* 230–233.

Ilgen, D. R., and Hollenback, J. H. "The Role of Job Satisfaction in Absence Behavior." *Organizational Behavior and Human Performance,* 1977, *19,* 148–161.

Johns, G., and Nicholson, N. "The Meanings of Absence: New Strategies for Theory and Research." In B. Staw and L. L. Cummings (Eds.), *Research in Organizational Behavior.* Vol. 4. Greenwich, Conn.: JAI Press, 1982.

Kaplan, A. *The Conduct of Inquiry: Methodology for Behavioral Science.* San Francisco: Chandler, 1964.

Kazdin, A. E. "Single-Case Experimental Designs in Clinical Research and Practice." In A. E. Kazdin and A. H. Tuma (Eds.), *Single-Case Research Designs.* San Francisco: Jossey-Bass, 1982a.

Kazdin, A. E. *Single-Case Research Designs: Methods for Clinical and Applied Settings.* New York: Oxford University Press, 1982b.

Latham, G. P., and Pursell, E. D. "Measuring Absenteeism from the Opposite Side of the Coin." *Journal of Applied Psychology,* 1975, *60* (3), 369–371.

Latham, G. P., and Pursell, E. D. "Measuring Attendance: A Reply to Ilgen." *Journal of Applied Psychology,* 1977, *62,* 234–236.

Lindman, H. R. *Analysis of Variance in Complex Experimental Designs.* San Francisco: Freeman, 1974.

Moch, M. K., and Fitzgibbons, D. E. "Automation, Employee Centrality in the Production Process, the Extent to Which Absences Can Be Anticipated, and the Relationship Between

Absenteeism and Operating Efficiency: An Empirical Assessment." Unpublished manuscript, University of Texas at Dallas, 1982.

Morrison, D. G., and Schmittlein, D. C. "Predicting Future Random Events Based on Past Performance." *Management Science,* 1981, *27,* 1006–1023.

Muchinsky, P. M. "Employee Absenteeism: A Review of the Literature." *Journal of Vocational Behavior,* 1977, *10,* 316–340.

Newman, J. E. "Predicting Absenteeism and Turnover." *Journal of Applied Psychology,* 1974, *59,* 610–615.

Nicholson, N. "Absence Behavior and Attendance Motivation." *Journal of Management Studies,* 1977, *14,* 231–252.

Nicholson, N., Brown, C. A., and Chadwick-Jones, J. K. "Absence from Work and Job Satisfaction." *Journal of Applied Psychology,* 1976, *61* (6), 728–737.

Roberts, K. H., Hulin, C. L., and Rousseau, D. M. *Developing an Interdisciplinary Science of Organizations.* San Francisco: Jossey-Bass, 1978.

Runkle, P., and McGrath, J. *Research on Human Behavior: A Systematic Guide to Method.* New York: Holt, Rinehart and Winston, 1972.

Scheflen, K., Lawler, E., and Hackman, J. "Long Term Impacts of Employee Participation in the Development of Pay Incentive Plans: A Field Experiment Revisited." *Journal of Applied Psychology,* 1971, *55,* 182–186.

Smith, F. J. "Work Attitudes as Predictors of Specific Day Attendance." *Journal of Applied Psychology,* 1977, *62* (1), 16–19.

Smulders, P. G. W. "Comments on Employee Absence/Attendance as a Dependent Variable in Organizational Research." *Journal of Applied Psychology,* 1980, *65,* 368–371.

Steers, R. M., and Rhodes, S. R. "Major Influences on Employee Attendance: A Process Model." *Journal of Applied Psychology,* 1978, *63* (4), 391–407.

Terborg, J. R., and others. "Extension of the Schmidt and Hunter Validity Generalization Procedure to the Prediction of Absenteeism Behavior from Knowledge of Job Satisfaction and Organizational Commitment." *Journal of Applied Psychology,* 1982, *67* (4), 440–449.

Thorndike, R. L. "The Analysis and Selection of Test Items." In D. N. Jackson and S. Messick (Eds.), *Problems in Human Assessment.* New York: McGraw-Hill, 1967.

Winer, B. J. *Statistical Principles in Experimental Design.* New York: McGraw-Hill, 1971.

Winkler, D. R. "The Effects of Sick-Leave Policy on Teacher Absenteeism." *Industrial and Labor Relations Review,* 1980, *33* (2), 232–240.

# 3

# Methodological Problems and Strategies in Predicting Absence

## Frank J. Landy
## Joseph J. Vasey
## Frederick D. Smith

In this chapter, we would like to outline the correct methods for gathering, analyzing, and interpreting absence data. We would like to—but we cannot. As you will see shortly, there are some serious problems inherent in dealing with the phenomenon of absence. It is not at all clear whether all of these problems can be overcome. We hope that they can, but it will be for the reader to decide.

In this chapter, we will identify *some* of the major methodological, analytical, and interpretive obstacles in absence research. We will concentrate on two in particular—the marginal distribu-

*Note:* The authors would like to express their appreciation to Kim Hedrick, Rene Bellamy, and Will Weissman for help in collecting and analyzing the absence data that were used in the chapter. We would also like to thank Paul Goodman, Chuck Hulin, and Nigel Nicholson for comments on earlier versions of this chapter.

tions of various measures of absence and the stability of individual absence measures. There are others, to be sure. Nevertheless, these two issues represent substantial threats to the integrity of inference in absence research. For illustrative purposes, we will use some of our own data. These data were gathered in three different settings: a state highway maintenance department, a university clerical pool, and a university maintenance pool.

Even though it is not our intention to support any particular theoretical position, it will be clear that we have chosen to address the standard "proneness" hypothesis. This hypothesis has guided much of the past research in industrial absence. In one form or another, it suggests that individuals can be characterized by a value that represents their individual propensity to be absent from their job. We address this hypothesis for two reasons. First, since it has been the most popular hypothesis (both explicitly and implicitly), it is useful for demonstrating both the limitations and advantages of alternative methods of analysis. In addition, our data limit us to such considerations, since we do not have information concerning such things as job satisfaction, worker performance, or group membership for our subjects. For the purposes of this chapter, this does not represent a serious problem. Through our data, we hope to sensitize the readers to issues that may affect their methods of data collection, analysis, and interpretation. We will leave other substantive discussions for the authors of the remaining chapters of this volume.

## Overview

There are two major issues with which we will deal in this chapter. The first issue is related to the problems inherent in dealing with a low-base-rate phenomenon. In most settings, absence is uncommon. Typical absence rates run about 4 percent in most industrial organizations. As a result of this low base rate, the normal distribution with which most behavioral scientists are so familiar is of little value in analysis or inference. Instead, other distributions must be identified that are more relevant to the variable at hand. We will consider how these other distributions might be used to answer some broad questions regarding absence patterns.

The second issue strikes directly at the heart of absence research. The question is whether absence is a stable phenomenon at the individual level, and, if it is stable, whether there are any constraints or bounds to that stability. Is there some regularity or predictability to the absence record of individuals over a fixed period of time? The issue here is not whether absence can be predicted by some other variable, such as job satisfaction or group norms, but whether absence rates in a given time period can be predicted from absence rates in prior periods. In the past, the issue of stability has been raised in the context of the reliability concept implied by the distribution of true scores and error scores in "classical reliability theory" (Ghiselli, Campbell, and Zedeck, 1982). As you will see in later sections of the chapter, the issue of reliability is inextricably bound together with the issues of validity and accuracy when one considers the phenomenon of absence. To put the matter most simply, *assuming* that absence can be measured accurately (an assumption that implies that the phenomenon can be *defined* to everyone's satisfaction — an unlikely state of affairs at present), is there any reason to suspect that it *should* be reliable in the classical sense? But the issue is not that simple. In fact, one might reasonably propose that there are multiple influences on absence patterns of individuals and that *one* of those factors may be a predisposition to be absent. The issue then becomes the extent to which that *one* factor may influence observed absence patterns. Even if that *one* factor is reliable in the classic sense, are the other factors equally reliable? The situation may be similar to a football game. Each team enters with an offensive and defensive game plan. The offensive plan may involve a particular balance between passing and running. The defensive plan may include a tendency to put only three defensive players on the line of scrimmage. This plan, however, represents a backdrop for the more dynamic aspects of the game. On any particular series of offensive plays, the balance suggested by the game plan may be ignored. On any particular series of defensive plays, there may be four or five or even seven defensive players who occupy positions at or near the line of scrimmage. Similarly, absence behavior may represent a combination of a plan or predisposition and a complex set of situational influences. Under such constraints, what is the highest value one might reasonably expect for a traditional reliability index? As you will see, our plan for exploring this question is to decompose absence data into subsets. We will examine various aggregation periods, absence indexes, and administrative absence categories in the search for stability. This search for stability does not necessarily imply a theoretical position. Historically, attempts to identify the absence-prone employee have been common. This portrays absence as a trait. An alternative nontrait individual-differences approach might propose that individuals who have hot or noisy jobs will be absent more frequently. In this case, we would expect moderated stability. If we could measure the extent of heat and noise on a job, we could demonstrate that people with hot or noisy jobs are absent consistently and that those with more appealing work environments are present consistently — a stable behavior. Finally, even if we take a nonindividual-differences approach — perhaps one similar to the social-exchange notions of Chadwick-Jones, Nicholson, and Brown (1982) — stability is still an important issue. It should be possible to show that if the rules of the exchange are learned and if the forces to comply with those rules are strong, then the behavior of the parties to that exchange should be stable or consistent — at the very least, stable with respect to their perception of the rules. Viewed in this light, the search for stability transcends broad theoretical frameworks.

These, then, are the two major issues that will be addressed in this chapter — distributions of absence and the stability of absence patterns under different sets of constraints. These issues hold some importance for most of the other chapters in this volume. For example, Atkin and Goodman (Chapter Two) suggest that one choose a time period for aggregation based on knowledge of the organizational patterns or "natural" observation periods. If time period is to be taken seriously, empirical investigations should be done to confirm the implicit hypotheses of Atkin and Goodman about periodicity. We provide such a framework. In the chapters by Rosse and Miller (Chapter Five), Latham and Napier (Chapter Eight), and Fichman (Chapter One), the individual-differences model that Chadwick-Jones, Nicholson, and Brown (1982) attack so vigorously is implicit. It is assumed that there is something stable about the absence behavior of individuals. If this is the case, it should be possible to demonstrate this presumed stability empirically. This is not to say that absence behavior is a trait. It simply says that if we hope to develop individual-differences models of absence behavior or interventions that can reduce absence rates among subgroups of employees, it is necessary to demonstrate that the behavior in question has stability under certain circumstances. Avery and Hotz (Chapter Four) present a discussion of how a data set might be analyzed. They suggest that data be gathered on a daily basis and by category for hints of consistency. We agree and have done just that in the present chapter. Finally, consider Table 7.1 of the Goodman and Atkin chapter (Chapter Seven). From their listing of the consequences of absenteeism at the individual level, it should be obvious that they imply a *pattern* of absence behavior when considering at least some of the consequences. If I am ill for a day, my job perceptions are not substantially altered. If I am gone for a week or a month, they may well undergo some transformation. Similarly, Goodman and Atkin are probably not interested in the fact that you might have taken off from work one day seven years ago to replace the brakes on your car, even though this might be an example of meeting a nonwork-role obligation. They would be more interested in examining individuals who regularly or consistently make these work-role/nonwork-role choices. Once again, we return to one of the major themes of this chapter: It should be possible to identify the boundary conditions for stability of individual absence behavior.

The overview makes it seem that we will take a rather traditional empirical view of absence analysis. This is not the case. We will be arguing, instead, that the data represent a puzzle to be solved. The solution is not in the data. It is in the head of the analyst. The data can only provide hints. In order to solve the puzzle, it will be necessary for the investigator to be clever at asking questions rather than careful in recognizing answers. We will suggest some types of questions about absence data that are not commonly asked. We hope to demonstrate that by asking these nontraditional questions, the analytical skills of the *investigator* can be greatly enhanced.

## Distributions of Absence

*The Conceptual Issue.* Absences, like accidents, are an example of a low-base-rate event. This is painfully true over short time periods at the individual level of measurement. It is less obvious for a group index of absence and for an individual absence record over a long time period—for example, five years. As we indicated above, in most organizations, absence rates are of the magnitude of 4 percent of scheduled working hours. In practice, this means that, on any given day, there are very few people absent from work. Similarly, it means that at the end of a specific period of time (for example, a week, one month, three months), many people will have no absences. As a result of low absence rates, recorded absences seldom follow the normal bell-shaped distribution with which most of us are familiar. If absences were high-frequency events (for example, if the average worker missed two or three days a week), one might expect that, during a given week, absences might actually be described by a bell-shaped distribution such as the dotted line in Figure 3.1. This represents a hypothetical distribution of absences for a sample of individuals across a sample of days. In such a situa-

Figure 3.1. Hypothetical Distributions of Absence of
Varying Durations Assuming High Base Rates.

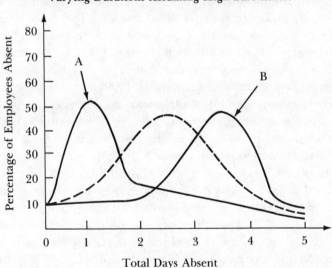

tion, it would be possible to detect "abnormal" absence patterns by comparing an observed distribution of absences to this expected pattern. In Figure 3.1, the two distributions depicted by the solid lines represent departures from the expected distribution. One distribution (A) illustrates a situation where there are fewer long absences than expected. In other words, fewer people are accumulating two days of absence per week than one might expect. The other distribution (B) illustrates a situation where there are more long absences among employees of the organization than one might expect. Keep in mind that the simple detection of differences between an observed and expected distribution does not necessarily provide substantive information about possible *causes* for that discrepancy.

Now let's switch from high- to low-base-rate events. Since we know that absences are *not* common for the average employee of the average organization, we must look for comparison distributions other than the traditional normal distribution. If a department of 100 people is average, one might expect that, in the course of a given work week, there may be a total of 20 absences. If we assume that these absences are somehow distributed randomly with respect to individual, organizational, or situational variables of psychological interest, then we would expect that most people would have no absences during that week, some people would have one absence, some fewer number might have two absences, and a very small number might have three absences. The expected distribution might look like the dotted line in Figure 3.2. This line approximates a Poisson distribution. In fact, the Poisson distribution is a reasonable expected distribution for low-base-rate events under certain circumstances (Froggatt, 1970c). It represents a nonproneness assumption. Put another way, if a manager distributed a fixed small number of absences to the records of unit employees using a random-numbers table, the distribution might look very much like the dotted line in Figure 3.2. This means that it is possible to compare obtained absence distributions with an expected Poisson distribution as a preliminary step in assessing the unique nature of absence patterns within a data set. Consider the two solid lines in Figure 3.2. These lines represent a circumstance in which the observed frequency of no absences is greater than one might expect (A) and a circumstance in which the observed frequency of two absences is greater than one might expect (B) — both interesting

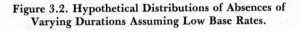

Figure 3.2. Hypothetical Distributions of Absences of
Varying Durations Assuming Low Base Rates.

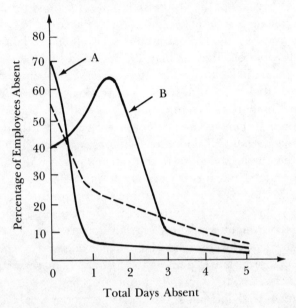

situations. Significance tests can tell us whether these discrepancies are likely to depart from the Poisson distribution as the result of sampling error or whether they may signal more substantial influences unrelated to sampling error. Once again, as was the case with the normal distribution, the simple fact of a significant discrepancy does not provide any information about the *cause* of that discrepancy. Nevertheless, the discrepancy represents a point of departure for follow-up analysis. For example, one might look at demographic characteristics, such as age, that distinguish individuals with no absences from individuals with two absences. Similarly, one might look for co-variation between absence patterns and job-satisfaction patterns for evidence of possible causal relationships. These examinations might include age or experience or a particular job characteristic as one variable of interest and absence as the other.

Typically, absence distributions are examined in order to identify any trends toward absence-proneness in some subset of employees. Managers frequently make such comparisons implicitly. They observe that some people have been absent more frequently than others for a fixed period of time and assume that a discrepancy exists between that observed pattern and some expected pattern. Implicitly, they accept the proposition that some (few) people are a disproportionate cost to the organization by virtue of the number of days they are absent. They accept this proposition even though the Poisson distribution suggests that, for any fixed time period, some (few) people are likely to accumulate a larger than average number of absences; that is, their absence rates will be *proportionally* higher than some comparison group's. But this is nothing more than the recognition that there is some within-group variance to absence for a fixed time period. Consider a coin-flipping analogy. The issue is whether the observed departure from the expected is due to systematic or random influences. Let's say you engaged in several sessions of coin flipping. Further, assume that each session consisted of ten flips. One session might result in eight heads and two tails; a second session might result in eight tails and two heads; the outcome most frequently observed would be five tails and five heads. It would be inappropriate to point to the first or second session as evidence of a biased coin. Only if the number of eight-head/two-tail or eight-tail/two-head outcomes exceeded expectations would a charge of a "biased" coin have any credibility (although there would be alternative hypotheses to explore as well; for example, the bias might be introduced by the method of flipping rather than by the coin itself). This is the problem with dissecting the distribution of absences and labeling some people as high on some absence-proneness factor and others as low on that factor. Unless a consistent *pattern* of absence over time for the same individuals can be demonstrated, this proneness inference is circular. The observation of above-average absence becomes the *explanation* for the phenomenon! The real issue is whether or not the *same* people accumulate multiple absences across *several* fixed observation periods. It is for this reason that absence distributions are examined. If some people are accumulating significantly more absences than one might expect, there may be some reason to explore the hypothesis of proneness in greater detail. The point we are making is that the phrase "significantly more than one might expect" is crucial to the inference of proneness. Many managers are looking for absence-prone employees, and they use incomplete data in making the proneness inference. They see it because they believe it. Nisbett and Ross (1980) and Kahneman and Tversky (1973) have documented the problems of inference that the typical person encounters in analyzing everyday data. This is simply an example of one of those problems.

*Earlier Research and Illustrations.* The statistical issues involved in distributions of absences can be quite complex and will be dealt with to some extent in the later chapter by Avery and Hotz (Chapter Four). Similar discussions have been presented in earlier work on both accidents (Greenwood and Yule, 1920) and absence measurement (Arbous and Sichel, 1954; Froggatt, 1970a, 1970b, 1970c; Pocock, 1974a, 1974b). Rather than reviewing the statistical intricacies of the issue of absence distributions, we will instead address the issue from a conceptual perspective.

The most complete and relevant treatment of the use of distributional comparisons for absence-proneness inferences has been presented in three articles by Froggatt (1970a, 1970b, 1970c). In the last of these articles, Froggatt (1970c) identified several theoretical distributions that might be used to characterize absence data. One distribution assumes a "random allocation of events in a homogeneous group of individuals with different liabilities or risks for changes equally for all subjects" (p. 298). This distribution is the Poisson distribution, which was introduced earlier in the discussion. Another distribution assumes that there is a relatively homogeneous grtoup of individuals with different liabilities or risks for absence. Like the Poisson distribution, it assumes that the environment is stable or changes equally for each subject and that the liability of each individual does not change (or at least changes quite slowly) over the period of examination. This is commonly known as the *proneness* distribution and is more formally known as the *negative binomial* distribution. If absences are distributed along a liability dimension, and if we have some reasonable variance in liability in our sample, then those individuals with higher liabilities should accumulate more absences than those individuals with lower liabilities. In other words, the high-liability subjects should be accumulating a high proportion of absences. If that were the case, one might expect to see a distribution much like distribution B in Figure 3.2. In this case, *liabilities* might be randomly distributed among individuals (based on principles of genetic transmission or allocation to environments or composition of work group), but absences would follow the pattern of liability distribution in the group of subjects examined. In this case, absences would not be randomly distributed — they would be systematically distributed with respect to liability. Of course, even in that data set, absences might still be randomly distributed with respect to an infinite number of other variables, such as phase of the moon, number of children born in Nebraska, or flights from New York City to Bucharest, Romania, on the days in question.

There are other distributions in addition to the Poisson and negative binomial distributions that could also be considered. These two distributions simply represent common "theories" of absence. The Poisson distribution represents an equal-liability model of absence and the negative binomial distribution an unequal-liability model. If one were to find that a data set followed the Poisson distribution, it might be concluded that there was little evidence of absence-proneness in the distribution. As we suggested earlier through the dotted line in Figure 3.2, even if every person's liability or risk for absence were the same, some people would be expected to accumulate one absence during the period of examination, still fewer would be expected to accumulate two absences, still fewer three absences, and so on. If one were using a random-numbers table to "dispense" 100 absences to a group of 1,000 people gathered in a room, some of those people would be given several absences, some only one absence, and most no absences. This can be contrasted with the negative binomial distribution, which assumes that some people are more vulnerable (or have a higher liability) than others. This model assumes differences in the "liability of individuals, in an otherwise homogeneous group, to incur an event" (Froggatt, 1970c, p. 298). Under the conditions of this model, it is assumed that the mean number of absences incurred by an individual in an observational period is directly proportional to the length of that period (Arbous and Sichel, 1954). In practice, this means that one subset of individuals (the group with the highest liability) would be more likely to accumulate multiple absences than another subset of individuals (the group with the lowest liability). In our example of dispensing absences to 1,000 people in a room, it would be as if the person dispensing them were partial to short people and gave more to the short people in the room than to the tall people. If this were the case, the distribution of absences would follow a negative binomial form rather than that of a Poisson distribution.

In Froggatt's (1970c) analysis of the short-term absence patterns of British industrial workers, he concluded that the negative binomial distribution was the "best fit" to the observed absence data for one- and two-day absences. From a statistical perspective, he could only conclude that *proneness* (and by that he meant a psychological trait) was still a viable hypothesis, but he was quick to point out that there were several other alternative explanations for the obtained negative binomial distribution *other than* proneness. For example, among the individuals studied, there was the possibility that some individuals had a greater exposure to risk than others. This would mean that some individuals would accumulate more "real" symptoms of illness than others. Consider the differences between an accounts clerk and a bus driver. An accounts clerk may come in contact with 3 individuals per day and a bus driver 3,000. The risk of contracting an illness carried by another individual is much greater for the bus driver than for the accounts clerk. (In fact, bus drivers have one of the higher absence rates of service-industry employees.) Thus, an examination of the absence distributions for a major urban bus company might suggest that account clerks are not prone to absence but drivers are. In this case, it is less the result of a psychological trait than a situational risk. The way around this inferential problem is to look at the distribution of absences *within* particular risk groups. Risk groups might be identified by age, or by job title, or by height and weight (as might possibly be the case among police officers or professional football players). If the variance of absence rates *within* each risk group is substantially reduced, then differential risk is the more viable inference. Froggatt suggested that additional explanations for the obtained negative binomial distributions might be differences in "tendency to report" absences among departments or supervisors as well as "contagion" explanations (that is, the possibility that one absence changes the liability for another absence *within* an individual). He suggests methods for testing those alternative explanations as well.

Froggatt's analysis and discussion of short-term absence

illustrate both the strengths and the weaknesses of the distributional analysis of overall absence data. Unexpected *unconditional* distributions of absence by themselves may represent nothing of interest to the behavioral scientist. On the other hand, they do signal cause for interest or further and more detailed consideration of various *conditional* distributions. The concept of the hypothetical distributions of absence under differing sets of assumptions has considerable significance for data analysis. It should be clear that a very useful first step in analysis of absence data is curve fitting. Initially, one may examine absence data by determining the extent to which proneness may be present. The question is whether some people have accumulated more absences that one might expect if everyone were equally liable to have an absence. If the data follow a Poisson distribution, then the presence of proneness is not supported. On the other hand, if the data follow a negative binomial form, it would appear that there is the possibility of differential absence liability among the people being considered that is psychological in nature. At this point, it would be necessary to consider other explanations (such as differential risk, differential tendency to report, or contagion processes) and systematically attempt to eliminate them as viable explanations by examining various conditional distributions in an attempt to identify sources of co-variation.

We have applied the techniques of distributional analysis to the data set describing the absence patterns of skilled and semi-skilled maintenance workers at the Pennsylvania State University. Hedrick (1983) was interested in testing the hypothesis that skill level and gender affected absence rates. In addition, she wanted to know whether the main effects or interactions were more obvious in certain absence indexes (for example, one-day absences versus two-day absences) than others. It has often been suggested that shorter absences are motivationally based and longer absences the result of physical illness. (In fact, researchers occasionally label one-day absences as motivational and two-day absences as physical without even looking at the recorded reason for absence). Therefore, she examined the absence distributions for the maintenance workers separately for half-day, one-day, two-day, and three- to five-day absences. Figures 3.3, 3.4, 3.5, and 3.6 illustrate what she found. The half-day, one-day, and three- to five-day absences all followed a

Figure 3.3. Observed and Expected Negative Binomial Distributions for Half-Day Absences.

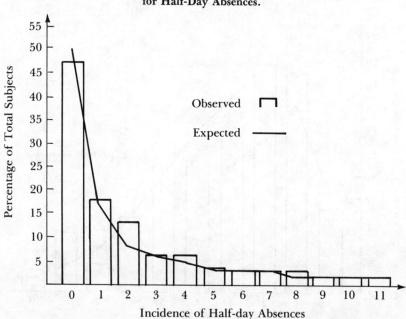

negative binomial distribution. In contrast, there seemed to be little support for the proneness concept in two-day absences, and she concluded that this type of absence followed an equal-liability model. The most parsimonious explanation is that the two-day patterns were genuine physical-illness patterns. Each individual was equally likely to become ill and incur a two-day absence to recover. On the other hand, some individuals were more likely to have half-day, one-day, and three- to five-day absences than others. These overall analyses were followed by more specific tests of the skill level and gender hypotheses. These substantive hypotheses were based on various applications of the Hackman and Oldham job-characteristics model (Hackman and Oldham, 1980), the Chadwick-Jones, Nicholson, and Brown (1982) social-exchange model of absence, and the propositions of Hall (Hall, 1972; Hall and Gordon, 1973) regarding competing role demands for females in the work force. Skill level was found to affect absence rates, with semi-skilled workers incurring significantly greater absences. On the

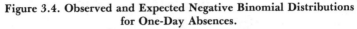

Figure 3.4. Observed and Expected Negative Binomial Distributions
for One-Day Absences.

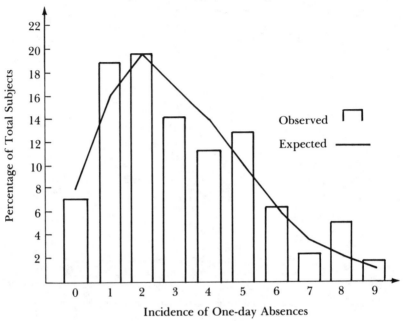

Incidence of One-day Absences

other hand, gender was not found to be a main effect in absence
rates, nor was it implicated in any interactions with skill level.

The illustrations provided by the data of Froggatt and Hedrick highlight the processes involved in considering absence distributions. The point is that one must compare expected to observed
distributions. There is one rather common example of the practical
implications of such comparisons. Most managers believe that
Monday is the day when the absence-prone employees are likely to
be absent. Many managers extend this belief to include Fridays, as
well as the day before and/or after a holiday. Chadwick-Jones and
others (1971) have even extended the concept to cover a statistically
determined worst and best day for a particular work group or organizational unit. Using this framework, an individual absent on a
day when everyone else is present is thought to be more absence-
prone (that is, have a higher absence liability) than an individual
present on a day when many other people are absent. For the sake
of illustration, however, we will limit the example to Monday

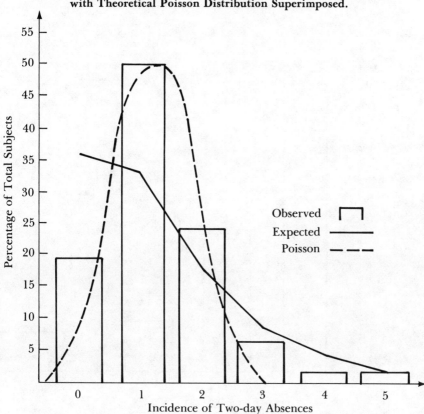

Figure 3.5. Observed and Expected Negative Binomial Distributions
with Theoretical Poisson Distribution Superimposed.

absences. Managers use high Monday absence rates as excuses to "clamp down" on sick-leave abuse. In addition, they may examine attendance sheets in order to identify "sick-leave abusers." The fact is that these managers have usually made a correct observation but an incorrect attribution. In many organizations, Monday absences *should be* higher than any other day of the week. In an organization characterized by a five-day, forty-hour operation, a Monday absence is 2.5 times more likely than an absence on any other day of the week if individuals have equal liability to absence (that is, there is *no* proneness—psychological or other). This follows from the fact that the probability for an absence on a Monday is 38.4 percent but that it is 15.4 percent for the other four days of the week.

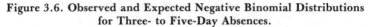

Figure 3.6. Observed and Expected Negative Binomial Distributions for Three- to Five-Day Absences.

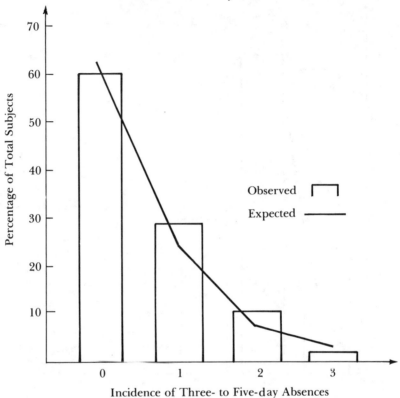

Pocock (1974b) has demonstrated this circumstance in an analysis of the fluctuations in daily absence rates examined by day of the week. The reason for these differential rates is relatively straightforward. If you become ill on a Saturday or a Sunday, the first day that your employer can notice this will be on a Monday. You have not been expected to come to work on Saturday or Sunday, so your illness is not recorded as an absence. This means that the higher rate of absence on Mondays is actually the result of the aggregation of illnesses that began on Saturday, Sunday, or Monday rather than the desire of the dissatisfied or unmotivated employee to avoid work. Under these circumstances, "clamping down" on absences is unlikely to have a major effect on overall absence rates. In fact, as we will describe in a later example, it may actually have the opposite effect and *increase* absence rates. In effect, by incorrectly interpreting Monday absence rates, the manager may *create* organizational and attitudinal problems that did not previously exist! At the very least, the intervention program will be a needless "cost" in departmental or organizational operations. In addition to the analysis of the fluctuations in absence rates by day of the week, similar examinations have been conducted for seasonal absence data. Pocock (1974a) illustrated the differential expectations with regard to length of absence as well as probability of absence based on various types of illnesses. He suggested that summer illness absences were shorter, since they commonly resulted from gastrointestinal disorders, while winter absences, commonly due to respiratory disorders, were of longer duration. He suggested methods of analysis that permit the identification of random, seasonal, and nonseasonal components of absence variation. Once again, we are left with the general conclusion that the interpretation of absence rates demands comparison with some expected distribution. As you will see in later chapters, these expected distributions really represent implicit theories of absence.

## The Stability of Absence Patterns

As we indicated in the earlier discussion of absence distributions, researchers and managers are common allies in the search for the absence-prone employee. To the researcher, absence represents a complex puzzle — something to be understood. To the manager, absence represents a cost — something to be reduced. One common theme of absence research has been to identify individual differences of a psychological nature that might help solve the absence puzzle for the researcher and reduce absence costs for the manager. These individual differences might be represented in such variables as job satisfaction, self-esteem, job involvement, or even a preference for discontinuity.

It has also been common to analyze surrogate variables in absence research. These surrogate variables have commonly been demographic or environmental factors, such as age, gender, marital status, job title, or work-group size. We call these *surrogate variables* because they stand as convenient replacements for more basic psychological variables. The fact that women are absent more frequently than men or the fact that older employees have fewer absences than younger employees is of no direct interest to the psychologist. What is of interest is the psychological process that might co-vary with age or gender and might potentially influence absence patterns.

The manager hopes to identify individuals more likely to be absent from work and not hire them in the first place. Alternatively (or additionally), attempts might be undertaken to identify subgroups of individuals whose absences can be reduced through some form of organizational intervention. The intervention might involve improving working conditions, providing rewards for those who accumulate fewer than the average number of absences, or threatening to punish those who accumulate more than the average number of absences.

In the earlier discussion of absence distributions, we described methods for identifying unexpected absence patterns that might signal the presence of the elusive "proneness" component in absence rates. If some individuals accumulate more absences than one might expect (as would be the case if a negative binomial distribution fit the data well), this suggests that leave taking or absences might be a regular characteristic of the individuals in question. Certainly, if we examine absence data for one month and find that several people seem to be absent at least once each week, we might suspect that this is a stable characteristic of their behavior. The real issue in proneness is the replicability of the pattern. Do the same people accumulate proportionally greater than average absences time (period) after time (period)? This is the issue that strikes at the heart of the traditional psychological-proneness hypothesis. If it turns out that some individuals are habitually absent and some are habitually present, then the search begins for explanations.

A traditional method for identifying these habitual-absence patterns has been through interperiod correlations of absence rates. These correlations have commonly been labeled *reliability coefficients,* and reported values have ranged anywhere from +0.15 to +0.90. There are many problems associated with considering these interperiod correlations as reliability estimates. Nevertheless, there are many intriguing instances in which the coefficients are sufficiently high as to suggest some stability to absence patterns. In the following section, we will explore the implications of interperiod correlations of absence rates.

*Reliability and the Concept of Parallel Measures.* Consider the design of most studies that examine the stability of absence patterns. Absences accumulated during one time period are correlated with absences accumulated during another time period. If one accepts the standard notion of reliability, values of 0.70 and above might be considered "acceptable"; values of 0.50 and below might be considered "unacceptable." These interperiod correlations are usually considered to be instances of test-retest or split-half reliabilities. This immediately raises the issue of parallel measures or tests, a sine qua non from the perspective of classical reliability theory. Ghiselli, Campbell, and Zedeck (1982) describe parallel tests as "a series of operations of measurements or tests that measure the same trait to the same degree, i.e. tests that evoke the same psychological processes" (p. 192). In the case of absence, the "test" is really a fixed time period, and the "trait" is absence. The critical question then becomes whether the two time periods chosen for data collection "measure the same trait to the same degree." Therein lies the problem. As a simple example, consider two distinct time periods of three months' duration. One time period may consist of three months in the winter and another of three months in the summer. If we assume that there is an underlying psychological variable that influences the probability that an individual will come to work, is it safe to assume that this variable is unaffected by seasonal differences? If we accept the notion of an interaction between differential liability (proneness) and seasonal variation, the seasonal differences may prohibit one from examining the behavior in question in "the same degree" as required in the definition of a parallel test. If this is the case, it is not possible to consider the resulting coefficient as a reliability coefficient.

Consider an additional illustration of the same problem. Again, assume that we are examining two three-month time periods. In one three-month period, the individual worker has an accident resulting in nine days of lost time. In addition, during that three-month period there are three legal holidays, and the worker takes two vacation days. In the second three-month period, the worker has no lost-time accidents and takes no vacation days, and there are no legal holidays. Do these two three-month periods represent parallel measures? It would appear not, since they cannot measure the behavior "to the same degree." There was a greater opportunity for an absence to occur during the second period than during the first. If the three-month periods each encompassed sixty-five working days, then the worker had the opportunity to be absent only on any of fifty-one days in the first period but could have been absent on any of sixty-five days in the second period. If we now extrapolate this type of interperiod inequality across a sample of 100 employees, such that similar threats to parallel tests obtain for each subject in the sample, the the requirement of parallel tests (time periods) is not likely to be met. Under these conditions, it would not be surprising to find low interperiod correlations, regardless of what they are called.

The two examples given above represent very different problems. The first problem is conceptually more difficult. If the behavior in question (absence) changes as a function of external variables (such as season or accumulated absences or work-group absence rate), then the notion of a *trait,* at least in the traditional sense, becomes somewhat fuzzy. At best, we are faced with the suggestion of a trait-by-situation interaction. At worst, we are left with the environmentalist or situationist position, one commonly at odds with the individual-differences approach. We use the term *at worst* in a very special way. It is at worst only for the traditional trait approach to proneness. If there is a trait-by-situation interaction, regularity will appear (and interperiod correlations or stability coefficients will increase) only to the extent that these environmental or situational factors are permitted to appear in the analysis. They might appear either in the form of variables (as might be the case in a multiple-regression analysis) or in the form of constants (in which case analyses might be performed *within* levels of a moderator variable). In other words, the issue may be less one of reliability than one of construct validity. The issue of the *validity* of absence measures is raised in other chapters of this volume.

As indicated above, a second problem with the notion of a parallel test (or time period) relates to the issue of the *opportunity* for a nonmedical absence to occur. Here, the problem is less conceptual than operational. If the "tendency to be absent" is a trait with a low-base-rate manifestation, and I observe an individual for one period of time (say one week) and then a second independent period (say one month), one might reasonably expect a low correlation between these two scores for a sample of subjects similarly measured. The periods of observation are substantially unequal. This is a more "legitimate" reliability problem, not because the behavior in question is inherently unreliable but because the circumstances surrounding the reliability calculations were inappropriate.

The solution to this inequality problem would seem to be careful data cleaning. It is important to match periods in order to assure that the opportunities to incur a nonmedical absence were equal both within and between subjects. Thus, one would make sure that the data were adjusted for things such as lost-time accidents, days off, vacation days, military service, and similar distorting influences. Unfortunately, this creates at least two additional problems. First, in balancing time periods, one may be forced to unbalance calendar periods. For example, in order to equate opportunity for absence for individuals A and B, it might be necessary to add two calendar weeks to the aggregation period of individual B (to make up for two weeks of vacation time). This inevitably confounds the interpretation of the resulting stability index. In addition, the problem of what factors should be used in balancing will eventually arise. If your theory of absence involves factors such as stress or some need for discontinuity, how should one treat a single vacation day? It may represent an attempt to reduce stress or satisfy a discontinuity need. Each solution creates a new problem. We may be overstating the importance of some of these concerns. Nevertheless, one should be aware of the problems inherent in simply picking a period of time and correlating it with a similar calendar period, assuming that the two periods represent parallel opportunities for absence (or parallel tests).

*The Issue of Stability.* To say that one is studying the stability of a particular behavior leaves many questions unanswered. In the case of absence measurement, a major question that remains involves the limits or conditions of stability. As we have seen above, there are some serious problems in searching for stability by choosing a block of time and computing a correlation coefficient between that block and a randomly chosen block of time that is similar in certain superficial or cosmetic respects (for example, a one-month time block with another randomly chosen one-month block). But choosing two equal calendar blocks randomly is only one way of computing a stability coefficient. There are others. For example, it would be possible to construct sampling distributions of interperiod correlations. This could be accomplished in one of two ways. First, a month could be chosen at random and the correlations between the absence rates for that month and each other month calculated for a given data set. Thus, if one has a year's worth of absence data, it would be possible to compute eleven individual interperiod correlations. This would represent a sampling distribution of stability coefficients, and the mean of that distribution would be a better estimate of the true one-month interperiod correlation than any single value (interperiod correlation). This proposition follows directly from the central limit theorem. We have calculated these stability coefficients and constructed such a distribution for the highway data. The distribution appears in Figure 3.7. It is interesting to contrast the median value of this distribution $(r = 0.00)$ with the value that would have been reported if the two months chosen for comparison were April and June $(r = 0.70)$ or June and September $(r = 0.49)$. As you can see, there is a discrepancy of substantial magnitude. If we consider the median value, we would conclude

Figure 3.7. Observed One-Month Interperiod Correlations.

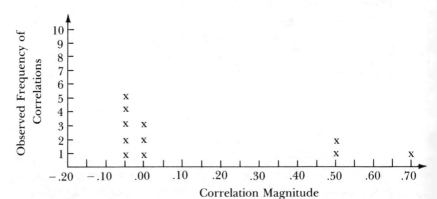

that there is no stability for one-month absence blocks. Instead, if we decided to estimate stability by calculating the correlation between two one-month periods chosen at random, we might conclude that there is substantial ($r = 0.70$) or moderate ($r = 0.49$) stability of absence rates in time periods as short as one month. In the latter case, we would be in error, since the stability does not hold for *any* comparison of one-month blocks (although it *may* be true for specific calendar-month comparisons).

The fact that the April/June correlation was dramatically higher than the median of the distribution of one-month correlations is of no particular importance. Sometimes the single value will be higher than the median value, sometimes it will be lower, and sometimes it will correspond closely with the median of the sampling distribution. The point is that the median of the sampling distribution is a better estimate of the actual stability for the particular time period chosen. We have constructed a similar distribution of stability coefficients for one-week time periods from the same data set (yielding a sampling distribution of fifty-one points). This distribution appears in Figure 3.8. As you can see, some of these values are reasonably high ($r = 0.60$), but most are close to zero. Had we chosen two particular weeks in estimating stability, our inferences about stability might have been quite different than they would be if based on the median of the sampling distribution ($r = 0.00$).

Although the sampling distribution of the correlations between a particular time period and all other similar time periods (such as the one presented in Figure 3.7 or 3.8) is instructive and more credible than a single-time-period correlation (such as the ones presented in Table 3.1), the estimate could be improved still further. In Figures 3.7 and 3.8, we have begun with a *specific* time block (for example, the month of April or the twenty-seventh week of the year). But what might the distribution have looked like if we had chosen another specific time block (for example, the month of December or the fifth week of the year)? It should be obvious that the estimate of the stability of absence for the time period could also be influenced by this initial choice as well. This distortion can be eliminated by looking at every possible combination rather than a particular one. In the case of the weeks in a year, this would yield a

Figure 3.8. Observed One-Week Interperiod Correlations.

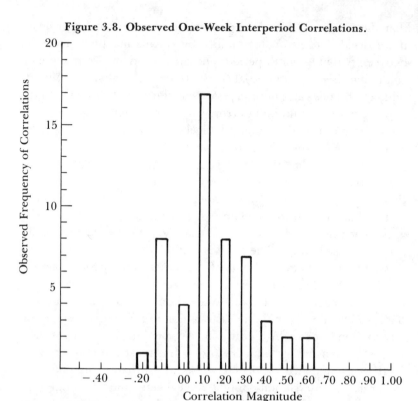

sampling distribution with 1,326 points [$N(N-1)/2$], and the median of this distribution would provide the best estimate of stability coefficients, since all possible combinations are considered. Consider the case of three-month or quarterly reporting periods. In our highway data, we looked at a randomly chosen interperiod correlation (which turned out to be Quarter 1 with Quarter 3). For this analysis, we considered one particular type of absence, called *personal days*. This category represents a paid nonillness absence (a fringe benefit included in the union-negotiated employment contract). The stability coefficient for the Quarter 1–Quarter 3 comparison was – 0.02. Contrast this value with the three stability coefficients that were obtained from correlating the Quarter 4 absences with those in Quarters 1, 2, and 3. These values were – 0.33, – 0.42, and – 0.52, respectively. Finally, consider the entire matrix of correlations comparing each quarter with every other quarter. The median of that matrix was – 0.25. These coefficients paint an interesting picture. They tell us that depending on any *one* interquarter correlation would be potentially misleading. Further, they suggest that there is a modest negative correlation between quarters (as one might expect if employees had a fixed and small number of personal days to "spend" in the calendar year). Finally, they suggest that Quarter 4 is most heavily influenced by the other quarters. The more days used in other quarters, the fewer taken in Quarter 4, and vice versa. The raw data suggest that employees save days for Quarter 4.

There is still another method for aggregating absence data across fixed time blocks that deserves a comment, although we will not illustrate it with our data. If we chose to examine the stability of absence across a fixed time period (for example, one month), we could *artificially* construct that time block by aggregating randomly chosen assigned working days. If we are interested in a period of twenty or thirty working days, it is a simple enough procedure to randomly choose one day at a time without replacement until we have accumulated twenty or thirty days. In order to construct a second, equal period (parallel test), we could construct a second set of twenty or thirty days from the working days remaining in the same manner. This would rule out most periodic or harmonic variations and might satisfy more closely the requirements of a parallel test.

The methods described above for approaching stability assume that the behavior in question should not vary from one time period to another. With absence, that may not be a reasonable assumption. For example, it may be that there are cyclical variations within a calendar year that repeat year after year. Examples might include trout and deer seasons, periods when the risk of influenza is great, summer months, holiday seasons, or other influences tied to environmental change. If this were the case, one might want to examine stability not in terms of combinations of all months or weeks but in terms of *particular* matching months or weeks from one year to the next. Thus, one might correlate first-quarter absence rates for 1980 with first-quarter absence rates for 1981, or March of 1979 with March of 1980, or the week before Christmas in 1982 with the same week in 1983. If the correlation coefficients are substantially higher than the mean of the sampling distribution for that aggregation period (as outlined in the previous section), one might reasonably conclude that there are certain cyclical factors operating in the phenomenon of absence. In effect, we are now examining conditional distributions rather than unconditional ones. A more general method that might achieve the same end might be to look at distributions of stability coefficients such as those appearing in Figures 3.7, 3.8, and 3.9 and concentrate on the high values, looking for possible moderators or co-variates. For example, if one examined the sampling distributions for a two-year period of time and found that most of the high-stability coefficients were matching time blocks from each calendar year, harmonic variation might be inferred. In this circumstance, it would be necessary to modify or qualify the meaning of the word *stability*. Such evidence would be extremely useful in pursuing a substantive theory of absence, since it points the way toward certain environmental influences that might be examined. The data presented above on quarterly stability for personal days is an example. One might investigate the choice patterns that individuals use in allocating those absence days. Similar choice patterns might apply to other categories of absence that are not constrained by work agreements.

A final notion of stability might include the concept of half-life. Some absence theories suggest specific relationships between one time period and the next consecutive time period. In a contagion or inertial theory, a positive relationship would be expected under certain circumstances. In other words, the fact that you were absent today might increase the probability that you would be absent tomorrow — a body at rest tends to remain at rest. In a stress-reduction theory of absence, a single absence might relieve work-related stress and allow the positively valent aspects of the work to "pull" the person back to the work setting. In this case, one might expect a negative relationship between absence rates in one period and absence rates in the next consecutive period. In fact, the data that we presented about the interquarter correlations for personal days could be interpreted within such a framework rather than an administrative-control framework. A more complex variation of the administrative-control explanation would be that initial absence instances are unrelated, but as the individual uses up permissible absences, the relationship between each absence and each subsequent absence becomes increasingly stronger. This is exactly the point made in the chapters by Fichman, Atkin and Goodman, and Avery and Hotz. In any event, the point is that correlation coefficients between consecutive or ordered periods provide very different information than is provided either by correlations between matched time periods or by means of sampling distributions of all possible time periods of equal length.

It is impossible to identify a "correct" aggregation period, but it is possible to examine data and determine where stability exists and where it doesn't. For a large data set, it would be a simple matter of breaking out subsets of data and calculating stability indexes for various aggregation periods (for example, two weeks, one month, two months, three months, and so on). These stability coefficients could then be examined for estimates of stability, using one or more of the methods described above. The investigator is bound by his or her data. Although it may not be possible to increase stability, it is possible to estimate what the stability of the absence measure is. This is critical in evaluating the relationship between absence and any other variable.

*Additional Parameters of Stability.* In the following discussion, we will ask you to suspend disbelief for the sake of illustration. Let's assume that we are working with data that permit the development of parallel tests (or time blocks) as the term is used in classical reliability theory. Further, let's assume that recording is accurate, at least in the sense that the person recording an absence takes at face value the reason provided by the employee and does not alter that report in any systematic way (although we need not assume that the records are perfectly accurate; random clerical errors are acceptable). The actual reason given by the person for an absence may be the result of a negotiation (either implicit or explicit) between the employee and the organization. Alternatively, it might represent an instance in which the employee has learned a certain set of organizational rules and applies those rules to cover a particular absence incident. Whether the rules are being *honestly* or *correctly* interpreted by the employee may be less important for the psychologist than whether the rules are being *consistently* interpreted by that person.

Even if all of the assumptions above are met, there may still be limits to the stability coefficients imposed by one of three different

parameters. The first is *aggregation period*. As is the case with any
measure, one needs an adequate observation period in order to feel
confident that the "true" score has been reliably assessed. For example, a test of 3 items would be expected to show lower reliability
than a test of 100 items, assuming they measured the same construct. The equivalent argument in absence research is the appropriate aggregation period for estimates of absence tendencies. You
will note that, once again, we beg the question of absence tendency
as an individual difference. All other things being equal, it is likely
that there is a lower limit to the number of observations (or periods
of observation) that might produce stable estimates of absence-
proneness. It is not unreasonable to assume that there is some
lower limit and that this limit is influenced by the fact that we are
dealing with a low-base-rate event. Thus, it is likely that a week is
too short a period. But what is long enough?

We have explored that question by systematically varying
aggregation periods from one week to one year and looking at the resulting stability coefficients. Consider the correlations in Table 3.1.
They were computed from the absence records of 174 highway
workers. As you can see, the values are quite low for one week, two
weeks, and one month. There is a substantial jump between one
and three months. One might conclude from these figures that one
month or less would be too short a period for gathering absence
data but that three months or more might be acceptable. In fact,
three months is a common aggregation period for absence research,
although it does not always yield stabilities similar to the ones
reported in Table 3.1. In a recent analysis of stability indexes for
varying aggregation periods, Hammer and Landau (1981) found
very low three-month coefficients (for example, 0.12, 0.14, 0.25).

Table 3.1. Stability Coefficients for Various Aggregation Periods.

| Aggregation Period | Coefficient |
| --- | --- |
| One week | 0.10 |
| Two weeks | 0.16 |
| One month | 0.13 |
| Three months | 0.58 |

Their results might be explained by our earlier illustration of the effect of choice of comparison periods. They chose monthly blocks using a calendar-based scheme. As we suggested above, this is questionable with respect to the *actual* number of observations available. As another example of low stability for a three-month period, in a study of the relationship between satisfaction and absence, Ilgen and Hollenback (1977) reported a three-month stability coefficient of less than 0.20. It is likely that such correlations will vary substantially from one organization (or study) to another or possibly even from one department to another within a single organization. In that sense, it is not likely that a particular period of aggregation is "best" for all settings or organizations. We have begun a meta-analysis of stability coefficients that appear in published studies to see whether there are any general parameters, such as sample size or absence index, that might help us to understand coefficient fluctuation over fixed time periods.

There is no doubt that stability coefficients will be influenced by base rates of absence. The lower the absence rate, the lower the coefficients. In many countries, absence rates are considerably higher than in the United States. In many factories in Yugoslavia and Romania, the absence rates run as high as 20 percent; Sweden's industries have experienced high absence rates for decades. as a result of a social welfare program that eliminates penalties for absence. In these countries, it is likely that there is some stability to absence behavior for relatively short aggregation periods, possibly as short as one month. In the typical U.S. employment setting, there may simply be insufficient variance in absence over short periods of time. This would greatly influence the observed value of the stability coefficient. This implies something very basic about the study of absence: It is best done in organizations where there is some variance to the phenomenon. This does not mean organizations with high absence rates overall but, instead, organizations where there is substantial variance in individual absence distributions.

As we indicated above, aggregation period alone may not be the only parameter or limit to stability coefficients. In some instances, three months may be sufficient; in other instances, it may be unnecessarily long; and in still other cases, it may be too short. A second parameter of absence measures has been suggested by several researchers — the *index of absence*. It is possible that various indexes of absence show different patterns of stability. For example, it has been suggested that some indexes may represent more psychologically meaningful measures than other indexes. Chadwick-Jones and others (1971), Muchinsky (1977), and others have suggested that the number of periods of absence is the most sensitive measure for psychological analysis, since it is the *inception* of an absence period that is most likely to be influenced by psychological variables. Over the years, many different indexes have been suggested. These include such measures as total days absent per unit time, number of absence spells per unit time, the ratio of days to absence spells (yielding an average duration measure), the number of one-day absences, the number of two-day absences, the number of half-day absences, the number of Friday absences, the number of Monday absences, and the number of Friday *and* Monday absences. It is easy to see the theory implicit in many of these measures. For example, Monday and Friday absences imply a desire on the part of the individual to extend the weekend by one or two days. Similarly, one-day absences are often considered "dispositional" and thus "avoidable," while two-day absences are thought to be more closely related to physical illness. In several of our analyses of absence data, half-day absences appear to be sensitive and stable measures.

As was the case for aggregation periods, it is possible to examine the stability of absence rates for each of several indexes separately. In Table 3.2, we illustrate the form that such an analysis might take. In that table, you will find stability coefficients for the various indexes listed above. These coefficients were computed for a three-month aggregation period and for total absence (excluding tardiness). They represent the correlations between the index for one three-month aggregation period and that index for another randomly chosen three-month period within the same calendar year. These data are part of our highway-worker data set and represent the attendance records for maintenance workers from various counties. The first and second rows break the data down by county. The third row represents the stability coefficients for all sixty-seven counties in the state. There are some interesting similarities and differences between rows. For example, when one

Table 3.2. Stability Coefficients for Various Indexes of Absence.

| | | | | Index | | | | | |
|---|---|---|---|---|---|---|---|---|---|
| | Days | Incidents | Ratio | Monday | Friday | Friday/ Monday | Half Day | One Day | Two Days |
| County 1 (N = 88) | 0.52 | 0.51 | 0.80 | 0.48 | 0.43 | 0.18 | 0.57 | 0.53 | 0.47 |
| County 2 (N = 86) | 0.30 | 0.57 | 0.06 | 0.22 | 0.50 | 0.03 | 0.59 | 0.57 | 0.43 |
| Total sample (N = 7,694) | 0.11 | 0.43 | 0.05 | 0.13 | 0.24 | 0.02 | 0.56 | 0.42 | 0.10 |

considers only the index of *total days lost*, the stability coefficient for County 1 is moderately high, the stability coefficient for County 2 is moderately low, and the overall stability coefficient for all sixty-seven counties is lower still. In contrast, the index that represents *incidents*, or spells of absence, is substantial for the two individual counties and for the entire data set. Similarly, *one-day* absences seem stable for both counties as well as for all sixty-seven counties taken as a whole. Finally, the *half-day* absence measure also seems reasonably stable over a three-month aggregation period. The stability coefficient for *Monday* absences is relatively high in County 1 but low in County 2. For the data set as a whole, there is little or no stability for the *Monday* index. One interesting index for County 1 is the *ratio* of days off to periods of absence. An inspection of absolute absence rates shows that in County 1, the number of *one-day* absences is considerably greater than in County 2. As a result, the average length of absence is a good deal less variable in County 1 from one period to the next. On the whole, one gets the feeling that the absence patterns in County 1 and County 2 are different in some important respects. Finally, the data for all sixty-seven counties suggest that *two-day* absences are not particularly stable across three-month time blocks.

It is tempting to conclude that these data relative to indexes of absence suggest subcultural influences on absence patterns. Stabilities appear in the county level that are not apparent in the data set as a whole. Similarly, there are interesting differences between counties on some indexes. Since we are picking and choosing stability values in order to illustrate potential modes of analysis, it is not appropriate to interpret these values in any substantive manner or from any particular theoretical perspective. Instead, the coefficients suggest hypotheses to be tested in independent data sets. One inference that can be drawn from these data is that alternative indexes of absence vary in stability. These data encourage the researcher to break data sets down into subunits, such as departments, shifts, plant locations, or, in our case, work locations, in examining absence pattern. We are confronted with the possibility that the only general conclusion about stability that can be reasonably made is that no general conclusion is possible.

There is a final parameter that might be considered in examining the stability of absence rates — *recorded reason for absence*. Keep in mind that we have asked you earlier in this section to suspend disbelief for purposes of discussion. We are not so naive as to believe that recorded reasons are to be taken at face value. Nevertheless, we do believe that there is some value in dealing with actual administrative categories themselves (such as excused sick leave, unexcused personal day, vacation day, and so on) rather than evaluations of those categories by researchers or organizational conventions (for example, aggregations of certain categories into a "voluntary" or "avoidable" category and others into an "involuntary" or "unavoidable" category) or with total absences regardless of reasons. From the psychological-proneness standpoint, there is every reason to believe that some categories (for example, unexcused personal absences) might display greater stability than others (for example, absence due to physical illness). Again, we hasten to add that we realize that such speculation is tantamount to testing a hypothesis that derives from a particular theoretical perspective.

It is difficult to justify the use of overall absence rates from a logical perspective. When you consider overall absence rates, it is obvious that there are an enormous number of variables that compose the aggregate value. Some obvious variables might be acute illness, chronic illness, acute or chronic positive factors in nonwork settings, acute or chronic negative factors in work settings, illness of a spouse or child, and so on. There is no reason to think that these factors are all operating in a similar manner or on the same cycle such that an overall absence figure would display some stability over a given time period. As an example, remember the interquarter correlations for the personal days category of highway workers presented above. The correlations were consistently negative. For other categories for similar interquarter comparisons, the correlations were uniformly positive. What could be the value of combining administrative categories of absence that would seem to have such different properties? There is no reason to expect a high correlation between overall absences for one three-month period and overall absence for another three-month period unless that overall figure happens to be dominated by one particular type of absence, such as illness.

The use of dichotomous categories to characterize absence is widespread and popular. Consider the various binary choices presented in Table 3.3. There is an unmistakable motivational flavor to the majority of these categorizations. These binary categories involve a reduction from many categories to only two. A set of absence data is transformed into binary information using some coding rules. So, for example, jury duty, illness documented by a doctor's note, or death of a family member may be considered "legitimate," "certified," or "excused" absence. On the other hand, reported illness with no doctor's note, a missed day to care for a sick spouse or child, or a day missed with no reason given may be considered as "illegitimate," "uncertified," or "unexcused" absence. Here we have still another behavior entering into the absence arena—

**Table 3.3. Some Commonly Used Categories of Absence.**

---

Scheduled versus unscheduled
Authorized versus unauthorized
Certified versus uncertified
Avoidable versus unavoidable
Justified versus unjustified
Contractual versus noncontractual
Sickness versus nonsickness
Disability versus nondisability
Medical versus personal
Injury versus noninjury
Chronic-illness versus acute-illness
Long-term versus short-term
Repeater versus nonrepeater
Voluntary versus involuntary
Intentional versus unintentional
Explained versus unexplained
Excused versus unexcused
Official versus unofficial
Compensable versus noncompensable
Insured versus noninsured
Occupational versus nonoccupational
Legal versus illegal
Reasonable versus unreasonable
Illness versus self-induced illness
Certified illness versus casual illness
Monday/Friday versus midweek
Reported versus unreported
Employee-centered versus management-centered

---

the behavior of the person doing the coding or constructing the coding rules. There is every likelihood that the implicit theory that the coder holds regarding absence will influence the nature of the categories' definitions. Consider a day off to take care of a spouse who has a bad cold. The employee honestly reports the reason, and it is coded as a personal day off without pay. One researcher might consider that a legitimate day off, that is, one not "under the control" of the worker. Another researcher might consider the same absence illegitimate, because the worker should have been able to find a neighbor or relative to look in on the spouse if necessary. In the second instance, it is assumed that the individual has missed work for "motivational" reasons. The point we are making is not that one researcher is correct and the other incorrect but that one researcher excludes this particular absence from examination (by considering it legitimate), and the other researcher includes it in the data set to be examined (by considering it illegitimate). This may have the effect of further muddying an already murky river. It may be advantageous to deal with individual administrative categories independently, at least until there is some reason — logical or empirical — for collapsing them.

The fact that many studies of absence are conducted on coded or transformed data has made it very difficult to aggregate studies and draw any firm conclusions. That does not mean that this earlier research is worthless. Instead, it means that the reader must be sensitive to the issue of coding and categorization. On a more positive note, it would seem that absence research is a prime candidate for meta-analysis. Since many researchers are careful to indicate what coding rules were used in data analysis, it should be possible to examine findings in light of these coding strategies. In addition, one might consider variables such as aggregation period, company size, and job titles in the meta-analysis.

As we have indicated above, there are problems in dealing both with overall absence data and with data that have been dichotomously coded. An alternative might be to consider absence data by administrative category. Most organizations use a multicategory system for coding absences. These categories usually include sick leave, vacation, leave without pay, personal excused leave, personal unexcused leave, funeral leave, and so forth. Since most studies of absence are conducted within a single organization, the idiosyncratic nature of the category labels or definitions is not likely to create problems for analysis. Consider Table 3.4. This table contains stability coefficients from two different studies. The top row of Table 3.4 includes data from an analysis of the absence rates of university clerical employees ($N = 70$). The bottom row includes data from state highway workers ($N = 167$). Clerical workers show low stability for sick leave but high stability for funeral leave. In contrast, highway workers show low stability for funeral leave and high stability for sick leave. (These two categories are the only two that are defined similarly in the two data sets.) The coefficients are based on three-month aggregation periods. These coefficients are not offered as answers to questions or support for a particular theory. Instead, they suggest hypotheses that might be tested in other data sets from the same organizations. For example, it is unlikely that the friends and relatives of the clerical workers die with the regularity implied by the three-month stability coefficients. It is more likely that this category is used in a very special way by supervisors, possibly as a reward for good work or loyalty. It may also be used in a creative way by the clerical worker, depending on the guidelines for the use of this category. As an example, a bus driver we know searches the obituary column of a major urban newspaper regularly in the hope of finding someone with his name who has recently died. He then requests day off to attend the funeral. Since he has a very common name, he requests several funeral days off each year.

One might also examine the differences between the clerical workers and the highway workers with respect to sick-leave use from an instrumentality perspective. It may be that the clerical workers are permitted to accumulate sick days for long periods of

Table 3.4. Stability Coefficients for Two Administrative
Categories in Two Samples.

|  | Administrative Category | |
|  | Sick Leave | Funeral Leave |
| --- | --- | --- |
| Clerical workers | 0.21 | 0.62 |
| Highway workers | 0.74 | 0.02 |

time or receive partial payments for sick days not used at the end of each year and that highway workers can accumulate sick days for a shorter period or cannot receive payment for sick days not used. In such a case differences would be mediated by organizational variables rather than individual differences. These differences should be apparent in the absolute frequencies of absence in the various administrative categories.

The type of data presented above, broken down by aggregation period or index or administrative category, contains both good news and bad news. The bad news remains the same: Researchers are unlikely to find any general principles that apply to various categories of absence. The good news is that absence data might prove to be a sensitive barometer to various aspects of organizational life. As an example, Nicholson (1976) examined the effect of "clamping down" on sick leave use by production workers in a food-processing plant. Workers received verbal warnings, written warnings, and finally dismissals for frequent periods of absence. The result was interesting. The absence periods were less frequent, but the length of an absence increased appreciably. In fact, for the year following the clamp-down, absence was 5 percent higher than the year before the clamp-down. Nicholson interpreted these results as examples of organizational learning. Once the employee had a doctor's certification of illness, he or she was likely to take an extra day or two. Nicholson's data support his conclusion. There was a 55 percent decrease in the frequency of one- to two-day sick spells after the clamp-down but an increase of 18 percent in three- to five-day sick spells, an increase of 18 percent in six- to ten-day spells, and an increase of 27 percent in eleven- to fifteen-day spells. In another study, involving rotating shift workers, Nicholson, Jackson, and Howes (1978) were able to show that absence rates varied as a function of a worker's shift (for example, day, afternoon, or evening), as a function of where the worker was in the shift cycle (for example, first two days versus last two days of the particular shift rotation), and as a function of the day of the week. The analysis demonstrated that there was a significant three-way interaction including these components.

Data such as these suggest that examinations of decomposed or segmented absence data can be quite valuable in understanding the dynamics of an organization. Similarly, within an organization, it should be possible to compare and contrast departments, shifts, and even work groups on absence statistics by category and develop hypotheses about intragroup dynamics. We have chosen to highlight the use of stability coefficients for this purpose, but, as Nicholson's analysis shows, absolute absence rates can be equally useful.

To this point, we have considered several potential parameters of stability independently. By implication, there are interactions of these main effects to consider as well. Consider the data cube that appears in Figure 3.9. This figure suggests that any particular stability coefficient is an interaction of circumstances. It is influenced by choices made along three dimensions — period of aggregation, index, and administrative category. The best way to illustrate such interactions is to compare stability coefficients for fixed values of two effects while allowing the third effect to vary across levels. For example, we might consider the stability coefficients for a particular administrative category (sick leave) and a

Figure 3.9. Coefficients of Stability.

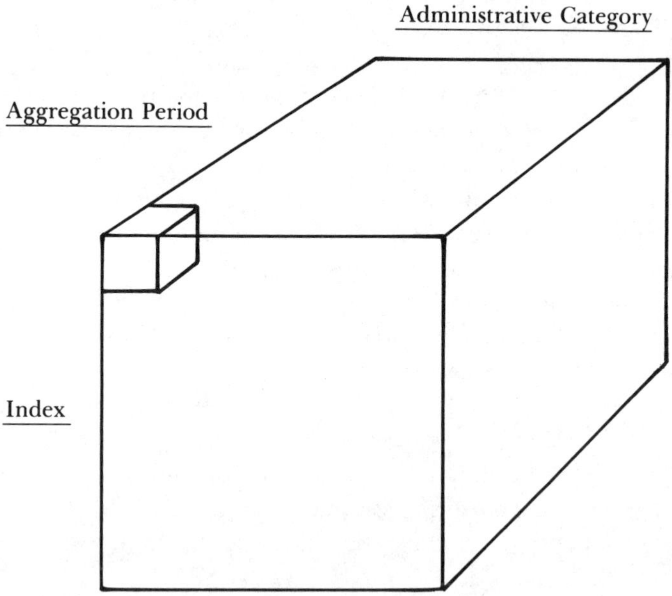

particular aggregation period (three months) for the full range of indexes (one-day, two-day, number of days, number of incidents, Monday, and so on). Similarly, we could consider stability coefficients for a particular administrative category (sick leave) and a particular index (half days) for varying aggregation periods (one week, two weeks, one month, three months, and so on). By considering the change in stability coefficients as a function of the parameter allowed to vary, we gain some insight into the nature of the absence measure being considered as well as an occasional hint about organizational dynamics that may be operating.

Let's consider some examples from the highway workers' data. In Tables 3.5 and 3.6, we have allowed two parameters to vary while holding the third constant. Specifically, we have varied aggregation period and index while holding administrative category constant. In Table 3.5, the administrative category is sick leave. In Table 3.6, the category is AWOL (unapproved absence). The data represent the attendance records of a subset of our highway workers.

There are a number of interesting aspects to these tables. In the first place, the index *Days* appears to be more stable than the index *Incidents* at three-month aggregation periods for the sick-leave matrix. This is surprising, since several earlier studies have found the *Incidents* index to produce greater stability (for example, Hammer and Landau, 1981). This presents an excellent opportunity to demonstrate how empirical results can provide substantive direction. One explanation for the observed difference between the *Days* and *Incidents* indexes might be derived from the social exchange framework of Chadwick-Jones, Nicholson, and Brown (1982). If there is an exchange between the organization and the employee, there must be some bookkeeping involved. In addition, these books must be occasionally balanced. If we assume that, from the employee's point of view, the exchange involves simply time off, then there might be no reason to see stability in *Incidents*. The employee would simply add up the total days and see if they fall short of or exceed expectations for a fixed period of time. From one fixed period to another, that *total* number might remain the same (much like the set-point theory of obesity), although the average length of an absence might vary from one period to another. If that

**Table 3.5. Stability Coefficients: Sick Leave.**

| | | | | Index | | | | | |
| Aggregation Period | Days | Incidents | Ratio | Monday | Friday | Friday/Monday | Half Day | One Day | Two Days |
|---|---|---|---|---|---|---|---|---|---|
| One week | | | | | | | | | |
| Two weeks | | | | | | | | | |
| One month | | 0.18 | | | | | | 0.22 | |
| Three months | 0.74 | 0.42 | 0.50 | | 0.33 | 0.40 | 0.47 | 0.39 | 0.30 |

*Note:* Only significant ($p = 0.05$) values appear in the table.

**Table 3.6. Stability Coefficients: AWOL.**

| | | | | Index | | | | | |
| Aggregation Period | Days | Incidents | Ratio | Monday | Friday | Friday/Monday | Half Day | One Day | Two Days |
|---|---|---|---|---|---|---|---|---|---|
| One week | | | | | | | | | |
| Two weeks | | | | | | | | | |
| One month | 0.54 | 0.33 | | | | | | | |
| Three months | 0.65 | 0.68 | | 0.48 | 0.40 | | 0.68 | .071 | 0.42 |

*Note:* Only significant ($p = 0.05$) values appear in the table.

were the case, one would expect stability for *Days* but not necessarily for *Incidents,* as occurred in our data. Of course, it is necessary to assume that set points vary from one individual to another (or there would be no variance, and the stability coefficient would be close to zero). The notion of a set point—a constant number of days to which the employee feels entitled—is a novel one. It represents a hypothesis that emerged from data analysis. We could speculate even further: perhaps, instead of looking at an *aggregation period*—a term that implies control by the sampler or investigator—we are actually looking at a *balancing period*—a term that emphasizes the role of the employee in controlling absence rates. From this perspective, we might conclude that employees balance the exchange books over three-month or quarterly blocks. Of course, this is speculation—but not completely idle. It is compatible with a theoretical framework (social-exchange theory) and is suitable for generating designs that will allow for its disconfirmation.

To return to the data matrix, both indexes seem equally stable for the AWOL category. The half-day and one-day indexes also seem to display differential stability for the two administrative categories. These indexes are considerably higher in the AWOL matrix than in the sick-leave matrix. Note also the difference in the *Monday* index for sick leave versus AWOL. From many perspectives, the AWOL category seems to be qualitatively different from the sick-leave category, at least with respect to stability coefficients. This difference becomes most apparent at the three-month aggregation period.

The implications for analysis from tables such as these can be serious. For example, these data suggest that both the sick-leave and the AWOL categories have potential for proneness analysis. In addition, it appears that there might be some value in developing a composite index that includes the half-day and one-day indexes in the AWOL category. One thing that is suggested by these data is that overall absence measures must obscure specific stable characteristics of more specific absence measures.

The data in Tables 3.5 and 3.6 are unique in some important respects. They represent a particular organization—one that adopted a "clamp-down" policy the year before the data were gathered. In addition, this organization has taken pains to develop a very detailed form for recording absence data, with as many as twenty-five different administrative categories. Finally, the organization is a public-sector service organization that functions in a civil-service framework with specific definitions and penalties for absences of various types. In addition, the workers in question are represented by an aggressive labor union. All of these factors undoubtedly play a role in the absence statistics that we have analyzed. As such, they limit the generalizability of any broad statements about absence.

Although we promised not to make any substantive claims regarding the phenomenon of absence, we must be allowed some additional speculation on the various data sets that we have examined. When aggregation periods exceed one month, stabilities begin to arise in most of the data sets we have seen. The stabilities seem idiosyncratic to the data set, however. In one set, it might be half-day absences; in another set, Monday absences may appear stable; in a third data set, it might be funeral leave. This is not simply the result of sampling error, since it occurs in both large and small samples. Tables 3.2, 3.5, and 3.6 are examples. One general hypothesis might be that the rules of social exchange differ from organization to organization (or even work group to work group).

An additional implication of the discussion above is that care should be taken in the design of an instrument to collect absence information. Our experience with many different data sets as well as our empirical findings with respect to various indexes and administrative categories suggest that researchers interested in absence research in an organization might consider introducing a particular form for recording data rather than taking data from the form currently in use in that organization. Categories should be well defined and clerks and/or supervisors trained in the use of those categories. We realize that we continue to beg the question with respect to whether employees or supervisors *will* be honest and responsible in the use of that form, but for the purposes of this chapter, we can assume no other circumstance.

What have we tried to say in this chapter that has not been said before? Several things. First, we have explored both the measurement and analytical obstacles to individual-differences investigations of absence patterns. As a result of those explorations, we think that we have demonstrated the pitfalls of choosing aggregation periods, indexes, and administrative categories on the basis of convenience. The resulting stabilities will vary dramatically. In addition, we have tried to demonstrate that attempts to predict absence using typical individual-difference measures are at a disadvantage, since the criterion often defies consistent description or measurement. We have also suggested alternative methods for conceptualizing stability, using various methods of aggregating, each method based on different assumptions. Finally, we have suggested that generalizations such as "Incidents are more reliable measures of absence than total days" may be ill advised. Most studies of absence are conducted *within* organizations. In some senses, that is equivalent to saying *within cultures*. Until we begin to identify patterns that transcend organizations (or cultures), generalizations should be considered with some caution.

Throughout the chapter, we have used an individual-differences model of absence. This might have implied that stability is important only for individual-differences models. This is not the case. Even in the social-exchange model of absence, one would expect that, when the rules or guidelines for the exchange are learned by all parties, stable patterns can be recognized in absence data. The problem for the psychologist is in trying to figure out how to operationalize those rules for data analysis. Once this operationalization occurs, it should be possible to use methods of correlational analysis to demonstrate consistent patterns of behavior.

### Concluding Comment

Applied psychology dug itself into a hole in the 1940s and 1950s. The era, retrospectively labeled the "dust bowl empiricism" period, was characterized by witless number crunching and endless iterative data analysis with no concern for theory. This led many researchers into the trap of developing and testing a theory on the same data set. One significant correlation was chosen from a set of dozens of nonsignificant values and used as the cornerstone for a theory that presumed to explain that correlation. We have presented several examples of how such activity can mislead the theorist. A single correlation of $+0.70$ extracted from a larger matrix simply represents an extreme value in a sampling distribution whose mean is considerably closer to 0.00. Correlations of this magnitude are to be expected with a specific frequency as a simple function of sampling error. Thus, the interpretation of single values must be put in some perspective. We have tried to provide that perspective.

Unfortunately, the abhorrence for "dust bowl empiricism" often produces an error of equal magnitude but in the opposite direction. Many researchers are reluctant to engage in *any* speculation based on preliminary analytical efforts. In the development of a theoretical position, there are no limits to the sources of hypotheses. In the case of absence, the would-be theoretician might retrospectively consider his or her own absence patterns, talk with chronically present and absent employees in a particular organization, or analyze data sets using operations similar to those we have described in this chapter. In fact, most researchers engage in all three activities, often simultaneously. Data sets do not build theories of behavior—behavioral scientists do. Our examinations of various absence data sets have served many purposes. We have become more aware of the limitations of this type of data than we had been before. In addition, we have begun to form some positions with respect to the notion of psychological proneness. We have also developed some appreciation for the relative integrity of various measurement and analytical techniques in absence research. Finally, and most importantly, our examinations of particular relationships have encouraged us to test certain hypotheses in new data sets.

In the research community, there is a general reluctance to take absence data at face value. Many believe that manifest absence rates or patterns have nothing to do with reality. As an example, an abundance of two-day or one-day or half-day absences may simply reflect an organizational control policy—a property of the environment rather than a property of the person. This position does not do justice to the phenomenon. In most instances, individuals still make decisions about coming to work or not coming to work. To be sure, they make these decisions in the context of certain environments. Nevertheless, when we consider the phenomenon of absence, in most important respects it is the behavior of a person, not of an environment. If stability is uncovered at some level of aggregation, for one or more indexes or for specific categories of absence, influences on this stability should be explored. The regularity is the stimulus for exploration. The fact that the label for that regularity (for example, excused or AWOL or bereavement absence) may be arbitrary or distorted does not diminish its potential for a better understanding of the phenomenon.

From a practical point of view, the implications of what we have said in this chapter seem relatively direct. The analysis of overall absence figures is not likely to lead to any insights in underlying absence patterns or any increased control over the phenomenon. We do not mean to imply that absence is necessarily something that must be eliminated. If the stress approach to absence proves viable (suggesting that certain absence rates should be increased through some intervention), we still have the same problem. Any attempts to modify absence patterns, regardless of whether the modification implies an increase or a decrease in some absence rate, will require a firm understanding of what the data actually mean. For that reason, we would suggest that organizations develop solid and understandable schemes for measuring and coding absence information. A second implication is the importance for the individual manager to understand his or her own data set rather than "absence data" in some abstract sense. Absence patterns do seem to have situational and organizational constraints or boundaries. Finally, we would suggest care in the selection of an index and aggregation period. The greatest threats to the individual manager in the treatment of absence data are errors of induction. We hope that the chapter has illuminated some of the more common inductive errors and methodological pitfalls.

## References

Arbous, A. G., and Sichel, H. S. "New Techniques for the Analysis of Absenteeism Data." *Biometrika*, 1954, *41*, 77–90.

Chadwick-Jones, J. K., Nicholson, N., and Brown, C. *Social Psychology of Absenteeism*. New York: Praeger, 1982.

Chadwick-Jones, J. K., and others. "Absence Measures: Their Reliability and Stability in an Industrial Setting." *Personnel Psychology*, 1971, *24*, 463–470.

Froggatt, P. "Short-Term Absence from Industry. I. Literature, Definitions, Data, and the Effect of Age and Length of Service." *British Journal of Industrial Medicine,* 1970a, *27,* 199–210.

Froggatt, P. "Short-Term Absence from Industry. II. Temporal Variation and Inter-Association with Other Recorded Factors." *British Journal of Industrial Medicine,* 1970b, *27,* 211–224.

Froggatt, P. "Short-Term Absence from Industry. III. The Inference of 'Proneness' and a Search for Causes." *British Journal of Industrial Medicine,* 1970c, *27,* 297–312.

Ghiselli, E. E., Campbell, J. P., and Zedeck, S. *Measurement Theory for the Behavioral Sciences.* San Francisco: W. H. Freeman, 1982.

Greenwood, M., and Yule, G. U. "An Inquiry into the Nature of Frequency Distributions Representative of Multiple Happenings, with Particular Reference to the Occurrences of Multiple Attacks of Disease or of Repeated Accidents." *Journal of the Royal Statistical Society,* 1920, *83,* 255–279.

Hackman, J. R., and Oldham, G. R. *Work Redesign.* Reading, Mass.: Addison-Wesley, 1980.

Hall, D. T. "A Model of Coping with Role Conflict: The Role Behavior of College-Educated Women." *Administrative Science Quarterly,* 1972, *17,* 471–486.

Hall, D. T., and Gordon, F. E. "Career Choices of Married Women: Effects on Conflict, Role Behavior and Satisfaction." *Journal of Applied Psychology,* 1973, *58,* 42–48.

Hammer, T. H., and Landau, J. "Methodological Issues in the Use of Absence Data." *Journal of Applied Psychology,* 1981, *66* (5), 574–581.

Hedrick, K. E. "The Influence of Gender and Job Type on Absenteeism." Unpublished master's thesis, Department of Psychology, Pennsylvania State University, 1983.

Ilgen, D. R., and Hollenback, J. H. "The Role of Job Satisfaction in Absence Behavior." *Organizational Behavior and Human Performance,* 1977, *19,* 148–161.

Kahneman, D., and Tversky, A. "On the Psychology of Prediction." *Psychological Review,* 1973, *80,* 237–251.

Landy, F. J., and Farr, J. L. *The Measurement of Work Performance: Methods, Theories and Applications.* New York: Academic Press, 1983.

Muchinsky, P. M. "Employee Absenteeism: A Review of the Literature." *Journal of Vocational Behavior,* 1977, *10,* 316–340.

Nicholson, N. "Management Sanctions and Absence Control." *Human Relations,* 1976, *29* (2), 139–151.

Nicholson, N., Jackson, P., and Howes, G. "Shiftwork and Absence: A Study of Temporal Trends." *Journal of Occupational Psychology,* 1978, *51,* 127–137.

Nisbett, R., and Ross, L. *Human Inference: Strategies and Shortcomings of Social Judgment.* Englewood Cliffs, N.J.: Prentice-Hall, 1980.

Pocock, S. J. "Harmonic Analysis Applied to Seasonal Variations in Sickness Absence." *Applied Statistics,* 1974a, *23,* 103–120.

Pocock, S. J. "Daily Variation in Sickness Absence." *Applied Statistics,* 1974b, *23,* 375–391.

# 4

# Statistical Models for Analyzing Absentee Behavior

*Robert B. Avery*

*V. Joseph Hotz*

The purpose of this chapter is to outline a series of statistical models of the process generating an individual's absenteeism behavior over time. While attention has been given to the formulation of behavioral models of the absenteeism process (see Muchinsky, 1977; Johns and Nicholson, 1982; and Atkin and Goodman, 1983, for surveys of these models) as well as to alternative ways of measuring absenteeism (see Chapter Two of this volume), there do not appear to be any systematic discussions of appropriate statistical models for the analysis of absenteeism data. (One exception is the recent paper by Hammer and Landau, 1981, which questions the appropriateness of the use of regression analysis in analyzing data on individuals' absenteeism behavior and suggests a model from the limited

*Note:* We wish to thank Mark Fichman, Robert Atkin, and Paul Goodman for helpful discussions while writing this chapter and Stephen Fienberg and Steven Garber for comments on a previous draft.

dependent-variable literature.) In this chapter, we attempt to fill this void. To focus our discussion, we begin by noting what appear to be four generally accepted statements about the absence process: (1) *The occurrence of an absence is a relatively infrequent and discrete event* (see Chapter Six of this volume). This feature of absences, from a modeling point of view, may hinder our ability to utilize standard regression and analysis of (co-)variance techniques. (2) *The propensity for an individual to be absent will differ according to the individual's characteristics and the types of jobs he or she holds* (see Chadwick-Jones, Nicholson, and Brown, 1982). That is, the "proneness" of certain types of individuals (members of certain demographic groups) and/ or members of certain occupational groups (for example, coal miners) to be absent may systematically differ. (3) *The process generating an individual's work attendance over some period of time is truly dynamic* (see, for example, Garrison and Muchinsky, 1977, and Mowday, Porter, and Steers, 1982). That is, the process generating absences at the individual level is not generally found to be static; the likelihood of an individual being absent is apt to change over time due to changes in the work environment or as a function of a worker's past work (or absence) history. (4) *Finally, there is a large component of the occurrence of any absence that is random and cannot be predicted by either the individual or those who are trying to analyze the individual's data.* That is, while it may be that certain types of individuals with certain types of work histories are more likely to experience an absence, it is still the case that they are stochastic events. The importance of each of the above four assertions for characterizing absenteeism behavior arises from existing empirical studies of absenteeism behavior. While, to our knowledge, there exists no theoretical model of absenteeism behavior that provides a coherent explanation as to why we would observe these features, their apparent importance in empirical analysis suggests that our statistical models of absenteeism data should accommodate them. That is, it would be appropriate to utilize statistical models for the analysis of individual-level absenteeism data that could accommodate the infrequent and discrete nature of the absence events, that should allow for heterogeneity (of both observed and unobserved forms) in the determinants of behavior, and that allow for dynamic variation in the determinants of a worker's absenteeism history.

In this chapter, we attempt to systematically outline the set of statistical models that are appropriate for the analysis of behavior, such as absenteeism, that has the above characteristics. We describe a set of models called "event-history" models, in which the focus is on the stochastic processes generating history of some event (in this case, an absence) for various types of individuals. The models discussed below have recently become popular for the analysis of various social and economic phenomena. For example, recent work in sociology has utilized these sorts of models to address the effects of welfare programs on a person's changes in marital status over time (see Hannan, Tuma, and Groeneveld, 1977, 1978; and Tuma, Hannan, and Groeneveld, 1979, for a discussion of these results) and job switching in work careers and interindustry occupational mobility (see Spilerman, 1972; Sorensen, 1975; Tuma, 1976; and Blumen, Kogan, and McCarthy, 1955). In the study of economic behavior, event-history analysis has been utilized to study individual employment (unemployment) histories (see Heckman and Borjas, 1980; and Flinn and Heckman, 1982, for examples of this approach) and individual histories of participation on welfare (see Plotnick, 1983). In demography, this technique is being utilized to analyze the timing of marital dissolution (see Menken and others, 1981), the duration of an infant's life in underdeveloped countries (see Trussell and Hammerslough, 1983; and Olsen and Wolpin, 1983), and the timing of births for individual women (Finnas and Hoem, 1980), as well as women's history of contraception utilization (see Littman and Mode, 1977). In the areas of epidemiology event history (or "survival analysis"), techniques have been utilized to study malarial infection histories (see Cohen and Singer, 1979) as well as other chronic diseases (see Kalbfleisch and Prentice, 1980; and Manton and Stallard, 1980). In addition, very similar approaches have been utilized to study accident histories of individuals (see Bates and Neyman, 1951).

The cornerstone of event-history analysis is specifying a stochastic model of a rare event in terms of the rate (or probability) at which an event (absence) occurs at time $t$ when the last event for the person occurred at $t'$. The primary focus in this approach is on the probability of an event occurring rather than on outcomes such as the number of absences per year. As we will show below, focus on the rates of events occurring allows one to make inferences about outcomes, such as the number of absences per time period. We show that one can use probability laws with varying degrees of complication to characterize these event probabilities in order to deal with the potential importance of individual differences (or heterogeneity) and/or past histories (historical dependencies) in the description of absenteeism data on individuals. We start by considering the simplest of stochastic models, in which we assume that a worker's absence events are generated by a homogeneous Bernoulli process. In such a model, there are no sources of heterogeneity or historical dependencies in the event process. We then consider models in which, based on observed characteristics, the probability laws generating an absence history may differ across individuals. We next consider event processes that incorporate historical dependencies; that is, the likelihood of an absence at time $t$ truly depends upon an individual's absence history prior to that date. Finally, we examine ways in which unobserved sources of heterogeneity can be incorporated in event-history models and what complications are likely to be entailed by their presence. In each of these discussions, we offer a description of the statistical model and how it might be parameterized, indicate what sorts of data (aggregate, individual-level cross-section, longitudinal) will be needed if one is to be able to estimate such models, and finally describe what sorts of estimation strategies are available to estimate the parameters of these models.

Before we begin, some important caveats are in order. In this chapter, we offer no behavioral rationale for the statistical models considered here. For a discussion that begins this task, see Chapter One in this volume. Our goal is to offer a set of statistical approaches that may provide, at a minimum, empirical results that are good descriptions of absenteeism behavior and, more hopefully, stimulate thinking as to the sort of behavioral theories that will "rationalize" the probability models set forth in this chapter. We also avoid offering any "ranking" of the models given as to the "best" way of modeling absenteeism. Some models are more complicated than others, requiring more data and/or more sophisticated estimation techniques. Whether the simpler models are best for a particular data set is not an easy question to answer. Much more depends upon the analyst's priors or the existing evidence on the important features of the process generating the outcomes in the data set under examination than on the simplicity or complexity of the models under consideration. While we cannot offer much guidance on model selection, we do discuss some relatively simple model specification tests that the analyst might employ to examine whether unobserved sources of heterogeneity or historical dependencies are important features in the data.

## Models Without Historical Dependence

In the next two sections, we offer an overview of a number of different models and statistical methods that have potential applicability to absenteeism. In order to simplify the discussion, it will be useful to define several terms and concepts that run throughout most of the presentation. Our focus will be on modeling individual absences or lost workdays of individual workers. This will be the dependent variable of virtually all the statistical models we discuss. Clearly, there are other potential variables of interest, such as absence spells (a series of consecutive absence days) or work hours as a fraction of total potential work hours or aggregate absence days for a plant measured over a period of time. However, virtually all these variables can be derived from individual worker absence days and models for them developed as straightforward extentions of models of individual absence days.

Another simplification we make is to restrict the discussion to a single type of absence. Obviously, absences may be of many different forms, such as unexcused, sickness, annual leave, or compensatory. Many analysts may wish to specify different model forms depending upon the type of absence. It may be of interest to test parameter restrictions across models estimated for different absence types. Each of the model forms we present should be applicable to any absence type, although some may be more appropriate for some absence types than others. Finally, we do not distinguish in our discussion between absence measured at a single plant or location and that measured over a larger sample. Again, this is not a substantive restriction, as plant-level variables can easily be included as causal factors in most of our model forms.

In the remainder of this section, we present a number of different statistical models that potentially could be applied to absenteeism. We focus in this section on models without historical dependence, that is, models where individual absences have no impact on the likelihood of future absences. Thus, absence is determined solely by exogenous factors. We begin with the simplest model where all individuals have the same likelihood of absence, the *independent Bernoulli trials model.* We discuss the implications of the Bernoulli model for estimation and aggregate data and propose several different ways of testing its very restrictive assumptions.

We then extend the Bernoulli model to include heterogeneous probabilities of absence both across individuals and at different points in time. Several different models are proposed to link observed worker characteristics (or plant or seasonal factors) to different likelihoods of absence. These include the *linear probability model,* the *log-linear probability model,* the *logit model,* and the *probit model.* We argue that these models are similar in concept but differ in the functional form that links the independent and dependent variables. For each model, we discuss estimation and data requirements and compare implications of each for the impact of changes in the independent variables upon the likelihood of absence. We conclude the section with a very brief discussion of several other model forms that potentially could also be applied.

*Independent Bernoulli Trials.* The first model we discuss is the most simple. Concentrating on a particular type of absence (for example, absence due to sickness, unexcused absence, and so on), we assume that the process governing whether a worker is absent on any given workday is an independent random event for which the likelihood of occurrence is the same for all individuals. Using a more formal notation, this says that each individual $i$ is equally likely to be absent and that such absences are equally likely to occur on any day $t$. These assumptions imply that absences are generated by the independent Bernoulli trials model,

$$P_{it} = \bar{P} \tag{4.1}$$

Note that this probability could be allowed to vary by type of absence and by type of job (or occupation). To avoid undue notation, we shall ignore this complication in most of our discussion.

This model rests on a strong set of assumptions about the data. In particular, it assumes that: (1) there are no systematic differences across individuals; that is, all individuals are assumed to have their absences generated by the same random process; (2) the process generating absences is stationary; that is, the likelihood of an absence on any given day or stage in the worker's career is the same; and (3) for any given person, the likelihood of an absence is independent of his or her absenteeism history. The independent Bernoulli model is a restrictive (and parsimonious) model of behavior; we shall relax each of these assumptions later in this chapter. It is important to note the implications and predictions of this model for observed absenteeism behavior. First of all, the assumption of the simple Bernoulli model implies that aggregate absentee data will be distributed in an equally straightforward manner. If the process generating the absence of a single worker on a single day is the simple Bernoulli model, then total lost man-days aggregated over $N$ individuals and $T$ days will be distributed with a *binomial* distribution. Thus, the likelihood of exactly $l$ absent man-days is

$$PR\{l\} = \binom{NT}{l} \bar{P}^l (1 - \bar{P})^{NT - l} \qquad (4.2)$$

It follows immediately that the expected number of man-days lost is $NT\bar{P}$ with variance $NT\bar{P}(1 - \bar{P})$. Since the sample mean and variance depend only upon $\bar{P}$, the estimation of the sample mean completely characterizes the structure of the Bernoulli model. It also follows that the length of time between absences, for a given individual $i$, is distributed with a *negative binomial* distribution, with an expected value of $(1 - \bar{P})/\bar{P}$. This expectation does not depend upon the number of days since the previous absence. Analogously, the expected number of *absence spells* in a sample (one or more days of consecutive absences is counted as a single spell, regardless of duration) is $NT\bar{P}(1 - \bar{P})$. It also follows that the expected duration of the average spell is $1/(1 - \bar{P})$ days, and the expected number of workdays between spells is $1/(\bar{P})$.

Because the binomial distribution is somewhat unwieldy and not easy to use in testing, several alternative approximations to the distribution of aggregate absenteeism are worthy of mention.

With reasonable sample sizes, the distribution of aggregate lost man-days can be approximated by a normal distribution with a mean of $NT\bar{P}$ and a variance of $NT\bar{P}(1 - \bar{P})$. This approximation will generally be quite good if the number of measured absences per observation is at least twenty-five. The approximation may be improved slightly when either sample sizes or $\bar{P}$ are small by assuming a mean of $NT\bar{P} - \frac{1}{2}$. The normal approximation is convenient in that it allows approximate testing of whether different plants or jobs have different absenteeism rates utilizing standard and well-known normal distribution procedures.

The normal approximation will generally be quite adequate when data are aggregated at the plant, job, or department level, where measured absences for each data point will tend to be large. However, when smaller units of aggregation are used, such as individual worker absences per year, and thus many observations may have values of zero or one, the continuous time Poisson distribution may be a better approximation. Under the Poisson assumption, the distribution of absences, $l$, for aggregate data points of $N$ individuals and $T$ days is then given by

$$Pr\{l\} = \frac{(NT\bar{P})^l \exp(-NT\bar{P})}{l!} \tag{4.3}$$

The mean of the Poisson distribution is $NT\bar{P}$, with a variance that is also $NT\bar{P}$. (Note that the variance is slightly different from the true binomial.)

The Poisson approximation is quite good if the probability of absence is less than one tenth. It follows that if the number of absences is Poisson distributed, then the amount of time between absences, $v$, for a given individual follows the *exponential* distribution with density function:

$$f(v) = \bar{P}\exp(-\bar{P}v) \tag{4.4}$$

and distribution function:

$$F(v) = 1 - \exp(-\bar{P}v) \tag{4.5}$$

and has an expected value of $1/\bar{P}$.

The assumption of a simple Bernoulli model at the individual-worker level enables one to generate a number of absence statistics when the only data available are in aggregate form. However, this model has several potential drawbacks. In particular, it assumes that absenteeism probabilities are the same for all individuals and time periods and that the stochastic components are independent over time. More complicated and less restrictive specifications may be necessary to properly describe or understand absenteeism if these assumptions are violated. We discuss some of these in the next section.

*Models with Observed Sources of Heterogeneity.* One of the major problems with the simple Bernoulli model is its assumption that absenteeism probabilities are the same for all individuals. This assumption seems to be clearly at odds with the assertion that there is considerable variation in individual absence-proneness (see Atkin and Goodman, 1983, for example). This may be an important concern, however, only if it has a significant effect on empirical inferences. If the only objective is to predict aggregate missing man-days, the simple Bernoulli model may be adequate. However, inappropriate use of the Bernoulli model can lead to a number of biased inferences. For example, both the variance in days lost to absenteeism and the average number of days between absence spells will generally be estimated incorrectly from the simple Bernoulli model, leading, among other things, to biased test statistics. Similarly, if any variables such as production depend nonlinearly upon absences, they will be incorrectly estimated. Moreover, if individual characteristics are changing over time, the simple Bernoulli model will incorrectly forecast future absenteeism. Finally, descriptive analyses of absenteeism may be severely limited if they ignore individual differences, and such differences are important particularly from a corrective standpoint.

Unfortunately, modeling absenteeism at the individual level may require significantly more detailed data. Before expending effort collecting such data, some simple calculations can be done with aggregate data to determine whether the violation of the assumption of a homogeneous absenteeism probability is serious. Consider a sample of data consisting of the recorded absences over a year (250 man-days) for a sample of $N$ individuals. If the simple

Bernoulli model is true, the mean number of absences per individual is $250\bar{P}$. Similarly, the variance of absences across the individuals is $250\bar{P}(1 - \bar{P})$. Suppose, however, that the assumption of homogeneity of probabilities is false and that the probability of each individual, $\bar{P}_i$, is distributed randomly about $\bar{P}$. The expected sample mean probability is still $250\bar{P}$. However, the expected variance of absenteeism across individuals will now be larger than the simple Bernoulli variance by 250 times the variance of $\bar{P}_i$ about $\bar{P}$. This can be viewed as an analysis of variance. The average within-individual variance is the same for both the heterogeneous and homogeneous models. The between-individual variance is nonzero only for the heterogeneous model. Hence, total variance is larger by the between-individual variance. Thus, a comparison of the actual sample variance of absenteeism across individuals and that predicted by the simple Bernoulli model could provide evidence on the validity of the homogeneity assumption inherent in the Bernoulli model. (As we note later, however, there may be causes for this other than heterogeneity across individuals.) This observation was noted by Blumen, Kogan, and McCarthy (1955) in a study of industrial mobility. They found that an aggregate model without heterogeneity led to a serious underprediction of the length of time individual workers would stay in particular "states." They concluded that the population was, in fact, heterogeneous—made up of some individuals who moved a lot (movers) and those who always stayed in the same state (stayers).

In addition to the assumption of homogeneity of probabilities, the simple Bernoulli model may be inappropriate also because of its assumption that absenteeism probabilities are stationary over time. For example, certain days (such as Mondays or Fridays or the day after a holiday) or seasons of the year (the winter) may have significantly higher levels of absenteeism; such differences over time are inconsistent with the stationarity assumption. Problems arising from ignoring what might be termed "temporal heterogeneity" will be similar to those of individual heterogeneity. Again, it is worthwhile to consider simple methods of detecting this type of heterogeneity. If absenteeism data are available on a daily basis, perhaps the most direct method of detecting temporal heterogeneity is to use means tests to see whether the absenteeism rate is significantly different, for example, on Fridays than on Tuesdays. Alternatively, if only the distribution of daily absences is available, and' this cannot be linked to specific days, a test of temporal heterogeneity can still be performed. The variance of daily absences can be compared to that predicted by the simple Bernoulli model in a fashion identical to the test of individual heterogeneity. A larger variance than predicted would be a sign that absences tend to clump together at certain times. Interestingly, a smaller variance than predicted would also be informative. This might be a sign that supervisors are forcing workers to spread out their absences more than they would do by chance.

The most obvious way to deal with either individual or temporal heterogeneity is to explicitly model it. If data are available at the individual level, data on individual characteristics such as age, performance evaluations, marital status, or health might be hypothesized to fully explain variation of absenteeism rates across individuals. Similarly, temporal variation in absenteeism might be assumed to depend entirely upon measurable effects, such as day of the week. Heterogeneity across jobs could also be modeled as dependent upon measurable differences in job characteristics. Formally, these imply revised models,

$$P_{it} = f(x_i) \qquad \text{(individual)} \qquad\qquad (4.6)$$
$$P_{it} = f(x_t) \qquad \text{(time)}$$
$$\text{or}$$
$$P_{it} = f(x_{it}) \quad \text{(time and individual)}$$

where $x$ is a vector of independent variables.

Once the simple Bernoulli model is abandoned, a number of decisions must be faced. First and foremost of these decisions is the precise choice of independent variables. That decision will depend upon the views of the individual researcher and is not our primary concern here. A second decision, though, is the specification of the function $f(\ )$. There are a number of functional forms that have been used in the statistical literature, each with drawbacks and virtues. In the remainder of this section, we enumerate some of the more common functional forms and discuss their applicability to the study of absenteeism.

One obvious specification of the relationship between the

independent variables and the probability of absenteeism is the assumption that the probability is a linear function of the $x$ variables. For the moment, we shall ignore any forms of temporal heterogeneity. Using individual heterogeneity as an example, this implies that,

$$P_{it} = P_i = x_i'\beta \qquad (4.7)$$

This type of model is the *linear probability model*. Note that this specification implies that an expression for the actual dependent variable, $y_{it}$ (which equals one if an absence occurs and zero otherwise) can be written as the regression

$$y_{it} = x_i'\beta + \epsilon_{it} \qquad (4.8)$$

where $\epsilon_{it}$ is a random disturbance with a mean of zero. The advantages of the linear probability model are many. (1) If data are available at the daily level for individuals, then the model coefficients can be estimated easily by ordinary least squares (OLS). (2) The model implies that predicted probabilities and/or average probabilities of absences can be easily formed from estimated coefficients. (3) The coefficients are directly interpretable as partial derivatives, that is, the change in the probability of absence for a given change in each $x$ variable. (4) As with the simple homogeneous Bernoulli model, the linear probability model has straightforward properties with respect to aggregation across individuals. The model form implies that the observed absentee rate for data aggregated over time and/or individuals will also be a linear function of $x$ variables averaged over data aggregated in the same way. Thus, the underlying individual coefficients could be estimated directly from aggregate data.

There are, however, disadvantages of the linear probability model. From the point of view of estimation, the Bernoulli form of the equation error (which still holds even when $x$ variables are used) implies that error variances will be heteroskedastic if the model is fit with ordinary least squares. Thus, it is necessary to weight observations by one over the square root of the error variance in order to avoid bias in estimates of the coefficient standard errors. The error variance is $P_i(1 - P_i)$ if the model is fit at the individual level; it is $P_i(1 - P_i)/NT$ if data aggregated over $N$ individuals and $T$ time periods are used. A common procedure is to first estimate the model using OLS, then use these estimates to compute probabilities used in forming weights for second-round weighted least squares estimators. A second concern with the linear probability model is the fact that predicted probabilities are not constrained to be between zero and one. This may cause problems with the heteroskedastic adjustment, for example, and require adjustments for observations with predictions below zero and above one. A third concern, and clearly the most important, is the linear probability model's specification of the effect of variation in $x$ variables on the probability of an absence. It may be much more realistic in many problems, for example, to believe that changes in the $x$ variables will have smaller impacts on the behavior of individuals with either very high or very low absence probabilities than on those in the middle.

Given these criticisms, a number of alternative specifications of probability functions have been utilized in models of rare events. Perhaps the simplest is the *log-linear probability model*, where the *log* of the probability is assumed to be a linear function of $x_i$. That is:

$$ln(P_i) = x_i'\beta \tag{4.9}$$

or, equivalently,

$$P_i = \exp(x_i'\beta) \tag{4.10}$$

The log-linear model lacks the major virtue of the linear probability model — it cannot be estimated directly with ordinary least squares. However, it also avoids some of the drawbacks of the linear model. One of the virtues of the log-linear model is that the predicted probability range is restricted to positive numbers, although it still can exceed one. More importantly, the partial effect of change in an $x$ variable is no longer constant but is now proportional to $P_i$, that is, $P_i\beta$. In other words, the effects of changes in $x$'s on the probability of occurrence exhibit a diminishing impact (in absolute value) as $P$ approaches zero.

Estimation with the log-linear model is more complicated than with the linear model. With individual-level data (absence data by day), the model can be fit by nonlinear least squares. Observation-error variances will have exactly the same heteroskedastic form as in the linear model. Thus, a two-pass weighted nonlinear least squares estimator, with weights formed analogously to the linear model, could also be used. If data are in semiaggregate form, such as total absences per year for each individual worker, the log-linear model lends itself quite nicely to what is termed *Poisson regression*. Total absences per year are assumed to be distributed with the Poisson distribution given in (4.2), where the parameter $P_i$ is assumed to have the log-linear form of (4.9). Then maximum likelihood estimates of the regression coefficients, $\beta$, can be solved iteratively using commonly available software.

If the only information available is the number of man-days lost for some group of workers (within a plant or occupation), the log-linear model parameters could also be estimated using least squares. If observations are aggregates of $N$ individuals and $T$ time periods, estimation is almost identical to the linear probability model with aggregated data, except that the dependent variable is the *log* of the absenteeism rate for each observation. Again, these can be fit as heteroskedastic regressions with approximate error variances of $(1 - P_i)/(NTP_i)$ and estimated in a two-pass procedure. (Note that this is slightly different from the linear model.) This procedure requires data at a sufficient degree of aggregation that no (or few) observations have no absences. Another concern is that the use of aggregate data is proper only if the $x$ variables are the same for all individuals aggregated into an observation. Unlike the linear model, one cannot simply use average $x_i$ values, because the straightforward linkage between average $x$'s and average probabilities is destroyed by the log transformation.

Another model that is quite similar to the log-linear model is the *logit*, or *logistic probability*, model. In this case, the log *odds* are assumed to be linear in the $x$'s, that is

$$ln \frac{P_i}{1 - P_i} = x_i'\beta \tag{4.11}$$

Alternatively, the logit model can be represented as:

$$P_i = \frac{1}{1 + \exp(-x_i'\beta)} \qquad (4.12)$$

With the logit model, the predicted probabilities are restricted to the proper zero to one range. Furthermore, the effects of variation in $x$'s on the probability of an absence diminish (in absolute value) in both tails of the distribution, being proportional to $P_i(1 - P_i)$.

Parameters of the logit model will generally be estimable only with iterative maximum-likelihood methods or nonlinear least squares. If estimated by nonlinear least squares with individual data, observations will have the same error-variance heteroskedasticity as the linear and log-linear models, and similar two-pass methods can be used. Maximum-likelihood estimation is much more common, however, as there are numerous programs available, and parameter convergence is generally quick and inexpensive.

Coefficients of the logit model can also be estimated from aggregated data. If data are available in semiaggregate form, such as absences per year for individuals, parameters can be estimated from weighted individual logit observations. For example, a 250-day work year with 5 absences would be treated as two individual-level observations—an absence with a weight of 5/250 and a workday with a weight of 245/250. Under certain conditions (particularly with no variation of the $x$'s within observation), ordinary least squares can also be used in a fashion similar to the log-linear model. The dependent variable is the log of the ratio of absences to non-absences (the sample log-odds) for each aggregated observation. These will again be heteroskedastic regressions with approximate error variance of $1/(NTP_i)(1 - P_i)$.

The log-linear and logit models are virtually identical when $P_i$ is small. Indeed, the models differ only to the extent that $1 - P_i$ differs from one, and this occurs only if $P_i$ is large. Thus, in problems where most probabilities are small—as should be the case in virtually all absenteeism investigations—there will be little basis upon which to choose between the two models. Both models are likely to yield very similar predictions and fitted coefficients.

Another model seen quite often is the *probit,* or *normit,* model. The probability of absence is assumed to be given by the standard normal distribution function evaluated at a linear function of $x$,

$$P_i = \int_{-\infty}^{x_i'\beta} \frac{1}{(2\pi)^{\frac{1}{2}}} \exp(-u^2/2)\,du \qquad (4.13)$$

For a particular set of $x$'s, the probabilities from probit and logit models are very similar and are likely to differ only with extremely small or large probabilities. Coefficients are scaled differently, however, with the coefficients of the logit model approximately 1.8 times as large. Both have predicted probabilities restricted to the zero to one range. The effect of variation in the individual $x$ variables in a probit model will be proportional to the normal density function evaluated at $x_i'\beta$ and, thus, also will diminish in absolute value as one moves to probabilities of one or zero.

Estimation procedures for the probit model are also virtually identical to those of the logit. Parameters for the probit model can be estimated from individual-level data using maximum-likelihood methods or nonlinear least squares, with or without adjustments for heteroskedasticity. Semiaggregated data can be treated as weighted individual data and estimated accordingly. Conditions for the use of aggregate data are the same as those of the logit, but estimates are somewhat more cumbersome to compute. The dependent variable used in fitting aggregate regressions is the sample, "probit," $F^{-1}(y_i)$, where $y_i$ is the absentee rate for the observation, and $F^{-1}$ is the inverse standard normal distribution function. Unfortunately, this does not have a closed-form expression, but approximations are readily available. These regressions will have heteroskedastic error variances that can be approximated by $P_i(1 - P_i)/(NTf(P_i)^2)$.

There are other functional forms and models that have been used with data similar to absenteeism. These include the *gompit* model, where

$$P_i = \exp(-\exp(x_i'\beta)) \qquad (4.14)$$

Others are based on so-called "angular transformations," such as,

$$P_i = \tfrac{1}{2} + (1/\pi)\arctan(x_i{}'\beta) \qquad\qquad (4.15)$$

Still others include forms of linear and quadratic discriminant analysis. To a great extent, the choice of model form is arbitrary. Choice could very well be made on the basis of sample fit (a number of pseudo $R^2$ measures of fit are available) or on the availability of computer software. One crucial point that should not be lost sight of, however, is that the choice of functional form will fundamentally alter the predicted relationship between absences and the $x$ variables at the aggregate level. The linear model, for example, would predict that any two plants with the same average demographic characteristics (assuming that these are the $x$ variables used), would have the same total absenteeism rate. Moreover, a change in the $x$'s would have the same effect on absenteeism in all plants. If the logit model held, however, it would be necessary to know the entire distribution of demographic characteristics — not just averages — in order to determine aggregate absenteeism. The effects of a change in the $x$'s would now be predicted to vary from plant to plant and to depend upon preexisting conditions. If only plant-level independent variables are thought to be major determinants of absenteeism, these considerations may not be too important. However, if disaggregated individual-level variables are believed to play significant roles, inferences based upon aggregate average data should be viewed with caution. Indeed, unless one truly believed in the linear model formulation, correct estimates of the model and unbiased predictors could be computed only from individual-level data.

Once heterogeneity is included in the model, there are almost an infinite number of forms it can take. Data at the individual level could include age, health, number of years with the company, wages, job ratings, and similar variables. Seasonal variables to account for temporal heterogeneity could include dummy variables for days of the week, weather, hunting season, or measures of local labor market conditions. Perhaps the richest specifications are available with panel data — data where individual absences are available by specific day. With such data, the probability of absence can be made a function of both temporal and individual determinants.

## Models with Historical Dependence

Up to this point, we have modeled absenteeism as a function only of exogenous determinants. Differences in behavior across individuals, for example, are modeled as arising from demographic differences or absence-proneness. Similarly, differences in behavior over time have been modeled as functions of seasonal factors or traceable to changes in plant-level variables. In none of these cases is it assumed that absences themselves are likely to affect the likelihood of future absences. We relax this restriction in this section and consider models where an individual's absence history is allowed to influence the likelihood of absence. A number of such models are examined.

We begin by characterizing the simplest model of historical dependence, the *Markov model*. The Markov model provides an explicit but very simple mechanism for "persistence" to influence subsequent events. This provides an alternative motivation to absence-proneness for the empirical observation that a small number of individuals account for a large percentage of the per-period absences. We then extend the Markov model to allow for more general specifications in which the occurrences of past absences directly influence the current likelihood of an absence. Such models are said to exhibit explicit *occurrence dependence*. Such dependence might arise because of firm policies in which the penalties (or rewards) for absences (or the avoidance of absences) are explicitly dependent upon a worker's absence history. We also consider a second generalization of the Markov model by allowing the duration of time since the last absence to affect the current probability of an absence. This form of historical dependence is called *duration dependence*. This might arise, for example, when absences are a withdrawal mechanism to alleviate the tension that builds up in the workplace. In that case, the longer an individual has gone since his or her last absence, the higher we might expect the probability of experiencing an absence.

In the remainder of this section, we consider each form of historical dependence in turn and then discuss strategies for estimating each specification, as well as a general specification that nests each form of historical dependence as a special case. Finally, we conclude this section with an important note of caution about the ability to distinguish, empirically, between models in which the past history of absenteeism behavior affects current absenteeism and those in which sources of heterogeneity are unobservable and serially correlated over time for a given individual or job. As pointed out in recent work by Heckman and Borjas (1980) and Heckman and Singer (1982), one generally will need to impose nontrivial restrictions in order to distinguish between such phenomena.

*The Markov Model.* Each of the models discussed in this section is based on the assumption that current decisions are dependent upon past decisions. Although past plant-level history might be modeled, it makes the most sense to think about such models at the individual level. The first such models we discuss are of the general Markov form, where the probability of being absent today depends upon whether you were absent yesterday. These models can capture the "inertia" typically observed in data where people tend to persist in their behavior. This might be caused in absenteeism when there are "fixed" costs to absence. Once these costs are borne on the first day, it may be much easier to be absent on subsequent days. These costs may be physiological in nature, for sick leave, or psychological (see Heckman, 1981, for a further discussion of the fixed-cost argument). Persistence may also be caused by the fact that certain absences, such as annual leave, are taken in blocks. (An extreme example is bankers, who are required to take two weeks consecutive leave.)

The simplest Markov model is where the probability of absence depends only upon whether one was absent the day before. Thus,

$$P_{it} = \bar{P}^{\alpha} \tag{4.16}$$

if the person was *not* absent the day before, and

$$P_{it} = \bar{P}^{n} \tag{4.17}$$

if the person was absent the day before. Clearly, the model can be made more complex by also including exogenous explanatory variables of the type discussed in the previous section as determinants of $\bar{P}^\alpha$ and $\bar{P}^n$. The implications of this specification, however, can be seen even with the simple Bernoulli-type model.

Several important observations can be made about how sample statistics of the Markov model would be expected to differ from those of a Bernoulli model without historical dependence. For a random sample of $N$ individuals and $T$ time periods, the expected number of absent man-days is $NT\bar{P}$ where the expected sample absenteeism rate, $\bar{P}$, equals $\bar{P}^\alpha/(1 + \bar{P}^\alpha - \bar{P}^n)$. The expected variance also follows as $NT(\bar{P}[(1 - \bar{P}^n)\bar{P}^n] + (1 - \bar{P})[(1 - \bar{P}^\alpha)\bar{P}^\alpha])$. Of particular interest are the expected number of absence spells, which is $NT(1 - \bar{P})\bar{P}^\alpha$; the expected duration of spells, which is $1/(1 - \bar{P}^n)$; and the expected number of days between spells, which is $1/\bar{P}^\alpha$. These latter statistics suggest some simple tests that could be performed with aggregate data to test for the possible presence of historical dependence.

Suppose that data were available not only on total lost mandays due to absence but also on the total number of absence spells in a sample. Note that $\bar{P}^\alpha$ can be estimated by taking the ratio of absence spells to total workdays. $\bar{P}^n$ could then be solved for from the sample mean formula given above. Simple comparisons, therefore, might be made to see how different these numbers were. Substantial differences might be a sign that historical dependence was an important factor in absence determination.

The presence of historical dependence has some important implications in common with the concept of heterogeneity discussed in the previous section. Although their root causes may be quite different, both phenomena may produce similar effects in aggregate data. To see this, note that the larger $\bar{P}^n$ is relative to $\bar{P}^\alpha$ (thus the greater persistence), the greater the expected duration of the typical absence spell will be. This is likely to produce the same finding in aggregate data — that absence days are disproportionately distributed to a few people — as absence-proneness generated by heterogeneity. To see this further, note that the variance of the Markov model differs from that of the simple Bernoulli model, just as the variance of absence rates across individuals can differ from that of the Bernoulli model in the presence of heterogeneity. In fact, depending on $\bar{P}^\alpha$ and $\bar{P}^n$, the sample variance across individuals can create the same pattern as heterogeneity. See Blumen, Kogan, and McCarthy (1955) and Singer and Spilerman (1976) for more on this point.

These arguments suggest that historical dependence and heterogeneity may be indistinguishable in simple tests. However, with finer-tuned data or certain types of structural specifications, differences between the two may become apparent. If time-series data are available for individuals, a comparison of the average number of spells to absence days by individuals would provide an unambiguous test of historical dependence. If individual panel data are available, heterogeneity could be incorporated directly into the Markov model. $\bar{P}^\alpha$ and $\bar{P}^n$ could each be made functions of individual demographic or seasonal data using any of the models and estimation procedures discussed in the previous section.

*Models with Occurrence or Duration Dependence.* While the simple Markov model described above is a parsimonious and convenient model for describing temporal patterns of discrete events, it does have its limitations, even with the incorporation of heterogeneity. The model is memoryless in the sense that only yesterday matters in determining the probability of absences. We now wish to consider richer specifications, based on inclusion of measures of an individual's history. For convenience in presenting these models, we shall formulate the rest of the models in continuous time; that is, we will now act as if the smallest time unit we can observe, a day, is very small. (This formulation will prove mathematically convenient later. Substantively, it does not change the framework from the discrete time formulation used to this point.) We first consider the possibility that the *number of occurrences* of absences in the past might affect the probability of a future absence. For example, suppose that an individual is allowed to be absent, at most, $K$ number of days per year before disciplinary action (such as a suspension without pay) is taken against the worker. Then one might expect the probability of an additional absence to decline with the number of prior absences. One can formalize this form of historical dependence by adapting the Markov process model just presented. In particular, we now formulate the instantaneous rate of moving from working to absence as $P_{it}^k$, where $k$ indexes the number of absences that have occurred in the past, $k = 1,2,\ldots$ (Depending upon the institutional setting, one may want to allow an individual's entire past history of absences or the absences since some date $t'$ (the beginning of the year, for example) to affect the transition rates. One might also want to have transition rates indexed by the number of days of unpenalized absences the individual has remaining during some period.) This form of state dependence has recently been termed *occurrence dependence* by Heckman and Borjas (1980). Assuming that the approach of one's absence limit would decrease the likelihood of an additional absence, we would expect that $P_{it}^k \leq P_{it}^{k-1}$. This would also imply that the mean time between absences, that is, $(1/P_{it}^{k-1})$, will be lower for those with fewer past absences than for those with more.

The occurrence-dependence model, like the simple Markovian model, maintains the assumption that absence probabilities do not depend upon the length of time since the previous absence. Thus, for example, the probability that an individual will have an absence tomorrow given that it has been three weeks since he was last absent is assumed to be exactly the same for the same type of individual for whom the time since the last absence has been three years. While this specification is particularly simple, it is frequently observed in data on the time spent in a particular occupation, geographical locality, or the like that the longer one remains in the current state, the more likely one is to remain. Such a phenomenon is not captured by a stationary Markov model. An alternative proposal is to consider semi-Markov models that allow the absence probability to exhibit *duration dependence*.

Such models focus on the continuous-time analogue of the absence probability, the *hazard rate,* or *hazard function,* which is the instantaneous probability of an absence. Duration dependence implies that the hazard rate, $h_{it}$, for the $i^{th}$ individual at point of time $t$ will depend upon the length of time, $\tau$, since the previous absence, that is,

$$h_{it} = f(\tau) \tag{4.18}$$

The hazard function, that is, the probability of an absence, may exhibit *positive* or *negative* duration dependence, depending upon whether the partial derivative of the hazard with respect to $\tau$ is positive or negative, respectively. Thus, negative duration dependence implies, for example, that the longer an individual has been working without an absence, the less likely he or she is to be absent. Alternatively, positive duration dependence occurs when the longer an individual is working without an absence, the higher the chances of an absence.

The motivation for duration dependence is that it is consistent with data on the timing of a number of differing types of events, such as birth, accidents, spells of unemployment, and so on. However, one can also imagine behavioral theories that might motivate the existence of duration dependence. For example, suppose that one believes that absences are a way for workers to deal with job stress. Stress may be *cumulative* — the longer one is exposed to job pressures, the more stress increases, until relieved by an absence. This structure would give rise to positive duration dependence, since the longer the time since the last absence, the greater the accumulated stress and, thus, the higher the probability of a worker taking action to alleviate some of that stress. Such duration dependence is characteristic of environments in which there is the *renewal* of some dynamic process each time an absence occurs.

A number of specifications have been proposed to model duration dependence. We briefly enumerate the most common ones considered in empirical applications. (For more detailed discussions of the hazard models described, see Kalbfleisch and Prentice, 1980; Miller, 1981; Lawless, 1982; and Tuma, 1983.) One form is the *Weibull distribution,* which has the following hazard function:

$$h_{it} = \alpha \tau^\lambda \qquad (4.19)$$

where $\tau$ is the length of time since the previous absence, $\alpha$ is a constant, and $\lambda$ is a parameter less than one in absolute value. When $\lambda$ is negative, the hazard exhibits negative duration dependence; when it is positive, it exhibits positive duration dependence. If $\lambda = 0$, there is no duration dependence. Other specifications that exhibit duration dependence include the *Gompertz distribution,* for which the hazard function is:

$$h_{it} = \alpha \exp[\lambda\tau] \tag{4.20}$$

again with parameters $\alpha$ and $\lambda$, and the *log-normal distribution*, for which the hazard function is:

$$h_{it} = \alpha \frac{(2\pi\sigma)^{-\frac{1}{2}}(\tau)^{-1}\exp[-(ln\tau - \mu)^2/2\sigma]}{1 - \Phi([ln\tau - \mu]^2/2\sigma)} \tag{4.21}$$

where $\Phi(\ )$ is the cumulative standard normal distribution function with location parameter $\mu$ and scale parameter $\sigma$. The Gompertz distribution, which has been applied in modeling death rates as a function of age, exhibits an exponentially declining or rising hazard. The log-normal distribution exhibits the property of a non-monotonic hazard function that first rises and then falls with $\tau$.

Another specification, proposed by Flinn and Heckman (1982), is the Box-Cox flexible duration dependence specification, which has the following hazard function:

$$h_{it} = \alpha \exp\left(\left(\frac{\tau^{\lambda_1} - 1}{\lambda_1}\right)\gamma_1 + \left(\frac{\tau^{\lambda_2} - 1}{\lambda_2}\right)\gamma_2\right) \tag{4.22}$$

where $\gamma_1$, $\gamma_2$, $\lambda_1$, and $\lambda_2$ are parameters. This specification is quite general and allows for a large number of forms of duration dependence, including a nonmonotonic hazard with both positive and negative duration dependence over the range of $\tau$. These include a quadratic specification and both the Gompertz and Weibull forms as special cases.

Duration dependence can be combined with heterogeneity and independent variable co-variates for a very flexible model specification. The constant term $\alpha$ in (4.19) through (4.21) can be modeled as a function of independent variables that vary across individuals, time, or both. Any of the functional forms proposed in the previous section can be used and combined with any of the duration dependence specifications. Out of factors of convenience, the most common functional form used is the log-linear form, or the *proportional hazard model:*

$$h_{it} = \exp(x_{it}'\beta)f(\tau) \qquad\qquad (4.23)$$

This model form is very general and could be altered to include even occurrence dependence by including historical absences in the $x$ vector. *Lagged duration dependence* could be considered by including the length of previous absences or work spells as independent co-variates. More elaborate forms of duration dependence could also be modeled by interacting co-variates with the duration dependence specification. The hazard form,

$$h_{it} = \exp(x_{it}'\beta)\exp(z_{it}'\lambda\tau) \qquad\qquad (4.24)$$

for example, allows the Gompertz parameter of duration dependence to vary by the vector $z_{it}$.

Testing different hypotheses about absenteeism behavior is a relatively straightforward exercise with virtually any of the hazard function models just described. It is easy, for example, to test whether there is a real behavioral difference between different types of absences. Separate hazard functions, using one of the above parameterizations, could be estimated for each type of absence. The test of whether certain types of absence are different is simply a test of significant differences in the hazard function parameters across different types of absences. (See Flinn and Heckman, 1983a, who test whether unemployment and out-of-the-labor-force states are behaviorally different.) We can also test hypotheses concerning occurrence dependence. For example, if an individual's maximum number of unexcused absences per year is $K$, one might hypothesize that the number of previous absences may not affect the conditional probability of an additional absence until that number is greater than or equal to $K$. Finally, we may wish to test for the presence and type of duration dependence. Suppose, for example, that one thinks that the strength of the duration dependence in this model depends upon the monetary rewards the firm provides. A test of such a proposition can be made by interacting the compensation associated with the individual's job, say, with the Gompertz duration parameter $\lambda$. If compensation is a "compensating differential" for stress, one would expect the coefficient in this interaction term to be significantly negative. There clearly are other hypotheses that one might test. The important point to note here is the relative ease with which such tests can be formulated with this specification.

Estimation of duration dependence for the proportional hazard models is a straightforward extension of estimation procedures used for the discrete models proposed in the previous section. Generally, estimation of duration dependence models will require data of day-by-day absence patterns for individual workers and, for treatment of observed sources of heterogeneity, measures of individual worker characteristics. Typical data may be collected for a set of individuals measured over a specific period of calendar time. During this interval, one will presumably be able to determine the lengths of intervals between absences and the number of occurrences and type of absences occurring for each individual. For models of duration dependence, a word of caution should be exercised. Given this sampling plan, two pieces of information that have importance for estimation are missing—namely, the individual's absence history *before* and immediately *after* the sampling period. Both of these aspects of one's data are called types of *censoring,* and they can arise in any problem modeling the timing of discrete events. The implications of censoring for models with duration dependence depends critically upon whether unobserved heterogeneity (see the next section) is present. With unobserved heterogeneity, the problem is virtually intractable unless severe assumptions are made. Without unobserved heterogeneity, censoring can generally be accommodated in estimation, although it may be necessary to know the starting date of the absence or work spell a worker is in at the beginning of the sample. For a further discussion of the censoring problem, see, for example, Miller (1981), Kalbfleisch and Prentice (1980), and Flinn and Heckman (1983a).

Estimation of duration dependence or proportional hazard models such as several of those discussed in the previous section is generally likely to entail interactive solution methods (although, under certain conditions, simpler procedures can also be used). However, the estimation algorithm is pretty straightforward in most cases, and a number of applicable software packages are available (for example, Hotz, 1983). Further discussion of estimation can be found in Kalbfleisch and Prentice (1980), Cox (1972, 1975), Flinn and Heckman (1983b), Tuma (1983), and Hotz (1983).

## Unobserved Sources of Heterogeneity

Up to now, we have talked about the possibility of incorporating individual heterogeneity only through the use of observed exogenous variables. We now discuss ways of treating unobserved sources of heterogeneity. We consider several alternative specifications of how unobserved heterogeneity could enter the specifications of the probability of an absence occurring at some point in time and what impact they have for making inferences from absenteeism data. We consider a number of alternative specifications.

To extend the previous formulations of models with heterogeneity, we now assume that individual heterogeneity has both observable and unobservable dimensions. Thus, we shall assume that, in addition to observable characteristics, $x_{it}$, the probability of an absence is also a function of unobserved characteristics, $\epsilon_{it}$, which could potentially vary by person and time. The most straightforward way of incorporating the unobserved component is to treat it in a fashion parallel to the observed components. Thus, for example, the linear probability model could be written as:

$$P_{it} = x'_{it}\beta + \epsilon_{it}, \tag{4.25}$$

where $\epsilon_{it}$ can be viewed as characteristics for which we do not have observations but that influence the probability of an absence.

Given this general specification, a number of assumptions can be made about the way in which the $\epsilon$'s enter the probabilities. As examples of the former, one might assume, alternatively, that: (1) $\epsilon_{it} = \epsilon_i$, that is, a time-invariant person-specific effect; (2) $\epsilon_{it} = \epsilon_t$, a time-period effect; or (3) $\epsilon_{it} = u'_i\alpha$, where $u_i$ is a vector of latent variables and $\alpha$ is a vector of coefficients. This latter specification of unobservables is of the factor-analytical, or *latent-structure,* form, in which the $u$'s are latent factors and the $\alpha$'s are factor loadings that must be estimated. See Heckman (1978) and Flinn and Heckman (1982) for examples of the use of this specification in models of event histories both with and without historical dependencies. Alternatively, the $\epsilon$'s can be assumed to be nonstochastic, either time or person invariant, and freely correlated with the $x$'s. This specification, called a *fixed-effects* specification of heterogeneity, is equivalent to specifying a separate intercept term for each individual. As we shall now describe, the appropriate estimation strategies for the two models are very different.

The implications of unobserved heterogeneity for estimation of the parameters characterizing probabilities of absences depend upon both the functional form assumed for the probability and whether the unobserved variable or factor is a random or fixed effect. For example, if we assume a linear probability specification, then incorporating unobserved heterogeneity is relatively straightforward. In the case of a fixed-effect specification, a person-specific fixed effect can be estimated by measuring all variables as deviations from the person-specific means of the variables and for a time-specific fixed effect, by measuring all variables as deviations from the time-specific means. OLS estimation techniques are then applied to these "deviated" data. If a random-effects specification is assumed, the OLS estimates of the elements of $\beta$ are consistent; but the usual OLS standard errors are incorrect.

In models in which the probability function is a nonlinear function of $\epsilon_{it}$, such as the log-linear or logit, estimation of models with heterogeneity is generally much more complicated and may impose restrictions on the kind of data needed — for example, these models in which parameter estimation requires not only the presence of panel data (repeated observations on each individual) but also a large number of time periods in such data. (The one exception is the logit model with the person-specific fixed-effect form of unobserved heterogeneity. In that case, the presence of heterogeneity essentially requires no modifications. See Andersen, 1980, and Chamberlain, 1980.) For similar models, with random-effects specifications, the estimation is even more computationally burdensome. To proceed with estimation in this case, it is necessary to assume a particular distribution (generally called the "mixing" distribution) for the $\epsilon$'s and to integrate the influence of these variables in estimating the coefficients on the $x$'s. The convenience of different distributional assumptions will depend upon the probability model form used. The normal, log-normal, and gamma distributions are among the most common distributions for the random effect. If the probability function for absences is a function of a set of observed and unobserved characteristics and is denoted as

$P_{it} = P(x_{it}, \epsilon_i)$, then in place of $P_{it}$ in forming a likelihood function, we must enter:

$$P_{it}^* = \int P(x_{it}|\epsilon_i)m(\epsilon_i)d\epsilon_i \qquad (4.26)$$

where $m(\ )$ is the probability density function for $\epsilon$. In addition to the increased complexity of estimation, there rarely is much of an a priori basis for choosing the distributional specification of $\epsilon$.

If the inferences from statistical analysis were insensitive to the presence or absence of unobserved sources of heterogeneity, some of the estimation problems inherent in models with unobserved heterogeneity could be avoided. Unfortunately, this is generally not the case. To illustrate this fact, consider the following example. Suppose that the true model characterizing an individual's propensity to be absent is a Markovian model; that is, the individual's hazard rate is constant. Furthermore, suppose that individuals differ only in the value of their hazard rate, $h_i$, and that these hazard rates are distributed across individuals. Suppose that we ignored the heterogeneity in these hazard rates and estimated a hazard rate specification that was a function of the time since each worker's last absence, $\tau_i$. While it is the case that the individual hazard functions exhibit no duration dependence, the hazard function we estimated, which is an "average" hazard function, will generally exhibit *negative duration dependence*. Intuitively, this result arises because individuals with high absence probabilities are likely to be the first people absent subsequent to the beginning of their most recent work spell, and those individuals with low absence probabilities will tend to be left in the sample of those still "at risk" of an absence. Thus, the observed instantaneous transition rate from work to absence declines in a heterogeneous sample, even though the true model exhibits no duration dependence for each individual. In fact, more can be said about this bias toward negative duration dependence. The only way the observed hazard function can exhibit positive duration dependence is if some (but not necessarily all) individuals have hazard functions with positive duration dependence over at least some portion of the domain of the distribution of exit times.

Thus, the fact that determinants of an individual's absenteeism behavior have either not been measured or not been included in one's empirical analysis—obviously, the situation faced by most analysts—can have serious consequences for making inferences from absence data. As we have seen above, failure to explicitly deal with unobserved sources of heterogeneity in the analysis of data can lead to the inability to distinguish whether unobserved heterogeneity or duration dependence is the correct explanation. Yet, for managerial decision making, it may be crucial to distinguish between the two. If there is a problem of absenteeism or absence-proneness on the part of some workers, policy actions such as using longer trial employment periods can be used in order to identify such individuals, since they will reveal themselves by having a higher number of absences over some period of time than others. Alternatively, if absenteeism is a process that is heavily influenced by past events, policy actions could be taken to influence the actual events (such as using incentive schemes or providing ways of dissipating worker stress) rather than just to identify certain types of workers. Thus, while the estimation of probability models that account for unobserved sources of heterogeneity is more difficult, and the problem of which specification of heterogeneity to use has no ready answers, these arguments suggest that one may not want to ignore the influence of these unobservables in analysis of absence-history data.

## Conclusions

In this chapter, we have outlined a series of statistical models appropriate for the analysis of events such as absenteeism. We have attempted to provide the reader with a brief guide as to what models are consistent with certain types of assumptions concerning heterogeneity and historical dependencies in the processes generating absences. We have conspicuously avoided providing the reader with a "cookbook" discussion as to when to use which model and/or which set of assumptions will be "correct" or "best." Simple rules for what is the appropriate modeling strategy for analyzing the absence process do not exist. But the natural question arises as to how to proceed in actually undertaking an absenteeism study in light of this methodological discussion. In the remainder of this chapter, we attempt to respond to (but not fully answer) that question by outlining a series of issues that any empirical analyst of the absenteeism process should address before deciding which statistical approach to adopt.

The first issue concerns which type of and the degree to which heterogeneity is suspected to characterize the absenteeism behavior at the individual level for the population one wishes to analyze. One of the recurring themes in the preceding discussion is that differences in the probabilities of an absence — either across different types of individuals or across different time periods — lead to different models of behavior. Thus, an important issue to consider is the dimensions of heterogeneity characterizing the absence processes to be studied. For example, consideration should be given as to whether one suspects variability in "proneness" of individuals, occupations, and/or industries to be studied; what the possible sources of these differences are and for which of them measures exist; and whether there are differences in the propensity of absences by season of the year or day of the week. Suspicions of the importance of such sources may be driven by theoretical priors — for example, economic theories predict that individual differences in the opportunity costs of time relative to work will lead to different absence propensities — or may arise from diagnostic analysis of the data using tests for heterogeneity we presented earlier. To the extent that data are available that allow one to observe these differences and that there exist observable measures of these sources of heterogeneity, the models outlined above can be utilized to measure the influence of these differences on the absenteeism process. If the appropriate data do not exist or the analyst lacks measures of important sources of heterogeneity in absence propensities, the ability to make inferences from empirical analysis is more constrained. For example, we have discussed the fact that the parameters of models of absence occurrences that differ across individuals and/or time frequently cannot be estimated with data that are aggregated across individuals and/or over time. Furthermore, we have noted that sources of heterogeneity that are present but not accounted for in empirical analysis can seriously hinder the ability to interpret the data. Our point is simply that if heterogeneity — either individual or temporal — is suspected, empirical analysis should explicitly incorporate it; to the extent that it cannot be explicitly incorporated, more caution should be exercised in drawing inferences about the underlying absenteeism process.

A second issue concerns whether the dynamics of individual absenteeism processes involve the dependence on past history. We have described models in which, abstracting from heterogeneity, the actual past *experience,* or history, of a worker's absence behavior directly influences subsequent behavior. To the extent that it does, more detailed models and more detailed data are generally necessary to generate reliable inferences and predictions. Unfortunately, it is very difficult to determine whether historical dependencies are present in a particular set of data; in general, it is virtually impossible to "let the data tell you" whether they are there. For example, as discussed earlier, empirical evidence of duration dependence is generally also consistent with the data coming from a heterogeneous population. Thus, an analyst may want to rely more on the theoretical motivations (or lack of them) for judging the need to incorporate historical dependencies in statistical models for absenteeism analysis.

Finally, practical issues of what data are available and what sorts of costs are entailed in alternative estimation strategies cannot be ignored. In many cases, a researcher does not have control over what data — and their level of aggregation — are available for empirical analysis. Thus, even though strong a priori reasons may suggest that historical dependencies are present in the absence process in a population of workers to be analyzed, statistical models that include such dependencies will not be estimable with data such as total man-days lost per month for a given firm or subdivision of a firm. As discussed earlier, some models — the linear probability and log-linear models, in particular — tend to have better aggregation properties than others; thus, these models may prove especially attractive in situations where only highly aggregated data are available. More importantly, as we have mentioned above, to the extent that one's suspicion is that the underlying absenteeism process is more complicated than can be measured with existing data, one may want to temper the certitude of inferences made from empirical analysis. Secondly, the present level of tested and efficient computer software is a constraint on the utilization of the more sophisticated models given above. But as event-history analysis increases in popularity in the social sciences, such software is becoming more accessible for social scientists. For example, certain models in survival analysis can now be readily estimated using BMDP and/or more specialized packages, such as RATE, written by Nancy Tuma (see Tuma, 1980, for documentation), and CTM, written by George Yates (see Hotz, 1983, for documentation). More importantly, as research into the dynamics of social and life-cycle processes continues to develop in areas such as unemployment, fertility, and so on, the availability of behavioral and statistical models as well as computer software provides the potential for important cross-fertilization of areas that may, ultimately, benefit our understanding of the absenteeism process.

## References

Andersen, E. B. *Discrete Statistical Models with Social Science Applications*. Amsterdam: North-Holland, 1980.

Atkin, R. S., and Goodman, P. S. "An Issue-Oriented Review of the Research on Absenteeism." Unpublished report to the U.S. Bureau of Mines, Carnegie-Mellon University, 1983.

Bates, G., and Neyman, J. "Contributions to the Theory of Accident Proneness. II. True or False Contagion." *University of California Publications in Statistics*, 1951, *1*, 215–253.

Blumen, I., Kogan, M., and McCarthy, P. J. *The Industrial Mobility of Labor as a Probability Process*. Cornell Studies of Industrial and Labor Relations, Vol. 6. Ithaca, N.Y.: Cornell University, 1955.

Chadwick-Jones, J. K., Nicholson, N., and Brown, C. *Social Psychology of Absenteeism*. New York: Praeger, 1982.

Chamberlain, G. "Analysis of Covariance with Qualitative Data." *Review of Economic Studies*, 1980, *47*, 75–97.

Cohen, J., and Singer, B. "Malaria in Nigeria: Constrained Continuous-Time Markov Models for Discrete-Time Longitudinal Data on Human Mixed-Species Infections." In S. Levin (Ed.), *Lectures on Mathematics in the Life Sciences*. Vol. 12. Providence, R.I.: American Mathematical Society, 1979.

Cox, D. R. "Regression Models and Life-Tables." *Journal of the Royal Statistical Society, Series B*, 1972, *34*, 187–202.

Cox, D. R. "Partial Likelihood." *Biometrika*, 1975, *62*, 269–276.

Finnas, F., and Hoem, J. "Starting Age and Subsequent Birth Intervals in Cohabitational Unions in Current Danish Cohorts, 1975." *Demography*, 1980, *17* (3), 275–295.

Flinn, C., and Heckman, J. "Models for the Analysis of Labor Force Dynamics." In R. Bassman and G. Rhodes (Eds.), *Advances in Econometrics*. Vol. 1. Greenwich, Conn.: JAI Press, 1982.

Flinn, C., and Heckman, J. "Are Unemployment and Out of the Labor Force Behaviorally Distinct Labor Force States?" *Journal of Labor Economics*, 1983a, *1* (1), 28–42.

Flinn, C., and Heckman, J. "The Likelihood Function for the Multistate-Multiepisode Model in 'Models for the Analysis of Labor Force Dynamics.'" In R. Bassman and G. Rhodes (Eds.), *Advances in Econometrics*. Vol. 2. Greenwich, Conn.: JAI Press, 1983b.

Garrison, K. R., and Muchinsky, P. M. "Evaluating the Concept of Absentee-Proneness with Two Measures of Absence." *Personnel Psychology*, 1977, *30*, 389–393.

Hammer, T. H., and Landau, J. "Methodological Issues in the Use of Absence Data." *Journal of Applied Psychology*, 1981, *66* (5), 574–581.

Hannan, M., Tuma, N., and Groeneveld, L. "Income and Marital Events: Evidence from an Income-Maintenance Experiment." *American Journal of Sociology*, 1977, *82* (6), 1186–1211.

Hannan, M., Tuma, N., and Groeneveld, L. "Income and Independence Effects on Marital Dissolution: Results from the Seattle and Denver Income-Maintenance Experiments." *American Journal of Sociology*, 1978, *84* (5), 610–633.

Heckman, J. "Dummy Endogenous Variables in a Simultaneous Equation System." *Econometrica*, 1978, *46*, 931–959.

Heckman, J. "Statistical Models for Discrete Panel Data." In. C. Manski and D. McFadden (Eds.), *Structural Analysis of Discrete Data*. Cambridge, Mass.: MIT Press, 1981.

Heckman, J., and Borjas, G. "Does Unemployment Cause Future Unemployment? Definitions, Questions and Answers from a Continuous Time Model of Heterogeneity and State Dependence." *Economica*, 1980, *47*, 247–283.

Heckman, J., and Singer, B. "The Identification Problem in Econometric Models for Duration Data." In W. Hildenbrand (Ed.), *Advances in Econometrics*. London: Cambridge University Press, 1982.

Hotz, V. J. "CTMM User's Manual: A Program for the Estima-

tion of Continuous Time Multiple State Multiple Spell Models."
Program manual, Carnegie-Mellon University, April 1983.

Johns, G., and Nicholson, N. "The Meanings of Absence: New
Strategies for Theory and Research." In B. Staw and L. L.
Cummings (Eds.), *Research in Organizational Behavior.* Vol. 4.
Greenwich, Conn.: JAI Press, 1982.

Kalbfleisch, J., and Prentice, R. *The Statistical Analysis of Failure
Time Data.* New York: Wiley, 1980.

Lawless, J. F. *Statistical Models and Methods for Lifetime Data.* New
York: Wiley, 1982.

Littman, G., and Mode, C. "A Non-Markovian Stochastic Model
for the Taichung Medical IUD Experiment." *Mathematical Bio-
sciences,* 1977, *34,* 279–302.

Manton, K., and Stallard, E. "A Stochastic Compartment Model
Representation of Chronic Disease Dependence: Techniques for
Evaluating Parameters of Partially Unobserved Age in Homogeneous Stochastic Processes." *Theoretical Population Biology,* 1980,
*18* (1), 57–75.

Menken, J., and others. "Proportional Hazards Life Table Models:
An Illustrative Analysis of the Sociodemographic Influences on
Marriage Dissolution in the United States." *Demography,* 1981,
*18,* 181–200.

Miller, R. *Survival Analysis.* New York: Wiley, 1981.

Mowday, R. T., Porter, L. W., and Steers, R. M. *Employee-
Organization Linkages: The Psychology of Commitment, Absenteeism,
and Turnover.* New York: Academic Press, 1982.

Muchinsky, P. M. "Employee Absenteeism: A Review of the
Literature." *Journal of Vocational Behavior,* 1977, *10,* 316–340.

Olsen, R., and Wolpin, K. "The Impact of Exogenous Child Mortality on Fertility: A Waiting Time Regression with Dynamic
Regressors." *Econometrica,* 1983, *51* (3), 731–750.

Plotnick, R. "Turnover in the AFDC Population: An Event History Analysis." *Journal of Human Resources,* 1983, *18* (1), 65–81.

Singer, B., and Spilerman, S. "Some Methodological Issues in the
Analysis of Longitudinal Surveys." *Annals of Economic and Social
Measurement,* 1976, *5* (4), 447–474.

Sorensen, A. "Growth in Occupational Achievement: Social
Mobility or Investments in Human Capital." In K. Land and

S. Spilerman (Eds.), *Social Indicator Models*. New York: Russell Sage Foundation, 1975.

Spilerman, S. "Extensions of the Mover-Stayer Model." *American Journal of Sociology,* 1972, *78,* 599–627.

Trussell, J., and Hammerslough, C. "A Hazard-Model Analysis of the Covariates of Infant and Child Mortality in Sri Lanka." *Demography,* 1983, *20* (1), 1–26.

Tuma, N. "Rewards, Resources and the Rate of Mobility." *American Sociological Review,* 1976, *41,* 338–360.

Tuma, N. "Invoking RATE." Unpublished manuscript, Stanford University, January 1980.

Tuma, N. "Nonparametric and Partially Parametric Approaches to Event-History Analysis." In S. Leinhardt (Ed.), *Sociological Methodology 1982.* San Francisco: Jossey-Bass, 1983.

Tuma, N., Hannan, M., and Groeneveld, L. "Dynamic Analysis of Event Histories." *American Journal of Sociology,* 1979, *84* (4), 820–854.

# 5

# Relationship Between Absenteeism and Other Employee Behaviors

█▛█▜█▛█▜█▛█▜█▛█▜█▛█▜█▛█▜█▛█▜█▛█▜█▛█▜█▛█▜█▛█▜█▛█▜█▛█▜█▛█▜█▛█▜█▛█▜
█▙█▟█▙█▟█▙█▟█▙█▟█▙█▟█▙█▟█▙█▟█▙█▟█▙█▟█▙█▟█▙█▟█▙█▟█▙█▟█▙█▟█▙█▟█▙█▟

*Joseph G. Rosse*
*Howard E. Miller*

It is not surprising that absenteeism has attracted the abundance of research attention that it has. To the uninitiated, it seems to be a clear, discrete, overt employee response with significant practical implications. Moreover, it is a very convenient dependent variable, since data are generally collected by employers on a routine basis. Unfortunately, the seductive appeal of absence has led researchers to a simplistic characterization of the variable, the result of which has been a disappointingly small return on investment in understanding, predicting, and controlling absence behavior.

As a number of writers have pointed out, absence is not a unitary concept. The functional meaning of being absent from work depends upon the motivation attributed to the behavior, its timing, the frequency of its occurrence, and the social setting in which it occurs. A person may miss work because of illness (personal or of other family members); external constraints, such as inclement weather or transportation problems; or such goal-directed motives as receiving otherwise-forfeited sick pay, limiting one's income (perhaps for income tax purposes), or, most generally, the opportunity to engage in any behavior seen as more attractive than work.

Given this multidimensionality, absence researchers need to develop a conceptual framework encompassing the varying functional meanings of absence. Different definitions of absence may be more appropriate for different research questions. In fact, one may find more shared variance between certain forms of absence and other employee behaviors (for example, turnover, lateness) than among the various forms of absence. It is this issue of communality among absence and other "withdrawal" behaviors that we wish to explore in this chapter. (As we will discuss, *withdrawal* serves to obscure important distinctions among various forms of behavior. Nevertheless, there does not yet appear to be a comparable summary term in the literature. We will initially use the term to refer to such behaviors as lateness, absence, and turnover but will subsequently adopt *adaptation* as a more comprehensive label.)

Two forms of evidence may be useful in addressing this issue. The most obvious form concerns empirical associations between absence and other behaviors. This apparently simple question involves a number of theoretical and measurement issues that have operated as significant obstacles to obtaining a clear answer. One issue involves the range of behaviors to be studied. Organizational researchers have traditionally investigated only a limited set of behaviors. Withdrawal research has almost universally been limited to the study of turnover and absence, with a much smaller set of studies of lateness. Ironically, while literally hundreds of studies of absence and turnover have been conducted, only a handful of researchers have studied the two behaviors simultaneously. Multivariate studies that include measures of lateness are rarer still.

Another issue noted in most reviews of absence and turnover pertains to the methodological rigor of the research. Studies vary widely in their operational definitions of the behaviors, in the nature of the samples, in the time period over which the behaviors were aggregated, and in the precision with which they were measured. Moreover, many studies are characterized by small samples, unreliable measures, and restriction of range (particularly such low-base-rate events as absence and turnover). As Schmidt and Hunter (1977) have pointed out in the personnel selection area, these sources of error variance operate both to increase the variance across studies in results and to attenuate observed correlations. Under these conditions, a single-minded concern with the statistical significance of results is unwise. Across a reasonable sample of studies, a consistent pattern of even weak associations may be accepted as confirming evidence.

Research using the individual as the unit of analysis shows consistent support for the hypothesis of a positive correlation between absence and turnover (Beehr and Gupta, 1978; Burke and Wilcox, 1972; Farrell and Robb, 1979; Hill and Trist, 1955; Lyons, 1968, 1972; Melbin, 1961; Newman, 1974; Revans, 1964; Ronan, 1963; Rosse, 1983b; Van Zelst and Kerr, 1953; Waters and Roach, 1979); only Marsh and Mannari (1977) and Miller (1981) report nonsignificant relations. Similarly, evidence shows a consistent positive correlation between absence and lateness (Adler and Golan, 1981; Beehr and Gupta, 1978; Chadwick-Jones and others, 1971; Farrell and Robb, 1979; Rosse, 1983b). The scarce data pertaining to lateness-turnover relations are more equivocal; Beehr and Gupta (1978) and Farrell and Robb (1979) found weak positive associations, whereas Rosse (1983b) reported nonsignificant results.

It should be noted that the associations reported in these sources are generally not very strong; it is clearly the case that the behaviors are not surrogates for one another in any simple fashion. On the other hand, the consistency of empirical relations across investigators, samples, and conditions is itself a datum that should not be ignored. Indeed, given the multiple functions each of the behaviors may play and other problems in measuring the behaviors, we should, perhaps, be surprised that the correlational data are as strong as they are. Yet mere evidence of co-variance— however consistent—is weak grounds for establishing a theory linking together turnover, absence, and lateness. A more interesting question concerns the antecedents of these behaviors; it is to this second form of evidence that we now turn.

In reviewing research concerning common antecedents of absence, lateness, and turnover, one again faces the methodological caveats described earlier. In fact, three additional concerns make these cautions even more significant here than in the description of behavior intercorrelations. First, the antecedent variables introduce additional between-study measurement variance (for example, different researchers have used different measures of job satisfaction, of organizational commitment, and of labor market conditions). Second, even fewer researchers have attempted to assess the communality of antecedents of lateness, absence, and turnover than have studied the behaviors' interrelatedness. As a result, conclusions rely heavily on aggregated studies of the antecedents of one or another behavior. While useful, this approach is clearly less desirable than multivariate studies specifically designed to explore the overlap in the behaviors' causes. The third consideration refers to the term *antecedents*. Clegg (1983) has reviewed a number of methodological issues in the withdrawal literature relevant to the determination of causality and has noted that the design of many studies is inadequate to unequivocally establish the direction of causality. Thus, this discussion might most appropriately be described as a review of correlates assumed to operate as antecedents of withdrawal.

A number of major reviews of absence and turnover have converged on the conclusion that job-related affect operates as a more powerful predictor of withdrawal behavior than do objective characteristics of the individual, task, or organization (Brayfield and Crockett, 1955; Herzberg and others, 1957; Lyons, 1972; Muchinsky, 1977; Porter and Steers, 1973).

Specifically, global job satisfaction shows consistent negative relations with turnover (Marsh and Mannari, 1977; Miller, 1981; Miller, Katerberg, and Hulin, 1979; Mobley and others, 1979; Newman, 1974; Rosse, 1983a; Waters and Roach, 1971, 1973, 1979) and, to a lesser extent, absence (Giese and Ruter, 1949; Newman, 1974; Nicholson, Brown, and Chadwick-Jones, 1977; Talacchi, 1960; Waters and Roach, 1971, 1973, 1979; nonsignificant relations were reported by Ilgen and Hollenback, 1977; Miller, 1981; and Rosse, 1983a). In three studies of lateness, one showed a significant relation to global satisfaction (Adler and Golan, 1981), while the others reported nonsignificant results (Farrell and Robb, 1979; Rosse, 1983a).

Satisfaction with work content shows a similar pattern of results. For turnover, Miller (1981), Miller, Katerberg, and Hulin, (1979), Mobley and others (1979), Rosse (1983a), Waters and Roach (1971, 1973), and Wild (1970) have reported negative correlations, while the results were nonsignificant in a study by Hulin (1968). Relations with absence are also predominantly negative (Dittrich and Carrell, 1976; Garrison and Muchinsky, 1977; Miller, 1981; Rosse, 1983a; and Waters and Roach, 1971), although the findings of Nicholson, Brown, and Chadwick-Jones (1976) and Watson (1981) were inconclusive. Adler and Golan (1981) also reported negative correlations with lateness, while the results of Rosse (1983a) were nonsignificant.

Satisfaction with co-worker relations does not appear to be significantly correlated with either absence (Marsh and Mannari, 1977; Mobley and others, 1978; Rosse, 1983a; Waters, Roach, and Waters, 1976) or turnover (Garrison and Muchinsky, 1977; Newman, 1974; Nicholson, Brown, and Chadwick-Jones, 1976; Waters and Roach, 1973; Watson, 1981; significant negative relations were reported by Nicholson, Brown, and Chadwick-Jones, 1977; Rosse, 1983a; and Waters and Roach, 1971). A single study found a significant negative association with lateness (Adler and Golan, 1981), whereas the results of Rosse (1983a) were not significant.

Most researchers have reported nonsignificant correlations between satisfaction with supervision and absence (Garrison and Muchinsky, 1977; Newman, 1974; Nicholson, Brown, and Chadwick-Jones, 1976; Rosse, 1983a; Waters and Roach, 1971, 1973; Watson, 1981), although Miller (1981) has reported a weak but significant inverse association. The pattern of results for turnover is less clear, with approximately half the reviewed studies reporting negative correlations (Hom, Katerberg, and Hulin, 1979; Hulin, 1968; Ley, 1966; Miller, 1981; Rosse, 1983a; Saleh, Lee, and Prien, 1965; Skinner, 1969) and the other half reporting nonsignificant results (Koch and Steers, 1978; Kraut, 1975; Mobley and others, 1979; Newman, 1974; Waters, Roach, and Waters, 1976). For lateness, Adler and Golan (1981) reported a significant negative association, and Rosse's (1983a) results were nonsignificant.

The only facets of job satisfaction that show a clearly different pattern of relations for absence and turnover are satisfaction with pay and satisfaction with promotion. Most researchers have found satisfaction with these aspects of work to be inversely related to decisions to quit (Frielander and Walton, 1964; Hulin, 1968; Knowles, 1964; Ronan, 1967); Hom, Katerberg, and Hulin (1979) and Miller (1981) found only pay-satisfaction relations to be significant. On the other hand, satisfaction with pay and promotion seem to be unrelated to a person's decision to be absent (Garrison and Muchinsky, 1977; Hackman and Lawler, 1971; Newman, 1974; Nicholson, Brown, and Chadwick-Jones, 1976; Rosse, 1983a; Waters and Roach, 1971, 1973; Watson, 1981); only Patchen (1960) and Miller (1981) (for pay satisfaction only) reported negative correlations which were statistically significant. Adler and Golan (1981) report significant negative associations with lateness, while Rosse (1983a) found a non-significant relation.

A review of lateness/absence/turnover research thus leaves us with the following conclusions: (1) the three variables reliably covary, although the strength of relationships is generally weak, particularly for lateness; and (2) all three variables appear to share common roots in job-related affect, particularly overall and work content satisfaction. The consistency with which these findings are reported argues against the contention that they may be attributable to chance or to methodological faults alone. In fact, a review such as this probably provides a very conservative estimate of the magnitude of true association among variables because of its emphasis on the statistical significance of results. As Schmidt and Hunter (1977) have pointed out, when evaluating data such as these, we should be concerned with the attentuating effects of typically small samples, unreliable measures, and restriction in range. We speculate that if corrections for these sources of variance were provided as part of a meta-analysis of the job satisfaction–withdrawal literature, the magnitude and consistency of relations would provide even stronger substantiation for our conclusions.

Nonetheless, Mobley (1982) – among others – has noted a number of instances in which an absence–turnover correlation should not logically be expected: (1) when either behavior is due to positive attraction rather than avoidance; (2) when absence is required by nonjob demands; (3) when they share few consequences, or when one is constrained; (4) when either is a spontaneous, impulsive act; (5) when one's work role allows discretionary time away from the job setting; (6) when unused sick pay can be "cashed in" at time of termination; or (7) when absence is used as a "safety valve" that reduces the likelihood of quitting. While the actual moderating role of many of these variables remains an empirical question, Mobley's point reiterates the importance of conceptualizing withdrawal as a multidimensional construct. Associations should be stronger among behaviors sharing similar functional meanings. To the extent that researchers aggregate dissimilar forms of behavior, intercorrelation should be expected to be weak.

More fundamentally, however, there is a need for a model of withdrawal behaviors that takes into account the varying forms of withdrawal and explains the process by which one rather than another occurs. Such a model should include a comprehensive network of antecedent and intervening variables, a full range of behavioral responses, and an appreciation for the role of "process." Whereas models of the turnover process have recently begun to reflect more complexity (for example, Steers and Mowday, 1981; Mobley and others, 1979), it is unfortunately the case that the few approaches encompassing multiple withdrawal behaviors are much less fully articulated.

## Current Models of Withdrawal

A review of the literature suggests at least five conceptual models underlying current research and theory. (It should be noted that, for the most part, these "models" are implicit rather than formalized frameworks.) At one extreme, some writers have argued that absence and turnover should be unrelated to one another on the basis of either differences in causes (Porter and Steers, 1973; Steers and Rhodes,1978) or differences in consequences (March and Simon, 1958). This can be called the *Independent-Forms* model. As already noted, the empirical literature showing consistent, if weak, correlations among behaviors and between these behaviors and job-related affect casts doubt on this hypothesis. However, the possibility that withdrawal behaviors may or may not be related, contingent upon other factors, represents a version of the Independent-Forms model that deserves more attention.

At the opposite extreme, proponents of a generalized withdrawal syndrome (or *Spillover* model) propose that one should find positive intercorrelations among the behaviors, due to the similarity of their causes (Beehr and Gupta, 1978). An aversive work environment is assumed to create a nonspecific avoidance response in which any means of increasing distance from the noxious stimulus is sought. Moreover, there may exist a functional relationship among behavioral responses such that engaging in one behavior makes it more likely that the person will also perform others. For example, workers who have made plans to accept employment elsewhere may be more likely to be absent or late if they feel less threatened by the sanctions organizations employ for absence or tardiness.

Although the empirical literature cited previously does provide some substantiation for the spillover hypothesis, the weak magnitude and inconstancy of relations encourage caution. Moreover, recent evidence of the importance of other factors (for example, labor market perceptions) on the job affect–turnover linkage implies that the development of models more complex than a simple spillover effect is warranted, especially when attempting to account for variance in multiple behaviors.

The *Progression-of-Withdrawal* model has clearly been the most popular of the more complex conceptualizations of employee withdrawal. According to it, individuals engage in a hierarchically ordered sequence of withdrawal ranging from its most minor form to a complete break from the organization (that is, quitting). Despite its general popularity, the logic of the progression-of-withdrawal model has not been well specified. Possible explanations might include: (1) a worsening of organizational conditions, requiring progressively more potent forms of avoidance; (2) a new employee's gradual acknowledgment of a lack of fit with the organization; (3) an iterative adaptive process in which dissatisfied employees initially experiment with adaptive responses that hold the fewest negative consequences; or (4) "reinforced deviance," in which employees find the rewards of withdrawal greater than its costs and are encouraged to attempt progressively more rewarding forms (note, however, that this explanation does not necessarily account for a progression from absence to turnover).

A number of assumptions underlying these possible explanations have not been well articulated or tested. Perhaps the most obvious is that the progression *concept* should apply to a range of behaviors, which presumably are seen by organizational members to fall along a continuum of avoidance potential (or cost/reward). Yet nearly all research has investigated only absence and turnover; we are aware of only two recent studies of progression among more than two behaviors (Clegg, 1983; Rosse, 1983b). Nor has much research investigated employees' perceptions of the avoidance/reward value of such behaviors.

Given the ambiguity of the underlying theory, it should not be surprising that evidence regarding the progression hypothesis is of generally poor quality. Most of the cited support takes the form of a positive correlation between absence and turnover (Clegg, 1983; U.S. Department of Labor, 1972; Herzberg and others, 1957; Lyons, 1972; Melbin, 1961; Muchinsky, 1977). Adler and Golan (1981), Beehr and Gupta (1978), Chadwick-Jones and others (1971), and Clegg (1983) have reported positive correlations between absence and lateness. Such evidence is insufficient to distinguish between a simple spillover model and a progression effect. Four researchers have investigated the predicted "surge" in absence prior to quitting. Evidence of higher absence prior to quitting was reported by Waters and Roach (1979, using one-year intervals) and Burke and Wilcox (1972, using three-month periods). Miller (1982), using finer time intervals, found no evidence of a pretermination increase in absence. Rosse (1983b, using conditional probabilities based on weekly attendance) found evidence of a lateness-absence progression effect and concluded tentatively in favor of an absence-turnover progression. Adler and Golan (1981) found no evidence of a lateness-absence progression effect with cross-lagged correlational data using twelve-month time intervals.

The second type of more complex models of withdrawal suggests that the behaviors may be substitutable. Two models, incorporating different reasons for this substitutability, may be distinguished. According to the *Alternate-Forms* hypothesis, the probability of one form of response (for example, absence) is increased in the presence of constraints on an alternative behavior (such as quitting). Following March and Simon's (1958) model of turnover, most research has been concerned with the effect of perceived ease of mobility on turnover (Miller, Katerberg, and Hulin, 1979; Mobley, Horner, and Hollingsworth, 1978; Schneider, 1976) or its moderating effect on attitude–turnover relations (Dansereau, Cashman, and Graen, 1974; Miller, 1981). Miller (1981) and Rosse (1983b) more specifically tested the alternate-forms hypothesis by investigating the relations between ease of one variable and the frequency of the alternate behavior. Miller found a positive correlation between ease of absence and turnover but failed to find evidence of greater absence with barriers impeding turnover. Rosse found that ease of turnover had no effect on absence and had only a linear (rather than the predicted interaction) effect on lateness.

A second form of constraint consistent with the alternate-forms model is attitudinal. A negative attitude toward one's work may fail to translate into voluntary termination if the individual feels that quitting is an inappropriate response. Hom, Katerberg, and Hulin (1979), Newman (1974), and Miller (1981) have reported positive associations between favorable attitudes regarding quitting and actual turnover, although neither Newman nor Miller found a significant relationship between attitude toward attendance and absence. Miller and Newman also assessed the crossover predictions by correlating attitudes toward one behavior with incidence of the other. Contrary to the predictions of the alternate-forms model, both found weak but *positive* co-variance between attitude toward absence and turnover and nonsignificant associations between attitude toward quitting and absence. Rosse (1983b) found higher absence among workers with a negative attitude toward turnover but found no effects of behavior-specific attitudes on lateness or turnover. Thus, there appears to be little support for the alternate-forms model.

A second version of the substitutability hypothesis may also be identified. A dominant theme in much of the withdrawal literature is that employees purposefully decide to be late or absent or to quit as a means of avoiding a noxious work environment. If absence, lateness, and turnover all represent means of avoiding an undesirable stimulus, there should be no need to engage in more than one form of avoidance (Hill and Trist, 1955). As an example, it is sometimes suggested that absence provides a "relief-valve" function that reduces the likelihood of quitting. Following this logic, the *Compensatory* model predicts that behaviors that successfully allow avoidance of a distasteful work environment should be negatively interrelated. By implication, this avoidance should also have a feedback effect on subsequent job affect. If negative affect motivates avoidance behavior, successful avoidance should reduce negative affect. Surprisingly, this basic assumption has received almost no research attention. Clegg (1983) and Rosse (1983b) both found negative feedback effects on affect (that is, people who were late or absence reported more negative subsequent job attitudes), although these effects were not strong. Rosse (1983a) also found a positive feedback effect of withdrawal behavior on health symptoms.

It is significant that none of the models derived from the literature has received unequivocal substantiation. The lack of support for the independent-forms and spillover models is particularly interesting, because it highlights a growing suspicion that relations among turnover, absence, and lateness should not be expected to be simple. Neither traditional single-behavior models nor simplistic general withdrawal models appear to be suitable for understanding these behaviors.

The ambiguity regarding the more complex models may be attributed to a number of factors. A major one — that of accurate measurement of dependent variables — is addressed in other chapters and will not be discussed here (although some measurement issues of particular import to multiple-behavior models will be described in the concluding portions of this chapter). Another relevant factor is the small number of studies that have purposefully studied multiple withdrawal behaviors simultaneously. A cursory examination of the literature easily gives the false impression that these behaviors have been well studied. Whereas innumerable studies have included measures of absence or turnover, relatively few researchers have specifically designed their research to investigate their possible communality. This problem is substantially worse for lateness.

This lack of multivariate research may be symptomatic of our generally narrow view of dependent variables (see Staw and Oldham, 1978). For the moment, let us assume that lateness, absence, and turnover share the functional purpose of avoidance. If so, we need to ask whether these behaviors are adequate operationalizations of the avoidance construct. To the extent that a researcher's goal is the understanding of basic processes rather than the prediction of one or more specific behaviors, he or she should be concerned with developing multiple operationalizations of the construct of interest. Other plausible indicators of avoidance include such behaviors as leaving work early, daydreaming, taking lengthy breaks, loafing, finding ways of avoiding aspects of work (for example, one's supervisor, co-workers, or unpleasant tasks), or drinking on the job. Not only would developing a better awareness of the relations among such behaviors enhance our understanding of underlying constructs, it would also likely improve their predictability. Attitude theorists from Thurstone (1931) to Fishbein and Ajzen (1975) have repeatedly argued that there is no necessary relation between attitude toward an object and any specific behavior; rather, a person's attitude toward an object should be reflected in the overall pattern of his or her behaviors with respect to that object.

How then do we define the range of behaviors to be included as dependent variables? To date, our choice of measures seems to have revolved around narrow conceptualizations of behaviors of interest to management. The withdrawal concept has broadened this focus slightly to at least include a broader set of behaviors believed to be consequences of job satisfaction. While this is an improvement, it still suffers from the limiting assumption that avoidance must be the mechanism driving these responses.

The general assumption underlying withdrawal models is that people are absent or quit as a means of avoiding a noxious stimulus. In other words, the behaviors represent coping mechanisms intended to help a person *adapt* to his or her work environment. Framing our analysis in terms of adaptation rather than withdrawal offers a number of advantages. First, it forces us to consider the total range of adaptive behaviors from which a person may choose when faced with a dissatisfying work situation. Framing the question in this fashion suggests a number of behaviors that fail to fit well in theories of withdrawal but that do show negative associations with job affect. An obvious possibility is a proactive attempt to make changes in the work environment, or what Hirschman (1970) termed the "voice" option. Interestingly, investigation of such change attempts in relation to job attitudes has been limited largely to the filing of grievances (Dalton and Todor, 1982; Herzberg and others, 1957) and unionizing activity (Allen and Keaveny, 1981; Getman, Goldberg, and Herman, 1976; Hamner and Smith, 1978; Schriesheim, 1978). It seems likely that other forms of change attempts (for example, negotiating with one's supervisor or co-workers, making informal job modifications, learning new job skills) might also fit into a framework of adaptation.

Other potential responses to unsatisfying work conditions are acts of aggression. The psychological literature (Dollard and others, 1939; Miller, 1941) provides some support for the suggestion of Spector (1978) that much organizational "aggression" (for example, vicious gossip, refusals to cooperate, theft, sabotage, overt violence) is the result of frustration of workers' desires. Although limited, there is some evidence that dissatisfied employees are more likely to engage in sabotage and restriction of output (Bensman and Gerver, 1963; Dalton, 1970; Gouldner, 1954; Hickson, 1961; Roethlisberger and Dickson, 1939; Roy, 1952), theft (Hollinger and Clark, 1979; Sheridan, 1979), and other forms of "counterproductive" behaviors (Hollinger and Clark, 1979; Mangione and Quinn, 1975).

Even within the category of withdrawal, a variety of behaviors in addition to lateness, absence, and turnover could be considered. One general class of behaviors might be categorized as physical withdrawal, encompassing actions that allow a worker to put physical distance between him- or herself and the job. In addition to lateness, absence, and turnover, this category might include such behaviors as taking frequent or lengthy work breaks, leaving work early, or finding excuses to leave the work area. A second general class, psychological withdrawal, includes behaviors intended to place psychological distance between an employee and noxious aspects of work. Included in this category would be daydreaming while working, use of alcohol or other drugs, sleeping on the job, telephoning friends, and other escapist behavior. To date, empirical evidence of an association between job attitudes and these behaviors is largely limited to the use of alcohol and drugs (Cook, Walizer, and Mace, 1976; Hawthorne, 1977–1978; Mangione and Quinn, 1975; Perone, DeWaard, and Baron, 1979; Trice and Roman, 1978; Urban, 1973), although Hollinger and Clark (1979) also included some of the other behaviors in their measure of "counterproductive" behavior. Further research in this area is urgently needed.

One advantage, then, of using adaption as a unifying theme is that it encourages consideration of a wider range of behaviors. A second advantage is that, by broadening the range of potential responses, it forces our attention to the process by which one rather than another behavior manifests. A third potential benefit is that this framework explicitly includes consideration of a feedback loop between adaptive behaviors and the work environment. If a behavior is truly adaptive, it should reduce the source of dissatisfaction. If the behavior is not successfully adaptive, this fact should also have implications for future affect and behavior. In the following section of this chapter, we will develop a conceptual model that incorporates these issues more formally.

## A Model of the Adaptation Process

The model is appropriately called a behavior-adaptation-cycle model of individual action. Briefly, the cycle is started by onset of some stimulus that brings relative dissatisfaction into the person's awareness (see Figure 5.1). Awareness of the relative dissatisfaction prompts thoughts on what the person can do about the source of dissatisfaction. Behavioral alternatives are considered, with several factors influencing the extent and outcome of review. Some behavior is enacted as a result. The behavior operates on the environment, potentially influencing the future occurrence of the precipitating stimulus and completing one cycle. Repetitions of the cycle depend upon what the stimulus was, what response alternatives were available and enacted, and how the environment reacted to the behavior that resulted. Successful adaptation results when cycles of interaction between the individual and the environment cease with respect to the stimulus producing relative dissatisfaction. We turn to discuss each of the steps in the cycle in greater detail.

Figure 5.1. A Model of the Adaptation Cycle.

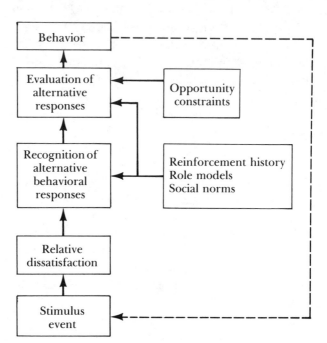

*The Stimulus.* The precipitating stimulus will usually be some event. Typical events might include receipt of a policy memo, the first warm, sunny day of spring (important here in Minnesota!), overhearing that Bill the Sluggard down the hall got a fat pay increase when you didn't, or watching a senior employee explain to a new member the importance of not being a rate buster, just after you turned in record performance for that shift. There are innumerable events that occur in work and other settings, and relatively few of them trigger adaptation cycles. The two characteristics of an event that identify it as an adaptation-inducing stimulus are that the person notices it and that it induces him or her to realize that he or she could be "better off" in a subjective utility sense.

The stimulus will, obviously, occur in some setting. With work-related behaviors as the set of dependent variables of interest here, it is reasonable to examine work-bound events when looking for triggers of adaptation. It would be artificially restrictive, however, to exclude other settings when seeking adaptation-cycle stimuli, Johns and Nicholson (1982), Steers and Rhodes (1978), and others have noted the importance of extra-work variables in the context of attendance models. Physical settings at home, the lake, the ball game, and commuter traffic all are suitable settings for an adaptation-cycle-inducing event. The only common tie among these settings is that they contain stimuli that trigger adaptation cycles involving work behaviors.

*The State of Relative Dissatisfaction and Adaptation.* The state of relative dissatisfaction experienced by the individual is a specific form of internal reaction, involving cognitive, affective, and connative components. It is *relative dissatisfaction* because the person realizes that he or she could be better off than in the current situation. The current situation could even be satisfying in the traditional job-satisfaction sense but suboptimal in the person's view. Such might describe the current situation of systems analysts, who make more than others in similar occupations but also know that they can achieve still higher wages by inducing competitive bidding among firms for their services. Relative dissatisfaction also includes the traditional notion of the employee dissatisfied with the current situation. The cognitive components of relative dissatisfaction include processing of the stimulus and realization of the new standard. Accompanying realization of the new standard is a measurable, negative affective response because one is not at the new standard. There continues to be considerable controversy about the interplay between affect and cognition (Birnbaum, 1981; Zajonc, 1981), and no generally accepted theory about the role of emotion in behavior exists as yet (Landy, 1983). We believe that the role of affect in adaptation is a testable proposition that does not depend precisely on the neurophysiological interplay between what is inferred as cognition and what is inferred as affect. The empirical contribution of affect in understanding adaptation does not hinge on resolution of the controversy enmeshing Zajonc and others.

The connative component of relative dissatisfaction reflects the core of what is intended as adaptation, reflecting an action tendency by the individual to attempt to achieve the new standard. This is clearly the strongest assumption in the model but is relatively straightforward to test. If people do not try to "fix"—defined from their perspective—relatively dissatisfying circumstances in the absence of constraints, we will know the model is wrong. In summary, the person will experience a mental state that involves (1) an awareness of a new standard, (2) negative affect because the person is not at the new standard, and (3) an action propensity to achieve the new standard. We will use the term *relative dissatisfaction* to summarize this internal mental state.

*Behavioral Choice and Enactment.* The relatively dissatisfied individual will consider what can be done to achieve the better state of affairs. While we are not in a position to speculate on the particular mental processes involved, we expect that four factors will influence the person's considerations. First, personal experience should influence both the range of behavioral alternatives considered and the value or utility associated with each of the alternatives considered. If one has experienced similar situations in the past, then knowledge about the likely consequences of various courses of action will help to sort among current alternatives. It is important to note that behavioral selection is based on perceived consequences. Errors in anticipating consequences are one mechanism for generating cycle repetition.

A second factor influencing behavioral choice is exposure to role models. People will model behaviors of others, particularly when then model is successful in resolving the source of relative dissatisfaction (Bandura, 1971; Weiss, 1977). There may be a trade-off between experience and role modeling, such that more experienced individuals will resort less to modeling the behavior of others.

A third factor influencing behavioral choice is the presence of clear social norms. For example, nurses working in hospitals maintain strong social norms against unexcused absenteeism because of the additional burden placed on co-workers and the added risk forced on patients in the unit. People do not have to experience or observe a behavior to judge its acceptability for adaptation.

Finally, the perception of constraints should influence behavioral choice. By *constraints,* we intend a fairly narrow interpretation of barriers to action, including ability-induced or environmentally induced limitations to behavior. For example, the employee frustrated with the company for laying him off cannot be absent from from work. Similarly, the drill-press operator pushed hard by management for ever-higher production cannot sabotage the machine by throwing it against the wall because it is too heavy. Perceived constraints force the probability of any one behavior toward zero.

The result of the person's considerations is a set of behavioral alternatives, ordered according to the perceived likelihood that they will result in the person being better off. It is convenient to think in subjective utility terms to describe the ordering of these behavioral alternatives. The *number* of different alternatives in the set can vary and will be idiosyncratic to the individual and the situation to which he or she is adapting. The behavior that is most likely to be displayed overtly will be that with the highest positive subjective utility, where *positive utility* is defined as the anticipation that the behavior will improve the person's situation. If a behavior has neutral or negative utility—the situation will remain the same or get worse—the person will not engage in it.

*Experienced Consequences of Behavior.* The enacted behavior will elicit counter-responses from the environment. The assumption of adaptation is that behaviors will be enacted that are expected to "fix" the situation—cause the source producing relative dissatisfaction to cease or be altered constructively. The experienced consequences of behavior can be classified according to whether reactions in the environment were in fact positive, negative, or neutral. A positive consequence occurs when the source of relative dissatisfaction becomes less likely to occur. A neutral consequence is one that leaves the probability, intensity, or duration of the source unaltered. A negative consequence accrues when the source of relative dissatisfaction becomes more likely in the future.

Enacted behaviors that are positive in effect should lead to a break in cycles, often with just one round occurring. Thus, the supervisor warns the employee about being late, prompting the employee—who was irritated by the warning because it was the first occasion of tardiness—to schedule a meeting to discuss the problem from both persons' viewpoints. Clearer, more reasonable expectations emerge on both sides, and future warnings are averted. A parallel between this adaptation-cycle pattern and Weick's (1969) discussion of self-correcting loops is clear.

A behavior that has a negative effect, such as being absent in response to the supervisor's warnings about being late, may produce further negative reprisals by the supervisor. A deviation-amplifying loop (Weick, 1969) has been identified. The employee's initial negative response to the supervisor's warnings would lead into cycles of increasingly negative behaviors and stronger negative sanctions, until the cycles were broken by resignation or termination. Such a pattern would fit a progression of withdrawal model. That an increasingly negative set of cycles is just one of the large array of cycle patterns that could unfold provides one reason why evidence in support of the progression hypothesis is scarce.

Neutral-consequence scenarios can arise from two different behavior patterns, either overt behaviors that do not influence the environment or a lack of overt behavior because no behavioral alternative with positive utility was perceived. Onset of future adaptation cycles would depend on the inherent stability of the source of relative dissatisfaction and on exogenous forces that may exist in the environment. In particular, forces other than the individual's adaptative response will influence the type of consequence experienced by the individual, providing another reason for repetition of cycles. More typically, the action taken by the individual will accrue positive consequences, causing the event that produced relative dissatisfaction to cease and adaptation cycles to stop. Indeed, if positive consequences were not the prevailing result, there would be substantially greater chaos in the workplace.

*Some Observations About the Model.* Although the perspective assumed in the model is that of the individual seeking to adapt to a source of relative dissatisfaction, it is interesting to think of interlocking adaptation cycles between people. Consider the political issue of unemployment compensation as business and labor political-action committees make their views known to a state legislator. Assume that any proposal for changes in tax structure will irritate some set of vested interests so that all courses of action are net negative in subjective utility. The legislator knows further that the funding bases of political-action committees are unstable, so that they might fold relatively soon regardless of what she does. A nonresponse is selected, and, indeed, pressure on the legislator is reduced in future sessions. If it is because business has moved to another state due to the nonresponse, we have an example of interlocking adaptation cycles rich with ramifications for other adaptation cycles. Mapping of adaptation cycles can clearly become complex.

It is assumed in the model that the individual will seek out the state providing greatest satisfaction. Strict interpretations of such an assumption generally have not fared well empirically if tests of expectancy-valence formulations are accepted as evidence. When cast in a behavioral-choice scenario, one for which few expectancy-valence theory studies exist, and when the person is predicted to maintain ordinal consistency in choosing one behavior over another, the prospects for empirical support are greater. We note that terms such as *maximum gain, minimum loss,* and *positive utility* are acceptable substitutes for *greatest satisfaction.* All convey the construct we intend.

Another point related to the rationality of the individual pursuing greatest satisfaction concerns the role of impulsive behavior as an adaptive response. Sometimes co-workers get assaulted for things they say, and some individuals do occasionally "take this job and shove it," to borrow a phrase from the vernacular. It would be difficult to predict such behaviors, regardless of whether the action would be interpreted as an adaptive response in retrospect.

The model is really concerned with behavioral shifts. It was initially developed to address the question, "What do workers do when they are dissatisfied?" Adaptation is expected to reflect a break from normal routine, as the individual is distracted from the task at hand. It is not designed to be a general theory of behavior, such as that offered by Naylor, Pritchard, and Ilgen (1980). Events precipitating relative dissatisfaction are expected to be nonroutine; otherwise, they will have difficulty competing for the attention of the individual.

It is important to note that relative dissatisfaction can result even when the current situation elicits positive affect upon reflection. This avoids the limitations of drive, need, and equity theories of motivation, which emphasize negative motivational states to the exclusion of positive influences on behavior.

Several interesting questions arise when we consider how the adaptation propensity is translated into specific overt behaviors. We expect that the behavior with the highest positive subjective utility will be enacted, all else equal. One question concerns what happens when no behavioral alternative is judged to have positive utility. Such might describe the circumstance of the person who feels trapped in a situation he or she can't do anything about. With a recurring stimulus, there are two likely consequences. One is that the person engages in cognitive readjustment or, in simple terms, gets used to it. The other possibility is that physiological symptoms of stress, such as headaches, fatigue, and ulcers, may appear. Specific information about the nature of the stimulus, behavioral alternatives, and so forth would be necessary to predict the more likely of the two alternatives.

A second question concerns the possibility that more than one behavior is judged to hold positive utility and that enactment of one behavior does *not* preclude enactment of others. A behavioral strategy of adaptation may include several courses of action, orchestrated in concert. This possibility illustrates the importance of not focusing exclusively on one behavior. It is generally true, as noted elsewhere, that single behaviors are hard to predict. Absenteeism is an excellent illustration of this statement. One of the strengths of the adaptation model is that it helps to shift focus from predicting specific behaviors to predicting broader response tendencies reflecting the adaptation construct. We expect that people will tend to select specific behaviors from a cluster of similar kinds of behaviors and that stable individual differences exist with respect to the clusters of behaviors considered for adaptive response. Identification of behavior clusters is an important empirical question. Withdrawal could be one such behavioral cluster, but indicators of this response tendency besides just absence, turnover, or tardiness would need to be considered. Clearly, these behaviors do not "hang together" as withdrawal theorists have proposed. Other behavior clusters might include problem solving, loyalty maintenance, or avoidance. An inductive empirical approach is necessary to begin identifying appropriate summary labels for these broad classes of response tendency with respect to adaptation.

A final point is that it is possible to reinterpret the five models inferred from the literature within the adaptation-cycle model. For example, consider the spillover model. Interpreting from an adaptation framework, one should find a number of behaviors that are positive in utility and neutral in effect on the precipitating event. In the first cycle of interaction, the behavior with the highest utility is enacted. As it is learned that the behavior did not fix the situation, the behavior's utility declines relative to other behaviors in the positive-utility set. In a second round of interaction, some other behavior has highest utility and is enacted. The cycles of interaction would probably continue until an exogenous shock changed the precipitating event. An important point is that behaviors would have to be monitored over time, which has not been done in studies advocating the spillover effect.

## Implications for Research

The model we have proposed suggests a number of implications for doing research on employees' adaptation to work. In this section, we will discuss four issues of particular importance: (1) defining the range of adaptive behaviors, (2) the importance of a within-subject research design, (3) the role of time in a process-oriented model, and (4) designing an operational test of the adaptation process.

Throughout this chapter, we have emphasized the importance of looking at absence as a specific manifestation of a more general construct, or latent trait. In our review of the literature describing relations between absence and other behavior, we suggested that the common theme linking together the behaviors is adaptation. At the operational level, it may be useful to hypothesize a small number of response tendencies comprising the adaptation construct. In factor-analysis terms, adaptation represents a general factor, under which are included multiple specific factors, or response tendencies.

Thinking in terms of response tendencies rather than specific behaviors offers a number of advantages. It encourages the researcher to search for a theory linking together behaviors, rather than arbitrarily measuring those that are readily available. Carefully formulated multiple-item measures provide a more reliable and more predictable representation of the construct of interest. Furthermore, the term *tendencies* implies a probabilistic relationship between relative dissatisfaction and any one of the behaviors. As indicated by the model, the specific response to relative dissatisfaction is conditioned by a number of intra-individual and contextual factors, so that the exact adaptive response taken by a particular person in a particular situation will be difficult to predict.

Studying these response tendencies raises a number of interesting research issues. What kinds of behaviors should be included?

How many response tendencies are necessary to summarize these behaviors? How should one measure the behaviors? Some progress in answering these questions has already been made. Gupta and Jenkins (1980) and Rosse (1983a) have attempted to provide a taxonomy of relevant behaviors. We are currently analyzing the responses of nearly 4,000 workers to a self-report measure of these behaviors. When completed, these analyses may provide better insight into the nature of behavior co-variance and the structure of response tendencies.

Another approach to studying these response tendencies is to investigate workers' perceptions of them. Farrell (1983) found that judges clustered twelve behaviors into Hirschman's (1970) categories of exit, voice, and loyalty and an additional category termed neglect. These categories appeared to be on two dimensions: active-passive and constructive-destructive. We are currently conducting a similar multidimensional scaling exercise with a wider range of behaviors. The results of studies such as these should facilitate progress in studying adaptation, although traditional issues such as validation of self-reported retrospective data remain.

One of the things to be learned from studies such as these is the generalizability of whatever response tendencies are found. While it would be very convenient to find that all individuals think in terms of similar response tendencies, this is not a necessity for the model. In fact, it should be noted that research appropriate to testing the model is necessarily of a within-subject design. Individuals are likely to differ in their perceptions of their work, of opportunity constraints, and of alternative behavioral responses. Research designs must acknowledge — indeed, capitalize upon — these individual differences.

The third important research implication concerns the role of time in a process model. Too often the term *process* is used to describe a model, but nothing is mentioned about the sequencing of variables or about how the process could recur. The adaptation model identifies cycles that, by definition, must unfold over time. Unfortunately, time as an aspect of behavioral processes in organizations is poorly understood (although Katz, 1980, and McGrath and Rotchford, 1983, have made contributions to improving our understanding). In particular, we speculate that researchers cannot use a chronological time orientation to decide when to measure aspects of the adaptation cycle. It is probable that cycle onset and duration are idiosyncratic to individuals, events, behaviors, and contexts.

Moreover, given the iterative nature of the process, the time span of study needs to include the whole process from the stimulus event that triggers an evaluation to the feedback that follows the chosen behavior (or nonresponse). The presence of the feedback loop is crucial to understanding that adaptation is a cycle, and, in a sense, is a never-ending process. A researcher may enter the cycle at any point, but understanding of the process is fostered by studying multiple complete cycles.

An example may help clarify this point. Susan has been a content and productive employee for over a year. But on Monday, she happens to read a confidential memo and learns that she is being paid substantially less than her male colleagues. She reacts with a sense of inequity and anger and considers the alternatives of (1) confronting her supervisor with the information and demanding a raise, (2) reducing her effort and attendance to a level that is consistent with her relative pay, or (3) resigning herself to the reality of sexual discrimination. She decides not to do (1), fearing that it might cost her a job that she really enjoys. She also rejects option (3), feeling that it is too passive. Reducing her level of effort, however, seems a fair response to an unfair situation. However, she soon discovers that she feels less fulfilled in her work and that it is no easier to pay her bills now than before. Thus, she remains dissatisfied and enters a second cycle of adaptation. The following week she hears of a woman in a similar professional position who has sued her employer for pay discrimination (role model) and learns that such discrimination is illegal (social norms). This new information prompts her to change her strategies and confront her supervisor with a demand for equitable pay. If the outcome of this confrontation is acceptable to Susan, a successful adaptation cycle has been identified. If it is not, we would expect a continuation of the process (perhaps with an enlarged set of alternative responses) until relative satisfaction is attained.

Note that the operational definition of successful adaptation is a positive change in relative satisfaction that may be reasonably attributed to previous behavior, not necessarily a change in the condition eliciting relative dissatisfaction. For example, suppose that Susan had complained to her supervisor, who had then explained to her that her male colleagues were actually performing substantially more demanding work. If Susan accepted this argument, her relative dissatisfaction would dissipate, representing a successful adaptation cycle, despite the fact the objective level of her pay relative to her male co-workers had not changed. An implication of this definition for designing research is that the work context must remain sufficiently stable to allow the inference that changes in relative dissatisfaction are due to the adaptive behavior and not to other events (such as Susan receiving a promotion that was unrelated to her adaptive behavior but that had the effect of removing relative dissatisfaction.

Considering all of the preceding points, what type of research is needed to evaluate the model we have proposed? The nature of our model specifies that such research must be of a longitudinal, within-subject design that permits analysis of (1) perceptions of work, (2) decision processes, (3) behavior, and (4) the consequences of that behavior on subsequent perceptions, affect, and behavior. Consideration must also be given to means of operationalizing all the variables indicated in Figure 5.1 (generally not a difficult task, except that few if any studies have attempted to measure all of them simultaneously). These parameters indicate rigorous, labor-intensive studies, which, with the finite resources generally available to researchers, probably implies relatively small samples in most studies. Although small sample sizes inevitably reduce statistical power and the opportunity for multivariate analysis, their trade-off for detailed, more "thick" description of cognition and behavior is probably justified. Aggregation across studies may then be used to compensate for small samples.

Three specific areas of research need to be addressed. The first deals with temporal processes in the model. One strategy would be to use retrospective reports to try to reconstruct event sequences. While the limitations of retrospection are well known, this approach would provide information not currently available, especially if several people were involved in an event sequence and were able to report on it. The alternative — trying to capture the process in real time — is fraught with hazards in the absence of a theory specifying probable time sequences. It may be best to formulate hypotheses about time sequences on the basis of retrospective reports that can then be tested in real-time research.

A second topic of research concerns the decision process through which a response is chosen. Among the many questions to be addressed here is whether a hierarchical decision process is used to first select a general response tendency and then a specific behavior from it, or whether a behavior is directly chosen. Decision-theory researchers should find this a fertile ground for exploring hypotheses concerning decision making under uncertainty and a host of other issues. A basic, exploratory strategy would be to use protocol analysis to talk people through a variety of scenarios in a role-playing fashion. This would provide a structured framework for measuring people's strategies and reactions to "natural" or manipulated series of events. This approach might also allow estimation of time sequences. As familiarity with temporal factors and decision processes is developed, the natural extension of this research would be to real-time analysis of behavior in the field.

The third major area — the logical extension of the first two — is analysis of the consequences of the behavior. As noted previously, successful adaptation is indexed by positive changes in relative satisfaction that may be attributed to a behavior. Research might profitably be directed to such issues as the scaling of behaviors with respect to their effect on job attitudes; the long-term effects of behaviors on future cycles (for example, whether people learn to habitually use a behavior that was initially successful, resulting in a shrinking behavioral repertoire); and the extent to which behaviors engaged in to satisfy one source of dissatisfaction also compensate for other areas of dissatisfaction (for example, whether stealing money will reduce dissatisfaction with co-workers as well as dissatisfaction with pay).

## Implications for Practice

While much work remains to be done before the empirical validity of the adaptation-cycle model is established, some practical implications can be foreseen in anticipation of supporting evidence. The reader is cautioned, however, that the implications are purely speculative at this time.

The first clear implication is that a practicing manager should look beyond behavioral symptoms before deciding on a course of action regarding some problem employee behaviors. She or he needs to consider the adaptation dynamics that lead to the overt behaviors engaged in by the employee, with a goal of isolating the initial precipitating event that ultimately leads to the behavior or behaviors. The importance of this is that one can break a non-productive adaptation cycle — one that produces "negative" behaviors in response to dissatisfying conditions — only by fixing the cause of the cycle in the first place. This advice stands in direct contradiction to that of traditional behaviorists, who advocate dealing with the overt behavior directly rather than looking for elusive causal mechanisms. The problem with the traditional behaviorist approach is that, if one behavior is modified by changing reinforcement schedules with respect to that behavior but the initial dissatisfying event is not addressed, then symptom substitutions are possible (under the right circumstances and patterns of adaptation). One example is the employee who is chronically absent because working a machine press is boring; bonuses for attendance are implemented, so he comes to work. Production does not improve measurably, however, because he needs frequent long breaks from the routine in order to do any work at all, and when strict break times are enforced, he severs a hand because he was too bored to watch what he was doing.

A second implication from the adaptation model flows from the realization that particular behavior patterns are probably idiosyncratic with respect to participants and settings. The direct implication of this for practice is that each "behavioral problem" should be treated as a case study, with concern for the unique circumstances that led up to the current behaviors and for the likelihood that precipitating events (and behavioral consequences) will continue in the future. Normative models and solutions may solve an absenteeism *rate* problem, but greater success would be achieved to the extent that problem diagnosis and treatment are tailored to each case individually. Furthermore, many behavioral patterns may be temporary and need not be fixed. Understanding the likelihood of future onset of the precipitating event is essential if one is to design treatments that are cost effective. Sometimes problems will go away without intervention because the conditions leading to the problem were fleeting.

A third implication concerns the types of behavioral models available in the work setting. As specified in the model, we expect substantial influence by role models in the narrowing of adaptation-behavior possibilities, especially on newer employees. Whenever possible, the manager can encourage and enforce constructive problem-solving modes within the work unit. Mechanisms for speedy conflict resolution, such as open-door policies and ombudspersons who have formal authority to force action, are concrete ways to encourage direct conflict confrontation and solving. The general point here is to provide paths for solving problems that are constructive, are preferred by both management and labor, and are the path of least resistance. The reader may recognize this as a path-goal leadership pattern applied to the particular circumstance of an employee confronted by a dissatisfying event.

A fourth implication follows from realization of the interdependence between the individual and his or her environment. Generally, one cannot simply focus on the individual or the environment in which he or she interacts. The problem behaviors result from the interaction of the two elements, and interventions may need to include modifications of the individual's approach to adaptation and also the environmental circumstances to which she or he is adapting.

If there is one strength of the model, it is that tracing adaptation cycles helps clarify how complicated interpersonal interactions really are, with the consequence that the easy or superficial solutions are rarely going to solve whatever problems are identified. This realization might be the most important practical implication of the model.

## References

Adler, S., and Golan, J. "Lateness as a Withdrawal Behavior." *Journal of Applied Psychology,* 1981, *66* (5), 544–554.
Allen, R., and Keaveny, T. "Correlates of Faculty Interest in

Unionization: A Replication and Extension." *Journal of Applied Psychology*, 1981, *66* (5), 582–588.

Bandura, A. *Psychological Modeling*. Chicago: Aldine-Atherton, 1971.

Beehr, T. A., and Gupta, N. "A Note on the Structure of Employee Withdrawal." *Organizational Behavior and Human Performance*, 1978, *21*, 73–79.

Bensman, J., and Gerver, I. "Crime and Punishment in the Factory: The Function of Deviancy in Maintaining the Social System." *American Sociological Review*, 1963, *28*, 588–598.

Birnbaum, M. "Thinking and Feeling: A Skeptical Review." *American Psychologist*, 1981, *36*, 99–101.

Brayfield, A., and Crockett, W. "Employee Attitudes and Employee Performance." *Psychological Bulletin*, 1955, *52* (5), 396–424.

Burke, R., and Wilcox, D. "Absenteeism and Turnover Among Telephone Operators." *Personnel Psychology*, 1972, *25*, 639–648.

Chadwick-Jones, J. K., and others. "Absence Measures: Their Reliability and Stability in an Industrial Setting." *Personnel Psychology*, 1971, *24*, 463–470.

Clegg, C. "Psychology of Employee Lateness, Absence, and Turnover: A Methodological Critique and an Empirical Study." *Journal of Applied Psychology*, 1983, *68* (1), 88–101.

Cook, R., Walizer, D., and Mace, D. "Illicit Drug Use in the Army: A Social-Organizational Analysis." *Journal of Applied Psychology*, 1976, *61*, 262–272.

Dalton, D., and Todor, W. "Antecedents of Grievance Filing Behavior: Attitude/Behavioral Consistency and the Union Steward." *Academy of Management Journal*, 1982, *25* (1), 158–169.

Dalton, M. "The Interlocking of Official and Unofficial Reward." In O. Grusky and G. Miller (Eds.), *The Sociology of Organizations*. New York: Free Press, 1970.

Dansereau, F., Cashman, J., and Graen, G. "Expectancy as a Moderator of the Relationship Between Job Attitudes and Turnover." *Journal of Applied Psychology*, 1974, *59*, 228–229.

Dittrich, J., and Carrell, M. "Dimensions of Organizational Fairness as Predictors of Job Satisfaction, Absence, and Turnover." Paper presented at 36th annual meeting of the Academy of Management, Kansas City, Mo., Aug. 1976.

Dollard, J., and others. *Frustration and Aggression*. New Haven, Conn.: Yale University Press, 1939.

Farrell, D. "Exit, Voice, Loyalty, and Neglect as Responses to Job Dissatisfaction: A Multidimensional Scaling Study." *Academy of Management Journal,* 1983, *26* (4), 596–607.

Farrell, D., and Robb, D. "Lateness to Work: A Study of Withdrawal from Work." Unpublished manuscript, Department of Management, Western Michigan University, 1979.

Fishbein, M., and Ajzen, I. *Beliefs, Attitude, Intention and Behavior: An Introduction to Theory and Research.* Reading, Mass.: Addison-Wesley, 1975.

Frielander, F., and Walton, E. "Positive and Negative Motivations Toward Work." *Administrative Science Quarterly,* 1964, *9,* 194–207.

Garrison, K. R., and Muchinsky, P. M. "Attitudinal and Biographical Predictors of Incidental Absenteeism." *Journal of Vocational Behavior,* 1977, *10,* 221–230.

Getman, J., Goldberg, S., and Herman, J. *Union Representation Elections: Law and Reality.* New York: Russell Sage Foundation, 1976.

Giese, W., and Ruter, H. "An Objective Analysis of Morale." *Journal of Applied Psychology,* 1949, *33,* 421–427.

Gouldner, A. *Patterns of Industrial Bureaucracy.* Glencoe, Ill.: Free Press, 1954.

Gupta, N., and Jenkins, G. *The Structure of Withdrawal: Relationships Among Estrangement, Tardiness, Absenteeism and Turnover.* Springfield, Va.: National Technical Information System, 1980.

Hackman, J. R., and Lawler, E. E. "Employee Reactions to Job Characteristics." *Journal of Applied Psychology Monograph,* 1971, *55,* 259–286.

Hamner, W., and Smith, F. "Work Attitudes as Predictors of Unionization Activity." *Journal of Applied Psychology,* 1978, *63,* 415–421.

Hawthorne, B. "Job Dissatisfaction: A Drug-Related Issue." *Drug Forum,* 1977–1978, *6,* 187–195.

Herzberg, F., and others. *Job Attitudes: Review of Research and Opinion.* Pittsburgh, Pa.: Psychological Services of Pittsburgh, 1957.

Hickson, D. "Motives of People Who Restrict Their Output." *Occupational Psychology,* 1961, *35,* 110–121.

Hill, J. M. M., and Trist, E. L. "Changes in Accidents and Other Absences with Length of Service." *Human Relations,* 1955, *8,* 121–152.

Hirschman, A. O. *Exit, Voice, and Loyalty: Responses to Decline in Firms, Organizations, and States.* Cambridge, Mass.: Harvard University Press, 1970.

Hollinger, R., and Clark, J. "The Quality of Work Experience: Its Relationship to Employee Theft and Production Deviance." Paper presented at annual meeting of the Society for the Study of Social Problems, Boston, Mass., Aug. 1979.

Hom, P., Katerberg, R., and Hulin, C. "Comparative Examination of Three Approaches to the Prediction of Turnover." *Journal of Applied Psychology,* 1979, *64,* 280–290.

Hulin, C. "Effects of Changes in Job Satisfaction Levels on Employee Turnover." *Journal of Applied Psychology,* 1968, *52,* 122–126.

Ilgen, D. R., and Hollenback, J. H. "The Role of Job Satisfaction in Absence Behavior." *Organizational Behavior and Human Performance,* 1977, *19,* 148–161.

Johns, G., and Nicholson, N. "The Meanings of Absence: New Strategies for Theory and Research." In B. Staw and L. L. Cummings (Eds.), *Research in Organizational Behavior.* Vol. 4. Greenwich, Conn.: JAI Press, 1982.

Katz, T. "Time and Work: Toward an Integrative Perspective." In B. Staw and L. L. Cummings (Eds.), *Research in Organizational Behavior.* Vol. 2. Greenwich, Conn.: JAI Press, 1980.

Knowles, M. "Personal and Job Factors Affecting Labor Turnover." *Personnel Practices Bulletin,* 1964, *20,* 25–37.

Koch, J., and Steers, R. M. "Job Attachment, Satisfaction, and Turnover Among Public Sector Employees." *Journal of Vocational Behavior,* 1978, *12,* 119–128.

Kraut, A. "Predicting Turnover of Employees from Measured Job Attitudes." *Organizational Behavior and Human Performance,* 1975, *13,* 233–243.

Landy, F. Personal communication, 1983.

Ley, R. "Labor Turnover as a Function of Worker Differences, Work Environment, and Authoritarianism of Foremen." *Journal of Applied Psychology,* 1966, *50,* 497–500.

Lyons, T. *Nursing Attitudes and Turnover.* Ames, Iowa: Industrial Relations Center, 1968.

Lyons, T. "Turnover and Absenteeism: A Review of Relationships and Shared Correlates." *Personnel Psychology,* 1972, *25,* 271–281.

McGrath, J. E., and Rotchford, N. L. "Time and Behavior in

Organizations." In B. Staw and L. L. Cummings (Eds.), *Research in Organizational Behavior*. Vol. 5. Greenwich, Conn.: JAI Press, 1983.

Mangione, T., and Quinn, R. "Job Satisfaction, Counterproductive Behavior, and Drug Use at Work." *Journal of Applied Psychology*, 1975, *60* (1), 114–116.

March, J., and Simon, H. *Organizations*. New York: Wiley, 1958.

Marsh, R., and Mannari, H. "Organizational Commitment and Turnover: A Predictive Study." *Administrative Science Quarterly*, 1977, *22*, 57–75.

Melbin, M. "Organizational Practice and Individual Behavior: Absenteeism Among Psychiatric Aides." *American Sociological Review*, 1961, *26*, 14–23.

Miller, H. "Withdrawal Behaviors Among Hospital Employees." Unpublished doctoral dissertation, Department of Psychology, University of Illinois, 1981.

Miller, H. "Some Evidence Concerning the Progression of Withdrawal Hypothesis." Paper presented at 42nd annual meeting of the Academy of Management, New York, Aug. 1982.

Miller, H., Katerberg, R., and Hulin, C. "Evaluation of the Mobley, Horner and Hollingsworth Model of Employee Turnover." *Journal of Applied Psychology*, 1979, *64*, 509–517.

Miller, N. "The Frustration-Aggression Hypothesis." *Psychological Review*, 1941, *48*, 337–342.

Mobley, W. "Some Unanswered Questions in Turnover and Withdrawal Research." *Academy of Management Review*, 1982, *7* (1), 111–116.

Mobley, W., Horner, S., and Hollingsworth, A. "An Evaluation of Precursors of Hospital Employee Turnover." *Journal of Applied Psychology*, 1978, *63*, 408–414.

Mobley, W., and others. "Review and Conceptual Analysis of the Employee Turnover Process." *Psychological Bulletin*, 1979, *86*, 493–522.

Muchinsky, P. M. "Employee Absenteeism: A Review of the Literature." *Journal of Vocational Behavior*, 1977, *10*, 316–340.

Naylor, J. C., Pritchard, R. D., and Ilgen, D. R. *A Theory of Behavior in Organizations*. New York: Academic Press, 1980.

Newman, J. E. "Predicting Absenteeism and Turnover." *Journal of Applied Psychology*, 1974, *59*, 610–615.

Nicholson, N., Brown, C. A., and Chadwick-Jones, J. K. "Absence from Work and Job Satisfaction." *Journal of Applied Psychology,* 1976, *61* (6), 728-737.

Nicholson, N., Brown, C. A., and Chadwick-Jones, J. K. "Absence from Work and Personal Characteristics." *Journal of Applied Psychology,* 1977, *62,* 319-327.

Patchen, M. "Absence and Employee Feelings About Fair Treatment." *Personnel Psychology,* 1960, *13,* 349-360.

Perone, M., DeWaard, R., and Baron, A. "Satisfaction with Real and Simulated Jobs in Relation to Personality Variables and Drug Use." *Journal of Applied Psychology,* 1979, *64* (6), 660-668.

Porter, L. W., and Steers, R. M. "Organizational, Work, and Personal Factors in Employee Turnover and Absenteeism." *Psychological Bulletin,* 1973, *80,* 151-176.

Revans, R. *Standards for Morale: Cause and Effect in Hospitals.* London: Oxford University Press, 1964.

Roethlisberger, F., and Dickson, W. *Management and the Worker.* Cambridge, Mass.: Harvard University Press, 1939.

Ronan, W. "Factor Analysis of Eleven Job Performance Measures." *Personnel Psychology,* 1963, *16,* 255-268.

Ronan, W. "A Study of and Some Concepts Concerning Labor Turnover." *Occupational Psychology,* 1967, *41,* 193-202.

Rosse, J. "Adaptation to Work: An Analysis of Employee Health, Withdrawal and Change." Paper presented at 36th annual meeting of the Industrial Relations Research Association, San Francisco, Dec. 1983a.

Rosse, J. "Patterns of Withdrawal Behavior." Paper presented at annual meeting of the American Psychological Association, Anaheim, Calif., Aug. 1983b.

Roy, D. "Quota Restrictions and Goldbricking in a Machine Shop." *American Journal of Sociology,* 1952, *57,* 427-442.

Saleh, S., Lee, R., and Prien, E. "Why Nurses Leave Their Jobs.: An Analysis of Female Turnover." *Personnel Administration,* 1965, *22,* 25-28.

Schmidt, F. L., and Hunter, J. E. "Development of a General Solution to the Problem of Validity Generalization." *Journal of Applied Psychology,* 1977, *62,* 529-540.

Schneider, J. "The Greener Grass Phenomenon: Differential Effects of a Work Context Alternative on Organizational Participation and Withdrawal Intentions." *Organizational Behavior and Human Performance,* 1976, *16,* 308–333.

Schriesheim, C. "Job Satisfaction, Attitudes Toward Unions, and Voting in a Union Representation Election." *Journal of Applied Psychology,* 1978, *63,* 548–552.

Sheridan, J. "Is There a Computer Criminal Working for You?" *Industry Week,* 1979, *200,* 69–76.

Skinner, E. "Relationships Between Leadership Behavior Patterns and Organizational Situational Variables." *Personnel Psychology,* 1969, *22,* 489–494.

Spector, P. "Organizational Frustration: A Model and Review of the Literature." *Personnel Psychology,* 1978, *31,* 815–829.

Staw, B. M., and Oldham, G. R. "Reconsidering our Dependent Variables: A Critique and Empirical Study." *Academy of Management Journal,* 1978, *21* (4), 539–559.

Steers, R., and Mowday, R. "Employee Turnover and Post-Decision Accommodation Processes." In L. L. Cummings and B. Staw (Eds.), *Research in Organizational Behavior.* Vol. 3. Greenwich, Conn.: JAI Press, 1981.

Steers, R. M., and Rhodes, S. R. "Major Influences on Employee Attendance: A Process Model." *Journal of Applied Psychology,* 1978, *63* (4), 391–407.

Talacchi, S. "Organizational Size, Individual Attitudes, and Behavior." *Administrative Science Quarterly,* 1960, *5,* 398–420.

Thurstone, L. L. "The Measurement of Attitudes." *Journal of Abnormal and Social Psychology,* 1931, *26,* 249–269.

Trice, H., and Roman, P. *Spirits and Demons at Work: Alcohol and Other Drugs on the Job.* Ithaca, N.Y.: Cornell University, 1978.

U.S. Department of Labor, Manpower Administration. *Suggestions for Control of Turnover and Absenteeism.* Washington, D.C.: U.S. Government Printing Office, 1972.

Urban, M. "Drugs in Industry." In National Commission on Marijuana and Drug Abuse, *Drug Use in America, Vol. 1.* Washington, D.C.: U.S. Government Printing Office, 1973.

Van Zelst, R., and Kerr, W. "Workers' Attitudes Toward Merit Rating." *Personnel Psychology,* 1953, *6,* 159–172.

Waters, L., and Roach, D. "Relationships Between Job Attitudes and Two Forms of Withdrawal from the Work Situation." *Journal of Applied Psychology*, 1971, *55*, 92–94.

Waters, L. K., and Roach, D. "Job Attitudes as Predictors of Termination and Absenteeism: Consistency over Time and Across Organizational Units." *Journal of Applied Psychology*, 1973, *57*, 341–342.

Waters, L. K., and Roach, D. "Job Satisfaction, Behavioral Intention, and Absenteeism as Predictors of Turnover." *Personnel Psychology*, 1979, *32*, 393–397.

Waters, L., Roach, D., and Waters, C. "Estimates of Future Tenure Satisfaction and Biographical Variables as Predictors of Termination." *Personnel Psychology*, 1976, *29*, 57–60.

Watson, C. "An Evaluation of Some Aspects of the Steers and Rhodes Model of Employee Attendance." *Journal of Applied Psychology*, 1981, *66*, 385–389.

Weick, K. *The Social Psychology of Organizing.* Reading, Mass.: Addison-Wesley, 1969.

Weiss, H. "Subordinate Imitation of Supervisor Behavior: The Role of Modeling in Organizational Socialization." *Organizational Behavior and Human Performance*, 1977, *19* (1), 89–105.

Wild, R. "Job Needs, Job Satisfaction, and Job Behavior." *Journal of Applied Psychology*, 1970, *54*, 157–162.

Zajonc, R. "A One Factor Mind About Mind and Emotion." *American Psychologist*, 1981, *36* (1), 102–103.

# 6

# Knowledge and Speculation About Absenteeism

## Richard M. Steers
## Susan R. Rhodes

Recent years have witnessed a marked increase in research on the topic of absenteeism in organizations. Some would argue that this increase is the result of heightened sensitivity to the problems of employees in the workplace that serve to foster alienation and withdrawal. Others would suggest that the increase results from organizations' increased interest in improving efficiency in the face of a more competitive international marketplace. Whatever the reason, the fact remains that the topic of employee absenteeism has "arrived" as a central topic of concern to organizational researchers.

The purpose of this chapter is to attempt to summarize the current state of knowledge with respect to research on absenteeism. In doing so, we feel it is important to recognize that such a summary deals with both knowledge and speculation. That is, it is necessary to identify what we know as well as what we think we know about absenteeism. Therefore, our overview of the available research will be classified in terms of these two topics. Moreover, it should be noted that this review focuses on trends in the more recent research and does not purport to represent an exhaustive review of all findings. (See Steers and Rhodes, 1978, for a review of earlier findings.) This is done in an effort to provide an integrative summary of the research literature so as to provide a backdrop for better understanding the conceptual and empirical discussions also presented in this volume.

### What Do We "Know" About Absenteeism?

To begin with, let's examine those aspects of absenteeism about which we feel fairly confident. There appears to be a series of facts concerning absenteeism that are worthy of review to set the stage for our examination of the more controversial or tentative results. Four such "facts" can be identified.

1. We know that absenteeism is pervasive both across organizational types and across international boundaries. As shown in Figure 6.1, although minor variations exist, absence patterns are fairly consistent across organizations of varying size, in different industries, and in different regions of the United States. Until about 1979, average absenteeism across all employees was approximately 3 percent, defined in terms of scheduled work time (U.S. Bureau of National Affairs, 1980). In some industries (particularly manufacturing), this figure climbed to as high as 15 to 20 percent per day. Over the past four years (see Figure 6.2), however, absence rates have steadily declined from an average of 2.9 percent in 1979 to 2.1 percent in 1982, this change being attributable to the increase in the unemployment rate over the same time period. The decreasing trend in absenteeism continued in 1983.

Further evidence suggests that absenteeism is truly a problem of international concern. In Western Europe, overall absence rates range from 14 percent in Italy to a low of 1 percent in Switzerland (Yankelovich, 1979). In Italy, for example, absenteeism has become so institutionalized that many organizations cannot cope with those rare days—usually twice a month on payday—when everyone shows up. This "problem" is serious enough to merit its own name, *presentisimo* and results because many Italian manufacturers must hire between 8 and 14 percent more workers than they

Figure 6.1. Absenteeism Rates by Organization Size, Industry Type, and Region, 1982 Twelve-Month Average.

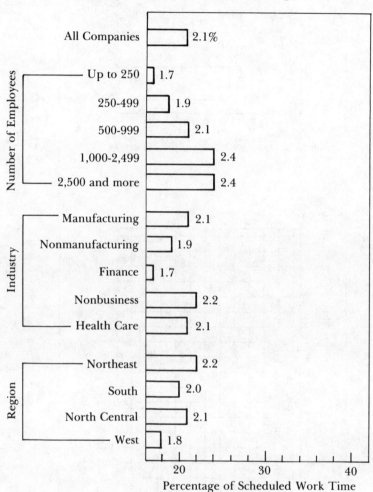

need just to get the work out (after controlling for absenteeism). When most everyone attends to collect his or her paycheck, there is not sufficient work (or work space) to go around. The situation in Italy reached its peak in 1982, when police began arresting some of the more serious absentees, charging them with fraud in claiming pay for hours not worked (Childe, 1982). Even so, a high-level commission impaneled to study the problem made little progress;

**Figure 6.2. Median Absence Rates by Year and Month.**

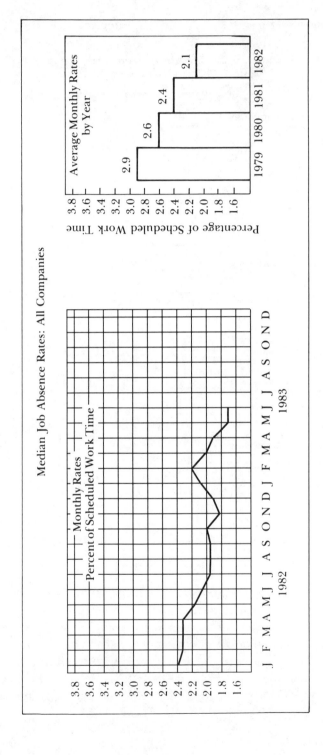

its first meeting had to be canceled because of poor attendance ("Maybe the No-Shows...," 1982).

France ranks second in Western Europe in absenteeism. One study found that one half of French workers never miss a single day of work. However, of the remaining half, over 80 percent take more than 40 "sick days" per year. And in England, it is estimated that over 300 million workdays are lost per year due to absenteeism (Roe, 1979). This figure amounts to about 13.5 days lost per employee. Clearly, then, absenteeism represents a problem of international concern.

2. We know that absenteeism can be expensive. Cost estimates can be calculated in many ways. Using 1977 estimates of total costs associated with each absence (Mirvis and Lawler, 1977), the estimated cost of absenteeism in the United States for that year was about $26.4 billion (Steers and Rhodes, 1978). The 1983 figure is probably closer to $30 billion. Similarly, in Canada, annual costs approach $8 billion (Gandz and Mikalachki, 1979). According to the *Oregon Business Barometer* of May, 1981, for every 0.5 percent of change in national absence rates in the United States, the gross national product (GNP) changes by $10 billion. Thus, however calculated, the costs to industry (and society) associated with absenteeism are high.

3. We know that a veritable constellation of diverse variables has been examined in relation to absenteeism at one time or another. Our own review of the literature has identified 209 such variables (see Table 6.1). Clearly, many of these variables are interrelated and overlapping (for example, we identified nineteen work-attitude variables that of necessity must be highly interrelated), and many nonsignificant correlations have emerged. Even so, researchers have thought enough of each one to pursue it in its own right as a possible antecedent.

The sheer magnitude of the number of antecedents suggests what is perhaps the basic problem of absenteeism research. If so many variables have been found to be related at one time or another to absenteeism, can we really conclude anything about causes that we can rely upon? This problem is at the heart of our discussion in the next section on what we think we know about absence behavior.

4. Finally, we know that absenteeism can at times have serious consequences in terms of performance for individuals, their co-

Table 6.1. Number of Variables Studied in Relation to Absenteeism.

| Category | Number of Variables |
|---|---|
| Work attitudes | 19 |
| Economic and market factors | 13 |
| Organizationwide factors | 26 |
| Immediate-work-environment factors | 37 |
| Job-content factors | 30 |
| Personal factors | 49 |
| External environmental factors[a] | 10 |
| Organizational change[b] | 25 |
| | 209 |

[a] External environmental factors are in addition to economic and market factors listed in the table and include temperature, hours of sunshine, geographical region, community support and recognition, and life satisfaction.

[b] Organizational-change studies represent efforts to reduce absenteeism through intervention activities. Variables are in addition to those included in other factors (for example, alcoholism programs, disciplinary programs, health examinations, employee ownership).

workers, and organizations. As discussed by Mowday, Porter, and Steers (1982, pp. 157–166) and Goodman and Atkin (Chapter Seven of this volume), when an employee is absent, consequences follow that can affect his or her own job or career, the amount of work his or her colleagues must perform, and the costs associated with production within the organization. These consequences can be both positive and negative. Since Goodman and Atkin address this issue, we simply pause to note it here.

In summary, then, we feel fairly confident in concluding that absenteeism is pervasive and expensive, that it is related to a rather long and diverse set of antecedents, and that serious consequences have been known to result from such behavior. In view of this, the next logical question to raise focuses on so-called "causes" of absenteeism.

## What Do We Think We Know About Absenteeism?

Moving from the realm of knowledge to speculation, we may now ask what we *think* we know about absenteeism. By this, we mean a review of the recent literature on employee absence behavior. We term this *speculation* rather than *knowledge* primarily because of the weak, tentative, or often contradictory nature of the findings on a particular variable or topic. In the absence of strong and consistent relationships, we shift from knowing to thinking and must of necessity summarize the results with reservation. Even so, we will attempt to provide an overview of such findings.

At least three conceptual models have been published that attempt to make sense out of the literature on absenteeism (Gibson, 1966; Nicholson, 1977; Steers and Rhodes, 1978). Each model is deductive in nature, and each recognizes clear limitations. Our own model, published in 1978, attempted to identify the major sets of variables as they contributed to an individual's decision to attend. It was based on a review of 104 empirical studies on the subject. A schematic of the entire model is shown in Figure 6.3.

While a detailed discussion of the model and its underlying framework goes beyond the scope of this paper (see Steers and Rhodes, 1978, for details), we should note here that the model suggests two primary forces for or against attendance: attendance motivation and perceived ability to attend. Attendance motivation, in turn, is thought to be a function of several factors, including: (1) satisfaction with the job situation; (2) economic and market conditions; (3) incentive and reward systems within the organization; (4) work-group norms concerning desirable attendance levels; (5) one's personal work ethic; and (6) one's commitment to the organization and its goals. Ability to attend, on the other hand, was thought to be influenced by: (1) illness and accidents; (2) degree of family responsibilities; and (3) possible transportation problems.

Subsequent to the publication of this model, a number of studies have appeared that shed new light on the absence process. We will attempt to summarize the major results from these studies. To do so, the review will be organized into seven parts: (1) work-related attitudes; (2) economic and market factors; (3) organizational control systems; (4) absence culture and work-group norms; (5) personal factors; (6) perceived ability to attend; and (7) multivariate studies examining the relative influence of different categories of variables.

*Work-Related Attitudes.* Overall job satisfaction, job involvement, organizational commitment, and several dimensions of job satisfaction (work itself, supervision, co-workers, pay, and promotion) have received the greatest research attention among the work-

**Figure 6.3. Major Influences on Employee Attendance.**

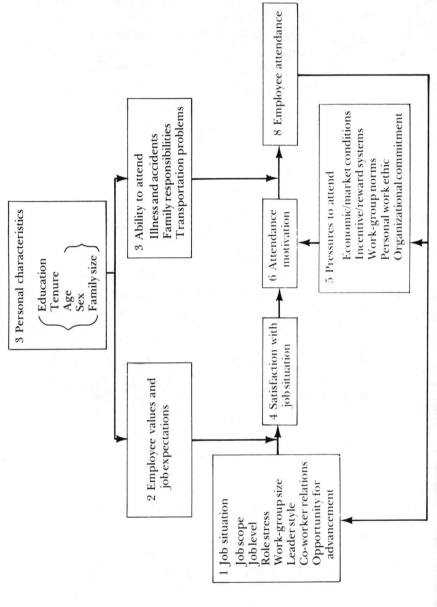

related attitudes as predictors of absence. Combining the studies reported by Rhodes and Steers (1977) and an updated literature search, we can identify thirty-one studies on overall job satisfaction, nine studies on job involvement, eight studies on organizational commitment, twenty-one studies on satisfaction with work itself, nineteen studies on satisfaction with supervision, sixteen studies on co-worker satisfaction, eighteen studies on pay satisfaction, and seventeen studies on promotion satisfaction.

A recent meta-analysis of the absenteeism–job satisfaction literature supports the assumption that employees who are dissatisfied with various aspects of their jobs are more likely to be absent (McShane, 1983). In particular, the relationship was strongest for overall satisfaction and work satisfaction. Moreover, in contrast to previous reviews (Muchinsky, 1977; Steers and Rhodes, 1978), satisfaction with co-workers, pay, and supervision was also related to reduced absenteeism. However, satisfaction with promotions was uncorrelated with absenteeism. Job satisfaction was found to be more highly related to frequency of absences than to number of days lost. It should be pointed out that the largest population-correlation estimate after correction for measurement unreliability was − 0.224, with satisfaction with work accounting for only 5 percent of the variance in frequency of absence. According to McShane, however, a number of measurement problems would lead one to believe that the true relationship between absenteeism and various aspects of job satisfaction is much greater.

In addition, job involvement appears to be a promising attitudinal predictor of absenteeism, particularly of absence frequency. In six out of eight instances, a negative bivariate relationship was reported between job involvement and absence frequency (Beehr and Gupta, 1978; Breaugh, 1981; Cheloha and Farr, 1980; Hackman and Lawler, 1971). For time lost and other measures of absence, results are evenly split between negative (Beehr and Gupta, 1978; Blumberg, 1980; Cheloha and Farr, 1980; Saal, 1978) and nonsignificant relationships (Breaugh, 1981; Hammer, Landau, and Stern, 1981; Siegel and Ruh, 1973).

Finally, studies examining the relationship between organizational commitment and absenteeism report either negative (Clegg, 1983; Hammer, Landau, and Stern, 1981; Rhodes and

Steers, 1981; Steers, 1977) or nonsignificant (Angle and Perry, 1981; Clegg, 1983; Hammer, Landau, and Sttern, 1981; Jamal, 1981; Miller, 1982; Rhodes and Steers, 1981; Steers, 1977) results. The results appear to be unrelated to the particular absence measure used.

In an extension of the Schmidt and Hunter (1977) validity generalization procedure, Terborg and others (1982) examined whether the weak work attitude–absenteeism relationship might be explained by statistical artifacts. Differences on variable means, standard deviations, reliabilities, and predictive validities were found for job-satisfaction and organizational-commitment measures collected on sales employees in six retail stores. However, little variability in validities remained controlling for six artifacts, including predictor and criterion unreliability, range restriction, sampling error, criterion contamination, and differences in factor structures between different measures of similar constructs. Specifically, they found that more than 50 percent of the variance in validities across situations was explained by situational artifacts. The situational-specificity hypothesis was rejected for satisfaction with promotion, satisfaction with supervision, and organizational commitment, with more than 75 percent of the variance in validities being accounted for. For satisfaction with work, pay, and co-workers, the situational-specificity hypothesis could not be rejected.

Is one attitude more salient in explaining absenteeism than others? Studies including more than one attitudinal variable provide some insight here. Blumberg (1980) and Hackman and Lawler (1971) reported significant negative bivariate relationships between job involvement and a time-lost index of absence and non-significant relationships between job satisfaction and absence. Breaugh (1981), on the other hand, found that only absence frequency and not time-lost absence was significantly related to job involvement, while job satisfaction was unrelated to either absence measure. Hammer, Landau, and Stern (1981) reported that only organizational commitment was negatively related to two measures of voluntary absence. Both involvement and job satisfaction were unrelated. In studies including both commitment and satisfaction, Terborg and others (1980) found commitment to be more important; Clegg (1983) and Jamal (1981) found job satisfaction to be more important; and Miller (1982) found nonsignificant relations between absence and both variables. Hence, there appears to be no one attitudinal variable that emerged as a more consistent correlate of absenteeism based on bivariate analyses.

Further evidence of the relative influence of different attitudinal variables on absenteeism is provided by two multivariate studies. First, in a study of workers in an employee-owned organization, Hammer, Landau, and Stern (1981) performed hierarchical regression analyses with three forms of voluntary absence as the dependent variables. Among the independent variables were job involvement, job satisfaction, organizational commitment, stock ownership, union as a voice, age, and educational level. Of the three attitudinal variables, only organizational commitment was a significant independent predictor of voluntary absence.

Second, Cheloha and Farr (1980) examined the relative influence of job description index (JDI) facets of job-satisfaction measures and job involvement on absenteeism for a sample of state government employees. According to zero-order correlations, both job satisfaction and job involvement were inversely related to absence behavior, but job involvement was more consistently related. Partial correlational analysis for the satisfaction-absence relationship, holding job involvement constant, and involvement-absence relationship, holding job satisfaction constant, revealed that job involvement was related to absenteeism but job satisfaction was not. The authors analyzed data in Saal's (1978) study using partial correlation and found similar results. It was suggested that the relationship between job satisfaction and absenteeism may be mediated by job involvement.

The causal direction of the attitude-absence relationship has been questioned by Clegg (1983). Despite the fact that Steers and Rhodes (1978) argued for a reciprocal relationship between attitudes and absence, of seventeen recent empirical studies on the subject, none considered the possibility that absence may influence work attitudes. Based on a sample of British blue-collar workers, Clegg found no evidence that attitudes (job satisfaction, organizational commitment) influenced absence behavior. On the other hand, absence independently predicted job satisfaction but not organizational commitment. Lateness was found to be the best independent predictor of absence.

In summary, there appears to be a fairly consistent, modest, and inverse relationship between work-related attitudes and absenteeism. Therefore, it can be concluded that attitudes must be recognized in any model of employee attendance.

*Economic and Market Factors.* In addition to work-related attitudes, a second factor worthy of consideration in this review is the general state of the economy and subsequent job-market conditions. Economic and job-market conditions often place constraints on employees' ability to change jobs. As a result, in times of high unemployment, there may be increased pressure to maintain a good attendance record for fear of losing one's job. Evidence suggests that there is a close inverse relationship between changes in unemployment levels within a given geographical region and subsequent absence rates (Behrend, 1953; Crowther, 1957; Behrend, 1951). Moreover, as the threat of layoff becomes even greater (for example, when an employee's own employer begins layoffs), there is an even stronger decrease of absenteeism (Behrend, 1951; Dijkstra, 1975).

On the other hand, when an employee knows that *he* or *she* is to be laid off (as opposed to a knowledge that layoffs are taking place in general), the situation is somewhat different. Specifically, Owens (1966) found that railway repair employees in a depressed industry who had been given notice of layoff because of shop closure had significantly higher absence rates prior to layoffs than a comparable group of employees who were not to be laid off. Owens suggests that, in addition to being a reflection of manifest anxiety, the increased absenteeism allowed employees time to find new positions. However, Hershey (1972) found no significant differences in absence rates between employees who were scheduled for layoffs and employees not so scheduled. Hershey argued that the subjects in his study were much in demand in the labor market and generally felt assured of finding suitable jobs. (Improved unemployment compensation in recent years may also have been a factor in minimizing absenteeism among those to be laid off.)

Thus, economic and job-market conditions may be largely related to attendance motivation and subsequent attendance through their effects on one's ability to change jobs. When *general* economic conditions are deteriorating, absenteeism decreases for several reasons. First, employees with poor attendance records may be among the first to be laid off. Second, remaining employees may be less likely to be absent for fear of reprisal. However, when the *individual* employee is to be laid off, absence rates are apparently influenced by one's perceptions of his or her ability to find alternate employment. When such alternatives are readily available, no effect of impending layoff on absenteeism is noted; when such alternatives are not readily available, absence rates can be expected to increase as employees seek other employment.

*Organizational Control Systems.* Organizational control systems involve those policies and procedures used by the organization to encourage attendance. Three such topics can be identified under this heading: (1) positive-reinforcement programs; (2) punishment and negative incentives; and (3) mixed-consequence systems. Since earlier reviews, there have been a number of studies published (both correlational and field experiments) that relate to this topic.

Positive-reinforcement programs: A recent review of the literature on positive-reinforcement programs as they relate to attendance was carried out by Schmitz and Heneman (1980). Ten such studies were examined, and in each case, implementation of the positive-reinforcement program led to a subsequent reduction in absenteeism. Reinforcers found to be effective included bonuses (Grove, 1968; Lawler and Hackman, 1969; Orpen, 1978; Panyan and McGregor, 1976), bonus points (Baum and Menefee, 1979), participation in lottery (Stephens and Burroughs, 1978; Johnson and Wallin, 1976), participation in poker hand (Pedalino and Gamboa, 1974), and food credit (Kent, Malott, and Greening, 1977).

In addition to the studies reviewed by Schmitz and Heneman (1980), five other studies have reported positive-reinforcement interventions. Reinforcers resulting in reduced absence included reimbursement for unused sick leave (Woska, 1972), a desirable work schedule (Reid, Schuh-Wear, and Brannon, 1978), and participation in a lottery (Robertson, Johnson, and Bethke, 1980). On the other hand, the introduction of bonus pay (Schneller and Kopelman, 1982) and participation in a weekly Bingo game (Carlson and Hill, 1982) did not lead to a reduction in absence.

To better understand the nature of the relationship between positive reinforcement and attendance behavior, several basic issues were raised by Schmitz and Heneman (1980). To begin with, in view of several characteristics of the programs or organizational settings, the results of these studies may actually understate the potential effectiveness of positive-reinforcement programs in reducing absence. That is, the baseline-period absence rates appear somewhat low in most studies. These low rates may have limited the extent to which decreases were possible (a "floor" effect). Therefore, we might expect larger reductions in absence rates with higher baseline rates.

Second, in many studies, all absences—voluntary and involuntary—were included in the baseline measure. Voluntary absences would probably be affected to a greater extent than total absences by the program. The results, therefore, would more than likely understate the impact of positive reinforcement on voluntary absences.

Finally, the monetary reinforcers were, for the most part, relatively small. For example, part-time cleaning employees received a $2.50 per week bonus (Lawler and Hackman, 1969). For organizations with paid-sick-leave programs, it would seem that the reward would hardly offset the sick-leave benefit. It is possible that even greater declines in absence might occur with larger rewards.

A number of problems with the studies noted by Schmitz and Heneman suggest caution in interpreting results. First, it is possible that failures are not so likely as successes to be reported in the literature. Hence, these studies may reflect a positive bias in the evidence. Second, both the lack of control groups and the inclusion of components in addition to positive reinforcement in a large number of interventions make it difficult to attribute results to the use of positive reinforcement. While in most programs the intended reinforcer was a monetary bonus, such additional features as feedback to employees, unconscious and conscious goal setting, and heightened supervisory attention to absence problems, along with verbal praise, could have accounted for reductions in absence alone or together with the bonus. Third, because most studies involved relatively short time spans of data collection in the postintervention period, there is little information as to the long-term effects of the rewards. Moreover, methods of data analysis were not suited for examining whether there was a tendency for absence levels to drift higher over time.

A final shortcoming of many of these studies was the absence of cost-benefit analyses, perhaps the best indicator of program effectiveness. Moreover, when cost-benefit analyses were performed, typically only direct costs, such as the costs of the bonuses, were assessed. Costs associated with developing, implementing, and monitoring the program were not provided. In summary, then, in spite of the consistent support for the association between positive-reinforcement programs and reduced absence, questions of causality long-term effectiveness, and cost effectiveness remain unanswered.

Punishment and negative incentives: Steers and Rhodes (1978) reported mixed results in the literature in regard to the effects of punitive sanctions on absenteeism. Since this review, three additional studies have appeared. In the first, an attendance-control policy incorporating a six-step procedure for unauthorized absences was implemented by Baum (1978) in a department of a large manufacturing organization. Two comparable departments served as controls. Results supported the effectiveness of the attendance-control policy among chronically absent workers. However, the policy did not lead to improvements in attendance among regular attenders. In contrast to Nicholson's (1976) findings that workers substituted certified for uncertified absences to avoid negative consequences of the sanctions, the attendance-control policy had no noticeable effect on either long-term illnesses or contractual absences. It was recommended that managers consider the possibility of designing multifaceted control policies that rely on both positive reinforcement and sanctions based on the motivational pattern of legal compliance.

Using a sample of school teachers, Winkler (1980) examined the influence of sick-leave policies on Monday-Friday absences and short-term absences (number of half-day absence episodes per teacher in the school year). Among the policy variables included in the analysis were whether they had to forgo the entire daily salary once the sick-leave allowance was used, the percentage of teachers in the school covered by an income-protection plan, whether the teacher had to provide proof of illness to the administration, and whether the absent teacher had to report directly to the principal. Multiple-regression results indicated a nonsignificant relationship between forgoing salary and both short-term and Monday-Friday absences. Percentage of teachers covered by an income-protection plan was positively related to both absence measures.

Reporting absences to the principal was negatively related to both absence measures. Finally, providing proof of illness was unrelated to short-term absences and negatively related to Monday-Friday absences.

In a final study, Dalton and Perry (1981) examined organizational-policy correlates of employee absenteeism in a sample of urban transit organizations. The organizational policies were formalized in the collective bargaining agreement. Bus-driver absenteeism (the ratio of the total number of absence hours to total hours worked) was found to be positively correlated with peak wage, sick-benefits accumulation rate, and the policy of not remunerating employees for earned but unused sick leave. No relationship was found between absence rate and organizational size or requiring proof of illness. In explaining the results, the authors suggest that certain collective bargaining policies relating to sick-leave provision have the effect of making absenteeism easier or more profitable for the employee, hence leading to higher absence rates for the organization.

In summary, Baum's study suggests that attendance-control policies can be effective in reducing absenteeism among chronically absent workers. Moreover, features of organizational policies, such as the accumulation rate for sick-leave benefits, remuneration for unused sick leave, and absence-reporting requirements, can affect attendance behavior.

Mixed-consequence systems: The third approach to absence-control systems is really a hybrid of the first two methods, that is, a combination of incentives and punishment. Four such studies have been identified. In Kempen and Hall's (1977) study, significant decreases in absenteeism were reported for 7,500 production workers in two plants after introduction of a mixed-consequence system. Absenteeism did not decrease significantly during the study period in comparison groups of salaried employees at the two plants and hourly employees at eleven equivalent plants. The intervention provided nonmonetary privileges to reinforce good and improving attendance along with progressive disciplinary warnings for excessive and worsening absenteeism. The use of nonmonetary rather than monetary reinforcers was deemed appropriate because any monetary incentive had to counteract a liberal sickness- and disability-benefit plan allowing full pay with a wage incentive bonus for three to twelve months. The nonmonetary privileges for good attendance included freedom from the requirement of punching in on the clock, one or two days off without pay, and immunity from disciplinary action for one year regardless of absence record. There was a greater drop in absence rates at one plant than the other. The researchers attributed this to differences in the absence-control plan. Although in both plants the absence problem was one of duration rather than frequency, only in the case of the plant with the greater improvement in attendance was the plan based on duration.

In a second study, a point-system absenteeism-control policy was instituted (Kuzmits, 1981). Under this system, employees received one point for each absence occurrence regardless of duration and partial points for tardiness and part absences. In addition, employees who failed to report their absence by a designated time received two points per infraction. If an employee accumulated perfect attendance for one month, that employee was rewarded by removal of one point. Disciplinary action was taken on the basis of accumulated number of points within a twelve-month period. Data were gathered for one year prior to and one year following introduction of the system, and a before-and-after comparison of multiple absence measures was made. A significant reduction in mean levels of absence occurrences, tardiness, part absences, and no-calls was found, but there were no significant changes in absence days or in absence days per occurrence.

In a third study, Kopelman, Schneller, and Silver (1981) reported a substantial decline in absenteeism after the introduction of a new time-off-with-pay system, the "Leave Bank" in a medical center. The medical center initially offered its employees ten to twenty days of vacation time, depending on rank and tenure, seven holidays, and twelve days of sick leave per year. Over a two-year period, sick hours taken as a percentage of sick hours earned increased from 22 percent to 65 percent. Under the "Leave Bank," vacation days, paid holidays, and five days of sick leave were combined and called *paid leave*. The remaining seven sick-leave days were assigned to a sick-leave account. Hence, employees still received twelve days of sick leave per year. The paid-leave account could be converted into cash. The sick-leave account was intended primarily for long-term illness. It could be used only after the paid leave account was exhausted and only with medical certification. In essence, it was similar to a savings account. The effect of the new plan was that employees, in reducing casual absences, were "rewarded" by having a longer vacation or cash payments. On the other hand, absences of more than five days were at the expense of vacation days and holidays. After introduction of the leave-bank system, paid sick hours ranged between 12 percent and 22 percent of sick hours earned for a two-and-a-half year period, a significant reduction over the previous 65 percent rate.

A final mixed-consequence intervention is reported by Harvey, Rogers, and Schultze (1983). Under this program, employees in a nonprofit organization who incurred no absences for four weeks received a bonus of four hours' pay. Casual absence was discouraged by nonpayment of the first eight hours of absence. The plan provided protection against serious illness by paying in full any illness time beyond eight hours up to two months, at which time a disability plan came into effect. For the one-year period after the introduction of the program, there was a 45.5 percent decrease in total sick leave used and a 55 percent reduction in total sick leave paid over the previous year.

A negative element of the program was an increase in average duration of sick leave from 9.6 to 20 hours, perhaps due to the fact that the program encouraged employees to take more than one day off to minimize their loss of eight hours' pay. While the amount of bonus paid under the program totaled $38,374, the plan resulted in a savings of $1,203, after taking into consideration savings from increased productivity and savings in sick-leave usage. Finally, in a survey administered one year after the introduction of the well-pay plan, employees indicated a preference for the well-pay plan over the sick-leave-accrual system. However, the results might have been biased by the stipulation that the sick-leave-accrual system would start with no time accrued, while, under the well-pay system, the sick-leave protection plan provided for paid sick leave after the first eight hours.

In summary, available results suggest that organizational control systems aimed at reducing absenteeism can be especially powerful in controlling such behavior. This is particularly true either when the controls involve a positive-incentive framework or when potential punitive sanctions are combined with a positive approach.

*Absence Culture and Work-Group Norms.* Previous research has pointed to the importance of work-group norms as an influence on absenteeism (see, for example, Gibson, 1966, and Steers and Rhodes, 1978). Moreover, Lawler (1971), in his job-attractiveness model of employee motivation, pointed out that members of highly cohesive groups often view coming to work to help one's co-workers as highly desirable. More recently, Johns and Nicholson (1982) have expanded this notion to incorporate the broader concept of absence culture (see Chadwick-Jones, Nicholson, and Brown, 1982).

Johns and Nicholson argue that much previous research on absenteeism has been "method-driven" and is often at odds with experiential accounts of absence behavior. Moreover, most research on absenteeism focused on an individual level of analysis and ignored group phenomena. As the authors note (1982, p. 161): "More enlightening may be the identification of distinctions between identifiable aggregates. As such, an 'absence climate' or 'absence culture' might be conceived as the net interactive effect of the normative forces that exist in the various relevant portions of employees' role sets and common nonnormative influences."

It is further argued that one reason for the weak or contradictory results in the absence literature may be the fact that there are many work settings in which there is little variation in absenteeism among the employees. In fact, in a study of absenteeism in sixteen plants, Chadwick-Jones, Nicholson, and Brown (1982) found few consistent relationships between attitudes and absence. Instead, their findings suggested that the plants differed in their "Causal climates." That is, in many instances, the differences between plants were more enlightening than the differences within them.

Absence culture is suggested as a variable of central importance in understanding absence behavior. It can be defined as " the set of shared understandings about absence legitimacy . . . and the established 'custom and practice' of employee absence behavior and its control" (Johns and Nicholson, 1982, p. 136). Viewed in this way, two important implications for the study of absence behavior emerge. First, absence culture exerts an influence over absenteeism that can be observed both within and across employees. Second, absence culture has the power to activate or suppress other variables that can influence employee attendance. In fact, Johns and Nicholson argue, for example, that organizational control systems (discussed earlier) affect behavior only to the extent that they influence or affect prevailing culture. Hence, absence culture clearly represents an important aspect of understanding withdrawal from organizations and is a fruitful area for future research.

*Personal Factors.* Personal factors constitute a category of variables relating the characteristics of individuals to absence behavior. While numerous studies have been published, few consistent findings have emerged. In particular, absenteeism has been generally found to be positively related to family size (Muchinsky, 1977), health problems (Kreitner, Wood, and Friedman, 1978; Pocock, 1972; Buzzard and Shaw, 1952), poor previous attendance (Breaugh, 1981; Keller, 1983; Morgan and Herman, 1976; Winkler, 1980), and age, particularly for males (Rhodes, 1983). The presence of day-care facilities is inversely related to absenteeism (Milkovich and Gomez, 1976), and females as a group tend to have greater absence rates than males (Steers and Rhodes, 1978).

In addition, a further influence on attendance is the personal value system of individuals (Rokeach, 1973). Some research suggests that a strong personal work ethic is closely related to attendance (Feldman, 1974; Goodale, 1973; Ilgen and Hollenback, 1977). Presumably, those individuals who feel morally obligated to work follow through in the form of actual attendance.

Finally, an interesting area of concern with respect to personal factors is the topic of the personal value of nonwork activities. Johns and Nicholson (1982) discuss this subject at length, suggesting that some absence may be attributable to the value individuals place on their "outside activities." For instance, Morgan and Herman (1976) found that absence was related to anticipated achievement of off-the-job social outcomes and leisure time. On the basis of such findings, Johns and Nicholson (1982, p. 151) argue that "attendance patterns may reflect an attempt to balance the quantity and quality of time spent in various endeavors."

Similarly, Youngblood (1984) proposed a model incorporating approach-avoidance conflicts associated with work and nonwork domains as they relate to withdrawal. It was found in the study that the value of leisure time was consistently related to absence hours, while work attachment was related to frequency of absence. Youngblood concluded (p. 106) that "the results generally supported the view that absenteeism is a function of motivation processes extant in work and nonwork domains." Hence, as we examine absence behavior, the role of the individual cannot be ignored.

*Perceived Ability to Attend.* The sixth and final variable, perceived ability to attend, represents a recognition that, in many cases, attendance motivation is simply insufficient to ensure actual attendance (Steers and Rhodes, 1978). There are many reasons — both real and perceived — why individuals may simply not be able to come to work.

This area of attendance research remains an area deserving further study; little has, in fact, been done on the topic. In the Steers and Rhodes (1978) review, it was suggested that at least three major factors are salient in this regard. First, clearly a major impediment to attendance is illness and accidents. In many cases, people may simply be physically unable to attend. Second, family responsibilities can impede attendance. For example, at least some absenteeism among women is traceable to illness among their children. As family size grows, we would expect this influence to increase. Moreover, as changing sex roles evolve, this reason may increase as an explanation for male absenteeism as well. Finally, a variety of transportation problems that influence ability to attend can be identified (car breakdowns, rapid-transit strikes, and so on). Hence, following the work of Herman (1973) and Smith (1977), we would expect real or perceived barriers to attendance to influence the relationship between intent to attend and actual attendance.

*Recent Multivariate Studies.* Some recent studies have examined the relative influence of different classes of variables (personal, organizational, attitudinal, work experience) on absenteeism (Breaugh, 1981; Fitzgibbons and Moch, 1980; Johns, 1978; Keller, 1983; Popp and Belohlav, 1982; Rhodes, 1978; Rhodes and Steers, 1981; Spencer and Steers, 1980). The results of these studies are summarized in Table 6.2 Included here are recent multivariate studies that do not purport to test the Steers and Rhodes (1978) model.

**Table 6.2. Summary of Recent Multivariate Studies of Absenteeism.**

| Study | Sample | Method | Results |
|---|---|---|---|
| Johns (1978) | 208 operatives in paper-products plant | Hierarchical regression | *Examined unique contribution of work attitudes over and above person, job, and leadership variables in explaining frequency of absence.* |
| | | | Overall job satisfaction and satisfaction with supervisor did not account for significant variance in absence over and above that explained by personal (sex, age), job (job identity, feedback), and leadership (leader consideration) characteristics. |
| Fitzgibbons and Moch (1980) | 264 production-department employees | | *Examined relative influence of organizational factors, individual context factors, social factors, and intrinsic satisfaction on excused, sickness, and unexcused absence (all frequency measures).* |
| | | Simple regression | For excused and sickness absence, intrinsic satisfaction, social factors (sex, dependents, primary wage earner), and organizational factors (tenure, shift) considered alone were significant predictors. |
| | | | For unexcused absences, organizational factors and individual-context factors (role support, role overload, probability of turnover, probability of layoff) considered alone were significant predictors. |
| | | Hierarchical regression | For excused and sickness absences, organizational factors and social factors made a unique contribution to explained variance. For unexcused absence, organizational factors made a unique contribution to explained variance. |

| Study | Sample | Method | Findings |
|---|---|---|---|
| Spencer and Steers (1980) | 200 hospital clerical and service workers | Multiple regression | *Examined relative influence of personal characteristics and work experiences as predictors of total days absent.*<br><br>Total number of days absent was better predicted by personal factors (organization and job tenure, sex, age, education [n.s.]) than by work experiences (group attitudes, met expectations, job challenge [$r_p = -0.15*$], personal importance, organizational dependability). |
| | | Hierarchical regression | Personal characteristics contributed significantly to explanation of total number of days absent over and above work-experience variables. |
| Rhodes and Steers (1981); Rhodes (1978) | 67 plywood-production worker-owners in producer cooperative | Analysis of co-variance | *Examined relative influence of personal characteristics and organizational commitment as predictors of frequency of absence.*<br><br>After controlling for the effects of marital status, age, and rural-urban background, organizational commitment accounted for a nonsignificant proportion of the variance in absence frequency, while personal characteristics accounted for a significant proportion. |
| Breaugh (1981) | 112 research scientists | Hierarchical regression | *Examined relative influence of past absenteeism and work attitudes as predictors of frequency and total days of absence.*<br><br>Work attitudes (overall job satisfaction, satisfaction with supervision, job involvement) taken together did not contribute significantly to explaining frequency and total days of absence over and above past absenteeism. Past absenteeism contributed significant variance when added after the work attitudes. |

**Table 6.2. Summary of Recent Multivariate Studies of Absenteeism, Cont'd.**

| Study | Sample | Method | Results |
|-------|--------|--------|---------|
| Popp and Belohlav (1982) | 174 manufacturing-plant employees (95 percent black) | Stepwise multiple regression | *Examined work attitudes, work-related information, and personal-history characteristics as predictors of total days lost, frequency, one-day, and severity of absence and an attitudinal absence ratio.*<br><br>1. Work-attitude indicators (overall satisfaction; satisfaction with amount of work, pay, supervision, working conditions, co-workers, and equipment; appreciation by community residents; expectations to stay with organization toward retirement) did not make significant contribution to prediction of absenteeism (total days lost, frequency, one-day, severity, and attitudinal absence ratio).<br><br>2. Significant predictors included tenure, previous military service, supervisory attitude toward absence, marital status, and amount of work. Job satisfaction was a significant predictor of absence frequency only.<br><br>3. Other nonsignificant variables included having a second job, distance to work, and number of children at home. |

Keller (1983)

174 supervisory, professional, clerical, and hourly employees in manufacturing plant.

*Examined prior absenteeism, job attitudes, demographic variables, and personality variables as predictors of absence frequency.*

Multiple regression

Tenure, marital status (married), group cohesiveness, self-esteem, and an internal locus of control were negatively related to absence frequency. Job satisfaction, job level, and age did not predict absenteeism.

Hierarchical regression

Prior absenteeism, group cohesiveness, and an interval health locus of control accounted for unique variance in absence frequency.

It should be pointed out that comparative analysis of these studies is somewhat problematical for several reasons. First, researchers are not consistent in naming the classes of variables. For example, *personal characteristics* (Johns, 1978), *demographic variables* (Keller, 1983), and *social factors* (Fitzgibbons and Moch, 1980) are terms that appear to be applied to similar variables. Second, and perhaps more severe, certain variables are categorized in distinctly different groupings from study to study. For example, Spencer and Steers (1980) and Keller (1983) treated tenure as a personal/demographic characteristic, while Fitzgibbons and Moch (1980) considered tenure to be an organizational factor. Finally, even when researchers use similar names for categories, they may use different sets of variables as representative of those categories. For example, Johns included sex and age as personal characteristics; Spencer and Steers included organization and job tenure, sex, age, and education; and Rhodes and Steers incorporated marital status, age, and rural-urban background.

It is with a certain amount of caution that we make the following generalizations based on these studies. First, prior absenteeism contributed significantly to the explanation of absenteeism when added after work attitudes (Breaugh, 1981; Keller, 1983) and demographic and personality variables (Keller, 1983). Second, personal/demographic variables were generally found to be important predictors of frequency of absence (Fitzgibbons and Moch, 1980; Johns, 1978; Rhodes, 1978; Rhodes and Steers, 1981) and total days lost (Spencer and Steers, 1980). Third, organizational (Fitzgibbons and Moch, 1980), individual-context (Fitzgibbons and Moch, 1980), leadership (Johns, 1978), and job (Johns, 1978) factors were found to be important sets of variables. Finally, and perhaps most important, when considered along with other variables, work attitudes generally were not found to be significant predictors of absenteeism. Attitudes in these studies were overall job satisfaction (Breaugh, 1981; Johns, 1978; Keller, 1983), job involvement (Breaugh, 1981), organizational commitment (Rhodes and Steers, 1981), satisfaction with supervision (Breaugh, 1981; Johns, 1978; Popp and Belohlav, 1982), and satisfaction with pay, working conditions, co-workers, and equipment (Popp and Belohlav, 1982). In Popp and Belohlav's study, overall satisfaction was a significant predictor of frequency of absence but accounted for the smallest amount of variance among the significant variables.

In conclusion, these studies suggest that there are multiple determinants of absenteeism. Moreover, there appears to be little consistency of results across studies in terms of specific variables. This inconsistency may in part be accounted for by uncontrolled statistical artifacts (Terborg and others, 1982) or, alternatively, by situational specificity. While attitudes do not perform well in general when compared with other variables, it would be too early to discard them, especially in view of McShane's (1983) meta-analysis, Terborg and others' (1982) validity-generalization findings, and the potentially promising bivariate results for job involvement (Cheloha and Farr, 1980).

## Implications for Model Development

Clearly, we have learned a great deal about absenteeism in the past several years. In fact, on the basis of these new studies, we can ask what implications have emerged for modifications or extensions of the original Steers and Rhodes (1978) model. This question can be answered in two ways. First, what studies exist that attempt to test the model itself? Second, on the basis of current literature, how may we wish to change the model? Let us first consider partial tests of the model.

*Partial Tests of the Model.* As noted by Fichman in Chapter One of this volume, the Steers and Rhodes model is difficult if not impossible to test in its entirety. It attempts to represent how a fairly large number of variables interact over time to influence a particular behavior. The same limitation of testability applies to models proposed by Nicholson (1977) and Fichman (Chapter One). However, a number of attempts have been made to examine empirically various aspects of the model.

The first, by Hammer, Landau, and Stern (1981), measured several of the variables noted in the Steers and Rhodes model (including job satisfaction, organizational commitment, job involvement, financial incentives, and demographic variables) and compared their power to predict employee absenteeism among 112 worker-owners in a small furniture cooperative. The results showed that attitudinal variables predicted *voluntary* absenteeism better than did individual or job characteristics. However, contrary to earlier findings in the literature, Hammer, Landau, and Stern found satisfaction and voluntary absenteeism to be *positively* related. In other words, the more satisfied the employee, the more likely he or she was not to come to work.

It was hypothesized on the basis of these findings that the less satisfied employees (who were simultaneously more committed to the company) felt compelled to come to work and try to improve the situation. Hence, commitment to the organization emerged as a more potent attitude in attendance than job satisfaction. Such findings suggest that job attitudes and various pressures to attend are, in fact, more important influences on attendance motivation than either job characteristics or individual differences. What remains to be explained in the study is the contraindicative job satisfaction–absenteeism relationship.

The second study that attempted to provide for a partial test of the model was carried out by Terborg and others (1980). This study was carried out among a sample of 259 retail employees. Several findings that emerged from this study are germane to the model. First, variables thought to index employee ability to attend were not found to be related to unpaid absenteeism. The absence of such a predicted relationship was explained in part by a restriction-of range problem with some of the study variables (for example, family size and distance from work) and in part by the fact that ability to attend was not assessed directly. Only surrogate measures were used. Even so, whatever the reason, Terborg and others failed to find support for the role of ability to attend in actual attendance.

On the other hand, variables used to index pressures to attend were found to influence attendance, although the magnitudes of the relationships were modest. Organizational commitment, for example was significantly and inversely related to absenteeism. Moreover, tenure with the organization (classified in this study as a pressure to attend) was also found to be inversely related to absenteeism. Overall, Terborg and others (1980) concluded that "the results for variables used to index pressure to attend were consistent with past research" (p. 15). In addition, the results with respect to job satisfaction were consistent with that segment of the Steers and Rhodes model. Satisfaction with work was negatively related to absenteeism.

Finally, Terborg and others found that different retail stores experienced different levels of absenteeism and were characterized by different mean demographic characteristics among their employees. Because of this, an argument is made against ignoring situational differences in studying employee behaviors. In considering the effects of situational factors, Terborg and others (1980) concluded: "We concur with Muchinsky (1977) and Steers and Rhodes (1978) in their request for more broadly based designs that include a variety of situational variables in the study of absenteeism. Our results convince us of the potential effects of situational factors. Situational factors might moderate the relationship between attitudes and behavior through affecting a person's ability to engage in the behavior. Or, situational factors may affect absenteeism directly... the consequences of being absent in this organization probably were more negative compared to consequences in other organizations. Yet, our review of the literature on absenteeism shows that only in a few limited cases have researchers either considered personnel practices as a factor or mentioned it in the discussion of their results" (p. 18). In conclusion, the Terborg and others study found some support for the various parts of the model, with the exception of the effect of ability to attend on actual attendance.

The third study was carried out by Watson (1981), who studied 116 production workers using a time-lost index. The general hypothesis of this study was that absenteeism was a joint function of personal characteristics, the job situation, and job satisfaction. It was not expected that this relationship would be overly strong, however. Indeed, the Steers and Rhodes model points to a number of other mitigating factors (for example, pressures to attend, ability to attend) that would lead one not to expect a strong relationship. No attempt was made to test the entire model. Although significant findings emerged in the multiple-regression results, the strengths of the relationships were not particularly strong. Moreover, satisfaction was found to be unrelated to time-lost absence for this sample. Since no variables measured pressures to attend or ability to attend (except for number of children), it is not possible to speculate about the extent to which these additional model-based variables would combine with the existing study variables to predict attendance levels.

A final study focused on eighty-one manufacturing employees and was carried out by Frechette (1981). Five personal characteristics (age, sex, marital status, family size, and educational level) were measured, as well as job satisfaction and job expectations. Ability to attend was estimated from company records concerning the reasons for employee absences (for example, illness, accidents, family responsibilities, transportation problems). Salary was the only pressure-to-attend variable used in the analysis. Multiple measures of absenteeism were taken. The results of this study showed a significant relationship between the predictor variables and a frequency-of absence measure ($R^2 = 0.25$, $p < 0.02$). The personal characteristics and the pressure-to-attend variable accounted for more of the variance here than did the satisfaction measures. In addition, it was found that the absence model being tested was able to predict absence frequency better than time-lost absence and was able to predict both voluntary and involuntary absence. In conclusion, Frechette concluded that "the model was able to predict absenteeism quite well" (p. 9).

Overall, then, these initial studies using correlational designs provide some support for the utility of the model. In fact, while support for the model is not universal, far more supportive findings have emerged than for any other absence model.

*Extensions of the Model.* In science, models are meant to be evolutionary, not static. Our proposed model of absenteeism is no exception. On the basis of recent research, it is logical to ask what modifications might be suggested to improve the overall utility of the model. Several suggestions emerge.

To begin with, a good deal has been written recently about the role of work-group norms and absence culture on attendance (see, for example, Johns and Nicholson, 1982). This is largely a conceptual argument in the absence of much empirical support. Even so, there is clearly a need to make recognition of the social context more explicit in absence research. While the original Steers and Rhodes model does, in fact, recognize work norms as a pressure to attend (see box 5 in Figure 6.3), we could have highlighted its presence more than we did. It is not true, however, as Chadwick-

Jones, Nicholson, and Brown (1982) have suggested, that current absence models such as our own are focused wholly on the individual decision maker without attention to the social context within which the person behaves. The issue concerns the *relative* importance of the group as a force in attendance, not its presence or absence.

Second, recent research suggests that, among job attitudes, job involvement may be a better predictor of absence than job satisfaction (see, for example, Cheloha and Farr, 1980). In view of this, and in view of the empirical overlap between these two variables, it may be more useful to talk in terms of work attitudes as they influence behavior instead of one particular attitude.

Third, the original model talked about ability to attend as a factor in actual attendance but failed to make explicit the fact that perceived ability may be more important than actual ability. That is, a snowstorm or a bad cold may or may not limit one's ability to come to work (see Smith, 1977). What is important is how the individual treats the event and how he or she interprets its impact on ability to attend.

Fourth, it has been suggested by some (see, for example, Rosse and Miller in Chapter Five of this volume) that we should be studying withdrawal processes rather than absenteeism. The argument is advanced that absenteeism, lateness, turnover, and so on all share similar roots and all affect behavior in similar ways. We disagree with this argument on several grounds (see also Clegg, 1983). For example, while Rosse and Miller assert that absence and other forms of withdrawal "share common roots" and "reliably co-vary," they are talking specifically about the relationship between withdrawal variables and attitudes. This approach ignores the multitudes of other variables in the equation that clearly have differential impacts on the various withdrawal categories. For example, illness has been shown to influence absenteeism far more than turnover. An absence-control policy may have little influence on turnover. In fact, several writers (for example, Mobley, 1982) have identified a number of reasons why an absence-turnover correlation should not be expected to be high. In view of the uniqueness of absenteeism as opposed to turnover as a category of behavior, it does not appear wise to us to attempt to model them with the same framework. This is not to say that the two forms of withdrawal are unrelated. Rather, it suggests that if we are to learn more about both behaviors, each may better be served by focusing attention on it as a category of behavior.

Finally, if we had it to do over again, we would probably have attempted to seek ways to make our points such that misunderstandings of the model would have been minimized. For example, Chadwick-Jones, Nicholson, and Brown (1982) reviewed our model and concluded that it failed to recognize the role of groups; it did not (see box in Figure 6.3). Fichman reviewed the model and concluded that it failed to recognize important economic variables; it did not (see box 5). Watson (1981) reviewed our model and concluded that it hypothesized that job satisfaction was the primary predictor of attendance; it did not (see boxes 4, 5, 6, 7, and 8). Our concern here, quite frankly, focuses on the degree of objectivity of the readers. (Note, for example, that Fichman in Chapter One in this volume claims that Clegg, 1983, "found little evidence for the Steers and Rhodes model." In fact, Clegg never claimed to test the model, and Clegg himself (p. 97) notes that his primary finding concerning reverse causation supports the feedback loops proposed by Steers and Rhodes.) If some have failed to understand our model as originally proposed, is it due to careless writing, careless reading, or motivated behavior? In order to attempt to overcome such problems and to recognize more recent research, we have depicted in Figure 6.4 a revised, simplified model that attempts to highlight what we believe to be the major clusters of variables that can affect attendance. It is meant to be an organizing framework for summarizing empirical findings such that future "misinterpretations" don't occur. It is hoped that it will assist interested readers in better understanding attendance behavior at work.

### Implications for Management

We have attempted above to summarize what we know and what we think we know about the causes of absenteeism. On this basis, questions are logically raised concerning implications for management. We will limit these implications to those that follow from the model we have proposed. Other contributors to this volume will discuss implications resulting from their own work.

Figure 6.4. An Organizing Framework for Understanding Absence Research.

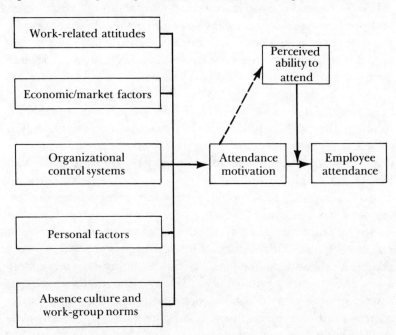

According to the findings reviewed above, several specific methods for reducing absenteeism can be suggested. The first suggestion deals with the approach that managers take to analyzing the problem. Specifically, instead of using "rules of thumb," managers can learn more about the causes of absenteeism in their own organization if they take a *systematic approach* to the problem. For example, one can use the model outlined in Figures 6.3 and 6.4 as a diagnostic tool and work through the process, asking at each juncture whether this aspect of the model may be causing the problem. What is the nature of the job situation? Are employees generally satisfied or involved in their work? What about the various pressures to attend? Do employees really have an ability to attend? Answers to questions such as these can help managers to pinpoint where the problems are, as well as where they are not.

If such a diagnosis indicates a problem with the *work-attitudes* component of the model, efforts can be made to improve such attitudes. Several techniques may be employed here, including enriching employees' jobs, reducing job-related stress, building group cohesiveness and co-worker relations, clarifying job expectations, and providing career counseling for employees. These techniques focus on the job situation and, if successful, should increase the likelihood that job expectations are met and positive attitudes develop over time.

If the diagnosis indicates that the major problem lies in the area of *pressures to attend,* again several techniques are available for use by managers. These include clarifying rewards for good attendance, reviewing sick-leave policies, encouraging an attendance-oriented work-group norm, fostering a personal work ethic, and facilitating employee commitment to organizations through an equitable exchange relationship. One of the more successful strategies here lies in the use of incentives for good attendance. For instance, in one experiment using operant conditioning, a sample of nurses were made eligible for cash-prize drawings of $20 if they had no absenteeism for a three-week period. As a result of this simple attendance-reward contingency, absenteeism declined significantly. In another study, it was shown that allowing employees to participate in the development of a bonus plan for perfect attendance also reduced absenteeism compared to a control group.

Should the diagnosis reveal that the major problem of absenteeism lies with employees' *ability to attend,* several additional strategies may be useful. For instance, organizations can encourage sound physical health (perhaps through company-sponsored exercise programs, physical examinations, and so on), institute employee counseling programs to foster sound mental health, be sensitive to problems of alcoholism and drug abuse and provide relevant programs where necessary, consider company-sponsored day-care facilities for employees with young children, and consider using shuttle buses for clusters of employees living in outlying areas. All of these techniques have been used successfully by organizations concerned about ensuring employees' physical health and ability to come to work in a timely fashion.

The point here is simple. By taking a diagnostic approach to solving problems of absenteeism, managers can focus their solutions and their limited resources on the major causes of the problem, instead of applying more general solutions that may not get at the heart of the problem. In this way, greater progress should be made toward reducing avoidable absenteeism and facilitating a work force that is more committed to the goals of the organization and more satisfied with the general work environment.

## Conclusion and Research Implications

It should be clear from this review of the literature on employee absenteeism that we know far less about absenteeism than we would like to. We know that it can represent a serious problem for organizaitons, but we know little about what to do about it. Moreover, the research that does exist is often flawed to the point where the utility, if not the validity, of the results is questionable. In view of this, it is logical to ask what we should do next. That is, what might guide absence research in the future in order to lead to more productive and useful results? Toward this end, we suggest the following:

Additional effort must be focused on the operationalization and conceptualization of absenteeism measures. For example, there is some disagreement concerning the relative preference for measures of absenteeism or measures of attendance. Latham and Pursell (1975, 1977) argue that measuring employee attendance (instead of absenteeism) leads to more stable measures over time and that the concept of attendance behavior is more appealing theoretically. Both of these assertions have been questioned by Ilgen (1977), however. In addition, as noted by Nicholson and Goodge (1976), various measures of absenteeism (such as total days lost, number of instances of absence, medically sanctioned absences) do not co-vary. Available data suggest that a frequency measure is preferable to time-lost measures or other indicators (Hammer and Landau, 1981). In any case, serious problems of interpretation emerge in attempts to compare results across various absenteeism studies. This problem is compounded by the reluctance of some investigators to specify clearly how absenteeism was measured in their own studies. Certainly, additional effort is needed to ensure that future research employs comparable (or at least multiple) measures of absenteeism so that greater integration of the various findings is possible. Finally, it would also be highly desirable if future studies reported the absence-control policies and sanctions that exist in the organization under study (for example, sick-leave policy, medical certification of absences). Such controls may have an important influence on study results that is often overlooked.

The reported test-retest reliabilities of various absence measures have typically been unduly low. Chadwick-Jones and others (1971), for example, report reliabilities ranging from 0.00 to 0.43 for various measures of absenteeism. Muchinsky (1977) reports reliabilities ranging from 0.00 to 0.74, with a median of 0.38. At least two interpretations of these data exist. On the one hand, it can be aruged that such low reliabilities clearly raise doubts as to the utility of the reported findings. On the other hand, it can also be aruged that attendance behavior over time is simply not a reliable phenomenon. Indeed, the model proposed here suggests several reasons why such behavior should *not* be stable over time. Although low test-retest reliabilities of absence measures increase the difficulty of dealing with such behavior, from both an empirical and a managerial standpoint, such instability may in fact reflect a reality that must be dealt with in future studies on employee absenteeism.

One characteristic attribute of absenteeism studies has been their focus on blue-collar and clerical employees. Managerial personnel have largely been ignored, either because of a lack of data or because absenteeism data that are available suggest that little problem exists with managers. However, in view of the increased autonomy that managers have, which makes short absences from work relatively easy, it may be useful to re-examine de facto absenteeism among such employees. This re-examination really suggests the need to consider the productivity of such employees. When an assembly-line worker is absent (or is present but not actually working), it is quite noticeable. However, when a manager is "in conference" or "working privately," questions must be raised concerning the extent to which he or she is really present on the job, psychologically as well as physically. Lenz (cited in Yolles, Carone, and Krinsky, 1975) argues that one of the prerogatives of managers is the right to be absent. "It is the right to sit around the office and talk, the right to take a slightly longer lunch 'hour' than anyone else, the right to run personal errands during the day while blue-collar workers must wait until Saturday" (p. 17). In short, it would be helpful to learn more about the active-participation levels of managers (and other employees), perhaps employing somewhat different measures of absenteeism. Such efforts may eventually lead to a call for a redefinition of absenteeism to reflect productivity on the job rather than mere presence.

Relatedly, of paramount importance in future research is the issue of frame of reference. Most previous research has assumed (either intentionally or unintentionally) a managerial bias. That is, the basic issue under study has been how to *control* absenteeism. An interesting quote from Johns and Nicholson (1982, p. 128) highlights the issue: "*I* am sometimes prevented from attending work through no fault of my own. *You* lack motivation to attend regularly. *They* are lazy malingerers, willfully milking the system." If we are to make progress in better understanding absence behavior, two things must follow. First, we must be clear (with both ourselves and others) about *whose* perspective we are taking. And, second, we should make every effort to adopt multiple perspectives in such analyses. It is easy for managers to discuss over coffee the absence patterns of shop-floor workers. Perhaps such managers (or even researchers) could learn more about the subject if they experienced the "problem" work environments firsthand and attempted to understand the varying perspectives on attachment to work. Until this is done, we will probably continue to see a proliferation of research and an absence of learning.

In addition, there is a prevailing assumption throughout much of the literature on absenteeism that all absenteeism is detrimental to organizational well-being. It is possible, however, that some absenteeism may in fact be healthy for organizations in that such behavior can allow for temporary escape from stressful situations (perhaps through the provision of personal days off), thereby potentially contributing to the mental health of employees (see, for example, Ivancevich and Matteson, 1980). In fact, rigid efforts to ensure perfect attendance (such as through behavior modification) may lead to unintended and detrimental consequences on the job, such as reduced product quality, increased accidents, and so forth. Hence, it would be helpful if future studies could examine the extent to which changes in absence rates have adverse consequences for other aspects of organizational effectiveness. If reduced absenteeism is accomplished at the expense of product quality, accident rate, strike activity, or employee mental health, serious cost-benefit questions must be raised concerning the desirability of initiating efforts aimed at reducing such behavior on the job.

Are there other variables that influence absenteeism but have yet to be studied systematically? One possible example is the problem of multiple commitments and possible conflicts among such commitments (Hall, 1976). That is, what effect does a strong commitment to one's family or a hobby (instead of to the organization) have on attendance motivation? Similarly, what effect does psychosomatic illness, possibly brought on by role pressures, have on actual attendance? Work by Staw and Oldham (1978) has touched on this subject. However, more detailed investigation is necessary. Additional work is also in order concerning the sustained impact of behavior modification on employee attendance. The influence of habitual behavior as it relates to attendance should also be examined. Finally, considerably more could be learned about the manner in which extraorganizational factors (for example, family responsibilities, pressures, and norms; friendship groups) influence the attendance decision (see Smulders, 1980).

As noted above, several conceptual models have been suggested, both in this volume and elsewhere, that rely primarily on an integration of somewhat fragmentary research findings. Very few comprehensive multivariate studies of absenteeism are to be found, although this trend may be changing (see, for example, Hammer, Landau, and Stern, 1981; Spencer and Steers, 1980). Moreover, very few studies have attempted to explore causal sequences among model variables. Clearly, there exists a need to test such models using longitudinal and multivariate methods if we are to make progress in the area.

Unlike other areas of intellectual concern, it is not necessary here to argue for additional experimental (as opposed to correlational) studies. In point of fact, there have been a number of experimental studies of absenteeism, particularly as it relates to job redesign (Steers and Rhodes, 1978) and positive reinforcement (Schmitz and Heneman, 1980). However, many of these studies used multiple interventions simultaneously (Glaser, 1976; Schmitz and Heneman, 1980), thus contaminating treatment effects. Moreover, the majority of experimental studies reviewed here failed to use matched control groups, and many failed to report the nature of the absence measures employed. Future experimental studies must therefore provide for a more rigorous test of the hypotheses by employing more stringent (and controlled) experimental designs, while clearly identifying and isolating the treatments. Confounding of variables remains a needless hallmark of studies of employee absenteeism. Moreover, in view of the inconsistency (and possible instability) of most measures of absenteeism, it would be highly desirable to cross-validate results. Evidence by Garrison and Muchinsky (1977) and Waters and Roach (1973) amply demonstrates the possible misinterpretation of results that can easily occur in the absence of cross-validation or replication of results.

With new and more systematic information such as that provided by the suggestions offered here, we hope to be able to move the field of absence research in a positive direction. If this is done, we can facilitate the development of work environments that are more conducive to both increased productivity and work attitudes and that develop attachments to work that are meaningful for all parties involved.

## References

Angle, H. L., and Perry, J. L. "An Empirical Assessment of Organizational Commitment and Organizational Effectiveness." *Administrative Science Quarterly*, 1981, *26*, 1–14.

Baum, J. F. "Effectiveness of an Attendance Control Policy in Reducing Chronic Absenteeism." *Personnel Psychology*, 1978, *31*, 71–81.

Baum, J. F., and Menefee, M. L. "An Experimental Study of Operant Conditioning and Absenteeism." Paper presented at 39th annual meeting of the Academy of Management, Atlanta, Ga., 1979.

Beehr, T. A., and Gupta, N. "A Note on the Structure of Employee Withdrawal." *Organizational Behavior and Human Performance*, 1978, *21*, 73–79.

Behrend, H. *Absence Under Full Employment.* University of Birmingham Studies in Economics and Society, No. A3. University of Birmingham, England, 1951.

Behrend, H. "Absence and Labour Turnover in a Changing Economic Climate." *Occupational Psychology,* 1953, *27,* 69–79.

Blumberg, M. "Job Switching in Autonomous Work Groups: An Exploratory Study in a Pennsylvania Coal Mine." *Academy of Management Journal,* 1980, *23,* 287–306.

Breaugh, J. A. "Predicting Absenteeism from Prior Absenteeism and Work Attitudes." *Journal of Applied Psychology,* 1981, *66* (5), 555–560.

Buzzard, R. B., and Shaw, W. J. "An Analysis of Absence Under a Scheme of Paid Sick Leave." *British Journal of Industrial Medicine,* 1952, *9,* 282–295.

Carlson, J. G., and Hill, K. D. "The Effect of Gaming on Attendance and Attitude." *Personnel Psychology,* 1982, *35,* 63–73.

Chadwick-Jones, J. K., Nicholson, N., and Brown, C. *Social Psychology of Absenteeism.* New York: Praeger, 1982.

Chadwick-Jones, J. K., and others. "Absence Measures: Their Reliability and Stability in an Industrial Setting." *Personnel Psychology,* 1971, *24,* 463–470.

Cheloha, R. S., and Farr, J. L. "Absenteeism, Job Involvement, and Job Satisfaction in an Organizational Setting." *Journal of Applied Psychology,* 1980, *65* (4), 467–473.

Childe, L. "Doctors Arrested in Swoop on Work-Shy Italian Bureaucrats." *London Daily Telegraph,* Feb. 27, 1982, p. 5.

Clegg, C. W. "Psychology of Employee Lateness, Absence, and Turnover: A Methodological Critique and an Empirical Study." *Journal of Applied Psychology,* 1983, *68* (1), 88–101.

Crowther, J. "Absence and Turnover in the Divisions of One Company—1950–55." *Occupational Psychology,* 1957, *31,* 256–270.

Dalton, D. R., and Perry, J. L. "Absenteeism and the Collective Bargaining Agreement: An Empirical Test." *Academy of Management Journal,* 1981, *24* (2), 425–431.

Dijkstra, A. "Reduction of the Employee Population of Business Firms and Sickness Absenteeism: A Longitudinal Secondary Analysis." *Sociologica Nierlandica,* 1975, *11* (2), 116–127.

Feldman, J. "Race, Economic Class, and the Intention to Work: Some Normative and Attitudinal Correlates." *Journal of Applied Psychology,* 1974, *59,* 179–186.

Fitzgibbons, D., and Moch, M. K. "Employee Absenteeism: A

Multivariate Analysis with Replication." *Organizational Behavior and Human Performance,* 1980, *26,* 349–372.

Frechette, H. M. "An Investigation of the Utility of Steers and Rhodes' Process Model of Attendance Behavior." Paper presented at 41st annual meeting of the Academy of Management, San Diego, Calif., Aug. 1981.

Gandz, J., and Mikalachki, A. "Measuring Absenteeism." Unpublished working paper, University of Western Ontario, 1979.

Garrison, K. R., and Muchinsky, P. M. "Evaluating the Concept of Absenteeism-Proneness with Two Measures of Absence." *Personnel Psychology,* 1977, *30,* 384–393.

Gibson, R. O. "Toward a Reconceptualization of Absence Behavior of Personnel in Organizations." *Administrative Science Quarterly,* 1966, *11,* 107–133.

Glaser, E. M. *Productivity Gains Through Worklife Improvement.* New York: Psychological Corporation, 1976.

Goodale, J. G. "Effects of Personal Background and Training on Work Values of the Hard-Core Unemployed." *Journal of Applied Psychology,* 1973, *57,* 1–9.

Grove, B. A. "Attendance Reward Plan Pays." *Personnel Journal,* 1968, *47,* 119–120.

Hackman, J. R., and Lawler, E. E. "Employee Reactions to Job Characteristics." *Journal of Applied Psychology,* 1971, *55,* 259–286.

Hall, D. T. *Careers in Organizations.* Santa Monica, Calif.: Goodyear, 1976.

Hammer, T. H., and Landau, J. "Methodological Issues in the Use of Absence Data." *Journal of Applied Psychology,* 1981, *66* (5), 574–581.

Hammer, T. H., Landau, J. C., and Stern, R. N. "Absenteeism When Workers Have a Voice: The Case of Employee Ownership." *Journal of Applied Psychology,* 1981, *66* (5), 561–573.

Harvey, B. H., Rogers, J., and Schultze, J. A. "Sick Pay Versus Well Pay: An Analysis of the Impact of Rewarding Employees for Being on the Job." *Public Personnel Management Journal,* 1983, *12,* 218–224.

Herman, J. B. "Are Situational Contingencies Limiting Job Attitude-Job Performance Relationships?" *Organizational Behavior and Human Performance,* 1973, *10,* 208–224.

Hershey, R. "Effects of Anticipated Job Loss on Employee Behavior." *Journal of Applied Psychology,* 1972, *56,* 273–274.

Ilgen, D. R. "Attendance Behavior: A Reevaluation of Latham and Pursell's Conclusions." *Journal of Applied Psychology,* 1977, *62,* 230–233.

Ilgen, D. R., and Hollenback, J. H. "The Role of Job Satisfaction in Absence Behavior." *Organizational Behavior and Human Performance,* 1977, *19,* 148–161.

Ivancevich, J. M., and Matteson, M. T. *Stress at Work.* Glenview, Ill.: Scott, Foresman, 1980.

Jamal, M. "Shift Work Related to Job Attitudes, Social Participation and Withdrawal Behavior: A Study of Nurses and Industrial Workers." *Personnel Psychology,* 1981, *34,* 535–547.

Johns, G. "Attitudinal and Nonattitudinal Predictors of Two Forms of Absence from Work." *Organizational Behavior and Human Performance,* 1978, *22,* 431–444.

Johns, G., and Nicholson, N. "The Meanings of Absence: New Strategies for Theory and Research." In B. M. Staw and L. L. Cummings (Eds.), *Research in Organizational Behavior.* Vol. 4. Greenwich, Conn.: JAI Press, 1982.

Johnson, R. D., and Wallin, J. A. "Employee Attendance: An Operant Conditioning Intervention in a Field Setting." Paper presented at 84th annual meeting of American Pyschological Association, Washington, D.C., Sept. 1976.

Keller, R. T. "Predicting Absenteeism from Prior Absenteeism, Attitudinal Factors and Nonattitudinal Factors." *Journal of Applied Psychology,* 1983, *68,* 536–540.

Kempen, R. W., and Hall, R. V. "Reduction of Industrial Absenteeism: Results of a Behavioral Approach." *Journal of Organizational Behavior Management,* 1977, *1,* 1–21.

Kent, H. M., Malott, R. W., and Greening, M. "Improving Attendance at Work in a Volunteer Food Cooperative with a Token Economy." *Journal of Organizational Behavior Management,* 1977, *1,* 89–98.

Kopelman, R. E., Schneller, G. O. IV, and Silver, J. J., Jr. "Parkinson's Law and Absenteeism: A Program to Rein in Sick Leave Costs." *Personnel Administrator,* 1981, *26* (5), 57–64.

Kreitner, R., Wood, S. D., and Friedman, G. M. "Productivity and Absenteeism Relative to Coronary Risk." *Arizona Business,* 1978, *25* (5), 11-14.

Kuzmits, F. E. "The Impact of a Legalistic Control Policy on Selected Measures of Absenteeism Behavior." In R. H. Kilmann and M. Jelinek, *The Eastern Academy of Management Proceedings of the Eighteenth Annual Meeting.* Binghamton, N.Y., 1981.

Latham, G. P., and Pursell, E. D. "Measuring Absenteeism from the Opposite Side of the Coin." *Journal of Applied Psychology,* 1975, *60* (3), 369-371.

Latham, G. P., and Pursell, E. D. "Measuring Attendance: A Reply to Ilgen." *Journal of Applied Psychology,* 1977, *62,* 234-236.

Lawler, E. E. III. *Pay and Organizational Effectiveness.* New York: McGraw-Hill, 1971.

Lawler, E. E. III, and Hackman, J. R. "Impact of Employee Participation in the Development of Pay Incentive Plans: A Field Experiment." *Journal of Applied Psychology,* 1969, *53,* 467-471.

McShane, S. L. "Job Satisfaction and Absenteeism: A Meta-Analytic Re-Examination." In G. Johns (Ed.), *Proceedings of the Annual Conference of the Administrative Sciences Association of Canada Organizational Behaviour Division.* Vancouver: University of British Columbia, 1983.

"Maybe the No-Shows Just Absent-Minded." *Eugene Register-Guard,* Sept. 7, 1982, p. 1.

Milkovich, G. T., and Gomez, L. R. "Day Care and Selected Employee Work Behaviors." *Academy of Management Journal,* 1976, *19,* 111-115.

Miller, H. E. "Some Evidence Concerning the Progression of Withdrawal Hypothesis." Paper presented at 42nd annual meeting of the Academy of Management, New York, N.Y., Aug. 1982.

Mirvis, P. H., and Lawler, E. E. III. "Measuring the Financial Impact of Employee Attitudes." *Journal of Applied Psychology,* 1977, *62* (1), 1-8.

Mobley, W. H. "Some Unanswered Questions in Turnover and Withdrawal Research." *Academy of Management Review,* 1982, *7,* 111-116.

Morgan, L. G., and Herman, J. B. "Perceived Consequences of Absenteeism." *Journal of Applied Psychology,* 1976, *61* (6), 738-742.

Mowday, R. T., Porter, L. W., and Steers, R. M. *Employee-Organization Linkages: The Psychology of Commitment, Absenteeism, and Turnover.* New York: Academic Press, 1982.

Muchinsky, P. M. "Employee Absenteeism: A Review of the Literature." *Journal of Vocational Behavior,* 1977, *10,* 316–340.

Nicholson, N. "Management Sanctions and Absence Control." *Human Relations,* 1976, *29* (2), 139–151.

Nicholson, N. "Absence Behavior and Attendance Motivation: A Conceptual Synthesis." *Journal of Management Studies,* 1977, *14* (3), 231–252.

Nicholson, N., and Goodge, P. M. "The Influence of Social, Organizational and Biographical Factors on Female Absence." *Journal of Management Studies,* 1976, *13,* 234–254.

Orpen, C. "Effects of Bonuses for Attendance on the Absenteeism of Industrial Workers." *Journal of Organizational Behavior Management,* 1978, *1,* 118–124.

Owens, A. C. "Sick Leave Among Railwaymen Threatened by Redundancy: A Pilot Study." *Occupational Psychology,* 1966, *40,* 43–52.

Panyan, S. W., and McGregor, M. "How to Implement a Proactive Incentive Plan: A Field Study." *Personnel Journal,* 1976, *55,* 460–462.

Pedalino, E., and Gamboa, V. "Behavior Modification and Absenteeism: Intervention in One Industrial Setting." *Journal of Applied Psychology,* 1974, *59,* 694–698.

Pocock, S. J. "Relationship Between Sickness Absence and Meteorological Factors." *British Journal of Preventive Medicine,* 1972, *26,* 238–245.

Popp, P. O., and Belohlav, J. A. "Absenteeism in a Low Status Work Environment." *Academy of Management Journal,* 1982, *25,* 677–683.

Reid, D. H., Schuh-Wear, C. L., and Brannon, M. F. "Use of a Group Contingency to Decrease Staff Absenteeism in a State Institution." *Behavior Modification,* 1978, *21,* 251–266.

Rhodes, S. R. "The Relationship Between Worker Ownership and Control of Organizations and Work Attitudes and Behaviors." Unpublished doctoral dissertation, Department of Management, University of Oregon, 1978.

Rhodes, S. R. "Age-Related Differences in Work Attitudes and Behavior: A Review and Conceptual Analysis." *Psychological Bulletin,* 1983, *93,* 328–367.

Rhodes, S. R., and Steers, R. M. *Summary Tables of Studies of Employee Absenteeism.* Technical Report No. 13. Eugene: University of Oregon, 1977.

Rhodes, S. R., and Steers, R. M. "Conventional Versus Worker-Owned Organizations." *Human Relations,* 1981, *34,* 1013–1035.

Robertson, D. E., Johnson, R. D., and Bethke, A. L. "Reducing Absenteeism with Fixed and Variable Interval Reinforcement." *Review of Business and Economic Research,* 1980, *15,* 73–82.

Roe, N. "Sham Illness Absenteeism Worries CBI." *Sunday Telegraph* (London, England), March 4, 1979, p. 3.

Rokeach, M. *The Nature of Human Values.* New York: Free Press, 1973.

Saal, F. E. "Job Involvement: A Multivariate Approach." *Journal of Applied Psychology,* 1978, *63,* 53–61.

Schmidt, F. L., and Hunter, J. E. "Development of a General Solution to the Problem of Validity Generalization." *Journal of Applied Psychology,* 1977, *62,* 529–540.

Schmitz, L. M., and Heneman, H. G. III. "Do Positive Reinforcement Programs Reduce Employee Absenteeism?" *Personnel Administrator,* 1980, *25* (9), 87–93.

Schneller, G. O. IV, and Kopelman, R. E. "Using Incentives to Increase Absenteeism: A Plan that Backfired." *Compensation Review,* Second Quarter, 1982, pp. 40–45.

Siegel, A. L., and Ruh, R. A. "Job Involvement, Participation in Decision Making, Personal Background and Job Behavior." *Organizational Behavior and Human Performance,* 1973, *9,* 318–327.

Smith, F. J. "Work Attitudes as Predictors of Specific Day Attendance." *Journal of Applied Psychology,* 1977, *62* (1), 16–19.

Smulders, P. G. W. "Comments on Employee Absence/Attendance as a Dependent Variable in Organizational Research." *Journal of Applied Psychology,* 1980, *65,* 358–371.

Spencer, D. G., and Steers, R. M. "The Influence of Personal Factors and Perceived Work Experiences on Employee Turnover and Absenteeism." *Academy of Management Journal,* 1980, *23,* 567–572.

Staw, B. M., and Oldham, G. R. "Reconsidering Our Dependent Variables: A Critique and Empirical Study." *Academy of Management Journal,* 1978, *21* (4), 539–559.

Steers, R. M. "Antecedents and Outcomes of Organizational Commitment." *Administrative Science Quarterly,* 1977, *22,* 46–56.

Steers, R. M., and Rhodes, S. R. "Major Influences on Employee Attendance: A Process Model." *Journal of Applied Psychology,* 1978, *63* (4), 391–407.

Stephens, T. A., and Burroughs, W. A. "An Application of Operant Conditioning to Absenteeism in a Hospital Setting." *Journal of Applied Psychology,* 1978, *63,* 518–521.

Terborg, J. R., and others. *A Multivariate Investigation of Employee Absenteeism.* Technical Report 80-5. Houston, Texas: University of Houston, 1980.

Terborg, J. R., and others. "Extension of the Schmidt and Hunter Validity Generalization Procedure to the Prediction of Absenteeism Behavior from Knowledge of Job Satisfaction and Organizational Commitment." *Journal of Applied Psychology,* 1982, *67,* 440–449.

U.S. Bureau of National Affairs. *Bulletin to Management: BNA's Quarterly Report on Job Absence and Turnover.* Washington, D.C.: U.S. Bureau of National Affairs, 1980.

U.S. Bureau of National Affairs. *Bulletin to Management: BNA's Quarterly Report on Job Absence and Turnover, 4th Quarter 1982.* Washington, D.C.: U.S. Bureau of National Affairs, 1983a.

U.S. Bureau of National Affairs. *Bulletin to Management: BNA's Quarterly Report on Job Absence and Turnover, 2nd Quarter 1983.* Washington, D.C.: U.S. Bureau of National Affairs, 1983b.

Waters, L. K., and Roach, D. "Job Attitudes as Predictors of Termination and Absenteeism: Consistency over Time and Across Organizational Units." *Journal of Applied Psychology,* 1973, *57,* 341–342.

Watson, C. J. "An Evaluation of Some Aspects of the Steers and Rhodes Model of Employee Attendance." *Journal of Applied Psychology,* 1981, *66* (3), 385–389.

Winkler, D. R. "The Effects of Sick-Leave Policy on Teacher Absenteeism." *Industrial and Labor Relations Review,* 1980, *33* (2), 232–240.

Woska, W. J. "Sick Leave Incentive Plans: A Benefit to Consider." *Public Personnel Review,* 1972, *33,* 21–24.

Yankelovich, D. "We Need New Motivational Tools." *Industry Week,* Aug. 6, 1979.

Yolles, S. F., Carone, P. A., and Krinsky, L. W. *Absenteeism in Industry.* Springfield, Ill.: Thomas, 1975.

Youngblood, S. A. "Work, Nonwork, and Withdrawal." *Journal of Applied Psychology,* 1984, *69,* 106–117.

# 7

# Effects of Absenteeism on Individuals and Organizations

*Paul S. Goodman*

*Robert S. Atkin*

The purpose of this chapter is to examine the consequences of absenteeism. Instead of asking what causes absenteeism, we want to identify the causal effects of absenteeism; that is, what effect absenteeism has on the individual worker, adjacent workers, the work group, the organization, other social organizations, and society. Our goal is to provide a better theoretical understanding of these questions. The literature in this area is quite sparse. While there are probably thousands of studies examining the determinants of absenteeism, there are probably fewer than twenty studies that directly examine the effects of absenteeism on other criteria, such as productivity, safety, and so on. Therefore, our focus in this chapter is more on understanding the theoretical issues underlying this question than on making sense of a robust literature.

*Note:* Support for this chapter was provided by the U.S. Bureau of Mines under contracts J0100069, J0328033 and J0123040.

This chapter is distinct from others in this book. The first series of essays (Chapters One, Two, Three, and Four) attempts to delineate the concept of absenteeism from a theoretical and methodological point of view. These analyses clearly bear on our analysis of the consequences of absenteeism, but their focus is primarily on providing a new perspective for thinking about absenteeism as a concept. The chapter on absenteeism as a form of withdrawal behavior (Chapter Five) appears similar in focus to this chapter. However, there are some important differences. The literature on employee withdrawal (for example, Beehr and Gupta, 1978) argues that there are a variety of forms of withdrawal behavior (such as absenteeism, lateness, turnover) and attempts to examine the interrelationships among these forms of behavior. One assumption in that literature is that there are a variety of ways to withdraw and that different conditions may evoke different withdrawal strategies. Our focus on consequences of absenteeism is different. First, we want to trace the causal relationship of absenteeism to some other criterion variable (for example, productivity) rather than look at the association among withdrawal behaviors. Second, the class of dependent variables in our investigation is different. Our interest is in variables such as productivity, quality, grievances, lost-time accidents, and so on, as opposed to turnover or lateness. The chapter on determinants of absenteeism (Chapter Six) captures the modal orientation of most absenteeism research — absenteeism is the dependent (or predicted variable) rather than the independent variable. This chapter treats absenteeism as the independent or predictor variable. Another way to distinguish our analysis of consequences of absenteeism is to contrast it with another area in the absenteeism literature and in this collection — the area of managing or controlling absenteeism. An assumption, either implicit or explicit, in that literature is that absenteeism is dysfunctional for the organization and needs to be controlled. One major theme in that literature is to identify procedures that will reduce the amount of absenteeism (Mikalachki and Gandz, 1982). Absenteeism is typically considered from the management or organizational perspective, primarily as a negative factor. The basic position in this essay is that absenteeism has different consequences for different constituencies and that these consequences may be positive or negative.

The rationale for studying the consequences of absenteeism should be obvious. First, there are very few empirical studies tracing the effect of absenteeism on other criterion variables, yet there are beliefs often articulated by managers on the dysfunctional effects of absenteeism on productivity and costs. Does absenteeism really reduce productivity, and, if so, under what conditions? Second, the literature in organizational psychology has a tendency to look into certain single-directional relationships, such as affect→behavior (for example, job dissatisfaction→absenteeism) and not explore reciprocal effects, such as behavior→affect or behavior→behavior relationships. Third, it is probably fair to say that most studies on absenteeism imply that it is something bad that should be reduced. This analysis of the consequences of absenteeism will highlight the positive benefits and thus ensure a more balanced cost-benefit analysis of absenteeism.

To accomplish our objective, a series of theoretical issues concerning the consequences of absenteeism will be delineated first. These include the dependent variable, defining the network of interrelationships, and establishing the meaning or representation of absenteeism. Then, the core of this chapter will examine in more detail a selected set of variables that absenteeism may affect. In each case we will (1) review what we know from the literature (including some new empirical information from our Carnegie-Mellon research project on absenteeism), (2) delineate the theoretical process underlying the relationship between absenteeism and the criterion variable, and (3) identify some strategic issues in researching these relationships.

## Theoretical Issues

*Selecting the Dependent Variable*

Our concern is to understand the effect of absenteeism on other variables. One task, then, is to enumerate the possible dependent or criterion variables. We need some systematic way to determine or organize the consequences of absenteeism. Our strategy is to borrow the constituency approach from the organizational-effectiveness literature (Goodman and Pennings, 1977) and organize the possible consequences of absenteeism by constituency. The possible constituencies include the individual who is absent, individual co-workers, the work group, the organization, the union, other social organizations, such as the family, and aggregate social units, such as the community and society. To each of these constituencies, absenteeism may generate positive or negative consequences. The importance of this exercise in categorization is that it will show that: (1) there are many consequences of absenteeism; (2) these consequences are *both* positive and negative; and (3) what may be a positive consequence to one constituency may be a negative to another. This section borrows and extends a listing of consequences developed by Mowday, Porter, and Steers (1982).

Table 7.1 lists positive and negative consequences of absenteeism by constituency. The list is meant to be representative, not comprehensive. We recognize that the different outcomes listed in this table may or may not be relevant to any given situation. The relevance of any of these outcomes would depend upon individual characteristics, the structure of the job, and the organization of work. We also acknowledge that there may be lagged effect between absence and any of these variables. For example, the effect of absence on productivity may occur on the day of the absence or several days later. We also recognize that the duration of the absence may differentially affect different outcomes. Lastly, we recognize that there is a complicated relationship among absenteeism and all the listed outcomes. We will elaborate on these points in the next section of this chapter.

The positive consequences of absenteeism, from the *individual* viewpoint, seem relatively straightforward and come from a variety of sources. There is some research that indirectly indicates that absenteeism is a form of withdrawal from job-stress situations (Staw and Oldham, 1978). If absence from work reduces stress, then it can be functional for the individual. In addition, much of our life is concerned with fulfilling such central nonwork-related roles as the parent role (when taking care of a sick child) or the marital role (when reducing marital stress). The valence and utility for performing many of these nonwork-role activities is likely to be strong (Naylor, Pritchard, and Ilgen, 1980). Completing these activities, which may require being absent from work, leads to

Table 7.1. Consequences of Absenteeism.

| | *Positive* | *Negative* |
|---|---|---|
| Individual | Reduction of job-related stress<br>Meeting of nonwork-role obligations<br>Benefit from compensatory nonwork activities<br>Compliance with norms to be absent | Loss of pay<br>Discipline, formal and informal<br>Increased accidents<br>Altered job perception |
| Co-workers | Job variety<br>Skill development<br>Overtime pay | Increased work load<br>Undesired overtime<br>Increased accidents<br>Conflict with absent worker |
| Work group | Crew knowledge of multiple jobs<br>Greater crew flexibility in responding to absenteeism and to production problems | Increased coordination problems<br>Decreased productivity<br>Increased accidents |
| Organization-management | Greater job knowledge base in work force<br>Greater labor-force flexibility | Decreased productivity<br>Increased costs<br>More grievances<br>Increased accidents |
| Union-officers | Articulated and strengthened power position<br>Increased solidarity among members | Weakened power position<br>Increased costs in processing grievances |
| Family | Opportunity to deal with health or illness problems<br>Opportunity to manage marital problems<br>Opportunity to manage child problems<br>Maintenance of spouse's earnings | Less earnings<br>Decline in work reputation<br>Aggravated marriage and child problems |
| Society | Reduction of job stress and mental health problems<br>Reduction of marital-related problems<br>Participation in community political processes | Loss of productivity |

positive benefits for the individual. Not all nonwork activities can be described easily in role terms. Some nonwork activities are inherently rewarding (for example, a hobby, fishing) and will at times be elected over work activities. In most organizations, norms exist that govern absenteeism behavior. In some organizations, informal norms exist that legitimate certain days of absence although these are scheduled workdays (for example, beginning of deer season). Taking these days off may be a way to avoid social sanctions; thus, absence may lead to a beneficial consequence.

The negative consequences of absenteeism to the individual are fairly straightforward. They may include loss of pay and disciplinary action for the individual. Accidents may occur to the individual when he or she returns to a less familiar work situation. A less obvious negative consequence, which has been suggested by Johns and Nicholson (1982) and Mowday, Porter, and Steers (1982), concerns the process of altered job perceptions. When confronted with an absence, even the employee may develop a reason (attribution) or justification for explaining the absence. The reason given may or may not correspond to why the employee was absent. If, over time, the justification or reason is rehearsed over other absence events and not controverted by any other information, we would expect that justification to become a permanent part of the individual's belief system. In the case of absenteeism, we would expect people to attribute the cause more to problems in their environment, such as a bad job, bad supervisor, and so on. So, to the extent that absenteeism leads to negative beliefs about the job or job environment that are not based on the reality of the situation, we would say that absenteeism indirectly creates negative consequences for the individual.

Positive and negative consequences fall to the *co-worker*. The absence of a worker may give co-workers a new opportunity to work on a different job, which would enhance job variety and skill development. In addition, if the work area is understaffed, there may be opportunities for overtime pay. On the negative side, the co-worker may have to do additional work, which is perceived as a burden, not a benefit. Overtime may be viewed as negative when it interferes with nonwork responsibilities. Accidents can occur when the co-worker is confronted with an unfamiliar machine or set of job activities. If any of the above negative consequences occur, they are likely to lead to conflict with the absent worker on his or her return. In addition, if the co-worker observes high absenteeism in the work group, an inferential process may be evoked to explain this absenteeism. If, as discussed earlier, the attributions are made about negative environmental conditions, the co-worker might develop negative beliefs about the work environment although he or she is not absent.

Some of the positive and negative consequences for the *work group* are the same consequences as for the co-worker. In this discussion, we view the group as characterized by task interdependencies among the members. Absenteeism is likely to create job switching within the group, which leads to a broader knowledge base among the work group. This knowledge base facilitates a more effective response to future absenteeism and day-to-day production problems. If job switching leads to a more flexible and productive group (Goodman, 1979) and absenteeism facilitates job switching, absenteeism may have positive benefits for the work group. On the negative side, replacing the absent worker, from either within or outside of the group, will lead to increased coordination problems. Productivity may decline in the short run, if the replacement worker is less skilled than the absent worker. In the area of productivity, we have made conflicting claims about consequences, which can be reconciled by noting the timing of their impact. If a less skilled worker replaces the absent worker, productivity should immediately decrease. If absenteeism increases the job knowledge of group members and, hence, their flexibility, in the long run we expect this type of group to be more productive than the crew where each member can perform only his or her job. In the area of accidents, we see a parallel. If absenteeism leads to a replacement who is unfamiliar with the job, an accident is more likely in an interdependent group. As group members become more familiar with other jobs, the effect of absenteeism on accidents will be less pronounced.

The positive and negative consequences for the *organization* parallel those for the work group. Some of the differences at this level include the costs of absenteeism. Hiring, training, and paying additional workers and maintaining records for, administering, and enforcing an absenteeism program all represent costs to management of the organization. We have observed in our own research that a variety of different arrangements or implicit policies develop with different classes of workers. The existence of absenteeism and any forms of absenteeism control policy are likely to generate grievances. Grievances, at least for the management, represent an additional cost of doing business.

Absenteeism can have consequences for the *union* and its officers. Absenteeism can be a tool for strengthening the power of the union with respect to management. Encouraging absenteeism (for example, "blue flu") can be used to increase management's costs and to extract gains for the union leadership and/or members. To the extent to which the union leadership is successful, we would expect increased solidarity among the members. In this specific example, absenteeism does not cause increased solidarity. Rather, it creates a condition that may facilitate the development of solidarity. A related scenario is one where an increase in absences is likely to create more grievances. To the extent to which the union wins the grievances, leader power is enhanced, and member solidarity may increase. Absenteeism also has negative consequences for the union. To the extent to which absences lead to grievances (Katz, Kochan, and Weber, 1982; Katz, Kochan, and Gobeille, 1982), costs in processing these grievances represent a negative consequence for the union. Also, if the union is unsuccessful in processing absence-related grievances, the power of the leadership is likely to decrease, as may the solidarity among members.

The constituencies related to absenteeism should not be solely work related. The *family* is another unit of social analysis that is affected by absenteeism. Absenteeism may be functional for the family in dealing with health, marital, or child-related problems. If incomes are rising, absenteeism may represent a way to consume positive leisure activities together. In the case of dual wage earners, absenteeism by one of the partners may be necessary to ensure the other spouse's job and earnings. On the negative side, absenteeism can lower earnings. Also, frequent absenteeism could lead to a poor work reputation, which may negatively reflect on family members. In some cases, absenteeism could aggravate marital and other family relations. If the absent worker interferes with the daily household routine, conflict may result.

The most common reference to the *societal*-level analysis is the cost of absenteeism (see Steers and Rhodes, 1978). Typically, one figures out an average cost per absence and multiplies this by the number of days lost per year. The problem with this analysis is that it really is drawn from the organizational perspective, not the national or societal perspective. For example, if absenteeism reduces job stress and mental-health problems, then there are certain cost savings to society in the sense of needing fewer mental-health facilities. If absenteeism helps minimize marital problems, then it has certain benefits to society. While we do not have any evidence to show that increasing absenteeism will reduce the societal costs for dealing with divorces, it is important in the total cost-benefit analysis to reflect these savings and not to think about costs solely from the management perspective. Similarly, absenteeism may reduce unemployment, which would affect the societal-level calculation of the costs and benefits of absenteeism. We also point out in Table 7.1 that absenteeism, particularly for workers on shift work, may provide a means for participating in community and political processes — a less quantifiable benefit to society. We can conclude this section by noting:

- There are many possible consequences of absenteeism.
- The consequences are both positive and negative.
- Positive consequences come from many sources — avoidance of stress, fulfillment of role obligation, rewards from work and nonwork activity, greater skills and flexibility, more power, and so on.
- Negative consequences come from many sources — loss of rewards, disciplinary action, accidents, greater work stress, lower productivity, greater costs, and so on.
- Both negative and positive consequences may exist simultaneously.
- Consequences to any of the constituencies may vary over time.
- Benefits to one constituency may represent negative consequences to another constituency.
- A constituency member may be unaware of the costs and benefits of absenteeism for other constituency members.

The purpose of this discussion was to identify possible dependent variables for our analysis of the consequences of absenteeism using a constituency approach. We have selected five that have been subject to research and are most common across all the constituencies: productivity, accidents, grievances, costs, and attitudes.

*Network of Interrelationships*

The preceding section identified many possible consequences of absenteeism. This section explores the complex relationship among the variables. We want to make explicit the complexity of the relationships as well as to state a strategy for empirically testing these relationships. Our analysis thus far has portrayed a simple relationship between an absence event and some consequences. We use the word *consequence* to mean something that follows from absenteeism, depends upon absenteeism, and is causally related to absenteeism. It is very unlikely that there is a simple one-way flow between absenteeism and the indicators in Table 7.1; therefore, we have outlined below some characteristics of the relationships.

*Reciprocal Causation.* One of the major problems with the absenteeism literature is that it has been grounded on the assumption that job dissatisfaction causes absenteeism. More recently, some authors have pointed out that the opposite may be true (Staw and Oldham, 1978; Clegg, 1983). We do not want to fall into this one-way trap. Many of the factors in Table 7.1 are both consequences of and causes of absenteeism. Absenteeism can cause accidents by creating a condition where a replacement worker is less familiar with the job activities. This is an example where absenteeism is a necessary but not sufficient condition for accident. Accidents (lost time) in turn cause absences, which in turn can cause accidents. In some of our research, there are data to suggest that family and marital problems lead to increased absenteeism. Now, if the time absent from work is used to repair the marriage (through an employee assistance program), absenteeism will create a condition to reduce marital conflict, which in turn should reduce absenteeism. It would be easy to go through Table 7.1 and illustrate these reciprocal relationships.

*Two-Plus Variable Relationships.* In most cases, we need additional variables to explain the relationship between absenteeism and its consequences. For example, the relationship between absenteeism and disciplinary punishment at the individual level depends upon whether there is an absenteeism-control plan, whether the plan is enforced, the individual's prior absenteeism record, the role of the union, and so on. Absenteeism can affect productivity, but other variables need to be considered. Absenteeism may increase productivity if the staffing policy normally creates excess slack in the work group or department. Absenteeism may have no affect on productivity if the job is highly motivating and variation in operator skill is not related to job performance (Moch and Fitzgibbons, 1982). Absenteeism in a central, highly skilled job may reduce productivity if comparably skilled labor is not available. While this point of identifying other main-effect variables and possible interactions appears noncontroversial, it has not generally been acknowledged in consequence studies (see Moch and Fitzgibbons, 1982, and Mowday, Porter, and Steers, 1982, for additional discussion on this point).

*Time Factor of Absenteeism.* Two time dimensions—duration of absenteeism and lagged effects of absenteeism—complicate the interrelationships between absenteeism and possible consequences. In the first case, the length of absenteeism may differentially affect the outcome variable under consideration. A short absenteeism spell may reduce stress, while a longer duration may increase stress. The effect of the lag structure of absenteeism on the possible consequence variables is another theoretical issue in understanding the models in this discussion. For example, accidents might occur in the beginning of the absence spell or later, when the replacement worker may be less vigilant.

*Alternative Explanations.* Our focus is on demonstrating the effect of absences on other variables. We have noted that the causal connections are complicated, and a careful model needs to be built linking absenteeism to any of the consequence variables. While there is some theoretical and empirical evidence to suggest that researching the absence-consequence link is potentially important, we should acknowledge that other variables may cause variation in the absenteeism and consequence variables and that these latter two variables may not be linked. For example, we have said that absences can cause lost-time accidents and that these accidents can cause absences. But it is possible for another variable, such as alcoholism, to cause directly both absences and accidents, and if the accidents are not lost-time accidents, there would be no connection between these two variables. In another case, it may be that poor supervision directly contributes to poorer quality and more absenteeism, without absenteeism and quality being connected.

The rationale for these illustrations is that the co-variation between absenteeism and accidents or absenteeism and quality may not signify that they are causally connected, and it is the responsibility of the researcher to acknowledge the existence of alternative explanations.

*Interrelationships Among the Consequence Variables.* The picture we have drawn about absenteeism and its consequences focuses on one consequence variable at a time. However, the consequence variables may be interrelated with each other and with absenteeism. This will further complicate our understanding of the absence-consequence relationships. Probably the best way to discuss this point is to draw a simple example between absenteeism and two consequence variables—production and accidents. Figure 7.1 illustrates some possible simple paths. The figure is drawn with the following format: starting at the bottom of an arrow, increasing that variable will have an effect on the variable at the head of the arrow, as determined by the sign. So, working from right to left, an increase in production should increase the number of accidents, which should increase absenteeism. Increases in absenteeism may have a direct effect on increasing accidents or an indirect

Figure 7.1. Possible Relationships Among Absenteeism,
Accidents, and Production.

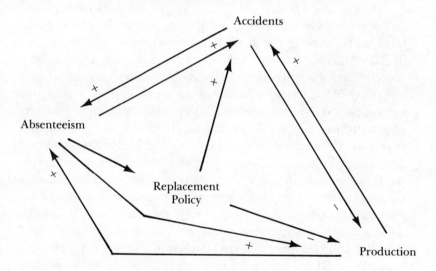

effect through the company's replacement policy; in both cases, accidents go up, which in turn should lower production. Increases in production (by increasing stress) can increase absenteeism, which can have a positive effect on production, which can increase accidents. The point of this illustration is simply that there are complicated relationships among the consequence variables and absenteeism. Note that the relationships in Figure 7.1 would be intolerably complicated if we added other consequence variables (attitudes, grievances) and specified functional relationships.

*Meaning or Representation of Absenteeism*

Two facts seem to emerge from the absentee literature. First, we have not done a particularly good job in empirically explaining variations in absenteeism. Second, there appears to be a trend toward better specified models; that is, researchers seem to recognize that different types of absenteeism operationalize in terms of content (for example, contract days, accidents) or frequency (and duration), which require different types of predictive models. While this move toward a more careful specification of absenteeism seems appropriate, studies adopting this point of view (for example, Moch and Fitzgibbons, 1982) have not recorded any major breakthrough.

In a new and refreshing look at the absenteeism literature, Johns and Nicholson (1982) go a step further in arguing that "absence means different things to different people in different types of different situations" (p. 134). Basically, they are arguing for a more idiographic approach to absenteeism; if we can get a better phenomenological representation of the person and environment at a given period, we can develop a better understanding or meaning of absenteeism at a given time. While there are as yet no studies that demonstrate the utility of the Johns and Nicholson theoretical argument, their position seems consistent with what we are learning from our own data set on absenteeism. We have absenteeism data on twenty-five organizations in the same industry, all operating under the same collective bargaining agreement, which includes an absenteeism control plan. Although it is the same industry and the same contract, the meaning attached to absence categories (for example, accident, excused, unexcused) differs across the twenty-five organizations. The same variation exists within different organizations of the same company. At the organization level, we see marked variations in category codes attached to different individuals with the same frequency and duration of absenteeism. We think this occurs because the coding of absenteeism by the organization represents a series of individual negotiations between individual workers and management.

The question that has motivated this discussion is: To what extent is the meaning or representation of absenteeism important for understanding the consequences of absenteeism? That is, do we first need to carefully delineate the meaning of absenteeism before we can understand the consequences? Regarding questions about reliability of absenteeism or predictability of absenteeism, we believe that the answer is emphatically yes — the meaning or representation of absenteeism needs to be determined first. In terms of the consequences of absenteeism, this central issue of determining the meaning of absenteeism may be less important. To illustrate our contention that a precise specification of the meaning of absenteeism may not be as important in studies of consequences of absenteeism, we will consider a selected set of consequence variables from the organizational, group, and individual perspectives. There are some reasons, both theoretical and empirical, to expect absenteeism to lower productivity. The principal explanatory mechanism is that absenteeism leads to understaffing, in number or skill, which should lower productivity. To test that assertion, one simply has to know whether a person is at work or not at work — the simplest definition of absenteeism. Now, anticipating this vacancy clearly will moderate its impact on productivity, simply because we manage the staffing problem more effectively. But anticipating a vacancy is not absenteeism. Our argument is that knowledge of the individual's subjective representation of absenteeism, the identification of unique patterns of absenteeism from company records, or delineating the construct of absenteeism does not appear to be essential to understanding whether the presence or absence of a person has an impact on productivity. In the analysis of absenteeism and accidents, the same conclusions can be drawn. The basic explanatory mechanism for accidents is whether the individual is familiar with the work and machinery. Unfamiliarity can be caused by absences. Knowledge of absence types, frequencies, and subjective representations of absences does not seem relevant. Basically, we need to know whether accidents create a level of unfamiliarity in the workplace. Knowledge of whether someone is present or absent seems sufficient.

At the group level, we indicated that absence could lead to greater job knowledge and greater group flexibility as members switch around to substitute for the absent worker. Whether job knowledge and group flexibility increase seems tied to whether absence occurs and to the company's staffing policy. A detailed understanding of the meaning of absenteeism does not seem important. It is at the individual level, particularly when the consequence variables are subjective indicators, that specifying the meaning of absence may be more important. Consider that absenteeism may permit the individual to fulfill role obligations, such as taking care of a sick child. Connecting this consequence to absence is very difficult if we know only whether the person was not at work or the type, frequency, or duration of absenteeism. Identification of the meaning of absenteeism for the individual at a particular time and in a particular situational context seems necessary. Similarly, absence can permit the fulfilling of desired nonwork activities (for example, a hobby). Understanding the process by which someone decided to allocate time to nonwork rather than work activities seems a necessary condition before we can link absenteeism and benefits from nonwork activities.

We have generated a discussion on the meaning or representation of absenteeism, since it is a central theoretical issue in absenteeism research. (See Chapter Two for more details.) We want to acknowledge its importance in redirecting our thinking about some questions about absenteeism — particularly the questions about measurement and explaining reasons for absenteeism. The essence of our argument is that, in explaining the consequences of absenteeism, we may be able to sidestep the specification of the meaning or representation of absenteeism. That is, we do not need a detailed delineation of the construct or the subjective representation of absenteeism to examine its impact on a variety of possible objective consequence variables, such as productivity or accidents. We did acknowledge that delineating the subjective meaning may be important in examining the impact of absenteeism on certain subjective indicators.

## Consequence Variables: Data and Theory

In this part of the chapter, we move from a general consideration of the theoretical issues about the absenteeism-consequence relationship to a more detailed consideration of variables that may be affected by changes in absenteeism. Our strategy is to focus primarily on variables that appear common to the constituencies enumerated in Table 7.1 and about which there is some empirical research. Basically, we are interested in three questions: What do we know about the relationship between absenteeism and some consequence variable? What is the underlying theoretical relationship among these variables? What is the research strategy to test each of these theoretical relationships? What motivates this section is a need to delineate fruitful research paths to examining the consequences of absenteeism. There is very little research in this area, although the problem is potentially interesting and policy relevant. By bringing together what we know and by identifying some research paths, perhaps we can help research in this area to grow.

### Productivity

What effect does absenteeism have on productivity? *Productivity,* in this discussion, will be defined as output over labor input. Also, we distinguish between productivity at the firm level, the group level, and the individual or job level. *Firm-level productivity* is defined in terms of total firm output (quantity and/or quality) over labor input; *group-level productivity* refers to the output of a particular group or crew over input; and *job productivity* refers to the output-input relationship for a particular class of job. It is important to distinguish among these levels, because in different types of technologies, a particular level of productivity assessment may be more central in the production process. For example, in coal mining, crew-level productivity may be more central than job-level productivity.

*Empirical Evidence.* There are very few studies of the impact of absenteeism on productivity. We have identified four studies, three of which are unpublished. Katz, Kochan, and Weber (1982) and Katz, Kochan, and Gobeille (1982) have developed data sets on manufacturing plants that include a variety of industrial-relations indicators, quality-of-working-life indicators, and organizational-effectiveness indicators over a ten-year period. Measures of quality and direct labor efficiency are available and can be considered productivity measures. The absence measure is calculated as a rate per year at the plant level. It includes days absent, excluding contract days off, over scheduled working days. Two different data sets are used in their research program, both drawn from the same company. They differ in number of plants and measures that are available. In their first data set (Katz, Kochan, and Weber, 1982; and Katz, Kochan, and Gobeille, 1982), regression analyses were run on the influence of variables such as total hours worked, grievance rate, absenteeism rate, quality-of-working-life rating, and plant dummies, on quality and efficiency. A positive significant coefficient appeared for absenteeism in respect to quality, and a nonsignificant relationship appeared for direct labor efficiency. In the second data set, absenteeism was significantly positively related to quality and negatively related to labor efficiency. The authors explain the positive relationship between absenteeism and quality by noting: (1) there was a general increase in both variables over the time of the study, and (2) cross-sectionally for any given year, the correlation between absenteeism and quality was negative but not significant.

Moch and Fitzgibbons (1982) also investigated the absenteeism, quality, and quantity relationships. Their research is directly focused on the consequences of absenteeism on production. Their basic hypothesis is that absenteeism and plant-level efficiency are negatively associated when (1) production processes are not highly automated, (2) those who are absent are central to the production process, and (3) absences cannot be anticipated. Data for this study were gathered from a manufacturing plant and cover two one-year periods. Results from this study are not completely clear. However, there is some evidence that absenteeism of more central people (for example, maintenance personnel) has negative impacts on productivity and that less automated production is more vulnerable to the negative effects of absenteeism.

A study by the Carnegie-Mellon Coal Project (1983a) also examined the impact of absenteeism on production. Data were gathered from an underground coal mine, where the crew or group is the primary production unit. The goal of this research was to explain variation in group performance. The analytical strategy was first to estimate the basic production function. In the production function, tons of coal is the dependent variable; the independent variables are number of laborers, physical conditions, machine availability, and a set of control variables. From a series of analyses it was learned that (1) a reasonable portion of variance in crew-level production could be explained by the production function $R^2 = 0.53$; (2) there were crew and departmental differences; (3) there were some significant nonlinear effects; and (4) there were significant effects due to different technologies. Given this baseline information, different measures of crew stability that reflect who worked on what job on what day in what crew were developed. These indexes indicate whether workers were present over time in their crew, job, and department. When the stability indexes were added into the baseline production-function run, they contributed to a significant increase in the $R^2$. While additional research is being conducted on the stability measure, there is some evidence that the presence of crew members (versus absence) contributes to production in interdependent work groups.

Staw and Oldham (1978) suggest that the absenteeism-performance relationship may be positive *and* negative. Very low attendance rates may be technically dysfunctional and reduce job performance. Absenteeism, on the other hand, may serve as a maintenance function and help the worker cope with job stress, in turn increasing job performance. They test this dual effect of absenteeism by examining the relationship between absenteeism and performance for those people likely to be experiencing stress on the job and for those that were not. For those people who were low in growth satisfaction and probably experiencing more stress at work, the relationship between total absenteeism and rated performance was positive. No relationship between absenteeism and performance appeared for those high in growth satisfaction. While this finding appears contrary to the results of the other studies, it should be noted that the other studies used record data (versus self-report data on production) and used more detailed analytical procedures to separate out the effect of absenteeism versus other variables.

What conclusions can be drawn from the empirical studies?

First it is amazing that there are so few studies about this relationship. Second, the findings tend to support a negative relationship, but there are a lot of nonfindings (that is, hypothesis not supported). Third, the idea of a positive impact of absenteeism on production is intriguing. Unfortunately, the design of the Staw and Oldham study does not permit testing that relationship. We need to look at daily absenteeism and production, controlling for other variables. Our guess is that stress would develop over time, leading to a decline in performance. An absence event should reduce tension, and performance should be high on subsequent days, declining again over time. Unless one can test this cycle of events, it will be difficult to support the positive effect of absenteeism on production.

*Theoretical Relationships.* The direct relationship between absenteeism and productivity is fairly straightforward. Absenteeism means that a job in the production process will be vacant. An understaffed production process should result in some decline in production. The organizational response to a vacant job could be a replacement. The skill level of the replacement relative to that of job incumbent should explain the amount and direction of the effect on production. A less skilled replacement would lower production, and a more skilled worker might improve production. In an overstaffed situation, if a vacancy occurs, production will probably remain the same, and labor productivity will increase.

The existence of a vacancy, the staffing policy, and the replacement policy seem to be the key factors underlying the absenteeism-production relationship. Of course, other variables can help refine the intersection between these variables. Some jobs are more central to the production process than others. *Centrality* means the degree to which performance on the job or a cluster of jobs affects the activities and performance on other jobs. In mining, the absence of the mine operator will affect all other crew jobs. If a utility person is absent, that person does not necessarily have to be replaced, at least in the short run. In the Moch and Fitzgibbons study, the mechanic was a key job. Absenteeism of this worker should affect the production process more than that of an assembly worker. The degree to which a job is programmed also will bear on the vacancy-replacement relationships. In highly programmed jobs, replacement is easier, and the impact on production should be less. In high-discretion jobs, replacement will be more difficult, and absenteeism effects should be more pronounced. The existence of a vacancy, the staffing policy, the replacement policy, the centrality of the job, and the level of discretion in the job affect the direct relationship of absenteeism to production. We noted earlier that absenteeism can affect other variables (for example, accidents) that in turn affect production. The focus here is on direct effects. The indirect effects (for example, absenteeism-accidents) appear later in this section.

*Strategies for Research.* How should we go about attacking the absenteeism-production relationships?

1. Begin with a common technology. Studying this question across different technologies will make the research overly complex.

2. Study the technology carefully. One needs to identify the primary production units and to have an intimate knowledge of job-skill requirements, the centrality of jobs in different settings, the extent to which jobs are programmed, the replacement strategy for that production unit, and the general staffing policy.

3. Design a data set that fits the theoretical process between absenteeism and production. Most of the studies we cited above (with the exception of the Carnegie-Mellon Coal Project) did not have a data set to address the research problem. When someone is absent, we need to know whether the person replaced has the skill experience of the replacement, which job is involved, and what the indicators of day-to-day production are. If you know only aggregate information (for example, yearly figures on absenteeism and productivity; Katz, Kochan, and Weber, 1982, and Katz, Kochan, and Gobeille, 1982) it will be difficult to shed any light on whether absenteeism causes changes in productivity and, if so, why that happens.

4. Develop a baseline model. Variation in production is a function of many critical variables. These need to be specified so that we can separate out the effect of absenteeism from other variables. In our work, we begin with the concept of the production function — in which production is a function of land, labor, and capital. In our mining research, this gets translated into physical conditions, number of laborers, and machine

availability. We think that these are the most critical and most proximate factors explaining productivity. After the production function is estimated, we then ask whether absenteeism had an additional effect on production variance.

5.  Examine alternative measures of production. Different measures may require different hypotheses. Measures of quality and quantity have been used in some of the studies we cited. Absenteeism may have greater effects on quality than on quantity in programmed jobs. In these jobs, the technology may drive the number of units but not necessarily the quality. Downtime is an example of an intermediate measure of production that should be investigated. We might expect that absenteeism may have more of an impact on the duration than on the incidence of breakdown. The job knowledge of the replacement is, of course, important, for the greater the job knowledge, the shorter the duration of downtime.

6.  Pay attention to linearity assumptions and lagged effects. We suspect that the effect of absenteeism on production does not have a simple linear form. For example, in coal mining, one can vary crew size within certain ranges without major impacts on production. However, changing size beyond that range will affect productivity. Similarly, the effects of absences on productivity may or may not be contemporaneous; there may be lags. For example, in coal mining, the total production cycle includes both a direct and an indirect component. If workers responsible for the indirect component were absent, production could proceed. However, after a point, the indirect work must be done. In this case, the effect of absenteeism would be lagged. The point is that the linearity assumption and possible lagged effects can be understood only if one has an intimate knowledge of the production process.

*Accidents*

What effect does absenteeism have on the number and severity of accidents? While many innovations have occurred in the area of machinery design and training to reduce accidents, there has been surprisingly little attention given to the relationship between absenteeism and accidents.

*Empirical Evidence.* We have found only a few studies dealing with the absenteeism-accident relationship. Some of these studies unfortunately do not address our interest in the effect of absenteeism on accidents. Hill and Trist (1953) studied the relationship between absenteeism and accidents, but their basic hypothesis was that accidents are a form of absenteeism. Some data were presented that indicated that accidents are positively motivated forms of absenteeism. In another study, by Allen (1981), the relationships between accidents and absenteeism are examined, but the focus is more on the effect of accidents on absenteeism than the reverse. His findings indicate that absenteeism rates are higher in plants with low wages and high occupational illness; absenteeism is a labor-supply adjustment to wage and employment hazards. While both of these studies examine the relationship between absenteeism and accidents, they do not deal with the research question in this chapter. Hill and Trist argue that accidents are one of the many forms of withdrawal (for example, turnover, tardiness). Allen provides data to demonstrate that organizations with bad safety records are likely to experience more absenteeism. Time is taken off to compensate for the higher risk of an accident; that is, plant accident rates lead to absenteeism.

The Katz and others study cited earlier (Katz, Kochan, and Weber, 1982; Katz, Kochan, and Gobeille, 1982) has some minimal data on absenteeism and accidents. Accident measures at the plant level included cost of sickness and accident benefits, number of injuries requiring more than minor first aid per 200,000 hours worked, and number of lost-time accidents divided by total hours worked. The simple correlations between absenteeism rate and these accidents showed a positive significant relationship with accident cost ($r = 0.29$, $p < 0.001$) and with lost-time accidents ($r = 0.15$, $p < 0.05$). Unfortunately, there are no multivariate runs that control for some important plant characteristics that may affect the absenteeism-accident relationship. These control variables were important in interpreting the correlation coefficients in the absenteeism-production discussion.

Some information on absenteeism and accidents appears in the Carnegie-Mellon Coal Project (1983b). Three questions are addressed: First, are people who are absent more likely to have an accident when they return to work? Second, if a worker is absent, is his or her replacement more likely to have an accident? Third, if a person is absent, is a worker interdependent with the vacant job or a replacement worker more likely to have an accident? Before we examined the first question, probit analyses were performed on a variety of accident measures to determine the effect of job and individual demographics on accidents. The results suggest that these demographics play a small role in explaining accidents. To see whether absences precede accidents, we looked at whether people were absent prior to an accident. Absence was measured as the day before, or the amount over the preceding five workdays. The data indicate that only a small number of accidents were preceded by absences. However, a large number of accidents were preceded by nonscheduled days, such as weekends. Further investigation of the magnitude and significance of these results is in progress.

The second and third questions concern whether the replacement worker or some adjacent worker is more likely to have an accident. To examine such a question, one needs a detailed data set that identifies who works on what job on what day and that gives information on accidents. This permits operationalizing whether an absence leads to a replacement and whether an accident occurred and if so, to whom. We are currently analyzing these data from a single organization, and it is not clear that replacements are more likely to have accidents. However, only preliminary analyses have been completed, and this type of analysis needs to be completed over multiple organizations to assess the degree of stability of the relationships among absences, replacement policy, and accidents. The empirical evidence in the literature on the absenteeism-accident relationship is very inconclusive. There are simply not enough studies with the appropriate data sets to answer the questions. The evidence on the absenteeism-production relationship is more convincing.

*Theoretical Relations.* The direct relationship between accidents and absenteeism follows some of the theoretical rationale for the absenteeism-production relationship. Absenteeism leads to a vacancy and, in most work situations, to a condition of understaffing. In a condition of understaffing, accidents may be more likely, because workers may have more work to do, experience more stress, cut more corners, and so on. This scenario is based on the assumption of no replacement; that is, absenteeism causes a condition of understaffing, which increases the probability of an accident.

Another explanation in the absenteeism-accident relationship concerns the concept of *familiarity*. *Familiarity* refers to the knowledge one has of intra- and interjob activities and the work environment. In the context of coal mining, for example, one can refer to the knowledge one has about one's job, equipment, co-workers, supervisor, and physical conditions. In the dynamic context of the work environment, changes in physical conditions may call for different job activities, use of equipment, or coordination activities. Familiarity with these events on a day-to-day basis should minimize chances for accidents. Unfamiliarity may increase the chances for accidents. Familiarity can be used to characterize the knowledge of the absent person or the replacement. In the former case, the person who was absent returns to work. The issue is the degree of familiarity that person has with the job activities or work environment. If the person has experienced a long absence and is therefore less familiar with the work, chances for an accident may increase for the focal individual and for an adjacent worker. In the latter case, we need to know the familiarity of the replacement with the job and work environment. Note that the unfamiliarity of the replacement worker has implications for that individual as well as for an interdependent worker. The unfamiliar replacement worker may cause an accident for the adjacent worker because different coordination mechanisms are being used. Unfamiliarity for the replacement worker then has implications for the accident rate of both that individual and of the adjacent worker.

Another factor that may underly the absenteeism-accident relationship is the concept of *vigilance*. *Vigilance* refers to the degree to which an individual consciously attends to all aspects of his or her work activity. Sometimes when driving a car, the work activity (driving) is done almost automatically, with low attention to each of the sequential activities. At other times, one pays careful attention to all the driving activities. In jobs with very low variety and standard routines, work may be done in a low-vigilance manner, while the opposite may be true in high-variety, unstructured jobs. Absenteeism may be functional for low-vigilance activities by "breaking set." After an absence, the worker may return to the job with renewed attention to the work activity, which lowers the probabilities for an accident. In high-variety, stimulating jobs, absence may be dysfunctional. In this case, after an absence interruption, it may take time to reach the optimal level of vigilance for the job, so that the possibility of an accident is increased. Duration of absence also may be related to vigilance and accidents. Long duration of absenteeism may initially increase vigilance of work. Long duration may make the contrast between nonwork and work roles more salient, so that the initial vigilance levels should be higher. Also, if the long duration was due to an accident, we would expect the worker to be more cautious, an aspect of increased vigilance.

The concepts of vacancy, familiarity, and vigilance should be fairly robust in explaining the absenteeism-accident relationship. However, as we mentioned in the discussion of production, there are other variables to include in the model. For example, the centrality of the job is important in explaining the absenteeism-vacancy-accident chain. When a vacancy occurs in a central job, failure to find a replacement will increase the number of production problems during that period, which may contribute to accidents. If a replacement is found, the degree of familiarity of the replacement should be associated with the frequency of accidents either for the replacement or for an adjacent worker. In a less central or peripheral job, a vacancy will have less effect on the production process, and a replacement is less necessary. So centrality affects the probability of a replacement and the number of problems and risks created by a vacancy. The degree to which the job is structured bears on the absenteeism-vigilance-accident chain. Absence in highly routine jobs may increase vigilance and lower accident rates, while the opposite may be true for nonroutine jobs. We also need to recognize that the relationship among these variables may not be linear and that there may be lagged effects among these variables. For example, long absence duration may contribute to initial vigilance, but the degree of vigilance may decline sharply after the first few days back at work.

*Strategies for Research.* The following are some key points in researching the absenteeism-accident relationship:

1.  Choose the appropriate data set. The theoretical discussion of the absenteeism-accident link requires that we be able to trace through the effects of absenteeism on vacancies and on replacements in specific jobs and at specific times in a particular organizational context. Simply collecting summary data at the firm level on absenteeism and accidents is inadequate.

2.  Reformulate the meaning of accidents. Most companies record accidents and indexes of lost-time accidents and no-lost-time accidents. Severity rates and accident costs are also generated from accident reports. The problem with these data is parallel to the problem with data on absenteeism. Companies use different types of reporting schemes. Within companies, different units adopt different conventions in labeling accidents. There is a natural bias to underreport accidents, since they are socially undesirable. At a more microscopic level, accidents may have different meanings to different people at different times in different situations. A worker with accidents that always occur on Fridays has a different accident profile from the worker who has the same kind of accidents that are randomly distributed over scheduled workdays. The different meaning ascribed in these two cases is important. If we want to model the absence-accident relationship, then the meaning we attach to accidents must be congruent with our model. One of our explanations is that absences cause unfamiliarity, which increases the chance of an accident. If our measures of accidents do not reflect our underlying concept of accidents, then prediction will be impossible. For example, unfamiliarity should contribute to an accident. But if our measure of accidents reflects withdrawal behavior (Hill and Trist, 1953), we will not be able to predict accidents.

3.  Develop a baseline model. The ideas in the discussion on the absenteeism-production relationship fit here as well. Before one attacks the absenteeism-accident relationship, some baseline model of accidents should be constructed. In the production analysis, the production function formed the baseline model. The analogy for accidents is less clear. We have approached the baseline in accidents by building an individual- and job-

demographic model for different types of absenteeism. Basically, we want to identify variables that would affect accidents even under perfect attendance. That is, given a common technology, there may be individual (for example, age) and organizational (for example, job shift) factors that affect accidents. Once that model has been estimated, one can pursue the analysis of the absenteeism-accident relations. That is, we want to determine the relative impact of absenteeism on accidents relative to the baseline model.

4. Examine alternative analytical techniques. Both absenteeism and accidents are low-frequency events, and this poses analytical problems in examining this relationship. In some of our data sets, we find that most employees have no accidents, those with accidents typically have one, and a very few employees have more than one accident. For example, on average, in all of our twenty-five data sets, absenteeism may run around 15 percent for all reasons. The majority of the workers (60 percent) have no accidents, and those with only one accident constitute much of the remaining work force (20–30 percent). If we take seriously the idea of refining the meaning of accidents (for example, in terms of withdrawal, uncontrollable accidents, and so on), then there will be fewer observations to study, at least within any common meaning of accidents. The problem is not only the low frequency of these events; their distributional qualities are also quite complex. Clearly, there are traditional statistical techniques for dealing with these data. We would begin our work by estimating a baseline model for accidents and then try to assess the impact of absenteeism. However, we may need to adopt new methods of study for accidents. In our own work, we are moving toward building rich case studies of absenteeism and accident behavior for a given work group. This type of qualitative representation captures the total experience of the work group in a given unit of time. The researcher can see all the complexities of these relationships unfolding within a particular social context. This more clinical approach may be used in addition to more traditional statistical approaches.

*Grievances*

*Empirical Evidence.* The study by Katz and others (Katz, Kochan, and Gobeille, 1982; Katz, Kochan, and Weber, 1982) on industrial relations and economic indicators provides some evidence about the relationship between absenteeism and grievances. Using plant-level data, they reported a correlation $r = 0.26$ ($p < 0.01$) between absenteeism and grievances. Unfortunately, this type of statistic does not speak to the causality of the relationship or what other variables may affect these two variables. In other related analysis, in a regression format, they report that grievances may have a negative effect on direct labor efficiency, a productivity measure. Unfortunately, we have found few other studies that bear directly on this relationship. There are peripheral studies that examine effects of the union on absenteeism (Allen, 1981), of the collective bargaining provisions on absenteeism (Dalton and Perry, 1981), and of the role of the union in representing employee interests on absenteeism (Hammer, Landau, and Stern, 1981), but none of these shed any light on the manner in which absenteeism may affect grievances.

*Theoretical Relationships.* The effect of absences on the number of grievances must be understood in an institutional framework. Many collective bargaining agreements have provisions that state the conditions under which an employee can be dismissed for absenteeism. The agreement also creates the distinction between legitimate absences (for example, holidays) and other kinds of absences. Typically, a worker can have a certain number of unexcused days before being put on probation. Subsequent absenteeism is usually the cause for discipline or discharge. Since these absenteeism-control plans are often formally part of the contract and one function of the grievance process is to deal with the administration of the contract, one would expect absenteeism-related grievances to increase with the presence of a formal plan and with greater enforcement of the plan. The problem is to assess whether the number is significantly larger than some base period (that is, than with no plan) and how large the increase is. The structure of the relationship between absence and grievance is as follows: Absences occur for a variety of reasons. The company counts and classifies the absences. If an absenteeism policy exists and the counts exceed a certain number, disciplinary action occurs, which creates conflict between labor and management. Grievances come into play because there are often ambiguities in the system of classifying absences, and there are likely to be conflicting precedents regarding how absences have been administered in the past.

A different theoretical view that may bear on the absenteeism-grievance relation comes from Hirschman's (1970) *Exit, Voice, and Loyalty*. His basic argument is that employees dissatisfied with some aspect of work can exit (temporarily or permanently) from the organization or can use their voice (via the union) to express their dissatisfaction in order to change the state of affairs. Employees are more likely to exit if they have little loyalty or commitment to the organization. If loyalty exists and there is a possibility for change, "voice" will be used. This framework provides some interesting hypotheses about absenteeism. If loyalty and a mechanism for change exists, there will be a positive relationship between job satisfaction and attendance. That is, dissatisfaction will not increase absenteeism, because a mechanism to address problems exists. A belief in the effectiveness of union representation also will decrease voluntary absenteeism (Hammer, Landau, and Stern, 1981).

While this framework and these hypotheses do not directly explain whether absenteeism causes grievances, they may bear on some of the underlying theoretical processes. The belief that the union is an effective mechanism for change may decrease certain types of absenteeism (Hammer, Landau, and Stern, 1981) that might lower the probability of absence-related grievances. This fact would not remove the relationship between these two variables, but the nature of the relationship may be attenuated. On the other hand, if the workers' belief that the union is an effective mechanism is connected to a belief that the union will be successful in process-ing grievances, then the fear of disciplinary action from absentee-ism will decline, and absenteeism and grievances will increase. Hammer, Landau, and Stern (1981) do not discuss this possibility. Our dilemma, then, with this theoretical position is that there are alternative positions about what will happen to absenteeism and grievances. The contribution of this position is that it focuses on whether the union is powerful in effecting change and raises some alternative hypotheses about satisfaction and absenteeism relationships. Also, the "exit-voice" position is not inconsistent with the institutional position discussed earlier. That position states that, as absenteeism increases, for whatever reasons, where there is some institutional policy about controlling absenteeism, grievances will increase in the course of administering the policy. A powerful union can both reduce the causes of absenteeism, which should decrease grievances, and encourage workers to take marginal absences.

Another possible explanation is that grievances precede absenteeism, and not the opposite. The idea is that grievances are a surrogate for industrial conflict, industrial conflict increases the unpleasantness of work, and absence is a way to avoid that unpleasantness. Earlier we noted that there was some empirical evidence that in low-wage/high-accident plants, workers would take more absences (Allen, 1981), and absence may be a labor market adjustment to low-paying and unsafe jobs. While there may be some appeal to the grievance→absenteeism relationship, there are a number of reasons why it may not be a highly probable or dominant relationship. First, grievances may not be as good an indicator of industrial conflict as strikes. Second, the incidences of grievances are not highly visible. Grievances affect the worker filing the action, the grievance committee, and certain levels of management. Unless a grievance precipitates a strike, it is unlikely that the work force in general would know the incidence rate, content, and disposition of grievances. Since grievance measures may be less visible to the work force than information about low wages or lost-time accidents, we would expect that they would have less impact on aggregate absenteeism.

Another possibility, which we acknowledged earlier in this chapter, is that a third variable may affect grievances and absenteeism. For example, the behavior of a supervisor may cause both absences (as a way to reduce interpersonal conflict) and grievances (by violating certain aspects of the contract). While this alternative explanation is viable, our focus for the rest of this section is on examining whether absenteeism causes grievances, the major theme of this analysis. While we have examined the merits of a variety of specifications of the grievance-absenteeism relationship,

the most viable one, given the context of this chapter, is that absenteeism precedes and/or leads to grievances. The critical factors
seem to be the existence and enforcement of an absenteeism control
plan and the role of the union. The stronger the plan and enforcement procedures, the more likely it is that grievances will occur. If
the union reduces sources of absenteeism, the relationship between
absenteeism and grievances may be alternated. If the union is
powerful and in conflict with management, the association between
these two variables may be strengthened.

*Strategies for Research.* Our position is that absences create
grievances when there is an institutional policy that specifies limits
on absence types and related penalties. To examine the relationship
between absenteeism and grievances, we need to develop a system
for recording grievances. In our current research program on absenteeism and in other research, we have not found good systems for
recording first- and second-level grievances. In most plants, later
stages of the grievance process are usually recorded, because there
are specific parties (arbitrators) and costs associated with grievance
processing. We have found few examples of good systems that capture all the steps in the grievance systems. We also need to assign
meaning to a grievance. This represents the same problem discussed
in respect to absenteeism and safety. Grievances are the result of
a complicated political and negotiation process. Our theoretical
position is that absenteeism leads to particular types of grievances
(absenteeism related), not grievances in general. The problem is
that, when we try to identify grievances related to absenteeism
policy, some may be self-evident, but the description of others may
be masked by some political agenda of labor or management.

In addition, we need to determine the existence of an absenteeism policy. The problem faced by the researcher is to determine
whether such a plan actually exists. We have found in our research
that public testimonials about the plan from either management or
labor tell us little about whether a plan is actually operational. We
see the process of recording an absence type or administering the
plan as a continual process of negotiation between individual workers and management. Separate deals are often made because of
special circumstances. If this characterization is true, one would
look for evidence not of a general policy but rather of different poli-

cies with different classes of workers. The task, then, is to infer the policy from the patterns of absences and the implementation of disciplinary action. A good approach would be to look for people who have similar patterns of absence where one has been disciplined and the other not. By looking at these contrasting cases, we may infer the rules governing the policies. If we can determine the existence of an absenteeism control policy, it would be useful to determine the extent to which there is a single rule or multiple rules for different workers. The greater the number of rules governing the absenteeism-control policy, the greater the number of grievances. If there is one set of rules used by all, there will be lower ambiguity in the policy and fewer grievances. In addition to determining the existence of a rule and the number of rules, some measure of the severity of the policy should be noted. Severity can be measured in terms of the number of people fired because of absenteeism over the total work force or people on the plan. The time elapsed between being subject to an absenteeism-control plan and being fired could be another measure of severity.

Finally, we should examine the institutional structure of the union and management. The institutional structure of the union and the character of labor-management relationships should moderate the absenteeism-grievance relationship and thus should be described. The degree of commitment with which the union grievance committee accepts and processes grievances will affect propensity to file grievances. Past success in winning grievances, position in the union power structure, and the need to reassert power or visibility, particularly in the time of an election, may contribute to the propensity to file grievances. The general character of labor-management relations should also be important. If union and management operate primarily in an adversary role, absenteeism and grievances should be highly related; if they operate in a more cooperative mode, the relationship should be alternated.

*Absenteeism Costs*

What effect does absenteeism have on company operating costs? It has been estimated that more than 400 million workdays are lost because of absenteeism each year. Cost estimates of absenteeism range from $8.5 to $26 billion (Steers and Rhodes, 1978).

*Empirical Studies.* There are only a few published empirical studies that include costs for absenteeism. Macy and Mirvis (1976) estimated the costs of absenteeism in a factory as between $55.36 and $62.49 per incident over a four-year period. Total estimated absenteeism costs for that firm varied from $289,360 to $570,453 per year during that period. Mirvis and Lawler (1977) estimated the costs of absenteeism for tellers in a Midwestern bank. The cost per incident was $66.45. While both studies are carefully done, they tell us more about the process of estimating than the actual costs. We would not expect their reported costs to be generalizable across industries or occupations.

*Theoretical Issues.* There is no well-developed theory on the relationship bewteen absenteeism and costs. Work in human-resource accounting provides one tradition in understanding costs of human resources (Flamholtz, 1974). The recent interest in evaluating the effectiveness of quality-of-working-life projects provides another intellectual tradition in assessing the costs of human resources. In both traditions, the problem is to find a realistic approach to portraying the costs of absenteeism to the firm.

There are several ways to classify the costs associated with absenteeism. The aggregate approach estimates the number of additional workers hired to offset the effects of absenteeism. For example, a firm may need 100 production workers to produce efficiently. However, if a certain percentage of these individuals are expected to be absent, the firm may hire an additional pool of workers (replacements) to offset absenteeism. The cost of recruiting, selecting, training, and paying these additional workers represents one way to estimate the costs of absenteeism. This aggregate approach to estimating absenteeism may overstate absenteeism costs. It is unlikely, at any period, that the pool of additional workers will always be replacing absent workers. Absenteeism rates are not constant over time, so there would be days when replacements may not be needed. In addition, absenteeism does not always lead to replacements. Therefore, the pool of the additional workers will be spending part of their time in other productivity activities, and this needs to be subtracted from costs of absenteeism.

Another approach, more individual in perspective, estimates the incremental costs (or benefits) per day associated with a specific absent worker. If a worker is absent and not replaced, the firm still incurs fringe-benefit costs. In addition, there may be costs incurred from lower productivity or greater chances of accidents for other workers who work in an understaffed situation. If a worker is absent and a replacement occurs, the task is to compare the marginal costs (benefits) that would have been incurred if the worker who was absent had come to work with the costs of the replacement worker. This enumeration includes both direct costs (salary, overtime, fringe benefits, supervisory costs and cost of recruiting and training replacements) and indirect costs (productivity loss, accidents, grievance costs, and physical overhead). In this approach, it is also important to recognize that absenteeism does not always lead to a replacement, so that direct labor costs may not be incurred.

There are a number of interesting theoretical issues underlying the absenteeism-cost relation. One is that there is a natural bias to assume that absenteeism increases costs. Consider the following case: A company hires additional workers to meet staffing needs in the face of absenteeism. That represents a cost. On the other hand, we have pointed to possible benefits to the company, as a function of absenteeism, in terms of short-run improvements in productivity and work group flexibility. This represents a benefit. The net effect may be a benefit. The issue is to recognize that the net effect of absenteeism is not always a cost.

A second issue concerns assigning costs to different meanings of absenteeism. Take the simplest case. Most collective bargaining agreements specify holidays and contract days that one may take and for which one will be paid. The costs associated with these days are costs of doing business. In one sense, they are no different from other labor or material costs. Many collective bargaining agreements give workers time off for bereavement or National Guard duty. Granting these days off reflects the firm's acknowledgment of obligations in the nonwork environment and, again, is an accepted cost of doing business. These types of costs that are agreed upon in the labor contract should perhaps be distinguished from absenteeism costs that are not sanctioned by the labor contract.

Another issue concerns who should be included in the enumeration of costs of absenteeism. Most absenteeism record systems concern nonexempt employees. Almost all studies on absenteeism focus on blue- or white collar workers. Record data are generally not kept on managers. One consideration in considering consequences of absenteeism, particularly the cost issue, is determining the appropriate population for investigation.

The last issue concerns the enumeration of categories for assessing costs. Most researchers (for example, Macy and Mirvis, 1976) include the items we have listed in the direct and indirect costs. A major difference among writers in this area concerns how to deal with costs such as supervisor time, recruiting, selection, and physical overhead. Mirvis and Lawler (1977) include these categories in the assessment of absenteeism costs; Goodman, Atkin, and Seabright (1982) do not. Whether to include these costs depends on how the organization deals with opportunity costs. That is, if a supervisor spends some time each day looking for replacements for absentees, should this time be allocated to the cost of absenteeism? Some argue that while this supervisory activity is being performed, other productivity activities cannot be, so that there is a cost to managing absenteeism. The opposing argument is that there is slack in supervisory jobs. If the supervisor spends time dealing with obtaining a replacement, there is still enough slack within the job to complete other activities without hurting productivity. This issue of allocating fixed costs appears in other areas, such as overhead charges, costs of training replacement workers, and so on.

*Research Strategy.* In developing a research strategy, the following steps should be taken into account.

1.  Develop new information systems. Traditional company accounting records are not designed to deal with the general issue of determining costs of absenteeism. On one level, the data may be there, but not in the desired form. For example, if worker A is absent and replaced by B, this state of affairs needs to be recorded, and then differential wages need to be calculated. In other cases, the data will not typically be collected. For example, in determining costs of absenteeism, we need to know the supervisory time related to absenteeism and the number of additional workers hired to deal with absenteeism. In both of these examples, new data systems would have to be created. That is an expensive task and one that companies may not cooperate with.

2. Estimate direct and indirect costs. To get the correct picture on costs of absenteeism, one must estimate both direct and indirect cost. Despite some of the problems we have mentioned in estimating direct costs of absenteeism, estimating indirect costs will be even more difficult. One must first estimate whether absenteeism changes productivity or accidents and then esti- mate the costs for that amount of change. Both estimation problems, particularly the former, make obtaining reliable estimates of indirect costs very difficult. Some strategies for estimating these indirect costs appear in this chapter and in Goodman (1979) and Goodman, Atkin, and Seabright (1982).

3. Relate costs to meaning of absenteeism. In the theoretical dis- cussion, we argued that it was probably better to separate costs of absenteeism by the types of meaning of absenteeism. Perhaps the simplest way of thinking about delineating mean- ing is to examine it from the point of view of the company and to distinguish between absenteeism that is paid for and legiti- mized by the company and all other kinds of absenteeism. We advocate making this distinction because the meaning of these permitted absence days is clear and represents an a priori agreement about the number and schedule of workdays. An employee may be legitimately absent from work. Other types of absences, such as accident days, excused days, and unex- cused days, are not formally legitimated, subject to multiple meanings from different constituencies, and should be costed separately. This discussion of costs is presented from the point of view of the firm. Different cost estimates would occur if we used different constituencies.

*Affective Reactions*

Does absenteeism affect the worker's affective state? Much of the absenteeism literature assumes the opposite—that negative affective states (for example, job dissatisfaction) can cause absen- teeism. In this section, we want to examine whether absenteeism leads to changes in affective states. The specific hypothesis is that absenteeism can reduce stress and lead to both positive and nega- tive attitude change.

*Empirical Evidence.* There are, unfortunately, very few empirical studies dealing with the absentee→affective reaction relationship. One study, by Staw and Oldham (1978), is interesting because it links absenteeism, attitudes, and performance. They argue that if a person is in an incompatible job (high stress), he or she may require some level of absenteeism to reduce stress. If a person is in a compatible job (low stress), then absenteeism will not serve the same function. They predict a positive relationship between absenteeism and performance in the incompatible jobs. Some empirical data are presented to support this differential hypothesis. While this study is important because it articulates theoretically the need to examine the absenteeism-attitude relationship and the positive consequences of absenteeism, it never directly tests the link between absenteeism and attitudes. That relationship is inferred from the sign of the association between absenteeism and performance for people in compatible and incompatible jobs.

A recent study by Clegg (1983) addresses the relationship between absenteeism and organizational commitment and job satisfaction. A basic thesis in this research is that researchers have focused too much on the attitude→absenteeism relationship rather than giving attention to the opposite causal path or some alternative explanation. Using a longitudinal design, some evidence was presented indicating that absenteeism was negatively related to job satisfaction and that job satisfaction was negatively related to absenteeism.

*Theoretical Relationships.* Absenteeism may have two effects on the individual worker. First, it may decrease or increase stress. Second, it may contribute to positive or negative attitude change. These two effects (stress and attitude change) may be experienced by the absent worker, a co-worker, or a replacement worker. There are many sources of stress at work. One mechanism for dealing with stress is some form of withdrawal, which would include absenteeism. While only a temporary way to manage stress, absenteeism may temporarily reduce experienced stress. This rationale is consistent with the Staw and Oldham (1978) paper. While an absence may reduce stress that is work initiated, prolonged absence may increase experienced stress at home. This stress may be caused by increased role pressures from family members or from the realization that one is not fulfilling the work role. Duration of absence may have consequences for the employee returning to work. The longer the duration, the greater the experienced stress when returning to work. The increased stress may occur because absence should lead to some "piling up of work," and activity levels of work and home probably differ, so that one would have to readjust to activity levels at work. This discussion of stress has focused on the absent worker, not the co-worker. Absence of an employee may increase role overload or stress for the remaining employees. If replacement workers are used, they are likely to experience some levels of role ambiguity given their unfamiliarity with the jobs at hand.

In this chapter, we have distinguished between work and nonwork outcomes. To the extent to which absenteeism permits the realization of valued nonwork outcomes, we would expect to see positive attitudes in these nonwork areas. Opportunities to be with one's family or to enjoy a hobby should lead to positive attitudes. The absent worker also may develop negative attitudes. To the extent to which workers are disciplined by their supervisor or co-workers for absence, interpersonal conflicts may develop, which may lead to negative attitudes toward one's supervisor or fellow workers. Absenteeism may also affect the attitudes of workers who do come to work. If absenteeism creates opportunities for other workers to work on different jobs and those jobs offer rewards such as greater variety, challenge, and skill development, we would expect a shift toward more positive attitudes about work in general. That is, absenteeism creates a rewarding opportunity that can affect attitudes. The critical issue, of course, is whether the new job activities are rewarding and how often the opportunity occurs.

Workers who remain at work may develop negative attitudes toward the absent worker or the company for a number of reasons. First, if the absent worker causes the work load of the present workers to go up, we would expect feelings of inequity and the development of negative attitudes toward the absent worker. Second, absence may be viewed by the employees regularly attending work as a form of inequity. That is, the "contract" is to come to work every day, but some workers come irregularly and still retain their jobs.

The above theoretical explanations focus on direct effects of absence on attitudes. We discussed earlier that the process of explaining absences by the absent individual may lead to attitude change. In this case, the person may attribute (correctly or incorrectly) the reason for absences to poor job or environmental conditions. The more often these attributions get rehearsed (as a function of absences), the more likely it is that they will facilitate the creation of attitudes.

*Strategies for Research.* Delineating the meaning of absenteeism is particularly important for understanding the absenteeism-attitude relation for the absent worker. If absenteeism represents a withdrawal from a stressful situation, we may expect to see a reduction in stress. If, on the other hand, absenteeism represents a planned consumption of nonwork activities (for example, fishing), we may not expect to see changes in stress, while we may expect to see changes in nonwork attitudes. The meaning of absence is less important in the analysis of the present workers' attitudes. In that case, the opportunity for working on another job and the character of that work are the key, not the reasons for the opportunity.

Analyzing this relationship requires a very detailed data set. If we want to examine the relationship among job stress, absenteeism, reduction of stress, and changes in attitude, we need frequent measures of these variables over time. If we want to see whether working on a new job as a result of absenteeism affects worker attitudes, we need measures on job characteristics, need dispositions, and job attitude before and after each job opportunity. While it is possible to develop such a data set, it differs from data sets typically found in the organizational literature.

Both work and nonwork attitudes should be measured. Absenteeism occurs because of work- and nonwork-related factors. To the extent that absenteeism creates the opportunity to perform valued nonwork activities, we would expect changes in attitudes about nonwork activities. Rousseau (1978) has shown that nonwork attitudes can affect absenteeism. Our interest is in demonstrating that absenteeism can affect both work and nonwork attitudes.

## Critical Issues

One of the issues in researching the consequences of absenteeism is identifying the set of consequences. We adopted a constituency perspective from the organizational-effectiveness literature and generated a list of positive and negative consequences for constituencies. While our analysis focused primarily on five consequences, many of the other variables mentioned in Table 7.1 are either included under the five consequence variables or are not central research problems. For example, benefits from compensatory nonwork activities, altered job perceptions, job variety, or skill development for co-workers could all be summed under changes in affective states. Greater crew flexibility or increased coordination problems would fit in the analysis of productivity. There are other consequences listed in Table 7.1 that are not really major research issues. Whether absenteeism leads to loss of pay for the absent worker or overtime for the co-worker is important, but it is hardly a challenging research question.

There are, however, important consequences we have not examined in detail. These consequences are found in social organizations outside the organization, such as the family or union. The omission of these variables is not surprising, since much of our research has a managerial or at least an organization-level bias. Table 7.1 acknowledges that there are other social organizations that are affected by absenteeism. A comprehensive analysis should develop theoretical models and data sets to assess the effects of absenteeism (positive and negative) on these social units. The research task appears to be manageable. Basically, it requires that we learn more about other social arenas, such as the family, and begin to develop data sets to trace through the effects of absenteeism.

The focus of our discussion has been on absenteeism as an independent variable. We have intentionally contrasted this perspective from the modal literature, which treats absenteeism as the dependent variable. However, we do not want to fall into the trap that characterizes most of the literature on absenteeism — that is, a one-way causal path. Absenteeism is both a cause of and a consequence of certain forces. In Clegg's research (1983), evidence for absenteeism as an independent and dependent variable is presented. In addition, in our theoretical discussions, it was pointed out that there are alternative variables that cause both absenteeism and other variables that appear to vary with absenteeism as well as variables that moderate the absenteeism-consequence relationship. The point is rather simple. The absenteeism-consequence relationship is more complicated than we have specified. However, given the amount of theory and research in this area, our strategy would be to focus on this one-way relationship and carefully study some selected relationships before examining forms of reciprocal causation.

Another issue is the population to be studied. Our discussion really focused on occupations where work unfolds in some specific time schedule; we talked about occupations where there are some formal expectations about coming to work at a certain time. Indeed, without these expectations, it is not clear what absence means. What about self-employed people whose occupations do not have specific expectations about time, such as artists? A version of this same issue is that some occupations are somewhat diffuse as to where work is performed. A manager might decide to work at home for a given day. Would that be considered absence? The point of this issue is that absenteeism gets defined primarily in ocupations where people work in a specific place at a specific time. If they are not there, then we observe an absence. The bias in the absenteeism literature and, to some extent, in this chapter is that we have focused primarily on the production worker, tangentially on the manager, and not at all on occupations where expectations about where and when to work are diffuse. In acknowledging this limitation, we also are suggesting some research opportunities. What effect does managerial absenteeism have on the manager's productivity or affective state? What is the relationship among absenteeism, nonwork satisfaction, and productivity for a research scientist or artist?

If we limit our theorizing to occupations where data on absenteeism are collected, one can still raise the question of generalizability. That is, do we expect absenteeism, for example, to have an impact on productivity and accidents across all work settings? The answer to that question should be evident from the theoretical analyses presented in this chapter. The argument was never derived from a particular work setting (for example, coal-mining crews). Rather, our theoretical focus was on variables or parameters that make a difference. For example, in the productivity analysis, the centrality of the job and the amount of discretion in the job are important in assessing the impact of absenteeism on productivity. In different work settings, we might expect to find different distributions of centrality or distributions within jobs and, therefore, different relationships between absenteeism and productivity.

If we can successfully understand the relationships between absenteeism and its consequences, we can focus our attention on other criterion variables. For example, much of the organizational-theory literature is concerned with determinants of performance. Yet we know little about the effect of performance on other variables. How do increases in performance affect absenteeism, accidents, affective states, and so on? What are the critical moderators? What is the nature of the functional relationship? All these questions are important, yet there is little systematic research addressing these questions. The point is that the strategy underlying the absenteeism-consequence relationship could be generalized to other variables, such as performance, turnover, or accidents. We are not advocating examining the interrelationships among a set of criterion variables, for that has been tried in the effectiveness literature with little success (Goodman, Atkin, and Schoorman, 1983). Rather, we are advocating a fine-grained analysis of variables that are traditionally dependent variables in most organizational research. We want to trace out their effects on the individual, work group, organization, and other social units.

## Implications for Practice

An important theme underlying this chapter is that absenteeism has positive and negative consequences at the individual, group, organizational, and societal levels. Unfortunately, many managerial approaches to absenteeism assume that absenteeism has primarily negative consequences. If one works on this assumption of negative consequences, the primary action implication is that absenteeism should be reduced. Our analysis of positive and negative consequences by constituencies indicates that this assumption and the implied course of action may not be correct.

A careful analysis of the benefits and costs of absenteeism may be a useful managerial activity. A careful analysis of both positive and negative effects might uncover an array of latent consequences not previously recognized by managers. We think that this type of analysis will set the stage for different action alternatives. For example, if one-day absences facilitate job switching and enhancement of multiple job skills per employee, the organization may not want to eliminate this form of absence. On the other hand, if one-day absences do not enhance the acquisition of multiple skills and serve primarily to assist in family activities (for example, child care), then action alternatives such as child-care facilities may be appropriate. Identifying the cause and consequence of absenteeism might help in selecting more appropriate action alternatives. If absenteeism does reduce productivity, then understanding the cause of this relationship will have obvious consequences for practice. One factor underlying this negative relationship is the role of the vacancy and/or the unfamiliarity of the replacement in causing lower productivity. One remedy for this situation is training replacements for specific jobs and thus reducing the amount of unfamiliarity when a replacement is necessary. If absenteeism causes accidents, then understanding the cause of this relationship will have obvious consequences for practice. If a worker is absent for a period and returns to a work situation unfamiliar with various aspects of work, the chances for accidents may be increased. One remedy, particularly for workers experiencing long spells of absenteeism, would be to provide some form of safety training prior to returning to work. Or, if absenteeism leads to the replacement of a worker by someone unfamiliar with various aspects of work, then some form of training for the replacement may minimize accidents.

In our analysis of grievances, we pointed out that the existence of an absenteeism-control plan probably will increase the frequency of grievances. The implication is not that one should throw out absenteeism-control plans. Rather, our analysis of absenteeism and grievances indicates that (1) the existence of an absenteeism-control plan may increase grievances, a potential cost to the organization and union; (2) it is difficult to administer an absenteeism-control program so that all employees are treated equitably; and (3) absenteeism-control plans are not quick solutions to reducing absenteeism. If an absenteeism-control plan is implemented, a major investment in training should be undertaken, and a feedback system should be installed to ensure that the program is working equitably over time.

In this chapter, we have shown that absenteeism can have a variety of positive and negative consequences for the individual, co-workers, and organization. We also believe that some levels of absenteeism will exist in any organization, and, therefore, some consequences that we discussed will follow. It may be possible in some cases, however, to alter some of the negative consequences through alternative organizational designs. For example, if absenteeism contributed to accidents and lower productivity in a work group, it may be that redesigning the group into an autonomous work group characterized by multiskilled members who are highly cooperative and cohesive would attenuate the absence-accident relationship. That is, these organizational interventions will not eliminate the consequences of absenteeism but surely will moderate their negative impact. This example is suggested to illustrate how alternative forms of work organization may be important in understanding the absenteeism-consequence relationship.

## References

Allen, S. G. "Compensation, Safety, and Absenteeism: Evidence from the Paper Industry." *Industrial and Labor Relations Review,* 1981, *34* (2), 207–218.

Beehr, T. A., and Gupta, N. "A Note on the Structure of Employee Withdrawal." *Organizational Behavior and Human Performance,* 1978, *21,* 73–79.

Carnegie-Mellon Coal Project. "Determinants of Group Productivity." Unpublished technical report to the U.S. Bureau of Mines, Carnegie-Mellon University, 1983a.

Carnegie-Mellon Coal Project. "Effects of Absences on Accidents." Unpublished technical report to the U.S. Bureau of Mines, Carnegie-Mellon University, 1983b.

Clegg, C. W. "Psychology of Employee Lateness, Absence, and Turnover: A Methodological Critique and an Empirical Study." *Journal of Applied Psychology,* 1983, *68* (1), 88–101.

Dalton, D. R., and Perry, J. L. "Absenteeism and the Collective Bargaining Agreement: An Empirical Test." *Academy of Management Journal,* 1981, *24* (2), 425–431.

Flamholtz, E. *Human Resource Accounting.* Encino, Calif.: Dickenson, 1974.

Goodman, P. S. *Assessing Organizational Change: The Rushton Quality of Work Experiment.* New York: Wiley-Interscience, 1979.

Goodman, P. S., Atkin, R. S., and Schoorman, F. D. "On the

Demise of Organizational Effectiveness Studies." In K. S. Cameron and D. Whetton (Eds.), *Organizational Effectiveness: A Comparison of Multiple Models.* New York: Academic Press, 1983.

Goodman, P. S., Atkin, R. S., and Seabright, M. "Issues and Strategies in Evaluating Employee Assistance Programs." (Contract J0100069, U.S. Bureau of Mines.) Carnegie-Mellon University, Oct. 1982.

Goodman, P. S., and Pennings, J. M. (Eds.). *New Perspectives on Organizational Effectiveness.* San Francisco: Jossey-Bass, 1977.

Hammer, T. H., Landau, J. C., and Stern, R. N. "Absenteeism When Workers Have a Voice: The Case of Employee Ownership." *Journal of Applied Psychology,* 1981, *66* (5), 561–573.

Hill, J. M., and Trist, E. L. "A Consideration of Industrial Accidents as a Means of Withdrawal from the Work Situation." *Human Relations,* 1953, *6* (4), 357–380.

Hirschman, A. O. *Exit, Voice, and Loyalty: Responses to Decline in Firms, Organizations, and States.* Cambridge, Mass.: Harvard University Press, 1970.

Johns, G., and Nicholson, N. "The Meanings of Absence: New Strategies for Theory and Research." In B. M. Staw and L. L. Cummings (Eds.), *Research in Organizational Behavior.* Vol. 4. Greenwich, Conn.: JAI Press, 1982.

Katz, H. C., Kochan, T. A., and Gobeille, K. R. "Industrial Relations Performance, Economic Performance and Quality of Working Life Efforts: An Inter-Plant Analysis." Unpublished paper, Massachusetts Institute of Technology, 1982.

Katz, H. C., Kochan, T. A., and Weber, M. R. "Assessing the Effects of Industrial Relations and Quality of Working Life Efforts on Organizational Effectiveness." Unpublished paper, Massachusetts Institute of Technology, 1982.

Macy, B. A., and Mirvis, P. H. "Measuring Quality of Work and Organizational Effectiveness in Behavioral-Economic Terms." *Administrative Science Quarterly,* 1976, *21,* 212–226.

Mikalachki, A., and Gandz, J. *Managing Absenteeism.* London, Ontario: School of Business Administration, University of Western Ontario, 1982.

Mirvis, P. H., and Lawler, E. E. III. "Measuring the Financial

Impact of Employee Attitudes." *Journal of Applied Psychology,* 1977, *62* (1), 1–8.

Moch, M. K., and Fitzgibbons, D. E. "Automation, Employee Centrality in the Production Process, the Extent to Which Absences Can Be Anticipated, and the Relationship Between Absenteeism and Operating Efficiency: An Empirical Assessment." Unpublished paper, University of Texas at Dallas, 1982.

Mowday, R. T., Porter, L. W., and Steers, R. M. *Employee-Organization Linkages: The Psychology of Commitment, Absenteeism, and Turnover.* New York: Academic Press, 1982.

Naylor, J. C., Pritchard, R. D., and Ilgen, D. R. *A Theory of Behavior in Organizations.* New York: Academic Press, 1980.

Rousseau, D. M. "Short Noted Relationship of Work to Nonwork." *Journal of Applied Psychology,* 1978, *63* (4), 513–517.

Staw, B. M., and Oldham, G. R. "Reconsidering Our Dependent Variables: A Critique and Empirical Study." *Academy of Management Journal,* 1978, *21* (4), 539–559.

Steers, R. M., and Rhodes, S. R. "Major Influences on Employee Attendance: A Process Model." *Journal of Applied Psychology,* 1978, *63* (4), 391–407.

# 8

# Practical Ways to Increase Employee Attendance

Gary P. Latham

Nancy K. Napier

This chapter is written from an advocacy viewpoint in a vein similar to that which is adopted by the legal profession when representing a client. The client in this instance is the employer. The point of view being advocated is that the person who accepts an offer of employment has a contractual obligation, ethically and legally, to come to the place of work.

*Plaintiff's Argument.* An advocacy position is being taken because the number of people who fail to meet this obligation is growing to a point that the world economy is being threatened. And the economic well-being of the world affects directly the quality of life of all of us. In the United States, for example, it is estimated that failure to come to work is costing organizations $15 to $20 billion annually (Cruikshank, 1976). This is because people who stay away from work disrupt work schedules, create the need for overstaffing, and thus add significantly to the labor costs of production. Where overstaffing does not occur, people work short-handed, and quality and costs suffer. In Canada, the Ontario Department of Labor estimates that the cost of absenteeism is one to three times the hourly rate of the absent worker (Manley and Duffy, 1983). In the U.S.S.R., Communist Party Chief Yuri Andropov initiated an ongoing campaign against employee inactivity and irresponsibility. In August 1983, the Kremlin stepped up the offensive by announcing measures aimed at increasing employee attendance ("Getting Everyone on the Wagon," 1983). Under the new rules, people who are absent from their jobs without a good excuse will lose a day of vacation for each day that they are not present. Missing more than three hours of work is treated as a full day's absence. Describing the new decrees, the party daily *Pravda*, according to *Time*, blamed not only workers but also managers who did not (1) set an example of discipline, (2) properly organize the employee's work, or (3) fully use the employee's time. One can only speculate as to the costs of lack of job attendance in Third World countries.

The purpose of this chapter is to describe behavioral interventions that organizations can use to increase the frequency with which people come to the workplace when they are required to do so. An axiom in psychology is that behavior is a function of both a person's ability and motivation. This chapter focuses primarily on the employee-motivation side of this equation with regard to attendance. Thus, absenteeism that occurs for physiologically related reasons (disability) is not discussed (for example, illness, alcoholism, drug addiction), because it is outside our area of expertise. Similarly, such issues as the inability of single parents to attend to their work because of the illness of children and the value of day-care centers as a redress are not discussed. Rather, discussion focuses on ways to motivate people to overcome obstacles, other than loss of physical health, so that they can attend work. In summary, this chapter describes contributions that organizational psychologists and human-resource specialists can make to increase the probability that employees will come to the workplace.

*Is More Better? Defendant's Argument.* Implicit in our advocacy position is that "more is better." This may be a very tenuous position and hence the weak point in our case. We concede (privately — not to the defendant) that attendance most likely has a curvilinear relationship with an organization's costs. Certainly, instances exist where this relationship is true regarding an employee's attendance and productivity. One of us found that as the attendance of employees in pulpwood crews in the South increases, the number of cords per employee hour decreases. Because of overstaffing due to high rates of absenteeism, "more" people on the job site meant that efficiency decreased. No employee was sent home for the day, because of the employer's fear that the person would quit the job in anger and seek employment elsewhere. Similarly, high productivity among the crews correlated significantly with low attendance. The employees were paid on a piece-rate basis. Employees worked until they earned enough money to stay away from the job. An axiom in psychology is that money that is contingent upon performance motivates people. But another axiom is that once a person is satiated with a reward, the reward no longer reinforces the behavior.

That "more" with regard to attendance is bad with regard to costs would appear to be an inference that has already been drawn in the airline industry. Pilots are not allowed to work a forty-hour week. A strong argument might be made by many (for example, patients) that surgeons, too, should be prohibited from working a forty-hour week. This argument, undoubtedly, could be made for other professions as well. Certainly, this is an area where a great deal of research is badly needed. How many hours a week should a person in a given profession work? We don't know the answer.

We do know that stress is a major contributor, either directly or indirectly, to coronary heart disease, cancer, lung ailments, accidental injuries, cirrhosis of the liver, and suicide — six of the leading causes of death in the United States. According to the American Academy of Family Physicians, two thirds of office visits to family doctors are prompted by stress-related symptoms. The cost of such symptoms in absenteeism, company medical expenses, and lost productivity, based on national samples, has been estimated at $50 billion to $75 billion annually, more than $750 for every U.S. employee ("Stress: Can We Cope?" 1983).

In preparing our arguments, we have anticipated that the defendants will charge that absenteeism may serve a maintenance function for them because they have difficulty coping with their work roles. Because their job is either too demanding or not demanding enough, they will state that they experience tension and stress and simply take an "unauthorized vacation" to cope with these feelings. Finally, they will state that attendance has a net negative effect upon their job performance, since attendance under highly unsatisfactory conditions may actually lead to more negative consequences than staying away on a short-term basis (Staw and Oldham, 1978). They will further charge that the plaintiff, in this case the employer, has an ethical obligation to provide employment that is conducive to coming to work.

Thus, we feel confident in our predictions of how the defendants will attempt to rebut our case; we do not feel confident in predicting the conclusion that the court will reach in resolving this debate over "more is better." Hopefully, we will be able to settle the argument out of court. Neither side is currently able to produce evidence showing what constitutes an optimal attendance period. However, if the defendants will agree to come to work, our client will agree to the following interventions: a realistic job preview, validated selection procedures, proper measurement of attendance, orientation training, provision of supervisors with counseling skills, uniform and consistent organizational controls, reinforcement for coming to work, flextime, job enrichment, stress-reduction training, and teaching of self-management to chronically absent employees.

These interventions were selected in accordance with Katz and Kahn's (1966) reasoning that, for an organization to remain in business, it must hire effective people into the system and motivate them to engage in behavior that positively affects the organization's ability to survive. Katz and Kahn classified possible motivational approaches under four major headings: legal compliance, instrumentality, job identification, and the internalization of organizational goals.

With legal compliance, employees follow rules that are perceived as stemming from legitimate sources of authority and that are enforced by legal sanctions. With instrumentality, rewards are the sine qua non of performance in that behaviors are reinforced by linking them to employee-desired rewards. With job identification, performance is so internalized that the activities themselves are reinforcing to the person. Additional incentives are not necessary. The internalization of organizational goals occurs when the goals of the organization represent the person's own personal values.

## Behavioral Interventions to Enhance Attendance

*Matching People to the Job*

*Job Previews.* A first step that can be taken to ensure that people are aware of the job that they will be accepting is to conduct a realistic job preview. The purpose of this job preview is to facilitate a dual matching process between (1) the applicant's capabilities and job requirements and (2) the applicant's individual needs and the organization's climate (Wanous, 1980). This is done by describing both positive and aversive aspects of the job to the applicant. This "realistic" information can be gathered from a variety of sources, such as exit interviews, attitude surveys, discussions about the job between applicants and former employees, and so on.

The realistic job preview can be effective from a self-selection standpoint. It gives the applicant information on which to make an intelligent decision as to whether to accept the employment offer. A person who chooses to accept the offer is likely to have greater commitment to that choice than to one that is made with external pressure and coercion (for example, when recruiters raise applicant hopes or expectations). Job previews can be very effective for reducing turnover (Wanous, 1980).

To date, we know of no study that has investigated the effects of a realistic job preview on subsequent motivation to come to work. However, to the extent that the preview affects commitment to the job, we would hypothesize that such a relationship should exist. Certainly, the concept fits the motivational model of Katz and Kahn (1966) with regard to the need to foster job identification, and it should make clear to the applicant the expected norms within the organization.

*Valid Selection Instruments.* A second step for increasing attendance is to develop valid selection instruments that will identify, prior to hiring, who is likely to come to the workplace frequently. One approach is to select people who are psychologically compatible with their work. *Compatibility* is defined as the extent to which the job content is congruent with the needs and goals of the applicant. Staw and Oldham (1978) hypothesized that people with high needs for growth and development at work are most likely to feel psychologically compatible in complex, involved jobs, whereas people with low growth needs are appropriately matched to simple, routine jobs. Incompatible situations occur when people with high growth needs are offered simple jobs and people who have low growth needs accept complex jobs.

A sample of 348 employees in blue-collar, white-collar, and professional jobs provided support for this hypothesis. Using the job diagnostic survey (Hackman and Oldham, 1975) to measure a person's desire for growth and development on the job, Staw and Oldham found that, when the job was incongruent with an employee's needs there was a positive correlation between absenteeism and performance. There was a negative correlation, however, when the needs of the individual were compatible with the job. With regard to our mock debate in the introduction to this chapter, these findings show that, in terms of performance, more attendance is not always better from either the individual's or the organization's standpoint. From a hiring standpoint, the job diagnostic survey (JDS) may prove useful as a selection tool.

A second selection tool that could prove useful for job attendance is the situational interview (Latham and others, 1980; Latham and Saari, 1984). Like the JDS, the situational interview emphasizes a person-environment interaction. The underlying premise of this interview is that a person's intentions predict behavior in given job situations. The interview is structured in that every applicant is asked the same questions. The questions are based on a systematic job analysis and hence are job related. A unique aspect of the interview is that a scoring key is developed for the interviewer. Thus, unlike the case with most interviews, the interviewer knows not only what constitutes a correct question but in addition what constitutes a correct answer.

Five studies have shown the situational interview to have acceptable interobserver reliability, split-half reliability, and criterion-related validity for predicting the job behavior of people in both entry-level and supervisory positions. Although attendance per se has not been the focus of these studies, it is hypothesized here that valid questions could be developed. The situational interview is also of value in providing applicants with a realistic job preview. Applicants are told that the questions asked of them describe situations that they can expect to experience as job incumbents.

*Measuring Performance*

*Purpose.* Measuring each person's performance serves a two-fold purpose, namely, validation of selection instruments and employee motivation. In order to validate a selection instrument, there must be a performance criterion. For example, if there is a significant correlation between how people perform in a situational interview and how frequently they come to work, the situational interview is a valid indicator of employee attendance. From the standpoint of motivation, measurement in itself may be the most highly effective, underused, and deceptively straightforward approach available for increasing employee attendance. The process is effective because "what gets measured gets done." The simple act of putting a measure on something focuses attention on that area. It tells people that this activity is important to the organization. It increases acceptance of legitimate authority (Katz and Kahn, 1966). It tells people that acceptance of this activity (for example, attendance) is a necessary condition for participation in the system. It emphasizes "the profound truth that the involvement of people in social systems entails generalized obligations to follow systemic demands" (Katz and Kahn, 1966, p. 342). Thus, measuring attendance is effective, according to Katz and Kahn's motivational typology, because it increases legal compliance. Legal compliance increases motivation to attend work to the extent that employees agree that there are specific organizational imperatives that all employees must obey. The act of measurement makes clear what these imperatives are (for example, coming to work).

An example may clarify this point. For several years, one of us wanted to investigate the relative effects on employee attendance of a monetary reward administered on a variable ratio, a variable interval, and a continuous schedule of reinforcement. With the union's permission, baseline data were collected. At the union's insistence, the details of the incentive program were explained at the time that the baseline data were collected. This was done to ensure that no employee could be "surprised" by management placing a new-found emphasis on attendance. Attendance increased immediately, even though the employees were aware that the bonus program would not take effect for another four weeks. It remained high throughout the winter months, when attendance was traditionally low. It remained high (98 percent) despite the fact that all the employees were women who had previously explained that some absenteeism on their part was necessary in order to care for family members who were ill. It remained high even though the bonus plan was never put into effect because the attendance problem no longer existed. It remained high the following year, when again with the union's permission and insistence, the details of the incentive program were explained during the baseline period, and an "apology" was once again given for its cancellation prior to its being put into effect because the absenteeism problem had disappeared.

These results with regard to measurement have been replicated at AT&T: "Management tried everything; the level of absenteeism wouldn't go down. Finally they put up a high, visible board with everybody's name on it and posted a gold star next to each name when people came to work. Absenteeism dropped dramatically — almost overnight" (Peters and Waterman, 1982, p. 268). Thus, we believe that measuring attendance and posting the results for each individual should increase overall employee attendance significantly.

The measurement of attendance is underused because people find the consequences aversive. From the organization's standpoint, it requires the hiring of clerical people to go through time cards and record by hand who is present and who is missing. The task is often assigned to company security guards "to give them something to do." Thus, it is not surprising that Manley and Duffy (1983) report that, in a study conducted by the Ontario Ministry of Labour in 1976, only 17 percent of the organizations reported that they compiled statistics on absenteeism.

With the greater use of computers, coupled with the traditional difficulties of enforcing a disciplinary action due to inadequate documentation, organizations may become less reluctant to record attendance. Supervisors, however, dislike recording absenteeism because they are called upon to make a judgment as to why the person was absent. This judgment is often questioned by the employee, the union representative, the personnel department, and even the supervisor's boss. Thus, the reluctance on the part of supervisors to record absenteeism is understandable. More will be said about this when we discuss the need to give supervisors counseling skills. At the present time, we believe that the act of measurement can be a highly effective intervention for increasing attendance and will more than offset clerical-computer costs inherent in its recording. And if attendance rather than the reason for absenteeism is recorded, supervisory judgment in this area will be minimized.

*Measurement.* The measurement of attendance, however, is not simple—at least for behavioral scientists. In fact, it has been labeled as one of the more severe measurement problems in psychology (Hinrichs, 1980). Among the proposed ways of looking at absenteeism are overall frequency, one-day absences, total time lost, a "blue Monday index," jury leave, and medical absences. The conclusion of such people as Huse and Taylor (1962) is that absenteeism measures generally lack reliability. The conclusion of Steers and Rhodes (1978) is that test-retest reliabilities of absenteeism measures should not be expected to be high. And the conclusion of Atkin and Goodman (1983) is that "it is not at all apparent that reliability, as traditionally considered, is an appropriate statistic" (p. 24).

Although we appear to be alone on this issue, we believe that these arguments are nonsensical. They are nonsense because they propose to throw away the problem (that is, reliability in measurement) because of an inability to solve it. Ignoring a problem will not make it go away. Test-retest reliability is critical in this instance because, to the extent that the absenteeism measure lacks stability, it cannot be predicted. The absence event takes on the characteristics of randomness. The outcome will be the discarding of effective predictors of and controls for attendance because they appear to have no relationship with it (Type II measurement error—an erroneous conclusion that the predictor/intervention was ineffective).

A primary problem with traditional approaches to measuring absenteeism is that researchers confuse cause and effect in their measure. That is, they make causal attributions, such as "attitudinal" reasons (Atkin and Goodman, 1983). In addition, researchers focus on measures that are heavily dependent upon self-report, thus precluding verification (that is, interobserver reliability). Making matters worse is the fact that there are almost always aversive consequences for employees who tell the truth, making factual self-report unlikely. How many people are likely to report that they did not come to work because they wanted to go fishing, work around the house, make up for lost sleep, or meet an interesting person of the opposite sex?

The solution to this problem is to choose a measure that is valid, reliable, free from contamination, and practical (Thorndike, 1949). Thus, Latham and Pursell (1975, 1977) have proposed measuring absenteeism from the opposite side of the coin — namely, attendance. This criterion is valid in that it truly measures what it purports to measure, that is, whether the person is on the work site. It is likely to have high construct validity in that it will have a high negative correlation with other measures of absenteeism to the extent that these other measures are reliable. The attendance measure has been shown to have high test-retest reliability (for example, 0.90). Interobserver reliability should approach 1.0. It is subject to contamination largely to the extent that there is error variance due to computational, typographical, and data transcription errors. But, even where this occurs, it is likely that consensus will be reached through discussion, as is done in observations of assessees by assessors in assessment centers. Attendance is a practical measure from an administrative standpoint in that all a person need do is record his or her presence. Thus, it can be self-administered rather than have clerks transpose the data from time cards.

To buttress our point regarding practicality and effectiveness, Miller (1978) reported a study conducted at Parkdale Mills, Inc. Prior to the study, people who were absent were reprimanded. Those who had good attendance records received no comments. A fifteen-week baseline showed that attendance averaged 86 percent. At the end of the baseline period, a daily attendance chart was placed in the work area. A blue dot was placed on the chart beside the name of each person who was on the job. A red dot was placed beside the name of each person who was off the job. A person who had been absent was welcomed back to the job by the supervisor. No oral or written reprimands were given. The supervisor maintained this graph daily. In addition, he posted a weekly attendance graph that showed the percentage of people who attended the job each day. From a baseline average of 86 percent, attendance averaged 94.3 percent for the following nine-week period. The costs of this program were less than $10.

The advantages of an attendance measure from a motivational standpoint are twofold. First, it accentuates the positive rather than the negative. This in itself, we believe, is to be applauded. Second, it minimizes judgments as to why the person is not on the job so that supervisors can be confident that they are unlikely to be punished for a "wrong guess." It is this second advantage that other researchers see as a disadvantage in using attendance as a criterion measure. Ilgen (1977, p. 232), for example, has argued that we need "to distinguish between absenteeism per se and absenteeism 'for what.'" An attendance measure is said to be obtuse because it is incapable of isolating the subset (cause) of interest.

Smulders (1980, p. 369) has echoed these points. An attendance "measure gives neither information on frequency per employee nor on the duration of the spells. In practice it is indeed almost impossible to construct and apply attendance frequency and duration measures (e.g., what to do with an attendance spell of ten years' duration?)" Our answer to Smulder's question is unequivocal: reward it. More will be said later on the subject of tying rewards such as praise and attention to attendance. Suffice it to say here that behavioral scientists have a penchant for wanting to confound cause and effect in their measures of absenteeism.

For us, our solution to these issues is no different from that which is followed regularly regarding the measurement of productivity. In the logging industry, for example, one measures productivity in terms of cords or cunits per employee hour. If productivity is low, one looks for causes. Causes are thus treated as a possible intervention or independent variable to be manipulated, rather than as a dependent variable to be measured because of primary importance in its own right. For example, the researcher interested in improving the productivity of loggers might look at ways of (1) tampering with existing equipment or introducing new equipment, (2) moving the people to different terrain, and/or (3) getting the people to set a specific challenging production goal.

The key difference between a predictor, or an independent variable, and a criterion, or a dependent variable, is that the former (for example, goal setting) takes on significance only in its relationship to (effect on) the latter (for example, cords per employee hour; attendance). In studies on attendance, one may very well want to look at various subsets as predictors (for example, illness) or independent variables (for example, access to medical specialists), but one would be well advised to look at employee attendance as the dependent variable. To do otherwise, as we noted earlier, is likely to lead to a Type II measurement error because of unreliability in the criterion (absence) measure. We believe that it is time for behavioral scientists to stop looking for reliable absence measures, to stop calling for new ways of looking at reliability simply because of frustration with the problem, and instead to devote our efforts to ways of increasing, when appropriate, employee attendance.

## Training

*Orientation.* Assuming that realistic job previews have been conducted, that the people are hired into jobs that are "right" for them, and that attendance measures are taken and made salient to the employee, the next intervention to ensure high attendance is orientation training. Rosen and Turner (1971) found that company-conducted orientation programs result in hard-core hires becoming as stable employees as those hired who had met "normal hiring criteria." Their training program was extensive. It consisted of twenty-one hours of exposure in fourteen sessions over a twelve-week period. The content of the training was job oriented and directed by company personnel. The strategy was to modify poor work habits and develop an acceptance and understanding of the organization's need for employee attendance. The benefits of working for the company were made explicit to the employees. The relevant rules and penalties for violating them were emphasized again and again. The rationale for the rules and penalties was discussed at length. Where there was a problem employee, the company trainer called the person aside and presented a clear picture of the consequences related to rule breaking but also interceded with the employee's supervisor on the employee's behalf.

The result, as noted above, was that after six months the hard-core became as stable a work force as people hired through the company's normal hiring channels. However, this was accomplished by loosening the company's standards regarding absenteeism during the orientation training period. This is further evidence that "more (attendance) is not always better." It was recognized by the company when the training program was initiated that habit patterns developed during extended periods of unemployment, particularly related to time, have to be extinguished before the hard-core hire can effectively operate within the constraints that a daily job imposes on one's personal freedom. Consequently, unauthorized absenteeism was higher in the hard-core group of employees during the orientation period than it was among the non–hard-core group.

The authors did not report follow-up statistics on attendance as a supplement to their research. However, it would appear reasonable to expect that such a study would show no significant differences in attendance between hard-core and non–hard-core employees once both sets of employees accepted organizational rules and regulations. Thus, a primary advantage of orientation training, using Katz and Kahn's (1966) motivational typology, is that it facilitates legal compliance.

*Supervisory Counseling.* In separate reviews of the literature, Hinrichs (1980) and the Educational Research Service (1980) found no consistent linkage between supervisory practices and employee attendance. However, none of the reviewed studies focused on teaching supervisors counseling skills to deal with attendance or other employee problems. We believe that such training is and always has been necessary for supervisors. In their study, discussed earlier, on the effects of orientation training, Rosen and Turner (1971) found that a company trainer was more effective than a university-based psychologist because the company trainer represented the company and could assess the rules realistically, particularly in terms of the supervisors that would be implementing them. Based on this reasoning, we would hypothesize that a supervisor would be even more effective than a company trainer in bringing about and sustaining a positive behavior change given that the supervisor has been trained in problem solving with an employee. Such training should also make supervisors willing to record and deal with attendance problems. An effective training methodology for teaching supervisors problem-solving skills is behavior modeling (Latham and Saari, 1979). Wexley and Nemeroff (1975) found that a decrease in absenteeism resulted from goal setting and feedback regarding role-playing exercises involving dealing with different employees who want to take vacation at the same time, telling employees that they are abusing coffee breaks, denying overtime to subordinates who insist upon it, and getting agreement among subordinates on how to maximize profits.

It is our opinion that supervisors are a key to keeping attendance rates high. It is they who should be responsible for keeping attendance records, so that a high attendance rate can be rewarded and a low attendance rate can be corrected. This is not likely to be done if the attendance data are buried in time cards, if the supervisor is continually second-guessed by others on judgments regarding the "why's" underlying an absence, if the supervisor is not trained in how to focus on problems rather than personalities, and if the rules regarding attendance are vague and subject to many interpretations.

*Control Programs*

A great deal of behavior can be predicted once we know the rules of the game. A job preview that is realistic will make the rules salient. An effective selection instrument will predict who is likely to follow these rules. If the rule is truly important to the organization, compliance with it should be measured on the part of each employee. In addition, orientation training should be conducted, and supervisors should be counseled on how to ensure that compliance occurs. The rules should define who constitutes a "problem" employee.

Legal compliance rests upon at least two conditions (Katz and Kahn, 1966). First, there must be minimum interpretation of what the rule is, or it will not be seen as having a character of its own, but rather as a means for obtaining individual advantage. This undermines the legitimate basis for compliance. Second, the individual must be involved in the social system.

*Discipline.* Another axiom in psychology is that behavior is a function of its consequences. If the consequences are aversive, the behavior is unlikely to be repeated. However, an axiom in case law is that the aversive consequences with regard to discipline programs must meet just-cause standards. In this regard, Rosenthal (1979) has noted the following:

1. The rules regarding an attendance policy not only must be published, but they must be communicated directly to the employees.

2. Clarity is essential. An arbitrator found a discharge to be without just cause because the rules required only "notice to management" regarding an absence without stating that the employee himself must do the notifying. The employee had had a friend notify the supervisor that he wouldn't be coming to work.

3. The organization must make it clear that it intends to enforce the attendance rules. Here is another value of making it clear to each person that his or her attendance is being measured daily.

4. Management discretion must be minimized. In one case, a company excused absences due to "acts of God." An arbitrator ruled that the company was remiss in not ruling an absence that occurred as a result of a snowstorm an "act of God."

5. Consistency must exist. Many company rules provide that, as the final step in progressive discipline, the employee is "subject to discharge." This discretion to discharge would appear reasonable and compassionate to most psychologists, but it makes the arbitrator's task of evaluating consistency exceedingly complex.

6. Length of employment is given little weight by arbitrators.

7. Progressive discipline steps should be followed, such as an oral warning, a written warning, and a suspension before termination occurs. Again, we see in this requirement the value of teaching supervisors problem-solving counseling skills. According to Rosenthal, arbitrators do not see excessive absenteeism in and of itself as just cause for discharging a person. "An employee may be discharged for just cause (excessive absenteeism) only if industrial due process (as that term has been interpreted by the individual arbitrator) has been afforded (p. 740).

   Legal issues aside, the question remains as to the effectiveness of sanctions on employee attendance. In a study involving classroom attendance, Baum and Youngblood (1975) found that when people were informed that attendance was expected and that it would affect the course grade and attendance was obtrusively taken each day, attendance was greater than in a class where this was not done.

In a review of the organizational-behavior literature, Beyer and Trice (1983) found only one field study that focused on the use of negative sanctions in industrial organizations. O'Reilly and Weitz (1980) looked at the effects of discipline on surrounding work groups rather than its effects on the problem employee. They found that the use of informal warnings, formal warnings, and discharges was positively related to group performance.

In a study involving nineteen locations of a large U.S. corporation that has a job-based alcoholism program incorporating progressive discipline, Beyer and Trice (1983) themselves found that only informal discussion had positive effects; written warnings had negative effects, and other forms had no effect on employee behavior. This finding supports Arvey and Ivancevich's (1980) conclusion that punishment of moderate intensity may be more functional than that of greater intensity.

In support of this conclusion, there is a before-after study by Nicholson (1976) that showed that the sudden imposition of management sanctions on blue-collar workers resulted in employees altering the form rather than the level of their absences. The employees simply stayed away from the workplace for longer time periods and provided medical support for the absence with greater frequency than they had done prior to the imposition of these sanctions.

Clearly, this is an area for fruitful research, since discipline is a fairly common occurrence in organizations, and its effects have yet to be systematically and thoroughly studied with regard to attendance. However, it would appear that an attendance-control policy, established by a legitimate source of authority and implemented with clear-cut, progressively enforced legal sanctions, should lead to significant improvements in employee attendance. The one study that looked at multiple behavioral outcomes showed that not only did attendance increase, but so did performance. Satisfaction with the supervisor on the job did not decrease as a result of the control strategy based on legal compliance. However, this one study involved college students (Baum and Youngblood, 1975); more studies similar in nature are needed.

*Employee Involvement.* Another approach to obtaining legal compliance is for employees to see sanctions against absenteeism as their sanctions. In this way, motivation to conform to them is so internalized that performance, in this instance attendance, is autonomous. To reject the rules of the system that they themselves developed is tantamount to rejecting the system itself, which includes one's peers.

Nadler (1981) has outlined several action steps that organizations can take to overcome employee resistance to change. These steps might be adopted as follows to develop a unified team approach to motivating people to come to work.

1. Identify and surface dissatisfaction with current attendance rates. People need to be "unfrozen" from their inertia about coming to work or they will not be motivated to change (Lewin, 1947). The greater the pain and dissatisfaction with the current state of low attendance rates, the more likely people will want to see change. This can be done by measuring attendance and showing employees how costs due to low attendance rates are affecting the organization, department, unit, and employee. At the time of this writing, the economic climate is threatening the survival of many companies. Several of our client companies are sharing cost data with supervisors, union representatives, and hourly employees in the hope that, together and individually, people will find ways of reducing costs in order to save jobs. Attendance is one way of minimizing costs. Peters and Waterman (1982) found that the "excellent" companies that have a policy of making such information available to employees stand in vivid contrast to typical management fears that the information will be abused by employees and that only competitors will benefit from it.

2. Build participation into the change. Participation facilitates the communication of information about what the change will be and why it has come about. Thus, one of our clients is asking the employees themselves to develop the rules regarding attendance and the appropriate sanctions for those who fail to

follow them. Employees and management representatives together determine whether and what type of sanctions should be applied to an individual who fails to come to work.

3. Reward attendance. People are motivated to behave in ways that they perceive as leading to desired consequences. Rewards such as bonuses, pay systems, promotions, recognition, job assignment, status symbols, and so on should be examined as ways to support high attendance rates. Peters and Waterman (1982, p. 268) cite William Manchester in describing his World War II experience as a foot soldier: "A man wouldn't sell his life to you, but he will give it to you for a piece of colored ribbon." In doing their research on top-performing American companies, Peters and Waterman were struck by the volume of contrived opportunities used by McDonald's, Tupperware, and IBM for showering employees with pins, buttons, badges, and medals. At Mars, Inc., an extremely successful consumer-goods company, every employee, including the president, receives a weekly 10 percent bonus for coming to work on time each day.

4. Finally, people need to be provided the time and the opportunity to disengage from the present stage (for example, organizational tolerance of low attendance rates). Change often creates a feeling of loss. People need to mourn the old system, when attendance was not critical in the company and the termination of an employee for absenteeism was all but impossible. Nadler argues that those advocating change must take the need for this time period into account by giving people information about the problems of status quo (costs of low attendance rates) and by allowing enough time in advance of a change to allow people to recognize the "loss" and prepare for it. The wisdom of this advice was underscored in our earlier discussion of orientation training for hard-core employees where attendance rules were temporarily relaxed, while the need for high attendance rates was repeatedly stressed.

In summary, it is our hypothesis that employee involvement in the formation of rules will help internalize them in employees and thus bring about routine compliance with the fundamental contract that exists between an employer and an employee, namely, employee attendance. We believe that this strategy is especially helpful for organizations that traditionally have not enforced attendance and now wish to do so. To the extent that employee internalization of rules takes place, Nadler's third step, involving the external reinforcement of attendance, should not be necessary. To the extent that employee involvement does not foster internalization of the rules, external reinforcement may be necessary.

*Instrumental Satisfaction*

A second approach to motivation in Katz and Kahn's typology is the linking of employee-desired rewards to organizationally desired employee behavior. Thus, a person's actions become instrumental in achieving specific rewards. This approach to motivation differs from legal compliance in that the latter is used primarily to remind people that they must meet organizational requirements because it is their duty to obey and because they will run afoul of organizational law if they do not (Katz and Kahn, 1966). The present approach focuses employee attention on the positive consequences of behavior. This approach to motivation, specified in Nadler's third step for overcoming resistence to high attendance, is exemplified in Skinner's (1953) *behavior modification* techniques. An initial step from the organization's standpoint is to examine the positive and aversive consequences of coming to work versus being away from work. For example, Morgan and Herman (1976) found that the positive consequences for staying away from work as perceived by people with low attendance included a break from the routine, personal business, and an increase in leisure time. In addition, they did not have to deal with transportation problems.

An axiom in behavior modification is that, if one changes the consequences, one can change behavior. Thus, a second step is to maximize the positive consequences of coming to work and to minimize the aversive. Concomitantly, one can maximize the aversive consequences of staying away from work and minimize the positive. One way of doing this, based on the data collected by Morgan and Herman, would be to make "free time" contingent upon attendance and to increase the absolute amount of loss of wages and benefits contingent upon absences for those employees whose attendance is poor.

The organization could also enforce discharges contingent upon a continuing pattern of low attendance. As Hinrichs (1980) has noted, a dispassionate analysis of the rewards associated with coming to work as opposed to staying away often indicates that the balance is in favor of staying away from work. Sick-leave programs in many organizations, in effect, provide built-in rewards for not coming to work, along with no aversive consequences. Thus, at the present time, most employees are rewarded in two ways for not coming to work: (1) rewards associated with nonwork activity and (2) rewards associated with sick-pay benefits.

There have been a multitude of studies showing that monetary bonuses contingent upon coming to work increase attendance (for example, Pedalino and Gamboa, 1974). However, Kempen (1982) has argued that such interventions are not always cost effective, because all perfect or near-perfect attenders receive the money, even though they cannot improve their attendance. To avoid this cost, Kempen suggests that two questions be asked: (1) What privileges would people like to have that they do not have now? (2) What do they find irritating or aversive in the work setting? The answers to these questions provide a list of possible rewards for reinforcing attendance. Kempen concluded his discussion with explanations as to how freedom from the requirement of punching a time clock, allowing a flextime work schedule, and granting a disciplinary immunity privilege can be made contingent upon high attendance. In addition, participating in employee-involvement groups could be made contingent upon high attendance.

It would appear that the steps used to obtain legal compliance combined with those used by behavior modification practitioners should be extremely effective for increasing attendance rates. A study by Kempen and Hall (1977) supports this view. In a large manufacturing company, employees were reinforced with nonmonetary incentives for good attendance. Progressive disciplinary warnings were used to punish low attendance. Attendance increased to 97 percent, higher than any rate previously achieved at the plant in its eighteen-year history.

*The Job Itself*

*Flextime.* A strong opposing view has been presented by Chadwick-Jones, Nicholson, and Brown (1982) regarding the idea that attendance can be effectively influenced by management intervention. They argue that absenteeism is a characteristic of blue-collar jobs primarily because there is little discretion given to holders of such jobs to leave work for a short time during the day to attend to critical nonwork-related duties. Professional and managerial employees, on the other hand, are not required to account clearly for their time and thus can more easily leave work to visit a doctor, attend to a child, get an automobile repaired, and so on.

Evidence to support the view that flextime work schedules reduce absenteeism includes a study on job sharing (Olmstead and others, 1979) involving civil service employees. The cost of employing two job sharers was $1,472 less than the cost of employing one full-time employee. In addition, job sharers used less sick leave than their full-time counterparts and had higher attendance rates.

On the basis of the extensive work done in Europe (Chadwick-Jones, Nicholson, and Brown, 1982) as well as many studies conducted in North America, it would appear that flextime and job sharing are effective interventions for increasing attendance. We would not go so far as to say that this is "the" intervention to use, but we would hypothesize that this procedure should minimize the use of aversive consequences on the part of organizations for increasing attendance and maximize the organization's use and effectiveness of positive reinforcers. What we don't know at the present time is the answer to the chicken-egg question. Should flextime and/or job sharing be made contingent upon high attendance rates, or is it more effective to implement flextime for everyone and reinforce high attendance with other rewards?

*Job Enrichment.* In writing this chapter, we have been struck by the paucity of evidence that staying away from the workplace is a problem with managerial and professional employees. This point was stressed strongly by Chadwick-Jones, Nicholson, and Brown (1982). It would appear that these people experience what Katz and Kahn (1966) term *job identification.* To arouse and maximize job identification, Katz and Kahn posit that the job itself must provide sufficient variety, sufficient complexity, sufficient challenge, and sufficient exercise of skill to engage the abilities of the employee. Internalization of organizational goals can occur to the extent that employees (1) participate in important decisions about group objectives, (2) contribute to group performance in a significant way, and (3) share in the rewards of group accomplishment (Katz and Kahn, 1966). When these three conditions are met, people can regard the group as theirs. We have touched upon this in our discussion of employee involvement in developing employee sanctions for low attendance. Job enrichment would appear to be a means of fostering job identification, because it focuses on employee desire for task identity, autonomy, feedback, variety, recognition, and advancement. Sociotechnical interventions should foster internalization of job/organizational goals, because the employee is involved in a group that designs the job/organization so as to maximize sociotechnological concerns.

In a review of the literature, the Educational Research Service (1980) cited a plethora of studies showing that these two related types of interventions do in fact increase attendance. However, they concluded their review with a quotation from Steers and Rhodes (1978, p. 394) regarding the lack of research rigor surrounding the studies, so that "we are left with largely hearsay evidence that job enrichment reduced absenteeism." On the basis of Katz and Kahn's motivational typology, we hypothesize that, when rigorous research is conducted, a relationship will be found between job enrichment and high employee attendance.

Similarly, we hypothesize that when rigorous studies are conducted on team-building interventions, high attendance rates will be found. Our optimism is based on the early work of Mayo and Lombard (1944), who found that attendance was highest for those people who were considered team players. Team-building is an intervention designed to get a group to agree on (1) work-related issues that need to be solved, (2) the solutions to these issues, and (3) goals and timetables regarding who will do *what* and *when* in implementing the solutions. In short, team building maximizes involvement of employees in decisions that affect them.

In using enrichment strategies, we are reminded of our earlier discussion regarding the need for valid selection instruments that take into account individual differences. We would agree that job identification and the internalization of organizational goals are at once the most effective of motivational patterns, as well as the most difficult to evoke in some employees. There are people who do not want responsibility and instead want minimal involvement in their work. Their primary identification is with other organizations, such as their union. They may see "enrichment" as a means of flattening the organization, thus denying them advancement opportunities to a leadman or supervisor position. These people may want only job security and to be left alone.

In this vein, even a very limited approach to enrichment may be effective. For example, in the tissue-napkin department of a paper-products company, employees who were allowed to set their own pace and make machine adjustments or corrections while processing was under way had less absenteeism than people who did not have this privilege (Fried, Weitman, and Davis, 1972). Regardless of whether there is a direct relationship between job-enrichment programs and attendance, we do know that the underutilization of a person's skills can lead to job stress (Gupta and Beehr, 1979).

*Stress Management*

As we noted in the introduction to this chapter, there are those who would argue that absenteeism is an effective means for coping with stress. That there is a correlation between job stress and absenteeism has been shown in a review of the literature (Educational Research Service, 1980). For example, Douglas (1976), in a study on teacher absenteeism, found that much of the absence reported as physical illness was a result of psychological stress.

Rather than encourage people to take time off from work and then subsequently return to the "problem," it would appear wise to provide people with training in stress management. Such programs have become all but faddish in their promulgation by corporate training departments, but effective programs developed by clinical psychologists do exist. Wolpe's (1958) well-known desensitization program using muscle-relaxation techniques, mental imagery, and the conditioning of relaxation responses to aversive stimuli is one such example. Smith's (1980) approach has been evaluated using both time-series designs and pre- and postmeasure designs with random assignment of individuals to training and control groups. The program involves five phases: (1) pretreatment assessment of issues affecting performance, (2) provision of a rationale for learning self-control and coping abilities, (3) training in voluntary muscle relaxation and deep breathing skills, (4) induced affect in which people are asked to imagine as vividly as possible a stressful situation taking place, and (5) coping skills that are taught in terms of relaxation and self-statements.

*Self-Management*

There is evidence that absenteeism is more likely to be spontaneous than carefully considered over time (Porter and Steers, 1973). Moreover, some employees may be absent chronically while others are not. A study at Hydro-Quebec found that one third of the work force were total nonabsentees and that repeated absences were limited to only 20 percent of the company's employees (Alain-Daniel, 1969).

Again, it would appear that there is a methodology in clinical psychology, namely, self-management, that would be useful to organizational psychologists and human-resource specialists in bringing about a behavior change. Self-management (Mills, 1983), also called "self-control" (Thoresen and Mahoney, 1974) and "self-regulation" (Slocum and Sims, 1980), implies responsibility over certain aspects of decision making and behavior on the part of individuals. Specifically, it is an effort by an individual to change his or her behavior in a way that is not what he or she would naturally have pursued (Thoresen and Mahoney, 1974).

The theory underlying self-management can be found in work by Bandura (1982) and Kanfer (Erez and Kanfer, 1983; Kanfer and Bursemeyer, 1982). Bandura has noted that people who judge themselves as inefficacious in coping with environmental demands imagine their difficulties (for example, transportation problems, caring of family members) as more formidable than they really are. In contrast, people who have a strong sense of efficacy focus their attention and effort on the demands of the situation and are spurred to greater effort by obstacles.

The use of self-management techniques may fall within Katz and Kahn's (1966) fourth motivational typology, namely, the internalization of an organization's goals regarding attendance. This is because a person's interest in attendance grows from satisfaction derived from fulfilling internal standards (presumably high) and from perceived self-efficacy gained from performance accomplishments (for example, arriving at work).

In Bandura's social learning theory, an important cognitively based source of motivation occurs through the use of goal setting and self-evaluative reactions. Thus, the focus of self-management is on internal comparison when performance is evaluated against personal standards. By making self-satisfaction conditional on goal attainment, employees create self-incentives for their efforts to come to work.

A pattern where competency goes unrewarded or is punished underscores the need to differentiate between self-efficacy, a belief that one can perform acts necessary for coping, and outcome expectancies, a belief that the environment will be responsive to one's efforts. Severe resentment and protest are likely to occur if the person believes that obstacles regarding attendance, such as child care, can be overcome but that the environment will be unresponsive (for example, supervisors will continue to see one as a "problem employee"). In extreme cases, employees may become so chronically preoccupied with self-depreciation that they "give up." This is why recognition-reinforcement of desirable behavior is so important.

Kanfer's model (Erez and Kanfer, 1983; Kanfer and Bursemeyer, 1982) focuses on two important components: (1) a sequence of goal-related events and (2) the source of control over the behavior or actions that an individual may take during those events. The sequence of goal-related events includes setting, monitoring, evaluating, and reinforcing behavior for goal attainment.

For self-management to be effective, not only must an employee have a goal and understand it, but this person must accept that it is a goal to be pursued. Otherwise, monitoring, evaluating, and reinforcing will have no impact on behavior. Self-management programs frequently include contractual agreements that are often written as a way to link external control and internal motivation (Erez and Kanfer, 1983). The purpose of these contracts is to

(1) clarify expectations for individuals and "external control sources," such as supervisors, (2) enhance commitment to the stated expectations for change, and (3) improve performance (Kanfer and others, 1974).

Self-management has been used effectively to change the behavior of smokers (Kanfer and others, 1974), drug abusers (Kanfer and others, 1974), alcoholics (Kanfer and Phillips, 1970) and sexual offenders (Kanfer and Phillips, 1970). Of relevance to this paper is that self-management has been used effectively to reduce anxiety and stress (Rehm and Marston, 1968). It is our hypothesis that self-management will also prove to be effective in increasing the attendance of chronic absentees.

## Issues for Research

It is reinforcing in our field to see the cup as either half-full or half-empty. To see the cup as half-full is rewarding for practitioners, because it enables them to function in organizational settings. To see the cup as half-empty is rewarding for academicians, because it enables them to do "more research."

In preparing a chapter on attendance, we decided to write from the practitioner's standpoint. This is because we were impressed by existing theories that enable the prediction, control, and understanding of attendance. We especially liked Katz and Kahn's (1966) motivational typology as a way of moving from legal compliance to the internalization of organizational goals. To be sure, these are not discrete categories; there are motivational techniques, such as behavior modification and self-management, that can be used as easily to inculcate internatization of organizational goals as legal compliance.

In addition, we were impressed by the wealth of rigorous empirical studies showing that attendance can be increased. This only strengthened our own protestant-work-ethic bias that people who accept employment and therefore, by implication, agree to come to work should in fact do so. But by adopting this position, we immediately tripped over issues that do in fact require "more research" before they can be adequately addressed. Included in these issues are the following questions:

1.  Is there an optimum number of hours that people in given professions should work? Is there a curvilinear relationship between attendance and costs? Would the question be more appropriately phrased if it focused on individual differences?

2.  Is it more effective to allow people to take time off from the job to reduce stress than it is to teach them stress-control techniques? Again, to what extent should attention be focused on individual differences? Matteson and Ivancevich (1983) have reported on a six-item scale that measures the rate at which people are able to leave job tensions quickly behind at the end of the workday. People who score poorly on the instrument miss more work and visit their physicians more often than do those who receive high scores.

3.  To what extent are job-enrichment sociotechnical interventions sufficient for reducing job tension and hence absenteeism because of a focus on reducing interrole conflicts? And there are always questions regarding sequencing and/or combining approaches involving valid selection instruments (individual differences), allowing people discretion in taking time off, teaching stress-control techniques, and involving employees in the design of their jobs.

4.  Where the primary focus is on legal compliance for increasing attendance, to what extent is measurement sufficient in itself to reduce absenteeism? There are so few organizations that measure attendance and absenteeism in any systematic way that we do not know the answer to this question. How ironic it would be if the huge costs resulting from low attendance disappeared with two relatively simple interventions: (1) the systematic measurement and posting of attendance data and (2) implementing flextime so that people can attend to important nonjob-related activities during the workday.

5.  Should an intervention such as flextime be made contingent upon high attendance, or should it be made available to everyone?

6.  Is orientation training an effective way to increase the attendance of people in entry-level jobs?

7.  Does teaching supervisors problem-solving counseling skills enable them to increase employee attendance?

8. Should disciplinary programs be explicit and rigid, with little or no room for judgment?
9. In increasing attendance, is it more effective to emphasize positive consequences, aversive consequences, or both?
10. Is Andropov correct in his emphasis on managers properly organizing an employee's time?
11. Can self-management be used as an effective method for increasing attendance?
12. If employees participate in the development and enforcement of sanctions for low attendance, how many people should do so? Should it be done on a department-by-department basis, without concern for uniformity and consistency across the organization? As new employees enter the department or organization, must they review and approve the sanctions?

We remain optimistic that organizations can increase employee attendance significantly and thus lower their costs due to absenteeism. We believe that organizational psychologists and other human-resource specialists can help organizations in this regard if they devote attention to answering questions such as these as they affect attendance, rather than continuing their blind pursuit of a reliable and valid measure of subsets of absenteeism.

## Overview

Two questions served as the basis for writing this chapter: How can we get people to come to work? How do we know that our efforts are successful? If we minimize discussions of ability, the first question leads to a focus on motivation. Consequently, we were drawn immediately to Katz and Kahn's (1966) typology of legal compliance, instrumental satisfaction, job identification, and the internalization of organizational goals. It could be argued that the word *how* is mechanical in that the emphasis is on prediction and control. It contrasts with the word *why*, which is aimed at understanding. But the interventions we recommended have implicit theories underlying them that explain why we believe people come to work.

For example, the implicit theory underlying the situational

interview may be in accordance with Hulin's (Chapter Ten) comments regarding an underlying trait. Specifically, our implicit theory in recommending this approach is that attendance is one measure of many regarding legal compliance. Legal compliance is a set of prosocial citizenship responses that are inculcated during a child's upbringing. It is manifested in the form of attendance in extremely bad weather, when people struggle to come to work when they could stay home without fear of sanctions (Smith, 1977). All of us know people who perceive their jobs as meaningless and repetitive but nevertheless come to work "no matter what" because it is the "right thing to do." Only ability factors (for example, serious injury) keep them from hobbling onto the job site.

Implicit in our discussion on orientation training, teaching supervisors counseling skills, and teaching employees self-management techniques is our belief that legal compliance can be taught to adult employees. Inherent in self-management is the concept of self-efficacy. It is our theory that self-efficacy in part explains employee attendance. People come to work because they are motivated to overcome perceived obstacles preventing them from doing so. Our recommendation to consider flextime is consistent with self-efficacy in that flextime strengthens it for people when they know that they can take time off from work to deal with nonjob-related issues.

Measuring attendance is based on our theory that one's cognitions and behavior are shaped by anticipated reinforcers and punishers. The advantage of employee participation in designing rules that affect the administration of reinforcers and punishers is that it increases employee understanding of the need for them and thus facilitates legal compliance.

In our discussion of the various interventions, we focused primarily on the employer and employee and were remiss in not mentioning the role of union shop stewards and business agents. Companies such as Weyerhaeuser and Scott Paper have held effective training courses teaching them how to counsel employees. A focus of this training is on counseling employees to overcome barriers in coming to work.

We are hesitant to recommend any one intervention over another, because any one prescription in itself may not be effective, but the "package" ought to be in the aggregate. In describing this aggregate, we attempted to tie the interventions together coherently. Thus, the interventions were drawn from the literature on selection (for example, situational interview), performance appraisal (for example, measuring attendance), training (for example, orientation, coaching supervisors, self-management), and motivation (for example, job enrichment). We hasten to stress the importance of not engaging in what might be termed "piecemeal human-resource management"—meaning managers shouldn't use participative goal setting to improve production and then fire people because excess productive capacity is uncovered. We must also acknowledge that we do not know the long-term effects of each of these interventions any more than the medical profession knows the long-term effects of its interventions (for example, birth-control pills). But the aggregate of the interventions we have recommended should have long-term effects on attendance behavior.

It is thus with considerable reluctance that we respond to an issue raised by a reviewer, namely, that our chapter does not rely enough on our own personal skill in selecting theory-based interventions. If we had a client with very limited resources to do everything that is recommended in this chapter, we would advocate the following: First, develop a situational interview that taps legal compliance. The situational interview measures employee intentions. Second, measure attendance. We believe that which gets measured gets done because people want to know that what they are doing is important. Measurement conveys importance. Third, allow employees to develop a system that acknowledges attendance and absenteeism. Participating in developing such a system will inculcate understanding of the system and the problems that it is designed to remedy. The system can be managed by employees and union officials. Where we have seen this operate, the employees are harder on themselves than are company officials. By allowing employee-union involvement in monitoring an attendance program, "deals" made by local management and union officials can be integrated successfully into the attendance program so that it is tailor-made for their situation. Fourth, find ways to allow people time off from work. Our experience is that union officials can be valuable problem solvers in this regard. Fifth, teach supervisors and union officials to teach self-management techniques to employees. We believe that the key to increasing attendance in organizations where jobs cannot or will not be made more meaningful to the employee is to focus on the concepts of legal compliance and self-efficacy. Goal setting, feedback, and recognition underlie the latter.

In the interest of space and our lack of expertise, we ignored discussion of the effects of alcoholism on attendance. Suffice it to say that self-management techniques and teaching supervisors and union officials how to teach these techniques are effective ways to deal with this issue (Marlatt, 1983). These programs do much more than simply teach people controlled-drinking skills. There is great emphasis on general intervention strategies, including the development of alternative responses to situations that might otherwise lead to excessive drinking.

The issue of costs to justify these interventions was dealt with in the introduction to this chapter. The mock debate was written with tongue in cheek. It was not our intention to imply seriously that failure to come to work is *the* primary reason for the world's economic recession. Nor was it our intention to imply that it's "those" employees and not "we" managers who are solely responsible for the recession. But we feel we are on solid ground in writing that the recession will be affected positively if people (boss-subordinate) do come to work. When people don't come to work they are, in our opinion, violating a legal contractual obligation. Organizations have every right to expect people to come to work. People have every right to know what is expected of them. This is why we recommended job previews and employee involvement in the development of control systems.

Nevertheless, the issue of costs remains. When is failure to come to work sufficiently severe that time and money must be devoted to interventions to correct it? The question is difficult, because even micro cost analyses can vary widely depending upon a number of assumptions. No one to our knowledge has an exact estimate for the percentage of loss that is incurred by an organization because of an absence that can thus be recaptured through an intervention(s). Because of this, we have recommended strategies that are not limited to attendance issues. In many instances, the words *employee performance* can be substituted for *employee attendance* under each intervention (for example, measuring and posting both performance and attendance). This is as it should be. We do not want people only to come to work; we want them to perform on the job after they arrive. To focus on the uniqueness of attendance issues, in our opinion, would be a mistake. Thus, it could be argued that a job preview will have little or no effect on attendance; it may have little or no effect on turnover. But it is ethical; it is humanistic; it is the right thing for an employer to do. We believe that the interventions we have recommended are the right things to do in that both the employer and the employee benefit by them. And when employees and employers do what is in the best interest of both parties, there is a spillover effect that affects both attendance and performance. We do not believe that any intervention that we have suggested will have an adverse effect on other dependent variables, such as productivity. We are reminded of work in the logging industry, where there was an initial fear that if logging crews set specific hard production goals, absenteeism and injuries might increase. This fear was unwarranted (Latham and Kinne, 1973). Productivity increased, and so did attendance. Injury rates were not affected.

The answer to our question as to how we will know whether our interventions are successful is straightforward. Measure performance. Measure turnover. Measure any dependent variable that the researcher-client believes may be affected by the intervention(s). But, above all, measure attendance rather than absenteeism. A fallout of studying ways of increasing attendance is that we will achieve an understanding of why people choose to stay away from the workplace. Because we fear that our position regarding the measurement of attendance will go unheeded, we ask the reader to consider the following statements by Fichman in Chapter One of this book:

1. "A heavy investment of research effort on absenteeism has failed to generate significant dividends, whether one's criterion is the prediction, explanation, or control of absence." (Quoting Johns, G., and Nicholson, N. "The Meanings of Absence: New Strategies for Theory and Research." In B. M. Staw and L. L. Cummings (Eds.), *Research in Organizational Behavior.* Vol. 4. Greenwich, Conn.: JAI Press, 1982.

2. "One needs a theory for predicting return to work, a different theoretical problem from being absent from work."

3. "Absence measures are often psychometrically unreliable."

4. "Absence phenomena are unstable, often not replicable, and difficult to treat statistically. . . . Difficulties are being recognized in defining absence events operationally and conceptually."

5. "Absence category schemes that attempt to identify the cause of an absence are conceptually flawed in a fundamental way, rather than merely being noisy and unreliable (that is, requiring refinement)."

6. "Absence is a socially defined event leading to interesting social responses. We may discover more consistency and clarity in the social definitions, categorizations, and responses to absence than in the event itself."

7. "The difficulty of characterizing behavior that is signaled by a nonevent is apparent. It is necessary to impute motives and causal factors to give meaning to absence events."

8. "To adequately explain an absence or lack of absence for [a] person, we need to know the full set of behavioral action options in the life space, not just the level of motivation."

The information needed for the researcher to make this kind of determination is forbidding.

Goodman and Atkin (Chapter Seven) have made the following statements:

1. "While [a] move toward a more careful specification of absenteeism seems appropriate, studies adopting this point of view . . . have not recorded any major breakthrough."

2. "The meaning attached to absence categories . . . differs across organizations."

3. "We think this occurs because the coding of absenteeism by the organization represents a series of individual negotiations between individual workers and management."

4. "Basically, we need to know whether accidents create a level of unfamiliarity in the workplace. Knowledge of whether some-

one is present or absent seems sufficient." "In terms of the consequences of absenteeism, this critical issue of determining the meaning of absenteeism may be less important."

In closing this chapter, we must remember that all we are looking for is a reliable measure on which to build theory, on which to evaluate the effectiveness of an intervention. Measuring attendance is one way to do this.

## References

Alain-Daniel, D. "Absenteeism: A Fact of Life." *Personnel Journal,* 1969, *48,* 881.

Arvey, R. D., and Ivancevich, J. M. "Punishment in Organizations: A Review, Propositions, and Research Suggestions." *Academy of Management Review,* 1980, *5,* 123–132.

Atkin, R. S., and Goodman, P. S. *An Issue-Oriented Review of the Research on Absenteeism.* Unpublished report to the U.S. Bureau of Mines, Carnegie-Mellon University, 1983.

Bandura, A. "Self Efficiency Mechanism in Human Aging." *American Psychologist,* 1982, *37,* 122–147.

Baum, J. F., and Youngblood, S. A. "Impact of an Organizational Control Policy on Absenteeism, Performance, and Satisfaction." *Journal of Applied Psychology,* 1975, *60,* 688–694.

Beyer, J. M., and Trice, H. M. "A Field Study of the Use and Perceived Effects of Discipline in Controlling Work Performance." Unpublished paper, New York State School of Industrial Labor Relations, Cornell University, 1983.

Chadwick-Jones, J. K., Nicholson, N., and Brown, C. *Social Psychology of Absenteeism.* New York: Praeger, 1982.

Cruikshank, G. E. "No Shows at Work: High-Priced Headache." *Nation's Business,* Sept. 1976, pp. 37–39.

Douglas, S. A. "Social-Psychological Correlates of Teacher Absenteeism: A Multi-Variate Study." *Dissertation Abstracts International,* 1976, *37* (11A), 7033.

Educational Research Service. *Employee Absenteeism: A Summary of Research.* Arlington, Va.: Educational Research Service, 1980.

Erez, M., and Kanfer, F. H. "The Role of Goal Acceptance in Goal Setting and Task Performance." *Academy of Management Review*, 1983, *8*, 454–463.

Fried, J., Weitman, M., and Davis, M. K. "Man-Machine Interaction and Absenteeism." *Journal of Applied Psychology*, 1972, *56*, 428–429.

"Getting Everyone on the Wagon." *Time Magazine*, Aug. 22, 1983, p. 39.

Gupta, N., and Beehr, T. A. "Job Stress and Employee Behavior." *Organizational Behavior and Human Performance*, 1979, *23*, 373–387.

Hackman, J. R., and Oldham, G. R. "Development of the Job Diagnostic Survey." *Journal of Applied Psychology*, 1975, *60*, 159–170.

Hinrichs, J. R. *Controlling Absenteeism and Turnover.* Scarsdale, N.Y.: Work in America Institute, 1980.

Huse, E. F., and Taylor, E. K. "The Reliability of Absence Measures." *Journal of Applied Psychology*, 1962, *46*, 159–160.

Ilgen, D. R. "Attendance Behavior: A Reevaluation of Latham and Pursell's Conclusions." *Journal of Applied Psychology*, 1977, *62*, 230–233.

Kanfer, F. H., and Bursemeyer, J. R. "The Use of Problem Solving and Decision Making in Behavior Therapy." *Clinical Psychology Review*, 1982, *2*, 239–266.

Kanfer, F. H., and Phillips, J. S. *Learning Foundations of Behavior Therapy.* New York: Wiley, 1970.

Kanfer, F. H., and others. "Contrasts, Demand Characteristics, and Self Control." *Journal of Personality and Social Psychology*, 1974, *30*, 605–619.

Katz, D., and Kahn, R. L. *The Social Psychology of Organizations.* New York: Wiley, 1966.

Kempen, R. W. "Absenteeism and Tardiness." In L. W. Fredericksen (Ed.), *Handbook of Organizational Behavior Management.* New York: Wiley, 1982.

Kempen, R. W., and Hall, R. V. "Reduction of Industrial Absenteeism: Results of a Behavioral Approach." *Journal of Organizational Behavior Management*, 1977, *1*, 1–21.

Latham, G. P., and Kinne, S. B. "Improving Job Performance Through Training in Goal Setting." *Journal of Applied Psychology*, 1973, *58*, 302–307.

Latham, G. P., and Pursell, E. D. "Measuring Absenteeism from the Opposite Side of the Coin." *Journal of Applied Psychology*, 1975, *60* (3), 369–371.

Latham, G. P., and Pursell, E. D. "Measuring Attendance: A Reply to Ilgen." *Journal of Applied Psychology*, 1977, *62*, 234–236.

Latham, G. P., and Saari, L. M. "The Application of Social Learning Theory to Training Supervisors Through Behavior Modeling." *Journal of Applied Psychology*, 1979, *64*, 239–246.

Latham, G. P., and Saari, L. M. "Do People Do What They Say? Further Studies on the Situational Interview." *Journal of Applied Psychology*, 1984, in press.

Latham, G. P., and others. "The Situational Interview." *Journal of Applied Psychology*, 1980, *65*, 422–427.

Lewin, K. "Frontiers in Group Dynamics." *Human Relations*, 1947, 1, 5–41.

Manley, J., and Duffy, J. "Controlling Absenteeism." Unpublished paper, Dalhousie University, 1983.

Marlatt, G. A. "The Controlled-Drinking Controversy: A Commentary." *American Psychologist*, 1983, *38*, 1097–1110.

Matteson, M. T., and Ivancevich, J. M. "Note on Tension Discharge Rate as an Employee Health Status Predictor." *Academy of Management Journal*, 1983, *26*, 540–545.

Mayo, E., and Lombard, G. F. F. *Teamwork and Labor Turnover in the Aircraft Industry of Southern California.* Boston: Graduate School of Business Administration, Harvard University, 1944.

Miller, L. M. *Behavior Management: The New Science of Managing People at Work.* New York: Wiley, 1978.

Mills, P. M. "Self Management: Its Control and Relationship to Other Organizational Properties." *Academy of Management Review,* 1983, *8,* 445–453.

Morgan, L. G., and Herman, J. B. "Perceived Consequences of Absenteeism." *Journal of Applied Psychology*, 1976, *61* (6), 738–742.

Nadler, D. A. "Managing Organizational Change." *Journal of Applied Behavioral Science*, 1981, *17*, 191–211.

Nicholson, N. "Management Sanctions and Absence Control." *Human Relations*, 1976, *29* (2), 139–151.

Olmstead, B., and others. *Job Sharing in the Public Sector.* San Francisco: New Ways to Work, 1979.

O'Reilly, C. A., and Weitz, B. A. "Managing Marginal Employees: The Use of Warnings and Dismissals." *Administrative Science Quarterly*, 1980, *25*, 467–484.

Pedalino, E., and Gamboa, V. U. "Behavior Modification and Absenteeism: Intervention in One Industrial Setting." *Journal of Applied Psychology*, 1974, *59*, 694–698.

Peters, T. J., and Waterman, R. H. *In Search of Excellence*. New York: Harper & Row, 1982.

Porter, L. W., and Steers, R. M. "Organizational, Work, and Personal Factors in Employee Turnover and Absenteeism." *Psychological Bulletin*, 1973, *80*, 151–176.

Rehm, L. P., and Marston, A. R. "Reduction of Social Anxiety Through Modification of Self Reinforcement: An Instigation Therapy Technique." *Journal of Consulting Psychology*, 1968, *32I*, 565–574.

Rosen, H., and Turner, J. "Effectiveness of Two Orientation Approaches in Hard-Core Unemployed Turnover and Absenteeism." *Journal of Applied Psychology*, 1971, *55*, 296–301.

Rosenthal, R. "Arbitral Standards for Absentee Discharge." *Labor Law Journal*, 1979, 732–740.

Skinner, B. F. *Science and Human Behavior*. New York: Macmillan, 1953.

Slocum, J., and Sims, H. "A Typology for Integrating Technology, Organization, and Job Design." *Human Relations*, 1980, *33*, 193–212.

Smith, F. J. "Work Attitudes as Predictors of Specific Day Attendance." *Journal of Applied Psychology*, 1977, *62* (1), 16–19.

Smith, R. E. "A Cognitive-Affective Approach to Stress Management Training for Athletes." In C. H. Nadeau and others (Eds.), *Skillfulness in Movement: Psychology of Motor Behavior and Sport*. Champaign, Ill.: Human Kinetics, 1980.

Smulders, P. G. W. "Comments on Employee Absence/Attendance as a Dependent Variable in Organizational Research." *Journal of Applied Psychology*, 1980, *65*, 368–371.

Staw, B. M., and Oldham, G. R. "Reconsidering Our Dependent Variables: A Critique and Empirical Study." *Academy of Management Journal*, 1978, *21* (4), 439–559.

Steers, R. M., and Rhodes, S. R. "Major Influences on Employee Attendance: A Process Model." *Journal of Applied Psychology,* 1978, *63* (4), 391–407.

"Stress: Can We Cope?" *Time Magazine,* June 6, 1983, pp. 48–51.

Thoresen, C. E., and Mahoney, M. *Behavioral Self-Control.* New York: Holt, Rinehart and Winston, 1974.

Thorndike, R. L. *Personnel Selection.* New York: Wiley, 1949.

Wanous, J. P. *Organizational Entry: Recruitment, Selection, and Socialization of Newcomers.* Reading, Mass.: Addison-Wesley, 1980.

Wexley, K. N., and Nemeroff, W. F. "Effectiveness of Positive Reinforcement and Goal Setting as Methods of Management Development." *Journal of Applied Psychology,* 1975, *60,* 446–450.

Wolpe, J. *Psychotherapy by Reciprocal Inhibition.* Stanford, Calif.: Stanford University Press, 1958.

# 9

# Unresolved Issues in the Study and Management of Absence from Work

ᏒᎱᏒᎱᏒᎱᏒᎱᏒᎱᏒᎱᏒᎱᏒᎱᏒᎱᏒᎱᏒᎱᏒᎱᏒᎱᏒᎱᏒᎱᏒᎱᏒᎱᏒᎱᏒᎱᏒᎱᏒᎱᏒᎱᏒᎱᏒᎱ

## *Gary Johns*

The other chapters in this volume represent potential pieces in the puzzle of measuring, modeling, predicting, controlling, theorizing about, and determining the consequences of absence from work. The goal of the present chapter is to somehow integrate these pieces, perhaps tentatively putting the puzzle together. However, there are at least two differences between accomplishing this task and assembling a jigsaw puzzle on the kitchen table. First, as noted, many of the pieces in the present puzzle are only potential pieces. The kitchen puzzle may lack some pieces, but it seldom contains spurious pieces. Some of the other chapters may contain spurious pieces just as this one will surely do. Secondly, the kitchen puzzle comes in a box with a picture on it, but I lack a box for the absence puzzle. Thus, I have modified my task to roughly sketch the picture on the box rather than pretend to solve the puzzle.

What follows is more Dali than Degas. It is impossible to do justice to each chapter in a sequential, linear, representational manner. Rather, five themes or ideas that the various chapters stimulate are presented, and reference is made to those chapters where appropriate. The first section is concerned with some pretheoretical work that is needed to precede or accompany the development of new forms of theory and research. The next three sections are concerned with a variety of theoretical viewpoints and methodological issues. The final substantive section concerns the management of absence.

### Pretheory and "New Look" Absence Research

In the traditional, prototypical research study of absenteeism, absence data from a particular level of a single organization are correlated with some combination of demographic variables and attitudinal variables that are measured with a questionnaire. The authors of the other chapters in this volume would probably agree that this general research approach is unlikely to yield further useful information. They would probably also agree that, until recently, there has been relatively little theory directed specifically at absence and that, at present, there is certainly no dominant theory. Fichman's well-rounded sketch of extant absence theory (Chapter One) supports these points.

One reason why there is no dominant theory in place is quite simply that there have as yet been relatively few empirical tests of the positions reviewed by Fichman. Thus, current theory falls much more into the "speculation" than the "knowledge" part of the Steers and Rhodes "knowledge and speculation" theme. This transition period between the demise of the traditional absence study and the establishment of a new tradition is an exciting prospect, because it permits the simultaneous development of creative theory unrestrained by ossified paradigms, as well as some useful pretheoretical work. This pretheoretical work should lead to the development of better absence theory and method, concerns of the three subsequent sections of this chapter.

Pretheoretical work in absence might be divided into the fine-grained analysis of absence data and asking workers direct questions about absence. The purpose of this work is to better immerse ourselves in our subject matter and, in terms that Landy has used, to rule out questions as much as to answer questions. An analogy might be the sociologist who engages in participant observation before doing a more rigorous and generalizable study of a phenomenon in question.

The research reported by Landy, Vasey, and Smith (Chapter Three) and that suggested by Avery and Hotz (Chapter Four) are examples of the fine-grained analysis of absence data. Speaking generally, this kind of work has some tradition in the United Kingdom but not in North America. It is possible that absence could profit from a re-examination of its "fine grains," especially given some of the emerging "new look" theoretical positions. However, in doing such work, there may be a strong tendency to isolate the data from their context, and some of the following advice is oriented toward avoiding this backward step:

1. Easy access to absence data at the individual level (that is, a complete, detailed "attendance calendar") may indicate that the system being studied is atypical. Robertson (1979) found in a survey of Ontario firms that only 17 percent assembled absence data for review. Thus, the record of Landy and his colleagues in obtaining such data is quite remarkable. The motto here is that we should "beware of businessmen bearing data," not because these data are unwelcome but because their ready availability may signal the existence of particular control systems or management concerns about attendance. In general, researchers should be aware of the precise nature of the control systems operating in the organizations they study.

2. Fine-grained analyses of absence data should be truly comparative, cutting across departments and other subunits within organizations, and comparing organizations as a whole. There is a strong need to understand which qualities of absence data are relatively invariant, which are typical of certain classes of jobs, occupations, and industries, and which are apparently unique to a setting.

3. Although the quality of the data is important in any research, problems of quality control are exacerbated in large-scale absence studies across multiple locations. To cite a personal example, "I once attempted to collect such [absence] information for lower-level managers in a large organization with branches across the country. This was a rare example of an organization which actually collected such data for managers, and on paper the report-

ing system looked commendable. However, the attempt had to be abandoned when headquarters personnel officers sheepishly admitted that the records simply weren't reliable—in some branches management absence was taken seriously and recorded accurately while in others it wasn't" (Johns, 1980, p. 53). In a similar vein, absence classification schemes that involve subjective causal attributions about why an incident occurred should be discounted, especially when comparing absence across levels or organizations.

4. Some careful attention must be paid to the *variance* in absence within and between identifiable aggregations of workers. Although low correlations between other variables and absence may be due to low reliability (the focus of Landy, Vasey, and Smith), they may also be due to restricted variance. Some theoretical positions, such as the absence-culture notion (Chadwick-Jones, Nicholson, and Brown, 1982; Johns and Nicholson, 1982; Nicholson and Johns, 1982), are especially concerned with patterned variation in absence.

Traditional test-theory concepts seem limited in their usefulness for describing absence data. Landy has admitted some ambivalence about the distinction between reliability and validity when dealing with such data. By the same token, I have trouble grasping some of Atkin and Goodman's suggestions for studying the validity of absence measures. I am in agreement with Fichman that absence is an interesting observable behavior and not a construct. As such, accurate observations of absence are *content valid* samples from the domain of "not coming to work." Of course, some kinds of absence are said to *reflect* certain constructs, such as a search for equity or withdrawal from aversive conditions. Here, it may be reasonable to speak of the construct validity of a particular absence measure, as in the case where frequency is posited to capture propensity to withdraw better than time lost.

In addition to the fine-grained analysis of absence data, the other aspect of pretheoretical work involves asking direct questions about absence. With a few notable exceptions (for example, Morgan and Herman, 1976; Nicholson and Payne, 1978), almost no studies of absence confront the subjects with the phenomenon being studied. In fact, it is safe to say that most subjects in such research never had a clue that their attendance was being scrutinized. This is really quite remarkable when it is observed that most studies of job satisfaction ask people how they feel about their jobs, and most recent studies of turnover challenge subjects to state their own intentions of quitting.

The prescription to ask people direct questions about absence is not made casually or arbitrarily. Rather, everyone has been absent from work and other social obligations, and everyone has had even more opportunities to observe the absence behavior of others. The clear-cut nature and consequent face validity of the behavior suggest that subjects will understand our questions and be able to provide valuable information if they trust our motives. Although some of this information may be biased and *inaccurate,* it should be a *valid* indicator of the person's phenomenological view of absence.

Many probes in organizational-behavior research confront subjects with rather exotic problems or tasks. For example, subjects in expectancy-theory research evidently have trouble providing independent estimates of instrumentalities and valences. Also, in turnover research, subjects' perceptions of their own mobility almost never operate as predicted by theory and common sense. In both cases, it is unclear whether the research results reflect true psychology or flawed methodology. In contrast, consider the straightforward questions about absence listed below. Answers to these questions can be verified objectively, and if subjects are incorrect, it is likely a function of mind rather than method.

Questions to be asked about absence include objective questions that tap knowledge and subjective questions that tap beliefs. Here are some examples of the former category:

1. Can workers accurately recall and predict their own attendance behavior? Do they know their own frequency and time lost for the previous year? Do they know how many days they have missed in the year to date? Do they know *when* they were absent? Can they recall how the organization coded these absences? Can they predict their own absence behavior in the near future?

2. Can workers accurately describe the absence behavior of their co-workers, including peers, superiors, and subordinates? Are

they accurate at the individual level, in the aggregate, or both? Can they accurately order the organizations' departments in terms of absence rates?

The researcher, of course, would also be interested in whether the accuracy of these answers varies across organizations, levels, occupations, and forms of control systems. Answers to the first set of questions bear upon certain theoretical views of absence, the cognitive effects of various control mechanisms, and the explanation of anomalous absence behavior.

Other factors equal, the use of absence as a stress-reduction mechanism would seem to have little bearing on one's awareness of one's absence record unless the stressor was regular and specific (inventory checks, budget preparations, and so on). By extension, the same argument would apply to theoretical views that absence represents withdrawal from generally aversive work conditions. However, theoretical views that see absence as consciously rational and calculated (especially as an element of economic exchange) would suggest heightened self-awareness of one's absence record. The first set of questions also bears upon how control systems might operate. Do such systems have a constant effect upon workers, or do they take effect only when the employee approaches some signal, such as $x$ sick days? If the latter is true, self-awareness should increase as $x$ is approached, with ignorance the rule otherwise.

Atkin and Goodman (Chapter Two) note in their mine research the apparent anomaly of workers taking unpaid absence days when they could have declared a paid day. It is possible that the miners (1) were confused about how many paid days they had left, (2) were confused about how previous absences had been coded, or (3) were trying to distribute paid and unpaid absences equally over the year. Answers to the first set of questions would aid in discriminating among such possibilities, and it is encouraging to see that Atkin and Goodman have adopted such an approach.

The second set of questions listed earlier is relevant mainly to the social or cultural view of absence causation (Chadwick-Jones, Nicholson, and Brown, 1982; Johns and Nicholson, 1982; Nicholson and Johns, 1982). In brief, if workers are unaware of the absence of their peers, in particular, it is unlikely that they have learned from or help support what Nicholson and Johns (1982) have termed a "salient" absence culture. But the same token, it is unlikely that an employee has modeled his or her absence on that of another co-worker (peer or not) if that person's behavior cannot be described accurately, although the time frame is an important qualifier here. Finally, we might consider the case in which a superior has perfect knowledge of subordinate attendance (unaided by records) but the subordinates haven't an adequate knowledge of their own behavior. On the surface, this would seem to suggest a frustrated control system.

In passing, it might be noted that *accurately* in the above questions could variously be interpreted to involve means, deviations, or correlations, and different measures provide different information. For instance, a worker might accurately rank order her co-workers in terms of time lost but badly overestimate the crew's mean absence to justify her own behavior to herself. In another setting, many workers might accurately estimate their department's mean absence rate via simple projection but be unable to rank order their co-workers in terms of time lost.

A final set of questions about absence that should be directed at workers in some sense taps beliefs about absence rather than knowledge. Although the answers to these questions may be impossible to verify, they may begin to provide researchers with valuable insight into the "popular psychology" of absence. First, there is an urgent need to know where people claim to *be* and what they are *doing* when they don't show up at work, measured under conditions of trust and confidentiality. For instance, a colleague is currently content-analyzing interviews conducted with nurses the day that they returned from either a scheduled or an unscheduled day off work. Potential differences in the activities reported under each condition are relevant to theories concerned with the adjustive and time-allocation functions of absence. In a similar vein, workers need to be confronted with detailed calendars of their own absence behavior over the past year or so and asked to explain the observed patterns (in conjunction with the kind of research proposed by Landy, Vasey, and Smith and by Avery and Hotz). The resulting data may provide us with new ways of classifying absence events or conceiving of the constraints and inducements relevant to absence.

For theoretical purposes, such information would surely be superior to that which can be found in the absence-classification schemes that shape personnel files.

Finally, it may be useful to systematically collect a series of stories, myths, and legends about absence and attendance in organizations. I have personally heard stories about heroic attempts to get to work in adverse conditions, about workers limiting their incomes for tax purposes through absence, and about how workers in remote sites contrived to be absent for days on end without detection. If localized, such stories may provide insights into the allowable causes of absence in a particular organization. However, Martin and others (1983) suggest that many supposedly unique organizational stories are in fact common across organizations. In this case, common stories about absence might reflect what Nicholson and Johns (1982) have called the societal dimension of absence cultures, those beliefs and ideas about absence that are current in the society at large.

If I seem to have dwelt overly long on so-called pretheory, it is because the clear description of absence behavior and its context is at least a corequisite to the successful accomplishment of "new look" absence research that is theoretically driven. By the same token, I see a less than obvious appreciation of the phenomenology discussed here in most of the other chapters, although the Carnegie-Mellon mines research has obviously been sensitive to the issue. This said, we can move from pretheory to theory.

## Does a Latent Trait Link Absence to Other Work Behaviors?

Hulin (Chapter Ten) has advocated the potential value of investigating a latent trait (arbitrarily, $\theta$) that might underlie instances of absenteeism, a theme implicit in part in the chapter by Rosse and Miller (Chapter Five). As Hulin noted, the essential argument here is that it is very difficult to study unreliable, low-base-rate behaviors except in extreme aggregation *or* as part of a syndrome of related behaviors. The latter approach is that of searching for a latent trait and eschewing the isolated investigation of a "specific behavior" (Hulin's words), such as not showing up at work. The related behaviors that contribute to the syndrome are also reflective of the underlying trait, although they may not have an equal probability of occurrence.

Disregarding recent advances in latent-trait theory and its associated methodologies, the general thrust of such an approach is common in psychology, where the search for psychological constructs is often viewed as more useful than the study of specific behaviors. Thus, it might be assumed that a latent trait underlies the construct of schizophrenia, which sometimes (but not always) stimulates delusions (as well as other reactions) on the part of the schizophrenic. Similarly, a latent trait might be seen to underlie the construct of intelligence, which sometimes (but not always) predicts a subject's response to item $i$ of an intelligence test (among other behaviors). In essence, studying the syndromes of behavior that comprise schizophrenia or intelligence is seen as more worthwhile than studying delusions or reactions to item $i$ in isolation.

Stated at this general level, it is difficult to argue against a latent-trait approach to the study of absence. Theoretically, the task is to choose specific behaviors that might reflect the latent trait, such as not showing up for work, daydreaming at work, sabotage, and so on. Empirically, the task is to examine the characteristic curves for these behaviors to see if they correspond to the hypothesized existence of the trait. Ultimately, such an approach could incorporate the notion that absence may have different meanings for different workers, such as a search for equity or conformity to norms (Johns and Nicholson, 1982). Similarly, it could confront the problem of the relationships among various "withdrawal" behaviors, the details of which are nicely described by Rosse and Miller.

Before buying the latent-trait approach wholesale, several of its actual or potential limitations should be noted. First, it is less than completely attractive to take an approach that is predicated in part on the low base rate of all absence events and then attempt to account for an even *smaller* subset of these events. Surely, this is what the isolation of any given $\theta$ would do, and this glorification of the construct at the expense of the specific behavior may satisfy some constituencies but not others. For instance, from the practitioner's viewpoint, some interventions could conceivably contribute to the management of absence regardless of the latent traits underlying its occurrence. Also, as Goodman and Atkin (Chapter Seven) point out, the consequences of absence are often independent of its specific causes, at least above the individual level of analysis. The point is not that practice should drive theory but that the way we frame the prediction and explanation of behavior will affect the range of control mechanisms we can conceive.

The remaining actual or potential limitations of the latent-trait approach are best discussed in the context of $\theta$ representing some tendency to avoid or withdraw from aversive work conditions. This hypothesis was suggested by Hulin and is considered directly by Rosse and Miller, although it is only one of several conceivable latent constructs that might affect absence.

It is essential to recognize that the measurement properties of the syndrome of additional behaviors that might comprise a withdrawal tendency may be even less favorable than those for absence itself. For example, reliable, accurate measurement of activities such as daydreaming, drug use, and sabotage is surely problematical. To return to the earlier analogy, conventional measures of intelligence are more reliable than conventional psychiatric diagnoses. It is relatively easy to form a pool of 1,000 parallel test items and to determine their measurement properties. However, the "parallel" behaviors that make up the schizophrenic syndrome may vary radically in observability and ease of reliable measurement. The investigation of a latent withdrawal trait would be susceptible to similar problems.

The existence of a latent withdrawal trait would dictate the occurrence of a negative relationship between job satisfaction and absence. McShane (1983) has recently performed a meta-analysis of eighty-nine correlation coefficients between satisfaction and absence reported in twenty-four studies. Correcting for unreliability in both measures, population estimates for frequency of absence ranged from $-0.22$ to $-0.03$, depending upon the job facet. Those for time lost ranged from $-0.15$ to $-0.03$. Some, such as Rosse and Miller, may find such figures an adequate basis from which to build a model or theory of withdrawal. I am less certain, especially considering studies in which job satisfaction was significantly correlated with absence but failed to supplement other predictors in multiple regression equations (Breaugh, 1981; Johns, 1978). Clegg's (1983) finding of reverse causality (absence influencing satisfaction) should induce even more caution. The point here is that the *precise* nature of the relationship between satisfaction and absence is open to question, and all answers to this question would not be equally beneficent to the conventional causal/withdrawal interpretation.

Of course, meta-analytical results are truly aggregate results by any standard of judgment, and it might be argued that a certain subclass of workers is particularly likely to exhibit absence in response to job dissatisfaction. However, when we isolate those in this group who also exhibit some of the other behaviors that comprise the withdrawal syndrome, we may be left with a very small proportion of workers. If this is the ubiquitous "low percentage of workers who account for a high percentage of absence," so much the better. However, Garrison and Muchinsky (1977) have shown that the core of such "absence-prone" workers changes gradually over time. If this proneness is at least in part a function of withdrawal from adverse conditions, parallel shifts in job satisfaction should occur, independent of nonwork demands on time, physiological risk, or other potential causes of absence. It might be noted that *managers* usually define proneness in terms of time lost rather than some other measure of absence, mainly because the costs of time lost are most easily conceived or calculated. However, McShane's (1983) meta-analysis indicates that the correlations between time lost and satisfaction are even lower than those for frequency. Thus, there is little guarantee that the isolation of a latent withdrawal trait would do much to solve organizational absence problems as those problems are defined by managers.

### Studying Absence Across Situations

A complement to the latent-trait approach is suggested by Hulin's commentary concerning how to study infrequent events — either study (1) syndromes of behavior or (2) aggregate behavior. While the latent-trait approach is primarily concerned with the study of syndromes, the complement under consideration here involves aggregation, conventionally across time and unconventionally *across situations or geography*. In other words, it would be valuable to study the attendance of individuals at social "obligations" in both the work and nonwork domains. Off-the-job attendance at parties, church, civic meetings, sporting events, and university classes might be examined in conjunction with work attendance, which could itself be further subdivided into attendance at department meetings, special seminars, and so on. In a similar vein, attendance before and after job changes, between the school/work transition, and across different types of jobs could be studied. The particular qualities of this approach include the following:

1.  Absence (and attendance) is granted status as a face valid measure of time allocation, whether or not this allocation is, in conventional terms, seen as intentional. Other than this, no excess meaning is attached in advance to instances of absence. Although Fichman restricts his proposed definition of absence to the work domain, his argument that all absence probably reflects the same basic *process* corresponds to the position taken here.

2.  More potential instances of absence can be observed. Even if absence is generally a low-base-rate behavior across situations, we will have a greater opportunity to see it exhibited in a given time frame.

3.  The interplay between work and nonwork behavior is explicitly recognized. Some of the more creative recent work on absence (Morgan and Herman, 1976; Nicholson, 1977; Youngblood, 1984) has profited from this recognition. Similarly, at the individual level, many of Goodman and Atkin's consequences of absence (such as stress reduction and the meeting of extrajob demands) are actually effected off the job.

4.  The approach increases the potential for variation in both the person's operative motives and his or her environment, including its constraints on absence. This increased variance (compared to the typical absence study) permits within-subject analyses to supplement between-subject analyses and should clarify the role of both person and environment in influencing absence.

This last point is particularly important, and it deserves elaboration. Smith (1977) calculated correlations between job satisfaction and attendance for a sample of Chicago and New York managers on a single day when Chicago was snowbound and New York was clear. The Chicago correlations were significant, while the New York correlations were not. As Fichman notes, this research represented a special opportunity to study absence *with the constraints against absence removed* (in Chicago). Under these conditions, attitudes toward the job were reflected in consonant behavior. Aside from the handful of studies of absence-sanctioning systems (for example, Baum, 1978; Nicholson, 1976), there has been little systematic attention paid to the issue of constraints.

Measuring the constraints against absence across various social obligations would profit from a multimethod perspective. First, a simple series of paired comparisons might be employed, asking respondents to report which one of each pair of obligations would entail the most constraints. Secondly, such constraints presumably involve the estimation of the consequences of an absence episode, and these consequences might be measured in an expectancy-theory format (see Morgan and Herman, 1976). If a fixed pool of consequences is developed, those proposed by Goodman and Atkin deserve special consideration, although it is unclear whether a generic set of consequences that pertain to both work and nonwork absence could be devised. Finally, it is possible to contrast objective constraints against absence in some social settings — work systems differ in whether they pay for an absent day, and professors differ in whether they factor attendance into student grades. However, the distinction between the practice and the letter of the constraint system is important, and comparisons of perceived and actual systems would themselves prove interesting. For instance, Nicholson and Johns (1982) have discussed how new employees may be socialized into an absence culture by observing discrepancies between what the organization says about absence and what it does.

At this point, the reader might imagine a 2 × 2 matrix, one dimension of which is the valence of a particular social obligation (high valence versus low valence) and the other the constraints against absenting oneself from that obligation (high constraints versus low constraints). From a within-subjects perspective, locating various obligations within the matrix yields straightforward predictions about their respective absence rates. From a between-subjects perspective, choosing a single social obligation (such as work attendance) and adopting a sampling strategy that maintains adequate variance on both dimensions, workers can be assigned to cells. Again, relative absence rates are predictable.

The various cells in the matrix are differentially relevant to certain theoretical viewpoints regarding absence causation. For instance, if employees would like to exhibit absence from work to withdraw from its aversive aspects but find that they can't, some theorists have suggested that they will substitute various behaviors for absence. If these activities (turnover, sabotage, and so on) are expressed anywhere, they are likely to be exhibited by those in the low-valence, high-constraints cell. Similarly, some have suggested that there is a habitual component to much attendance behavior. Conceptually, if one sought to isolate this elusive component, one might begin by examining those who exhibit atypically high attendance in low-valence jobs where constraints against absence are also low. Finally, reactance theory (Brehm, 1972) might explain a certain degree of absence from highly valent jobs where constraints against absence are also high. Workers who feel that the constraints limit their freedom may act to assert themselves even though this requires them to forgo the pleasure inherent in a day's work.

Adopting research methods that increase the variance in both valences and constraints across various social obligations may result in some interesting findings. Fichman raises a fascinating question about what the ambient or baseline rate of work absence would be if we could somehow hold its various causes and constraints constant. In lieu of this tricky task, we might attempt to measure extant absence rates across a variety of social situations that vary in terms of evoked motives and presumed constraints and see what we can learn. For instance, it is my experience that absence rates for social gatherings and parties for verbally committed invitees are as great as or greater than the time-lost figures that Steers and Rhodes (Chapter Six) cite for North American industry. Assuming that an occasional party is a highly valent event for most persons, one is left with the hypothesis that a lack of constraints on absence drives these people to less attractive but more constrained activities.

This last point suggests a theoretical negative relationship between attendance at social obligations — if one is attending $x$, one can't be at $y$ at the same time. Thus, it is certainly possible that the absolute number of social obligations that an individual has will limit the basic attendance predictions made by the "valence × constraints" matrix. For example, if an individual has a very large number of highly valent obligations that are perceived to be essential to attend, "something has to give." The underlying theme here is that of the finite nature of time, a theme that absence researchers might do well to keep in mind. However, again, some surprises may be in store for researchers who tackle the task of studying attendance or absence across social obligations. For instance, Wilensky (1960) has contrasted two possible hypotheses regarding the relationship between work and nonwork activities — compensation versus spill- over. Under the compensatory hypothesis, alienation at work is compensated by a socially active off-the-job life. The less intuitively obvious spillover hypothesis posits that alienation at work will cause isolation and alienation in the nonwork domain. Although the evidence for all hypotheses about the relationship between work and nonwork is equivocal (Kabanoff, 1980), Wilensky's contrast can serve as an analogy for those interested in time allocation across social obligations. The compensatory position is analogous to the view that time is finite and that negative relationships among absence events at social obligations will prevail. The spillover posi- tion, however, allows for the possibility that absence in one domain affects absence in other domains positively.

　　This brings us to a point that I have carefully avoided until now — the possibility that the degree of absence that a person ex- hibits is cross-situational. In other words, for example, are those who are absent from work also likely to be absent from other social obligations? The answer to this question is important for several reasons. For theorists, cross-situational absence would point to the possibility of a personality trait underlying many instances of absence or a "type" of individual who is destined to ignore social obligations. For empirical researchers, absence could be aggre- gated across situations, a convenient methodological tactic. And for managers, cross-situational absence would suggest a selection strat- egy to screen those who might be likely to exhibit high absenteeism. For example, school attendance records might be used to predict subsequent work attendance.

　　The issue of the cross-situational consistency of behavior

has had a long and sometimes acrimonious history in social psychology. The controversy has been fueled by a persistent paradox: Although it is "common knowledge" that people behave consistently across situations, research has repeatedly failed to demonstrate such consistency. More formally, studies by Bem and Allen (1974) and Mischel and Peake (1982) indicate "that raters agree substantially more about persons who identify themselves as cross-situationally consistent. However, these individuals do not show substantially greater cross-situational consistency in behavior than people identified as more variable. Here, again, shared intuitions about persons do not agree with the data" (Mischel and Peake, 1982, p. 749).

The chief recent figures in the behavioral-consistency controversy are Epstein, Bem, and Mischel (see Page, 1983). Briefly, Epstein (1980) feels that the problem is essentially one of reliability, and if behavior can be aggregated over sufficient instances to improve reliability, consistency across situations will be demonstrated. Bem (Bem, 1983; Bem and Allen, 1974) argues that an idiographic, within-person approach is necessary to predict the behavior of particular persons in particular situations. Mischel is the chief proponent of the view that behavior is not cross-situationally consistent. Recently, Mischel and Peake (1982) have argued that an illusion of cross-situational consistency stems from observers' unwarranted generalizations of *temporally* consistent prototypical behaviors.

Given previous research, it is safe enough to predict that conventional methodologies will reveal that absence is *not* cross-situationally consistent. However, the temptation to engage in the search may be strong, so I think it advisable to provide the reader with four specific arguments against such consistency:

1. A prerequisite for cross-situational consistency is *temporal* consistency within situations. The large body of research that has not been able to demonstrate the former has often been able to demonstrate the latter (Mischel and Peake, 1982). On the other hand, most measures of absence from work exhibit marginal reliability.

2. Johns and Nicholson (1982) have argued that absence from work has a variety of meanings within and across individuals — that it serves a variety of functions. If this argument can be

generalized to absence from other social obligations, it is highly unlikely that gross absence measures will exhibit consistency across situations.

3.  A good sample of social obligations, including that of attending work, should reveal a wide range in the degree of constraints against absence. As suggested earlier, this variety of constraints may itself reduce cross-situational consistency. Although it is impossible to ascertain the range of constraints against the behaviors in question in recent studies of consistency, one suspects that it is not large.

4.  Dudycha (1936) made over 15,000 observations of the punctuality of college students in attending various college functions, finding a mean cross-situational correlation of only 0.19. Although punctuality should not be confused with attendance, both variables have some similar properties with respect to the allocation of time.

In summary, the value of studying absence across situations will probably be diluted if we turn such study into an obsessive search for consistency.

In concluding this discussion about studying absence across situations, I might note an anticipated methodological problem. When researchers restrict their interest to absence from work, it is fairly easy to discriminate among absence, lateness, and turnover. The basis for this discrimination may be somewhat arbitrary, but it is usually grounded in conventional organizational definitions. Making such discriminations for other social obligations may prove difficult. For example, is the season-ticket holder who shows up for the last quarter of a Steelers game essentially late or absent? Is the person who hasn't attended church or exercise class for several months an absentee or a turnover statistic? Arbitrary guidelines for answering these questions may have little correspondence to the way people interpret their own behavior.

## Coming to Grips with the Social Dynamics of Absence

If there is a deficiency in the other chapters in this volume, it involves their reticence to come to grips with what might be called the social dynamics of absence. In this regard, it would be fascinating to know what a panel of anthropologists and sociologists would have to say about the problem under consideration. The theoretical positions espoused by Rosse and Miller and by Fichman seem exceedingly "individualized" or "privatized," although they would seem to be capable of incorporating a social dimension. By the same token, the implicit contract between the worker and the organization that Latham and Napier (Chapter Eight) invoke to justify the organization's response to absence is portrayed essentially as a series of individual contracts rather than a master contract with the work force. Furthermore, I have already alluded to the lack of attention to the variance properties of absence in the work of Hotz and Avery and Landy, Vasey, and Smith. I do see some recognition of the social dynamics of absence in the chapter by Goodman and Atkin. Many of the consequences of absence that they outline involve socially mediated feedback that could be expected to shape the patterning of absence for work groups, departments, or organizations. *Patterning* is a key word here, for it is the distribution of absence within and between identifiable aggregates that signals the potential social dynamics of absence.

Just what are the "social dynamics of absence"? These dynamics have generally been subsumed under the label of *absence culture*. Johns and Nicholson (1982, p. 136) define an absence culture as "the set of shared understandings about absence legitimacy in a given organization and the established 'custom and practice' of employee absence behavior and its control." Of course, departments, work groups, and organizational levels could also have distinctive absence cultures. The concept was first employed by Hill and Trist (1953, 1955) to describe how workers might learn to adjust their absence behavior to a pattern that would be acceptable to the employer. It was used subsequently by Nicholson, Brown, and Chadwick-Jones (1976) as a potential explanation for the pattern of relationships between job satisfaction and absence observed across a variety of organizational sites. The same authors later presented a detailed treatise regarding the social dynamics of absence (Chadwick-Jones, Nicholson, and Brown, 1982).

How do absence cultures develop? Nicholson and Johns (1982) suggest that each such culture has a societal dimension and an organizational dimension. The former is a product of the larger society's assumptions about employment, conceptions of self-control, and beliefs about absence itself. It is possible that these factors are partially responsible for the rather striking cross-national differences in absence rates reviewed by Steers and Rhodes, and probing the popular psychology of absence cross-culturally would prove illuminating. The organizational dimension of the absence culture is a product of a specific organization's technology, control system, status hierarchy, division of labor, and so on. The societal and organizational dimensions interact to determine the absence culture of a particular aggregation of workers. These cultures either affect absence patterns directly or serve as moderators of the extent to which individual-level variables can act to influence absence.

There are certainly no right and wrong ways to conceive of the operation of an absence culture. There are, however, more or less *useful* ways of conceiving of such cultures, and I would now like to address this issue. Several of the other papers, when alluding to the cultural position, discuss it as a separate and isolated theoretical stream. The operation of social dynamics on absence is then portrayed as a residual position, to be employed after we have exhausted the predictive power of individual differences. This position is counterproductive, because it suggests that the cultural argument will be invoked only when the social dynamics of absence are strong and obvious to the researcher. The term absence *culture* is perhaps unfortunate in that it seems to connote excess meaning along the lines of "exotic" or "unusual." Thus, on an intuitive basis, the reader would probably detect a cultural element in the following examples:

1.  In a South Wales town, bus drivers exhibited a high degree of absence. However, they were willing to go to work when the transportation company sent a car to their homes to pick them up. This became common operating procedure for the company.

2.  In an Indian university, students in large engineering laboratory sections would regularly "give proxy" by saying "present" for an absent fellow student and then allowing him to copy their notes for that day. It was understood by all students that proxy would be given as long as the process was freely reciprocated.

3.  In a Midwest university, professors in the management depart-

ment came in to work every weekday as well as Saturday mornings. Those who were absent on Saturday received much good-natured but not-so-subtle razzing on Monday morning.

Nicholson and I have termed such absence cultures highly *salient,* in that the social dynamics behind attendance behavior are clear, consistent, and powerful for the actors. In each case, obvious norms that govern attendance behavior have been developed. Also, in the first two examples, notice that "management" and "labor" have come to an implicit understanding about how attendance is to be managed — the bus company did not *have* to send cars for absentees, and the Indian lab instructors could have done away with the roll call or gone to great pains to accurately verify attendance.

The value of the absence-culture approach can be seen in the Midwest university, where it is extremely unlikely that individual differences in demographics or job satisfaction would predict Saturday attendance. To return to an earlier theme, the socially mediated constraints against absence outweigh the potentially low valence of the social obligation to show up for work on the weekend. It is important to understand, however, that there are also *low*-salience absence cultures that nonetheless conform to the previous definition. Such cultures are less obvious to the actor (and the researcher), but they also influence absence via social mechanisms. For example, consider a work force composed of men and women of dissimilar ages and ethnic backgrounds who are operating under an individual piece-rate pay system. Work stations are far enough apart to discourage regular interaction but close enough for workers to see who is at work and to follow exchanges between the boss and co-workers. The company has a strict written absence policy, but supervisors have a high degree of discretion in its application. Here, there is the potential for a fair degree of variation in absence, which would probably be predictable from individual differences such as job satisfaction, economic need, and relations with the boss, in conjunction with workers' observations of the boss's reaction to their own and others' absences. Thus, the payment system, technology, and social ecology interact to influence behavior. This absence culture is less obvious than those described above, but a culture nonetheless.

The previous discussion makes two important points. First,

absence cultures do not rely upon social norms per se for their existence. In some highly salient absence cultures, there may be explicit norms that regulate the degree of absence (as for the Midwest professors) or how absence is "shared out" (as for the Indian students). Equally probable, however, especially under low-salience cultures, is the form of influence covered by the label "social information processing" (Griffin, 1983; Salancik and Pfeffer, 1978; Thomas and Griffin, 1983). According to this viewpoint, the observed behavior of others is a persuasive and eloquent shaper of the observer's own work behavior and attitudes, often overpowering the influence of "objective" cues. In the current context, the boss's response to the absence of one's co-workers may influence one's attendance to a much greater degree than the firm's official absence policy, a supposedly objective behavioral cue. There is no requirement for consensus among sources of information under this perspective, and only one communicator has been used in most tests of social information-processing theory. However, in many work settings there would be pressures for consensus (for example, demands for equal treatment from the boss) that would gradually result in the development of explicit norms regarding attendance.

The second implication of the preceding discussion is that it is difficult to conceive of a work setting that would *not* have an absence culture, as long as it can be agreed that a low-salience culture is still a culture. Some may argue that this renders the absence-culture concept excess theoretical baggage and that it is only a heuristic device for conveniently describing an omnibus of individual-level effects. The corollary is that we should be able to adequately research absence using "new look" theory but sticking with traditional sampling strategies and individual-level methods. This position is absurd, since a single culturally determined variable (such as a norm) could account for almost *all* of the absence exhibited by a given aggregation of workers. Notice that traditional sampling strategies and research methodologies would not capture this fact, because there would be little variation in absence within the aggregation (a common phenomenon) and almost *no* variation in response to a questionnaire item that probed the existence of a norm. It is the sensitization to variance *between* versus variance *within* collectives that is the strength of the absence-culture concept.

It was the existence of reliable and distinctive absence patterns between various occupational groupings that led Chadwick-Jones, Nicholson, and Brown (1982) to advocate a cultural view of absence. I am in agreement with Fichman that this research does not conclusively demonstrate the social determination of absence. However, it would be possible to design such a study. For example, in Canada and the United Kingdom, a relatively small number of banks have hundreds of branches to serve the population. For a given bank, each branch would operate under a common formal absence-control policy, but the physical dispersion of the branches would provide ideal conditions for the development of more- and less-salient absence cultures. The task would be to draw a sample of high- versus low-variance branches, some where there is much interindividual variation in absence and others where there is little. Under most conceptions, little interindividual variation in absence would be a necessary but not sufficient condition for the existence of a salient absence culture. The next task would be to discover the variables that differentiate between the high- and low-variance branches, the basic prediction being that socially indexed variables would do a better job than aggregated individual-level variables. For example, branch cohesiveness should differentiate the groups better than mean satisfaction with co-workers. Similarly, variance in ages within the branches might perform better than the mean age of the branch employees. Also, in the low-variance branches, there should be agreement about the *content* of the culture (for example, extant norms) and accurate awareness regarding the behavior of others. Eventually, such information would permit us to predict levels of absence in a random sample of branches, indicating the conditions under which social versus individual causal variables would be prepotent.

## Can Absence Be Managed?
## Can It Be Managed Cost Effectively?

Speaking of the "management" of absence allows for the possibility that an organization might be interested in increasing, decreasing, or holding constant the occurrence of absenteeism among the work force. Traditionally, both managers and researchers have spoken of *controlling* absence, a term that in practice refers exclusively to reduction. However, Goodman and Atkin's consideration of the potential benefits of absence highlights the possibility that reduction may not always be advisable, especially when the costs of such reduction are calculated. This caveat having been offered, the remainder of this section will adopt the traditional perspective that equates management with reducing or maintaining at low levels the occurrence of absence.

It is noteworthy that the majority of the pages in the majority of the chapters in this volume are not concerned directly with the management of absence. Rather, the focus is on refining the measurement of absence, modeling absence, and determining the causes and correlates of absence via tests of theory. By implication, absence can be managed effectively only after these tasks are accomplished, with prediction and explanation preceding control. A contrasting position is seen to some extent in the chapter by Latham and Napier (Chapter Eight). This position suggests that, while absence may be a symptom of some underlying cause, this symptom can be treated directly without fear of dysfunctional "symptom substitution" (Kempen, 1982). In practice, such treatment usually involves rewarding attendance or punishing absence through a variety of sanctioning systems, disregarding specific explanations. The tension between these two positions is well known in psychology. For now, suffice it to say that "there exists no practical theory linking causes with interventions" (Johns, 1980, p. 54).

On the surface, there would appear to be plenty of stimulus for organizations to attempt to reduce absence. The combined U.S./Canadian estimate of $38 billion in direct costs cited by Steers and Rhodes is staggering. More easily conceivable is Kempen's (1982) estimate of $1 million in annual costs for a 1,000-employee organization with a 5 percent absence rate. In addition, one suspects that many of the other negative consequences of absence listed by Goodman and Atkin are more quantifiable than the positive consequences and thus more likely to capture management attention. Despite all of this, there is little evidence that most organizations devote more than passing attention to absence. For instance, recall again Robertson's (1979) survey of Ontario firms that showed that only 17 percent regularly compiled absence data for management review. Similarly, when was the last time the reader encountered a corporate annual report that discussed absence levels? As Kempen (1982) notes, American absence rates have not fallen in the past decade, in spite of the regular occurrence in practitioners' journals of cogent, practical articles calling attention to the problem (for example, Stone, 1980).

What is responsible for the lack of serious attention devoted to the management of absence in many organizations? It is possible that the answer to this question rests in assumptions about absence-proneness, the realities of organizational structure and politics, and doubts about the utility of many absence-management schemes.

The common observation that a fair proportion of absence can be attributed to a smaller proportion of the work force often signals "proneness" to line managers and personnel managers. This low-consensus, highly consistent behavior invites a dispositional attribution to proneness. In our society, there is a general norm that work organizations should intervene regarding employees' internal dispositions only when such dispositions have a direct effect on work behavior. If this is so, the most common absence "management" strategy should be post hoc, reactive, and individually oriented rather than proactive and comprehensive. A recent survey of 987 personnel managers (Scott and Markham, 1982) confirms this. The managers reported that individually targeted negative control strategies (such as progressive discipline leading to termination) were the most common *and* most effective methods used by their organizations. *However, a much smaller proportion of the personnel managers reported that their organizations maintained or analyzed daily attendance records!* Evidently, assumptions about proneness locate most absence-management systems in the realm of clinical psychology rather than management.

The relative infrequency of more sophisticated absence-management systems may also result from structural and political factors. As suggested, top management will not be aware of absence levels if data have not been collected and summarized by the personnel department. And top management will be unlikely to *ask* for such figures if shareholders or board members show no interest, a possibility reinforced by the lack of attention given to such matters in annual reports. If top management does acquire an interest in absence, that interest will almost always be oriented toward time lost, which is associated directly with costs. However, supervisory personnel will often be interested in frequency of absence more than time lost, since irregular, unpredictable attendance may have a greater impact on their day-to-day operations. Many rigorous absence-management systems place a premium on accurate absence classification and greatly increase the involvement of supervisors in monitoring attendance. Some smart managers may anticipate the possibility of collusion (an implicit recognition of the absence culture) and decide that such systems will simply be subverted. Finally, personnel departments do not have the reputation of suggesting interventions that are easy to evaluate objectively, and an absence-management system falls into this category. Critical discussions of the literature on organizational training provide a precise analogy.

A final reason for management's reticence to adopt sophisticated interventions to control absence may involve some intuitive doubts about the utility of such interventions. We as researchers and students of absence have generally ignored this issue. As Steers and Rhodes note, time lost in measured occupations in the United States averages around 3 percent. Since measured occupations tend to encompass blue- and lower-level white-collar jobs, this figure may actually be inflated. In any event, a certain amount of this 3 percent is due to legitimate sickness or other causes that are not susceptible to organizational control and are outside of the domain of psychology and organizational behavior. Based upon an inspection of frequency distributions and time-lost distributions from the same sample, it is occasionally argued that somewhere around 50 percent of time lost is theoretically susceptible to control. This, then, means that the base rate of controllable absence would average 1.5 percent and that the potential dollar savings in North America would shrink from $38 billion to $19 billion. Clearly, the 50 percent estimate is crude, and there are many settings where time lost exceeds 3 percent. The point, however, is that absence is a very-low-base-rate behavior by *any* standard.

If low base rates threaten the utility of interventions, so do low validity coefficients for the interventions themselves. Since most reviews of the correlates of absence do not report raw correlations or effect sizes, this argument must be handled indirectly. Many of the more complex, process-oriented interventions that are targeted in part at reducing absence (such as job enrichment or human-relations training for supervisors) are evidently supposed to work through increasing job satisfaction. However, as noted earlier, McShane's (1983) meta-analysis of the reliability-corrected correlations between job satisfaction and time lost (the form of absence most managers are concerned with) shows a range from $-0.15$ to $-0.03$. For the more operantly oriented control systems reviewed by Steers and Rhodes and by Schmitz and Heneman (1980), validity coefficients may be higher.

A final component of the utility equation is the cost of the intervention or control system. It is important to emphasize this point, often made in passing, because it is ignored in the prescriptions of Latham and Napier. It is common to talk glibly regarding the savings from reduced absence that could be realized if job satisfaction in a particular setting could be increased by some fraction of a standard deviation (Mirvis and Lawler, 1977; Terborg and others, 1982). However, these articles fail to consider the *costs* involved in implementing this increase, the technology for which is not well established. Moving to more direct, operantly oriented control strategies, there is evidence that "symptom substitution" may indeed occur and that these symptoms can be expensive. Nicholson (1976) found that the introduction of a sanctioning system preceded a shift to longer, medically certified absence spells. An even more striking example is provided by Harvey, Schultze, and Rogers (1983), who describe the implementation of a "well-pay plan" designed to reward employees for not using sick leave. In one year, this plan paid out $38,374 in well pay, for a net savings of only $1,203 over the previous year! Workers more than doubled the average duration of their sick-leave absences in order to override the one-day, no-pay policy that was part of the system. Operantly oriented observers may argue that such results can be patched up by revising contingencies. Skeptics may respond that there is a natural, adjustive level of absence characteristic of particular occupations and work settings to which workers will revert, although this has not been reported in the short-term experiments that relied solely upon positive control.

A final point regarding the cost effectiveness of absence-management systems involves opportunity costs. The purpose of such systems is to enhance organizational performance through improved employee performance. However, absence control may not be the most cost-effective way to do this when the money can be spent on other strategies. Recently, Schmidt and Hunter (1983) have shown that, for a variety of operative and clerical jobs, the best 5 percent of the work force produces about twice as much output as the worst 5 percent and that the standard deviation of productivity in dollars is around 40 percent of salary. Unlike the case for absence, there *does* exist a practical theory for translating the causes of this impressive variation into interventions — about 40 years of selection test theory.

None of the above should be taken to imply that absence can never be managed in a cost-effective way. However, the social and economic context of absence control has often been ignored. Ironically, most process-oriented absence researchers who have been concerned with the explanations for absence have done a better job of predicting frequency of absence, while most managers will remain concerned with time lost, if they are concerned at all.

## Conclusion

The larger picture that will ultimately provide a partial solution for assembling the pieces of the absence puzzle consists of a number of details. One of these details is the fine-grained description of absence behavior. Another is what absentees tell us about this behavior. A third detail involves the relationship between absence and other behaviors, perhaps examined via a latent-trait perspective. A fourth detail specifies how absence behavior varies across situations that include both the work and nonwork domains. A fifth detail includes an appreciation of the social context in which absence occurs. A final detail is a recognition of the psychological, political, and economic aspects of managing absence. If we can develop research to highlight these details, the solution to the absence puzzle should emerge.

## References

Baum, J. F. "Effectiveness of an Attendance Control Policy in Reducing Chronic Absenteeism." *Personnel Psychology*, 1978, *31*, 71-81.

Bem, D. J. "Further Déjà Vu in the Search for Cross-Situational Consistency: A Response to Mischel and Peake." *Psychological Review*, 1983, *90*, 390-393.

Bem, D. J., and Allen, A. "On Predicting Some of the People Some of the Time: The Search for Cross-Situational Consistencies in Behavior." *Psychological Review*, 1974, *81*, 506-520.

Breaugh, J. A. "Predicting Absenteeism from Prior Absenteeism and Work Attitudes." *Journal of Applied Psychology*, 1981, *66* (5), 555-560.

Brehm, J. W. *Responses to Loss of Freedom: A Theory of Psychological Reactance.* Morristown, N.J.: General Learning Press, 1972.

Chadwick-Jones, J. K., Nicholson, N., and Brown, C. *Social Psychology of Absenteeism.* New York: Praeger, 1982.

Clegg, C. W. "Psychology of Employee Lateness, Absence, and Turnover: A Methodological Critique and an Empirical Study." *Journal of Applied Psychology*, 1983, *68* (1), 88-101.

Dudycha, G. J. "An Objective Study of Punctuality in Relation to Personality and Achievement." *Archives of Psychology*, 1936, *204*, 1-319.

Epstein, S. "The Stability of Behavior. II. Implications for Psychological Research." *American Psychologist*, 1980, *35*, 790-806.

Garrison, K. R., and Muchinsky, P. M. "Evaluating the Concept of Absentee-Proneness with Two Measures of Absence." *Personnel Psychology*, 1977, *30*, 389-393.

Griffin, R. W. "Objective and Social Sources of Information in Task Redesign: A Field Experiment." *Administrative Science Quarterly*, 1983, *28*, 184-200.

Harvey, B. H., Shultze, J. A., and Rogers, J. "Rewarding Employees for Not Using Sick Leave." *Personnel Administrator*, 1983, *28* (5), 55-59.

Hill, J. M. M., and Trist, E. L. "A Consideration of Industrial Accidents as a Means of Withdrawal from the Work Situation." *Human Relations*, 1953, *6* (4), 357-380.

Hill, J. M. M., and Trist, E. L. "Changes in Accidents and Other Absences with Length of Service." *Human Relations,* 1955, *8,* 121–152.

Johns, G. "Attitudinal and Nonattitudinal Predictors of Two Forms of Absence from Work." *Organizational Behavior and Human Performance,* 1978, *22,* 431–444.

Johns, G. "Did You Go to Work Today?" *Montreal Business Report,* 1980, 4th Quarter, 52–56.

Johns, G., and Nicholson, N. "The Meanings of Absence: New Strategies for Theory and Research." In B. M. Staw and L. L. Cummings (Eds.), *Research in Organizational Behavior.* Vol. 4. Greenwich, Conn.: JAI Press, 1982.

Kabanoff, B. "Work and Nonwork: A Review of Models, Methods, and Findings." *Psychological Bulletin,* 1980, *88,* 60–77.

Kempen, R. W. "Absenteeism and Tardiness." In L. W. Frederiksen (Ed.), *Handbook of Organizational Behavior Management.* New York: Wiley, 1982.

McShane, S. L. "Job Satisfaction and Absenteeism: A Meta-Analytic Re-Examination." In G. Johns (Ed.), *Proceedings of the Annual Conference of the Administrative Sciences Association of Canada, Organizational Behaviour Division,* 1983.

Martin, J., and others. "The Uniqueness Paradox in Organizational Stories." *Administrative Science Quarterly,* 1983, *28,* 438–453.

Mirvis, P. H., and Lawler, E. E. III. "Measuring the Financial Impact of Employee Attitudes." *Journal of Applied Psychology,* 1977, *62* (1), 1–8.

Mischel, W., and Peake, P. K. "Beyond Déjà Vu in the Search for Cross-Situational Consistency." *Psychological Review,* 1982, *89,* 730–755.

Morgan, L. G., and Herman, J. B. "Perceived Consequences of Absenteeism." *Journal of Applied Psychology,* 1976, *61* (6), 738–742.

Nicholson, N. "Management Sanctions and Absence Control." *Human Relations,* 1976, *29* (2), 139–151.

Nicholson, N. "Absence Behaviour and Attendance Motivation: A Conceptual Synthesis." *Journal of Management Studies,* 1977, *14* (3), 231–252.

Nicholson, N., Brown, C. A., and Chadwick-Jones, J. K. "Absence from Work and Job Satisfaction." *Journal of Applied Psychology,* 1976, *61* (6), 728–737.

Nicholson, N., and Johns, G. "The Absence Culture and the Psychological Contract — Who's in Control of Absence?" Paper presented at 20th International Congress of Applied Psychology, Edinburgh, Scotland, Aug. 1982.

Nicholson, N., and Payne, R. "Attachment to Work and Absence Behaviour." Paper presented at 19th International Congress of Applied Psychology, Munich, Germany, Aug. 1978.

Page, M. M. (Ed.). *Personality — Current Theory and Research: 1982 Nebraska Symposium on Motivation.* Lincoln: University of Nebraska Press, 1983.

Robertson, G. "Absenteeism and Labour Turnover in Selected Ontario Industries." *Relations Industrielles [Industrial Relations],* 1979, *34,* 86–107.

Salancik, G. R., and Pfeffer, J. "A Social Information Processing Approach to Job Attitudes and Task Design." *Administrative Science Quarterly,* 1978, *23,* 224–253.

Schmidt, F. L., and Hunter, J. E. "Individual Differences in Productivity: An Empirical Test of Estimates Derived from Studies of Selection Procedure Utility." *Journal of Applied Psychology,* 1983, *68* (3), 407–414.

Schmitz, L. M., and Heneman, H. G. III. "Do Positive Reinforcement Programs Reduce Employee Absenteeism?" *Personnel Administrator,* 1980, *25* (9), 87–93.

Scott, D., and Markham, S. "Absenteeism Control Methods: A Survey of Practices and Results." *Personnel Administrator,* 1982, *27* (6), 73–84.

Smith, F. J. "Work Attitudes as Predictors of Specific Day Attendance." *Journal of Applied Psychology,* 1977, *62* (1), 16–19.

Stone, T. H. "Absence Control: Is Your Company a Candidate?" *Personnel Administrator,* 1980, *25* (9), 77–84.

Terborg, J. R., and others. "Extension of the Schmidt and Hunter Validity Generalization Procedure to the Prediction of Absenteeism Behavior from Knowledge of Job Satisfaction and Organizational Commitment." *Journal of Applied Psychology,* 1982, *67* (4), 440–449.

Thomas, J., and Griffin, R. "The Social Information Processing
    Model of Task Design: A Review of the Literature."*Academy of
    Management Review*, 1983, *8*, 672–682.
Wilensky, H. L. "Work, Careers and Social Integration." *Inter-
    national Social Science Journal*, 1960, *12*, 543–560.
Youngblood, S. A. "Work, Nonwork, and Withdrawal." *Journal of
    Applied Psychology*, 1984, *69* (1), 106–117.

# 10

# Suggested Directions for Defining, Measuring, and Controlling Absenteeism

░░░░░░░░░░░░░░░░░░░░░░░░░░░░░░░░░░░░░░░

## *Charles L. Hulin*

This chapter contains a discussion of concerns about *definitional problems, theoretical/conceptual perspectives,* the *"meaning" of absence behaviors, distributional properties, statistical estimates of stability of absences, empirical/nomological networks* that empirically "define" absences, and *practical methods of absenteeism control* that are common to several of the preceding chapters. All of these concerns cannot be resolved by a few typewriter keystrokes or some nifty conceptual legerdemain. However, the perspectives and approaches represented in the chapters in this volume are convergent enough to make an integrated statement about absences possible. I shall not make the Herculean effort to integrate all of the preceding chapters. Instead, I shall dis-

*Note:* I would like to thank Fritz Drasgow and Stanley Wasserman for their helpful comments and assistance on the statistical/distributional problems in absence research, David Harrison for his comments and discussions of the general area of absence/withdrawal, and Mary Roznowski for reading and commenting on an earlier draft and for her readily shared views of my definitional legerdemain.

391

cuss the above themes that appear to be the bases of research and practical absenteeism-control problems. Solutions, where they exist, are suggested, and some directions for future efforts are indicated.

Absenteeism has been described as a social fact in search of a theory (Ås, 1962; Muchinsky, 1977). This observation very nicely raises the specter that absenteeism per se may be a social phenomenon and an organizational problem with costly and serious implications for organizational effectiveness and national productivity but with scant scientific or theoretical basis. I would therefore amend the observation to read that absenteeism is a variable, often mistaken by organizational researchers as a construct, in search of a theory. The amendment draws attention to what may be the central problem in this research area. Studies that concentrate on analyses of the antecedents, consequences, or even measurement of absenteeism per se may be inadvertently restricting the conceptual, empirical, and measurement progress that can be achieved. Concentrating on infrequent manifestations of an underlying theoretical construct creates methodological and theoretical problems of serious magnitude.

Such concentration on absenteeism as an observable realization of the underlying construct causes research problems related to the distributions of the events and has implications for the statistical estimates of stability. Concentration on manifest absenteeism also creates definitional problems about the "meaning" of the individual absence behaviors. Attention is focused on the binary variable as the central construct in a nomological network rather than on the underlying theoretical construct comprising a diverse set of behaviors with the potential to integrate different research areas.

## Definitional Considerations

Nearly all studies of absenteeism have used samples of hourly, clerical, or blue-collar employees below the level of professionals and supervisors (see comments by Fichman, Chapter One, and by Steers and Rhodes, Chapter Six). Absenteeism among managers is treated as if it does not exist or, if it does exist, as if it is of little importance. This limitation is a result of industrial/organizational (I/O) researchers not only letting organizations define their scientific research problems but also abdicating the data-gathering responsibilities in favor of personnel departments. Whatever the cause, the result not only limits the range of samples that can be studied, it tacitly accepts the organizational-context definition of the variable of interest.

Fichman defines absence behavior so that it can be observed and studied independently of any organizational context, as a set of behaviors that do not depend upon an organizational manager or decision maker noticing, encoding, recording, or otherwise acting on them. This definition stresses that absenteeism is an individual behavior and should be studied as such.

Consider the following: I am late with this chapter. It was due four days ago and I am still writing it. It is Sunday and I had planned to work on it yesterday and today. Unfortunately, yesterday was a very cold day, with ice crystals visible in the air. I spent most of the day trying to obtain photographs of Champaign County's rather plain scenery with this ice fog adding some photographic interest. I was absent from work according to a definition that stresses absence behavior as absence from planned work activity. No one noticed it except me. It was not encoded or entered into an organizational record alongside my name. Was it an absence? If we are going to study absences, is such an occurrence as reasonable for analysis as the absence of an assembly-line worker or a miner on a scheduled workday?

The difficulty of studying a variable defined as "an absence from any planned work activity" should raise warnings about the definition. It may make little sense for us to define a variable in a way that cannot be studied, in spite of the theoretical appeal. It has also been misleading in several instances—as when intelligence is defined as native ability or capacity but can be studied only by assessing the current repertoire of skills and knowledge individuals have. Misinterpretations by other researchers and the consumers of the research have had serious consequences for both theoretical research and public policy (Hulin, Drasgow, and Parsons, 1983). Scientific integrity may require that we define the term to be congruent with the way it can be studied using the best research procedures currently available. We must, however, recognize that by our definition we have limited the generality of our reserach findings. Research methods based on the watchfulness of Big Brother, a development this Orwellian year of 1984 makes especially salient, could substantially broaden our field of inquiry and limit the generality of our current findings.

On the individual side of the issue, we do not ask employees about the meaning of their vote in a National Labor Relations Board (NLRB) election before we record it as a vote for (or against) union representation. The "meaning" and understanding of the behavior are determined by the research process after the observations of the variables. Consistent definitions will allow the events to be recorded with a small degree of recording error. Once we have agreed upon the definition of the terms, we can debate the merits of various epistemological approaches to attributing meaning to the events.

We seem to be nicely impaled upon the horns of a dilemma. If we are interested in studying absenteeism as a binary behavior, we must define it consistently with our ability to record and study it. Such a definition practically excludes the attendance behavior of large segments of our work force from study. An alternative to this dilemma is to redirect our efforts to the study of the theoretical construct underlying observed absences. Studying a latent theoretical construct, labeled $\theta$ for convenience, that comprises many behaviors and responses that seem to form a coherent behavioral syndrome may offer a solution to our definitional problems.

### Theoretical/Conceptual Perspectives

The two theoretical perspectives offered by Fichman (Chapter One) and Rosse and Miller (Chapter Five) represent converging views of a theoretical perspective on absences, notwithstanding the diverging paths the authors took to these positions. Fichman propounds a view of the stream of behavior, infrequently encountered in empirical research in organizations, that stresses that rapid switching from one behavior to another is more to be expected of individuals' behavioral choices than are choices that lead to long-term stable behaviors. This highly molecular view of behavior is derived from the work of Atkinson and Birch (1970). The approach suggests that the problem for psychologists is not one of predicting activity, because this is the normal state of people, but predicting which, among the many possible activities, will be engaged in, for how long, and at what effort level, and which activity the individual will switch to next. This approach suggests that we rapidly and continuously switch among many different activities during all of our waking hours.

Within the infinite set of possible behaviors, there exist broad families of behaviors that we might label productive, recreational, family oriented, social (if different from family behaviors), withdrawal from work, and even self-destructive. A behavioral family consists of behaviors that are perceived to lead to the same goal. Some of these behavioral families are mutually incompatible; others are expected to involve the time and effort of individuals on a nearly simultaneous basis. Behavior within one family should display substitutability and generally occupy the same block of time.

Using utility analysis to explain individuals' behavioral choices (Naylor, Pritchard, and Ilgen, 1980), we would predict that an individual might choose activities from a general family of activities on the basis of the utility of the family of behaviors to the individual. The specific behaviors or activities chosen at any instant in time from a general family depend upon the activities recently engaged in, the slope of the utility function for specific behaviors for the next unit of effort or time spent on that activity, expectations about future rewards and need states, and *many* random minor factors. The choice of families of behaviors and the selection of individual behaviors within families define the research problem of time and effort allocation. Analyses of behavioral choice represent the fundamental research question within this general framework.

In this analysis, absenteeism is put into a perspective in which it may be seen as one specific element of a broad family of behaviors that might be termed *attendance behaviors* or *adaptation* or *withdrawal*. The specific label and the comprised behaviors will depend upon how broadly one wishes to define the behavioral family. The breadth of the framework will determine how the problem is structured. The tendency among most researchers probably would be to use absence to identify the specific binary variable or behavioral choice reflecting one element of the more inclusive behavioral family of adaption or withdrawal.

The convergence between Fichman's general theoretical exposition and the recommendations of Rosse and Miller is perhaps not readily apparent. Rosse and Miller essentially argue that employees make many — and retain some — responses in their attempts to adapt to their work environments. They make these arguments on the basis of empirical research evidence and general propositions about the selectivity, substitutability, and rationality of behavioral choices made by employees. Adaptation summarizes a general family of response tendencies. Withdrawal represents a subset of this general theoretical family. Individuals engage in different elements selected from the general family. Depending upon the outcome of these selected responses, they either repeat the behavioral choice at the next opportunity or eliminate it from their repertoire and choose another response from the same family at their next opportunity. Their behavioral choices are presumably made to reduce the anxiety, pain, stress, dissatisfaction, or other negative feedback they are experiencing on their job.

If behavioral choices within a family of responses are seen by the focal individual as partially substitutable for each other, or forming a hierarchy of responses, the individual should selectively engage in the behaviors from a general family more frequently than he or she would make behavioral choices from another general family. Thus, we should expect to find patterning or co-variation among the responses that compose the family Rosse and Miller have labeled *organizational adaptation.* Behaviors that represent individuals' attempts to withdraw from their work situation, if these are indeed a subset of the adaptation responses, should show very strong evidence of patterning and co-variation. (In this context, co-variance among different elements of general behavioral families can refer to relationships other than standard linear relationships.)

One difference between these two theoretical chapters is the degree of generality of the theoretical propositions. Fichman has presented a discussion of a very general theoretical perspective. Rosse and Miller have focused specifically on one hypothesized family of responses to stressful or distressing or dissatisfying work situations. They have hypothesized adaptation cycles that proceed from negative stimulus conditions to response selection that generates positive and negative rewards that influence future response selection. Rosse and Miller attempt to specify the content of the behaviors related to organizational adaptation and withdrawal. More importantly, perhaps, they stress the psychological process by which individuals learn about the utility functions that relate expected rewards to units of effort for the specific behavioral elements and for the general family and behavioral choices as a whole. Both of these chapters lack needed detail about the hypothesized families of responses and the response elements they comprise. More detail is also needed about the expected rates of switching by organizational employees from one behavior or response to another; research is at a very primitive stage regarding necessary details of the behavioral choices. This is less a criticism of the chapters than a comment that basic research is badly needed in which researchers may simply count and describe what individuals do in organizations (Campbell, Daft, and Hulin, 1982).

Rosse and Miller report research under way that attempts to specify the responses that define adaptation and withdrawal. The content and patterning among these different responses should provide evidence about both the existence of response families and the defining response elements. On the basis of their literature review, it is expected that patterns among response elements may reflect alternation, substitution, positive co-variance, or other possible patterns. Problems inherent in longitudinal research in ongoing organizations may make detection and description of the many expected patterns difficult; available cross-sectional studies are limited in the information they contain about these questions. Our lack of knowledge of organizational time cycles over which we should observe responses is a factor that limits the information in our empirical studies. Nontraditional research paradigms may offer some piecemeal solutions to a few of the empirical questions. Perceived sequences or hierarchies of responses, general social norms regarding appropriateness of behaviors for different groups of employees, and similar attempts to gain insights into how and why employees withdraw from organizations are badly needed. A series of limited studies, each designed to answer a specific question about the response elements that compose the relevant families of responses, may be an appropriate start on the specifications or descriptions of the underlying theoretical constructs involved.

The chapters by Fichman and by Rosse and Miller draw our attention away from the study of absenteeism per se and focus on the specification and theoretical meanings of different families of response tendencies. The theoretical and methodological advantages offered by this change in orientation alone should more than repay the effort involved in specifying and assessing these theoretical constructs. The methodological advantages are obvious. Studying continuously distributed responses, especially when such variables can be defended from a theoretical as well as a methodological perspective, will allow researchers to obtain much better estimates of the relation between a set of predictor variables and the theoretical construct manifested by an observed absence.

### Meanings of Absences

This epistemological problem can be put into context by noting the range of approaches to it. At one extreme, the radical empiricist might simply state that it is meaningless to even ask about the meaning of an absence, just as it is meaningless to ask about the truth of a verbal response to an item in a paper-and-pencil personality or interest scale. These are behaviors. One cannot ask about the meaning or truth of behaviors. One studies them, their antecedents, consequences, distributions, and reliabilities. The meanings are embedded in networks of antecedents, correlates, and theoretical laws. At another extreme, we might find an unreconstructed phenomenologist insisting that a researcher must ascertain the meaning of the act to the individual who was absent before the event can be categorized and studied.

The crucial issues in the meanings of absenteeism probably have less to do with the different epistemologies than with the sensitivity of our research techniques for inferring the meanings of absenteeism and related behaviors. Analyses of organizational cause maps (Bougon, Weick, and Binkhorst, 1977) to infer meanings of events as perceived by organizational participants enable us to examine perceived causes and consequences of such acts. A parallel effort conducted by a traditional organizational researcher might involve large-scale studies in which antecedents chosen from different classes of predictor information (biographical, motivational, attitudinal, organizational) were correlated with absenteeism aggregated across periods of time. Secondary meta-analyses of the correlates of absenteeism become grist for the mill of those who would infer meanings of absence events.

Both quantitative analyses of absenteeism cause maps and large-scale studies of the correlates of absenteeism can be no more meaningful than the raw data that generated the cause maps or established empirical relations among antecedents and absenteeism. In a world populated by rationalizing individuals who are likely to justify their nonconforming or deviant behaviors, statements about the personal "meanings" of absenteeism are suspect until proved otherwise. Large-scale studies attempting to establish correlates of absenteeism are equally flawed, but for other reasons — the serious limitations that extreme base rates impose on the maximum and expected values of the correlations of even the best predictors of absenteeism.

Individuals, whether in isolation, as members of an intact group, or as group members within a formal organization, seldom make responses that are unrelated to other things they say and do. In fact, the most striking characteristic of behaviors is the patterning and co-variation among the responses and acts of individuals; the nonrandomness makes their study scientifically interesting and compelling. The patterning and co-variation serve both as evidence about hypothesized underlying traits that generate the manifest responses *and* are used to estimate the strength or potency of the underlying trait possessed by individuals. When we speak about individuals' intelligence or job satisfaction or aggressiveness, we refer to a latent and unobservable construct that has meaning only in the sense that other mathematical abstractions have meaning. The meaning of the construct is to be found in the mathematical/ statistical rules governing the combination of responses into an estimate of a general construct.

Operationalizations of such constructs may generate the quantitative estimates of the constructs, but the meanings of the constructs are found in the co-variances among the different manifestations of constructs. Similarly, the meanings of the different observable manifestations of constructs are in terms of the relations between the observable variables and the construct itself (Drasgow and Miller, 1982). This approach to inferences about conceptual meanings of observed behaviors stressing analyses of co-variances among many different individual behaviors and responses may, in the long run, offer methodological benefits to the study of absenteeism that are as important as the gains in conceptual understanding. Theorists from Thurstone (1931) to Fishbein and Ajzen (1975) have commented on the folly of attempting to predict individual behaviors from a knowledge of attitudes (presumably) relevant to that behavior. Although the emphases of Thurstone and Fishbein and Ajzen were somewhat different, their points were similar. Any specific response or behavior of an individual contains a great deal of specific variance. However, when many co-varying individual behaviors are accumulated and quantified, the *common* variance among these individual behaviors is a better representation of the general behavioral orientation or disposition than is any one of the individual behaviors or responses. The proper dependent variable for one interested in the behavioral consequences of attitudes is these general behavioral dispositions represented by the common variance that more nearly matches the generality of the internal cognitive/motivational variables than does any specific response.

These arguments reflect *theoretical* propositions about the generality and consistency of behaviors. They are not made on the basis of psychometric considerations. Technical considerations involving distributional properties of the variables, reliability, and other statistical concerns are separate concerns and are discussed later.

The general problem of the validity of an individual behavior or scale as an estimate of an underlying construct has been addressed by Campbell and Fiske (1959) in their landmark article on convergent and discriminant validity. Although the major point of Campbell and Fiske was about the convergence among different methods of assessing the same underlying construct, analyses of their multitrait, multimethod matrix are often used to make claims about the construct validity of individual scales or variables. Drasgow and Miller (1982) have commented on this procedure and have derived methods of estimating the "fidelity coefficients" that reflect the relation of the observed variable to the underlying construct. However, both the Campbell and Fiske and Drasgow and Miller articles address issues of the relevance of scales and variables to theoretical constructs where the theoretical construct has been well specified and defined. Reliance on observations of simple binary behaviors, without specification of the theoretical construct, seems indefensible. Estimates of fidelity coefficients, construct validity, or information in the variable about the construct can be done only after we have specified and defined the construct. The construct should be defined in terms of the mathematical/statistical relations that specify the communality among the multiple manifestations of the underlying response tendency.

## Distributional Properties of Absences

In American industries, absences on any specific day or even aggregated across a number of days are low-base-rate phenomena. Studying low-base-rate events is an inherently difficult pursuit. Researchers need to set aside standard methods and techniques that were learned and developed for the usual class of normally distributed variables studied in large samples of individuals during a single time period. However, we can also take advantage of the infrequent occurrences of the events and extract all the information contained in the moments of the distributions.

Research and theory of accidents and accident-proneness benefited from rigorous examinations of the implications different theories of accidents had for distributions of accident occurrences (Mintz and Blum, 1949; Greenwood and Yule, 1920). The study of absences in different time periods, and the conditional distributions of absences across time periods, can similarly benefit from rigorous statistical examinations of the distributional properties of the events and the theoretically expected conditional distributions across times.

There are at least two different approaches to understanding and studying behavioral phenomena that are fundamentally at odds with each other. The first begins with a theoretical statement about the process that governs the distribution of the events. From this conceptual psychological model, one (and usually only one) distribution is derived (deduced). If the fit of the obtained empirical distribution to the theoretically expected distribution cannot be rejected, assuming sample sizes with sufficient power, it represents a powerful statement about the reasonableness of the assumed psychological/organizational process. It obviously does not ensure that the theoretical psychological process is the exact process by which absences are generated and distributed across individuals and time periods. It does, however, substantially increase our belief in the validity of the hypothesized process. More sophisticated versions of this deductive process would probably begin with two or more competing theoretical models and derive the empirical distributions associated with each model. Competing hypotheses in the form of expected distributions could be constructed (where possible) and tested to determine which of the theoretical models was more likely to have generated the empirical distributions.

The second inferential process is unfortunately more common. It begins with an empirical distribution and searches through a catalogue of theoretical statistical models until one is found whose fit to the data cannot be rejected. The implicit conclusion is reached on the basis of this process that this specific statistical model mirrors the process by which the absence events were generated and distributed across individuals and time periods. Obviously, there are a very large number of theoretical models whose fit to the data cannot be rejected. For every statistical model whose fit cannot be rejected, there may be several conceptual models of the psychological process. The finding that a specific statistical model provides a reasonable fit to the data says little about the reasonableness of the conceptual models that could have generated the data. Our interest is in the theoretical psychological models of absence, not the empirical realization of their associated distributions.

As an application of the first inferential process, consider a model in which the expected number of absences in any time period is controlled by social norms governing appearances at work, professionalism, and fulfilling obligations. Management control mechanisms can also be hypothesized. Further, consider that no individual in your sample is more likely to be absent than any other individual, that the individuals represent independent observations, and that experiencing an absence in time period $i$ neither increases nor decreases the probability of an absence in time period $i + 1$ (the time periods are independent replications). Formalizing this theoretical process, we might conclude that if $Y$ (the theoretical random variable representing absences) is distributed approximately as a binomial variable with parameters $N$ (the number of independent observations; in this case, the number of individuals) and $P$ (the probability of any one individual being absent during a time period), then the empirical realization, $y$, of our theoretical random variable $Y$ is distributed as

$$f(y \mid P) = \binom{N}{y} P^y (1 - P)^{(N-y)} \rightarrow \frac{\lambda}{y!} \, e^{-\lambda}$$

as $N \rightarrow \infty$, when $P$ is small, and $\lambda = NP$.

A simple hand calculator is sufficient technology to enable an investigator to calculate the expected number of individuals with zero absences, one absence, two absences, and so on. This expected distribution of absence and the fit of the data to the model can be tested. The familiar Poisson distribution is a special limit case of the binomial distribution when $P$ is very small and we have a very large number of independent observations. The conceptual model that generates a Poisson distribution assumes that no one person is more absent-prone than any other person, days or other time periods are independent so data can be aggregated or disaggregated over different time bases, and increasing sample size allows us to decrease the time bases over which we aggregate data so that $NP = \lambda$ remains constant. This is obviously the simplest model of absence behavior that is consistent with current knowledge of organizational environments and individual behavior. It is often taken as the baseline or benchmark model with many different classes of infrequent events as a basis for evaluating more sophisticated theoretical process models.

A slightly more complex theoretical model might hypothesize that $P$ was varied randomly from individual to individual, reflecting individual differences in the propensity to be absent. A variation on this theory would hypothesize that $P$ was varied by group or block of individuals. In the case where $P$ was varied randomly across individuals, the expected distribution of absences would follow a *mixed binomial* distribution. Where $P$ was varied by block or group of individuals, the expected distribution has been termed a *stratified mixed binomial* distribution (Kappauf and Bohrer, 1974).

This theoretical model of absences generates absence events

that are distributed approximately as a stratified mixed binomial with parameters $(P_1 n_1, P_2 n_2, \ldots P_k n_k)$. If the empirical distribution of absences fits the theoretical distribution within the limits of sampling fluctuations, the substantive research problem is to estimate $P_i$ for individuals in the general case of the mixed binomial, or for blocks or groups of individuals in the stratified mixed binomial. Hypothesizing $P_i$ as log-linear combinations of the demographic variables that define the blocks of individuals represents a possible approach to understanding the reasons for the differing values of $P_i$.

An interesting special case of mixed binomial distributions arises when $P_i$ is distributed across individuals as a *gamma* distribution. (A gamma distribution can be described verbally as a distribution of positively valued random variables, as $P_i$ must be, that is positively skewed. This is a reasonable, although imprecise, description of how $P$ might be distributed across individuals. A $\chi^2$ distribution is a special familiar case of the gamma distribution.) In the case of absences, assuming a gamma distribution of $P$ across individuals, absences should have a negative binomial distribution. Landy reports that two-day absences in his data follow this distribution.

Let us, however, reverse the direction of inference and work from theoretical psychological processes that might generate absences and derive the expected empirical distributions of the events. We might specify two distinct models. The first, which we will label as the *heterogeneity* model, specifies that $P$ is distributed across individuals as a gamma distribution. As we have seen, this process will generate a negative binomial distribution with parameters $(P, N)$. Our alternate process is a *contagion* model and hypothesizes that the rate of occurrences of an event arises from a fixed probability but depends upon the current state of the individual, absent or present. The two models, the *heterogeneity* and the *contagion* process models, are distinctly different in their psychological and organizational implications. The first states that individuals can be characterized by different probabilities of an absence, with future absence rates independent of their current state. The second specifies that individuals' absences are governed by a single probability but that the future events occur at rates that are dependent upon the current state of the system. Both theoretical psychological models, one specifying heterogeneous distributions of $P_i$ and the other specifying that events occur at system-dependent rates, will generate negative binomial distributions of absences with the same theoretical parameters. *Occurrences of events (absences) within one time period or block of time cannot distinguish between the two models* (Wasserman, 1983). Their realized empirical distributions cannot be used to distinguish between theoretical models as divergent in their theoretical and organizational implications as these two models. From this development, it can be seen that the information in absence distributions about theoretical psychological processes that generate absences may be very limited or even misleading. Distribution analysis should be preceded by rigorous conceptual development to develop competing hypotheses where possible and followed by other analyses that compare other statistical properties (such as correlation or conditional distributions) to theoretically expected values.

It is possible, however, to distinguish between the heterogeneity and the contagion process model by appropriately designed longitudinal studies in which conditional distributions of events are examined and correlations among events in different periods are compared to the expected correlations derived from the different models. Wasserman (1983) presents an extended discussion of these two theoretical processes along with different methods of distinguishing among them. Markovian process models are useful in this area.

More complex models can be considered in which $P_i$ is varied across individuals or blocks of individuals and $P_j$ is also distributed across days according to specified functions. Depending upon one's theory of absences, weekends might have a probability of absence approaching 1.0 or might be excluded from the data set. Christmas, Yom Kippur, the opening day of trout season, and other religious holidays might similarly have probabilities of absences approaching 1.0. (In the case of the opening day of trout season, the probability of an absence might interact with demographic characteristics of individuals, so that for males in certain regions of the country, the probability of an absence on this day would approach 1.0; for female workers or for those living in urban or aquatically deprived areas, the probability might be no different from what it would be for any other day of the year.)

Dynamic theoretical models could also be constructed in which the probability of an absence on a day following an absence would be increased or decreased depending upon the psychological function that absences were hypothesized to fulfill. The probability of an absence could increase (or decrease) following strings of absences (or attendances) to reflect psychological inertia, stress reduction, or other theoretical psychological processes.

Parameter estimation is a serious problem in complex models of absence behavior. In the simple binomial or Poisson distribution, only one parameter must be estimated. In the case of the stratified mixed binomial distribution, one parameter for each group or block of individuals must be estimated. If probabilities of absences are varied across days, one parameter for each day must be estimated in addition to the parameters for each individual.

In this regard, the chapter by Avery and Hotz (Chapter Four) is particularly important. They discuss increasingly complex theoretical models and the associated structural parameters of data sets. Derivations of expected distributions of absences from these theoretical models and estimated structural parameters can be obtained. Avery and Hotz do not emphasize problems of estimating the parameters required by these complex models. Very large samples of individuals (300 to 500) observed across a large sample of days or other time periods (say 1,000) may be required before the maximum likelihood estimates of the parameters converge to the true values with sufficiently small errors of estimation. The behavior of the parameter estimates of very-low-base-rate events at preasymptotic levels is not well known. These estimation problems suggest special care be exercised.

Simulation studies are needed in which data are generated by assuming the validity of different theoretical models. Comparisons of estimates of parameters of the simulated data (with the true parameter values that were used to generate the data) often reveal that the binary data are poor reflections of the theoretical models. Root mean squared errors between the parameters and the parameter estimates frequently suggest extremely large sampling variances. Empirical research should be accompanied by analyses of simulated data at every step to determine whether the available estimation procedures and algorithms are capable of recovering the parameters in moderate sample sizes. If we cannot recover the known parameters in our simulated samples of perfectly reliable absence events with moderate sample sizes, our chances of success when working with empirical data are poor.

Alternatively, for many theoretical research and practical application purposes, it may not be necessary to estimate the parameters for every individual and time period, even under the assumption that these parameters are varied across both individuals and times. It is often sufficient to estimate the *variance* of the parameters across individuals and times. If, for example, the variance of the probabilities of an absence across individuals is small compared to the variance across days or time periods (excluding opening days of deer and trout season and other "unusual" days), then theories of absence control that operate on assumptions of absence-proneness differing by individual or similar psychological mechanisms might be unlikely to produce the desired results or research knowledge.

If researchers decide that studying absence behaviors is a reasonable course to pursue, the problems caused by the relative infrequency of the events must be addressed. Limiting our observations to realizations of the underlying theoretical random variable places severe limitations on the ability of the investigator to achieve high degrees of prediction of these events. Our techniques for studying such low-base-rate events are not well developed (Hulin and Rousseau, 1980). Routine application of standard research techniques developed for other purposes in other content areas may fail badly when applied to this specific problem area.

### Estimates of Stability of Absences

I have argued that low base rates create special problems for the study of absence behaviors. These low base rates combine with our lack of knowledge about certain essential properties of organizations to jointly conspire against the rigorous study of the stability of absence behaviors across time. Once again, the problematical meanings of these stability estimates can be traced, partially at least, to the choice and treatment of the dependent variable. It is

well known that imposing a dichotomy on a continuously distributed variable also imposes limitations of the relations that can be
observed between the dichotomized variable and any other variable,
even the continuously distributed variable that gave rise to the
dichotomized variable.

Let us assume there is a normally distributed *latent absence
variable* $Y_i$ for each individual in the sample that underlies each
observed dichotomous variable $y_i$ by the relation

$$y_i = 1 \text{ if } Y_i < \tau$$
$$= 0 \text{ otherwise.}$$

If an individual's latent propensity to be absent is greater than
$\tau$, the individual does not come to work that day. If the latent propensity is less than or equal to $\tau$, the individual does come to work.

Olsson, Drasgow, and Dorans (1982) show that the correlation between an observed polychotomous variable $y_i$ (a dichotomous
variable is simply a special case of their more general formulation)
and its corresponding latent propensity variable $Y_i$ is influenced
very strongly by $\tau$. For example, if absences have a base rate of
0.03 (see Steers and Rhodes' Chapter Six for this estimate of the
proportion of workers absent on any given day), the correlation
between $Y_i$ and $y_i$, the correlation between the theoretical variable
and its empirical realization, is only 0.399. In other words, the
*maximum* correlation between observed absences and the latent
variable underlying observed absences is less than 0.40. There is
little information in $y_i$ about $Y_i$. Limiting our empirical studies to
the observable manifestations of the underlying theoretical variable
severely limits what we can learn about the theoretical construct
latent absence propensity.

Attempts to estimate stability of absences across time periods
illustrate another aspect of this problem. In this case, two very
infrequent variables are correlated that represent manifestations of
underlying latent propensities. The ceiling on our empirical correlations depends upon both the underlying correlation between the
theoretical variables *and* the cutting scores that dichotomize these
underlying absence propensities into our observed behaviors. The
empirical correlations probably tell us as much about the base rates
for absences in the two time periods as they do about underlying
theoretical correlations.

Consider the phi coefficient between absences on two days when the base rate on day $i$ was 0.05 and the base rate on day $j$ was 0.01. (When dealing with extreme base rates, a small change in the absolute numbers of individuals absent can change the proportion by a large amount.) The *maximum* phi coefficient that could be observed between days with such base rates is only 0.23 (Wiggins, 1973). With base rates of 0.01 and 0.03, the maximum phi is 0.57. Routine computation of maximum observable coefficients not only provides a benchmark for the evaluation of the obtained empirical coefficients, it provides evidence about the information contained in such coefficients about the underlying theoretical relation between the theoretical constructs.

A potential solution to the theoretical maximum values imposed on phi coefficients by base rates is offered by tetrachoric correlations $(r_{tet})$. Tetrachoric correlations express the correlation between two theoretical underlying normal distributions when both distributions have been dichotomized to produce the observed binary variables. The assumption of two underlying, normally distributed variables is crucial. However, the addition of the normality assumption is not greatly restricting. However, $r_{tet}$ has a sampling distribution that is particularly sensitive to frequencies of individuals in all four cells of the two-by-two matrix. Unless there is a minimum of forty or fifty individuals in *each cell*, the sampling distribution of $r_{tet}$ may be several times larger than the sampling distribution of phi coefficients. If absences on two selected days are independent, for instance, the expected frequency in the absent/absent cell is equal to the product of the two base rates. If both base rates are 0.04, the expected proportion in the absent/absent cell is 0.0016. With sample size of 1,000, the expected frequency is approximately 2. Sample sizes of several thousand would be required before the smallest cell frequency was large enough to provide an acceptably small sampling error.

A frequent solution to the problems created by extreme base rates is to aggregate absences across a number of days to generate absences per week, per month, per quarter, or some other time period (Hulin and Rousseau, 1980). Landy, Atkin, and Goodman have all commented on the aggregation problem. It needs emphasis, however, because of our lack of a theory of organizational time. When absences are aggregated across time periods, the selection of the time period may be as important in determining the empirical results, such as stability coefficients, as any underlying co-variance among absences in different time periods. If we interpret stability coefficients of absences across time periods as reflecting something like reliabilities, then we must select time periods that are both organizationally meaningful and parallel (in the sense that tests are defined as parallel when used to estimate reliability of measurement).

Parallel tests are defined statistically. The expected scores, the variances, and the co-variances among the items making up the parallel tests must equal (Gulliksen, 1950). Some of these requirements can be relaxed to define other kinds of equivalent tests. The main point, however, is that the definition of parallel tests rests on equal expected scores, variances, and co-variances, not on whether one individual took a vacation or was on sick leave during one of the time periods but not in another. It similarly is irrelevant whether one individual had a crashing hangover when he or she took an admission test and had, on that occasion, a score much lower than he or she might have had on another test at another time. All that is required is that *expected* scores be equal across many such parallel tests. Individuals with anomalous scores can always be found, but that does not negate the parallelism of the tests or the inferences that can be made about correlations between parallel measures.

Note, however, that selecting *meaningful* time periods for absence aggregation requires a theory of organizational time. What is a meaningful organizational time period for the recording of absences? The answer might range from half days to quarters. If half days are selected, is the parallel measure for any specific half day the other half of the same day? If we aggregate absences by quarters, what is a parallel quarter? (Note that the idea of quarters as a base for aggregating absence data probably comes to us more from accounting and government taxing than from anything inherent in the life cycle and time periods of an organization.)

Correlations of absence events among different time periods need not be routinely compared to zero as the expected value of the empirical coefficients. Specific theoretical models that are reasonable explanations of absences, because of the fit of the empirical distribution of absences to the theoretical distribution, can also be

used to derive the expected correlations among time periods. Wasserman (1983) has shown that these theoretical correlations may or
may not depend upon the lag between the time periods. If we obtain
the ubiquitous superdiagonal (simplex-like) matrix of correlations
of absences across successive time periods but the theoretically
expected correlations generated by the psychological models depart
substantially from this characteristic pattern, we have learned that
the random growth process probably will not account for absence
behavior. Low-base-rate, binary events cause problems but are
often accompanied by opportunities to derive theoretically expected
results that cannot be accomplished with other classes of dependent
variables.

There is no situation so bad that we cannot take advantage
of it. If investigators are going to saddle themselves with the distributional problems of low-base-rate events, then they must take
advantage of opportunities offered by different conceptual processes
to establish benchmark models specifying expected correlations of
the events across different time periods. Random-growth models,
state-dependent models, and other theoretical processes should be
explored to determine the extent to which these different models
can account for observed coefficients of stability and change across
time as well as the empirical distributions of events.

### Empirical Correlates of Absenteeism

On the basis of an extensive literature review (Steers and
Rhodes, 1978) and an update discussed in this volume, Steers and
Rhodes have reported that we can be confident that absenteeism is
pervasive and expensive, is related to a long list of antecedents, and
is known to have serious consequences. They also report that
absenteeism steadily declined from 2.9 percent (aggregated across
all industries in the United States) in 1979 to 2.1 percent of scheduled work time in 1982. They assert that this decline is attributable to the increase in the unemployment rate over the same time
period (although no evidence in support of this assertion is provided). There are apparently stable differences in absenteeism rates
across different industries. The long list of antecedents to which
they refer includes over 200 variables. Many of the reported rela-

tions between antecedents and absenteeism are nonsignificant; those that reach significance are normally only weakly related to absenteeism.

Another way of summarizing this literature is to note that most of what we know about absenteeism is in the form of information about grossly aggregated absences — across years, industries, regions of the country. Although more than 200 variables have been investigated in terms of their relation with absenteeism, the relations between these variables and absenteeism are small, often nonsignificant, and the variance accounted for is often trivial even when the relations are significant. Meta-analyses of the empirical studies reduce somewhat the variation of the coefficients around their expected values, but the corrected relations of most variables with absenteeism are still small, albeit statistically significant. Job attitudes are a frequently studied antecedent of absenteeism and represent one of the more stable *individual* correlates of this form of behavior.

In spite of the comfort I/O psychologists seem to derive from conducting literature reviews to summarize what is known about a behavior or cognitive state, the usefulness of such activities is problematical in many areas of research. Meta-analysis (Hunter, Schmidt, and Jackson, 1982) offers an approach and a set of procedures that reduce the apparent noise in the literature and allow investigators to estimate more accurately the magnitude of signals that are present. These signals, indeed, allow secondary investigators to integrate and summarize the different categories and groups of antecedents that have been studied. Apparent conceptual development and progress represented by these boxes-and-arrows models is comforting. However, meta-analysis and conceptual models notwithstanding, such review of empirical literature seems to miss the point of research on absenteeism.

Conducting and summarizing literature reviews of the accumulated studies of the antecedents of absenteeism will generate evidence about the theoretical construct of absenteeism only to the extent that absenteeism itself contains information about the underlying construct. Unreported and unanalyzed organizational, social, and demographic variables influence base rates of absences. These factors also influence the observed relations between the antecedents and the behavior and normally cannot be used to adjust observed relations for artifactual variance. The information in an empirical correlation about an unobserved but theoretical correlation may be severely limited. Expected values of empirical correlations, theoretical maximum values based on base-rate information, and other statistical evidence about the artifactual influences on the observed relations must be analyzed to either correct or interpret the observed relations before a great deal of general theoretical value is learned.

Theoretical researchers and managers who wish to control and understand absenteeism can learn a great deal from the accumulated literature *if* these limiting factors are considered and used to correct the observations for different sources of bias. Without such cautions and corrections, the insights gained from the literature and the usefulness of models that are developed to explain the accumulated trends may be aimed at an empirical phenomenon with little relevance to an understanding of the theoretical problem.

Research techniques that are useful for studying other classes of behaviors and phenomena may be inefficient means of providing information needed for an understanding of absence behaviors. If examinations and interpretations of the available literature begin with badly flawed data, the output will itself be flawed to an unknown degree. Conceptual models that summarize our knowledge of absence behavior may be of limited value as scientific statements. Extreme caution must be used to avoid the pitfall represented by models that account for an empirical literature but are essentially irrelevant to an understanding of the underlying constructs that generate the manifest behavior.

## Absence Control

The practical aspects of this volume address the problem of decreasing or controlling absences — or increasing the frequency with which individuals come to work. (There seems but little advantage in discussing one rather than the other.) The conceptual and theoretical perspectives discussed in this as well as in other chapters supplement the practical recommendations made by Latham and Napier (Chapter Eight). These perspectives can be used to interpret and expand upon the shopping list of interventions they discuss. Latham and Napier seem to accept the validity of a general utility model to explain behavioral choice and even to accept the existence of a family of withdrawal behaviors that partially defines a latent absence-propensity variable. Thus, they recommend interventions that seem intended either to reduce the utility of behavioral choices that interfere with work attendance or to increase the utility of behavioral choices that lead to attendance. It is important in this respect that managers recognize that an entire family of behavioral choices is the target of the manipulation and not simply the attention-getting variable of absence from work. Even in this applied area, there are numerous practical advantages to considering perspectives offered by an expectancy/valence theoretical model (Naylor, Prtichard, and Ilgen, 1980) and the perspective that absence is but one of many behaviors that are observable manifestations of an underlying latent construct.

Individuals do not always engage in behaviors that have positive utilities associated with them. They make choices from among a number of behaviors; the chosen behavior is likely to be from among those with the largest positive utilities or smallest negative utilities. Employees also do not necessarily avoid all behaviors with a negative utility. They normally avoid those with the strongest disutilities but occasionally select those with negative utilities because these choices represent the least painful or costly of the alternatives available to them. These simple propositions relating behavioral choice to utility may seem obvious to a researcher. However, they also make the point that, simply because attendance is expected and rewarded, it will not necessarily be the behavior chosen. If employees can select an alternative competing or substitutable behavior that has a greater utility (or less long-term disutility), they will likely engage in that behavior rather than the behavior the organization would prefer (and is attempting to establish). Talking to organizational members, an activity that is inherently interesting as well as theoretically useful (Campbell, Daft, and Hulin, 1982), often reveals that the organizational programs that have been carefully structured to increase attendance are frequently perceived by employees to offer too few rewards for attendance *relative to the rewards offered by carefully selected absences*. Sanctions for nonattendance are often perceived as less costly to the employee than attendance. Otherwise well-designed programs often fail because they are designed to influence the utility of a set of behaviors with little consideration for the set of alternatives.

Focusing on the latent absence-propensity variable leads to at least two quite different types of organizational manipulations. One could recommend interventions to increase the threshold on the latent propensity variable at which the propensity becomes manifested as an observable absence. Alternatively, managers could attempt to systematically move individuals lower on the propensity continuum by rewarding behaviors associated with attendance or reducing the costs of behaviors associated with attendance. Employees, finding attendance to have greater amounts of utility than they had perceived, should be more likely to engage in attendance behaviors and to move lower on the absence-propensity continuum.

Goal-setting programs and manipulations offer quite different insights into the practical problem of controlling absences because of the psychological effects goal setting might be hypothesized to have. One interpretation of goal-setting effectiveness is that it influences the perceived utilities associated with small changes in behavior or effort around the point represented by the goal. In this case, the effects should be on the utilities of behaviors around that point on the latent continuum represented by an absence. Goal-setting interventions can be seen to introduce abrupt discontinuities into the functions relating utilities to behaviors and outcomes. Below the point on the outcome scale represented by the goal of perfect (or near-perfect) attendance, the utility to outcome regression may be small and have a moderately positive slope. Outcomes slightly above the goal may have very large perceived utilities, but the slope of the regression line may still be moderate. Variations in outcomes below and above the goal are associated with variations in utilities, but these variations are small when compared to the abrupt increase in utility associated with achieving the established goal of very high levels of attendance.

In a similar way, many of the intervention strategies discussed by Latham and Napier may, by making the goal of attendance salient to the employees, introduce a discontinuity in the utility to attendance (or absence) regression perceived by the employees. Variation in utility for many behaviors that reflect withdrawal or absenteeism tendencies may become very small when compared to the abrupt decrease in utility (or increase in negative utility) associated with a manifest absence. The influence of these programs on the utility to absence regression perceived by employees may be entirely concentrated in the region of the threshold for overt absenteeism.

Three courses of action to increase employee attendance thus are suggested on the basis of the theoretical perspectives represented in this volume. These interventions are directed toward increasing the threshold on the latent-propensity continuum at which the propensity to be absent becomes manifest, moving individuals lower on the latent-propensity-to-be-absent continuum, so that it takes more of a negative event or requires more input to move the individual up to the absence threshold, or increasing the slope of the utility to attendance function sharply in the neighborbood of the threshold, so that small changes in attendance behaviors or efforts result in large changes in utilities to the individuals.

Simple statements of what the interventions should be designed to accomplish are relatively easy to enunciate; they are neither easy nor inexpensive to implement. The behaviors associated with job withdrawal must be identified and specified. These costs include things that individuals want to do that they cannot do if they attend work. There is a large cluster of activities that are much more easily accomplished during working hours than during evening and weekend hours. Decreasing costs of attendance at work can be accomplished, at least in part, by increasing the ease with which these activities can be done by employees. Decreasing the costs of work attendance and increasing the costs of nonattendance should increase the threshold at which absence propensity becomes manifested as an absence.

Conversely, increasing the utility of behaviors associated with work attendance should move individuals lower on the absence-propensity continuum. That is, if those behaviors that either are required for work attendance or are associated with work attendance are made either less costly or more rewarding, then individuals should be moved lower on the absence-propensity continuum. Increasing the utilities of the behaviors that are associated with the construct of withdrawal should generalize from the individual behaviors to the entire construct and should eventually increase the perceived utility of attendance, even though attendance per se may never have been singled out and reinforced.

Basically, the utility of attendance and the disutility of nonattendance can be increased by applications of a behavioral utility model as elaborated by Fichman. The relations of the many behavioral choices to a general family of behaviors have been initially developed by Atkinson and Birch (Atkinson and Birch, 1970) and applied by Rosse and Miller. However, we learn how to implement these theoretical models and ideas by listening to practitioners such as Latham and Napier.

## Conclusion

In this chapter, I have concentrated on one major thesis, with related subhypotheses, that seems to address the root of many of the problems that plague researchers in this area. The lack of dramatic or even measurable progress toward understanding absenteeism may be seen to be caused by a focus on a specific and dramatic behavior rather than on a scientific, theoretical construct. As long as we continue to concentrate our research and conceptual efforts on models and studies of absenteeism measured as a binary behavior, we will be limiting the amount of progress we can make. In this regard, absenteeism researchers might be likened to researchers who attempt to understand the antecedents and correlates of knowing or not knowing the meaning of *sesquipedalianism* rather than the latent trait of verbal ability of which this specific word might be assumed to be a manifestation.

It was argued that any specific response, behavior, or decision made by an individual contains a small amount of variance that is common to a number of other responses, a large amount of specific or unique variance, and some error variance. Analyses of any specific response or behavior will necessarily amount to analyzing the components and antecedents of a great deal of specific variance. Because specific variance is, by definition, not common to other responses or variables, the limitations on the relations between antecedents and binary absence behaviors are obvious. On the other hand, assessments of a latent theoretical construct would rely on combinations of many different kinds of responses that share some common variance but little specific variance. Emphasis on general theoretical constructs representing general response tendencies offers both theoretical and methodological advantages over repeated studies of binary behavioral variables.

In addition to the general theoretical advantages, broadening our conception and assessment of the dependent variable in this area offers solutions to definitional problems, a way of integrating different theoretical behavioral models developed by Naylor, Pritchard, and Ilgen (1980), Atkinson and Birch (1970), Fishbein and Ajzen (1975), Thurstone (1931), and others with empirical research on absence behaviors. Defining families of behaviors or activities also permits investigators to develop the substantive or content meanings of the behavioral families. Substitutability of activities or behaviors within families is consistent with the bothersome common finding that the phenotypically most preferred, or highest utility, activity is not always the most frequently selected activity. Research on the broader response families is analogous to research on the variance common to the genotypical family of behaviors rather than a specific phenotype.

A substantial effort was devoted to discussing the specific problems caused by the infrequency or low base rates of absence behaviors. Notwithstanding the theoretical and methodological advantages of developing assessments of underlying response tendencies, it is entirely possible that researchers and managers will conclude that absenteeism is so expensive and has so many indirect consequences throughout the organization that we should concentrate our efforts on this binary variable, and the theoretical construct be damned. If this is the case, we must be prepared to deal with the distributional properties of absence behaviors. The distributional problems have implications for nearly all phases of research on absences ranging from substantive theories of absence-proneness to estimates of stability across time periods. At the same time, binary variables offer unique opportunities to develop mathematical models of psychological processes that generate absence behaviors. If we decide to tackle the problems of low-base-rate events, we must take advantage of every opportunity offered by properties of such binary variables. The advantages are not offered free of charge. To avail ourselves of them, we must engage in rigorous theoretical development that includes derivations of expected bivariate relations across time as well as the more commonly derived moments of univariate distributions.

## References

Ås, D. "Absenteeism: A Social Fact in Need of a Theory." *Acta Sociologica,* 1962, *6,* 278–285.

Atkinson, J. W., and Birch, D. *The Dynamics of Action.* New York: Wiley, 1970.

Bougon, M. E., Weick, K. E., and Binkhorst, D. "Cognition in Organizations: An Analysis of the Utrecht Jazz Orchestra." *Administrative Science Quarterly,* 1977, *22,* 606–639.

Campbell, D. T., and Fiske, D. W. "Convergent and Discriminant Validation by the Multitrait-Multimethod Matrix." *Psychological Bulletin,* 1959, *56,* 81–105.

Campbell, J. P., Daft, R. L., and Hulin, C. L. *What to Study: Generating and Developing Research Questions.* Beverly Hills, Calif.: Sage, 1982.

Drasgow, F., and Miller, H. "Psychometric and Substantive Issues in Scale Construction and Validation." *Journal of Applied Psychology,* 1982, *67,* 257–279.

Fishbein, M., and Ajzen, I. *Beliefs, Attitude, Intention and Behavior: An Introduction to Theory and Research.* Reading, Mass.: Addison-Wesley, 1975.

Greenwood, M., and Yule, G. U. "An Enquiry into the Nature of Frequency Distributions Representative of Multiple Happenings, with Particular Reference to the Occurrences of Multiple Attacks of Disease or of Repeated Accidents." *Journal of the Royal Statistical Society,* 1920, *83,* 255–279.

Gulliksen, H. *Theory of Mental Tests.* New York: Wiley, 1950.

Hulin, C., Drasgow, F., and Parsons, C. *Item Response Theory: Applications to Psychological Measurement.* Homewood, Ill.: Dow-Jones, Irwin, 1983.

Hulin, C. L., and Rousseau, D. M. "Analyzing Infrequent Events: Once You Find Them, Your Troubles Begin." In K. H. Roberts and L. Burstein (Eds.), *Issues in Aggregation.* San Francisco: Jossey-Bass, 1980.

Hunter, J. E., Schmidt, F. L., and Jackson, G. B. *Meta-Analysis: Cumulating Research Findings Across Studies.* Beverly Hills, Calif.: Sage, 1982.

Kappauf, W. E., and Bohrer, R. "Observations on Mixed Binomials." *American Journal of Psychology,* 1974, *87,* 643–666.

Mintz, A., and Blum, M. L. "A Re-examination of the Accident Proneness Concept." *Journal of Applied Psychology,* 1949, *33,* 195–211.

Muchinsky, P. M. "Employee Absenteeism: A Review of the Literature." *Journal of Vocational Behavior,* 1977, *10,* 316–340.

Naylor, J. C., Pritchard, R. D., and Ilgen, D. R. *A Theory of Behavior in Organizations.* New York: Academic Press, 1980.

Olsson, U., Drasgow, F., and Dorans, N. J. "The Polyserial Correlation Coefficient." *Psychometrika,* 1982, *47,* 337–347.

Steers, R. M., and Rhodes, S. R. "Major Influences on Employee Attendance: A Process Model." *Journal of Applied Psychology,* 1978, *63* (4), 391–407.

Thurstone, L. L. "The Measurement of Attitudes." *Journal of Abnormal and Social Psychology,* 1931, *26,* 249–269.

Wasserman, S. "Distinguishing Between Stochastic Models of Heterogeneity and Contagion." *Journal of Mathematical Psychology,* 1983, *27,* 201–215.

Wiggins, J. S. *Personality and Predictions: Principles of Personality Assessment.* Reading, Mass.: Addison-Wesley, 1973.

# Name Index

# Subject Index

## T

Theoretical specification: analysis of, 1–41; assumptions in, 12–14; background on, 1–4; criteria for, 14–16, 34–37; as disconfirmable, 15, 35; economic perspectives on, 9–10, 22–24; implications of, 37–41, 61–63; issue of, xi; literature review for, 4–12; and measurement, 57–63; for motivated behavior, 21–34; perspectives and developments for, 4–12, 394–398; and pretheory, 361–367; value of, 29–33

Time allocation: absence defined by, 20–21; as motivated behavior, 21–34

Time span: in adaptation process, 216–217; aggregation over, 85–87; choice of, and measurement, 50–54, 71, 83–87; and consequences of absenteeism, 286; and demand effects, 53; in dynamics model, 38; and policy effects, 52–53; and season effects, 53–54; and shift effects, 54

Training: and attendance, 333–335; in supervisory counseling, 334–335, 348, 351–352

Tupperware, and attendance, 339

Turnover, and absence, 196–200

## U

Union of Soviet Socialist Republics, increasing attendance in, 323

Unions: and attendance, 350, 351; consequences of absenteeism for, 280, 283

United Kingdom: absence culture in, 378, 379, 381; causes of absence in, 239; data analysis in, 362; distribu-

tion of absence in, 121; rate of absence in, 233

United Mine Workers of America (UMWA), 65, 66

U.S. Bureau of Mines, xvi, $1n$, $47n$, $276n$

U.S. Bureau of National Affairs, 230, 274

U.S. Department of Labor, 202, 227

## V

Vacancy: and accidents, 298–299; implications of, 318

Validity: issue of, 400–401; of measurement, 98–100

Vigilance, and accidents, 299–300

## W

Wage and benefit structure, and absenteeism, 9–10

Weibull distribution, in statistical models, 180, 181

Weyerhouse, and attendance, 350

Withdrawal: behavior categories of, 206–207; and causes of absenteeism, 259–260; concept of, 195; current models of, 200–207; issue of, xii; and latent trait approach, 369–370; and satisfaction, 197–199; in theoretical models, 6, 10–11, 12, 396–397. See also Adaptation

Work attitudes: as causes of absenteeism, 235–240; management implications of, 261–262

Work group: and absence culture, 247–248, 377–381; consequences of absenteeism for, 280–282

## Y

Yugoslavia, absence rate in, 139